Natural Resources as Capital

Natural Resources as Capital

Larry Karp

The MIT Press
Cambridge, Massachusetts
London, England

This book was set in Times Roman by Westchester Publishing Services. Printed and bound in the United States of America.

Library of Congress Cataloging-in-Publication Data

Names: Karp, Larry S., author.
Title: Natural resources as capital / Larry Karp.
Description: Cambridge, MA : MIT Press, 2017. | Includes bibliographical references and index.
Identifiers: LCCN 2016051902 | ISBN 9780262534055 (pbk. : alk. paper)
Subjects: LCSH: Natural resources. | Environmental economics.
Classification: LCC HC85 .K38 2017 | DDC 333.7—dc23 LC record available at
https://lccn.loc.gov/2016051902

10 9 8 7 6 5 4 3 2 1

For Heather, Duncan, Mischa, and Alexis

Contents

* These are sections that can be skipped at first reading.

Preface

The book is designed for upper division undergraduates and, with the appendices, for a masters level course. Prerequisites include intermediate micro-economics and a grounding in calculus. The book uses derivatives, and in a few cases, partial and total derivatives. Appendix A reviews the required mathematical tools. Asterisks identify sections with examples or with advanced material that can be skipped without loss of continuity.

The text covers standard resource economics topics, including the Hotelling model for nonrenewable resources and renewable resource models, such as fisheries. The distinction between natural resource and environmental economics has blurred and become less useful over the decades. This book reflects that evolution by including some topics that also fit in an environmental economics text, while emphasizing natural resources. For example, the problem of climate change involves resource stocks and therefore falls under the rubric of natural resources. Environmental externalities drive the problem, so the topic also fits in an environmental economics text.

Two themes run through this book. First, resources are a type of natural capital; their management is an investment problem, requiring forward-looking behavior, and thus requiring dynamics. Second, our interest in natural resources stems largely from the prevalence of market failures, frequently associated with incomplete or nonexistent property rights. "Policy failures" complicate matters; often policy does not adequately address, or even exacerbates, those market failures. The book emphasizes skills and intuition needed to think sensibly about dynamic models and about regulation or institutional remedies (e.g., the creation of property rights) in the presence of both market and policy failures. The opportunity cost of this focus is the omission of a detailed discussion of several important resources. This pedagogic decision reflects the view that students at this level are best served by acquiring a good understanding of concepts and tools that will help them think critically about a broad range of resource issues.

Standard Topics

Chapter 1 provides an overview of resource economics. Eleven chapters (3–5, 7, and 12–18) cover the nuts and bolts of resource economics and could stand alone as a mini-course. Chapters 3–5 and 7 cover nonrenewable resources. Chapters 3 and 4 study the two-period model, first in the simplest setting and then including stock-dependent costs. Chapter 4 explains the role of resource scarcity and stock-dependent extraction costs in determining resource rent. This chapter shows how to obtain the optimality condition using the perturbation method; chapter 5 adapts that method to the T-period setting to obtain the Euler equation, known in this context as the Hotelling rule. The perturbation method (the discrete time calculus of variations) enables students to perform constrained optimization almost without being aware of it: it is simpler and more intuitive than the method of Lagrange, dynamic programming, or the Maximum Principle. We use the two-period optimality condition to write the T-period optimality condition merely by replacing time subscripts. Chapter 5 also discusses the idea of the shadow value of a resource stock, and uses an example to show how the transversality condition makes it possible to completely solve the model. Chapter 7 presents the backstop model. Backstops are economically important, and this material gives students practice working with the Hotelling model while preparing for a subsequent policy-focused chapter.

Chapters 12–18 study renewable resources. I emphasize fisheries, because they provide a concrete setting and illustrate most of the issues found in other renewable resources. Chapter 12 defines and provides historical perspective on different types of property rights and then discusses the Coase Theorem. The rest of the chapter uses real-world examples and a one-period analytic model to describe the difficulties and the unintended consequences arising from fishery regulation. It discusses attempts to establish property rights in fisheries as an alternative to regulation.

Chapter 13 introduces the concepts needed to study renewable resources, including the growth function, steady states, (local) stability, and maximum sustainable yield. This chapter explains the relation between—and the relative advantages of—discrete time versus continuous time models, and it describes how the rest of the text uses these two approaches. Chapter 14 discusses the open access fishery, showing how the long-run effect of policy depends on the initial stock size. Chapter 15 introduces the sole-owner fishery, explains the Euler equation and steady state conditions, and discusses policy under multiple market failures. The chapter compares the open access and sole-owner steady states; it also discusses the effect of harvest cost and the discount rate on the sole owner's steady state(s). Chapter 16 shows how to analyze the sole-owner fishery outside the steady state. There we begin with a problem that can be studied using only the Euler equation and careful reasoning; we then move to a more complicated example requiring phase portrait analysis. Chapter 17 discusses water economics, showing how the tools developed for the fishery setting can be adapted to other resources. Chapter 18 explains concepts of weak and strong sustainability. There are several approaches to estimating social prices for natural resources without well-functioning markets. Measures of national income have been modified to assess sustainability.

Less-Standard Topics

Chapter 2 reviews topics in microeconomics needed to study resource economics. These topics include the concept of arbitrage, the use of elasticities, the relation between competitive and monopoly equilibria, and the use of discounting. Chapter 6 discusses empirical tests of the Hotelling model.

Chapters 8–11 introduce policy problems. Chapter 8 uses the Hotelling model to examine the "Green Paradox," an important topic in climate policy. In addition to its intrinsic interest, this material gives students practice in using the Hotelling model and more generally illustrates the use of models to study policy questions. The material promotes critical thinking by discussing limitations of the Green Paradox model.

Chapter 9 provides the foundation for policy analysis when market failures are important. It explains and illustrates the Theory of the Second Best and the Principle of Targeting, and it discusses the importance of political lobbying and the distinction between policy complements and substitutes. To present this material simply, examples in the chapter use static environmental problems instead of stock-dependent natural resource problems.

Taxes and other market-based instruments are becoming increasingly important regulatory tools. Chapter 10 introduces the principles of taxation in a static framework. We discuss tax equivalence, tax incidence, and deadweight loss. These basic ideas provide a conceptual framework for estimating the fraction of permits in a cap and trade scheme that would need to be grandfathered to compensate firms for the cost of regulation. Chapter 10 is essential for understanding taxes in the dynamic natural resource setting, the topic of Chapter 11. That chapter provides an overview of actual taxation (and subsidy) of fossil fuels and then explains how to synthesize the Hotelling model with the information on taxes studied in the static setting. A numerical example illustrates this synthesis.

Chapter 19 studies the role of discounting, emphasizing its role in recommendations for optimal climate policy. The chapter explains the difference between utility and consumption discounting. It discusses the Ramsey formula for the social discount rate in the deterministic setting, and then introduces uncertainty. I emphasize the importance, to the social discount rate, of projections of future economic growth. A concluding section introduces hyperbolic discounting and explains its relevance to climate policy.

International Issues

Under the view that students are better served by a solid foundation in the concepts of resource and environmental issues, rather than a smattering of information about a longer list of important issues, this book does not systematically treat international environmental and resource problems. However, the text touches on international issues in several places, providing instructors with an opportunity to extend those themes. Chapter 10 studies taxes in a closed economy, but appendix C.1 illustrates how trade changes tax incidence. Section 11.1 discusses international attempts to reign in distortionary fossil fuel subsidies. Section 11.3 discusses the potential of multinational investment treaties to alleviate the hold-up problem arising with international investment. Section 17.5 explains that water markets can increase overpumping, and thereby lower efficiency, when property rights to groundwater are weak. Building on that special case, the rest of the section introduces some important themes in the trade and environment/resource literature. The discussion of sustainability metrics in section 18.3 includes (briefly) cross-country comparisons and global metrics. Climate change policy, discussed in chapter 19, is of course a global environmental issue.

Acknowledgments

This manuscript benefited from comments by Sangeeta Bansal, Edward Barbier, Ron Griffin, John Hartwick, Beat Hintermann Michael Hoel, Stephen Holland, Derek Lemoine, John Livernois, Jeff Perloff, Deepak Premkumar, Wenfeng Qiu, Karolina Ryszka, Hiroaki Sakamoto, Jesus Marin Solano, Hilary Soldati, Marty Smith, Zhen Sun, Christian Traeger, Yacov Tsur, Cees Withagen, Molly Van Dop, Yang Xie, and Huayong Zhi. It also benefited from feedback provided by the 2013–2015 classes in EEP/Econ 102 at University of California, Berkeley. I also thank Richard Howitt, Marc Mangel, and Jim Wilen, for introducing me to resource economics, and Alex McCalla for introducing me to the theory of the second best.

1 Resource Economics in the Anthropocene

Natural resources are under threat of misuse and depletion, but human ingenuity makes it possible to devise rules and create institutions to protect them. Policies that harness the power of markets are more likely to be successful than policies that ignore market forces. Resource economics offers a framework for analyzing resource use and improving stewardship.

Natural resources are a type of capital: natural, as opposed to human-made capital. Resource use potentially alters the stock of this capital and is a type of investment decision. Change is a key feature of natural resources, requiring a dynamic (i.e., multiperiod) perspective. Natural resources, like other types of capital, provide services that affect human well-being. In some cases, as with burning oil or eating fish, we consume those services by consuming a part of the resource. In other cases, we consume natural resource services indirectly. Wetlands provide filtration services, reducing the cost of clean water. Transforming wetlands into farms or cities changes the flow of these services. Other resource stocks, such as birds, bats and pollinating insects, provide services essential to agricultural production. Reducing habitat or otherwise changing the ecosystem can diminish the stocks necessary for future pollination services.

These examples are anthropocentric, attributing value to natural resources only because they provide services to humans. Species or wilderness areas may have intrinsic value apart from any effect they have on current or future human welfare. Regardless of whether one begins with a purely anthropocentric view or a more spiritual/philosophical perspective, resource value depends on the remaining stocks: oil, fish, wetlands, pollinators, wilderness, and so forth. These stocks affect current and future flows of services. Spiritual or philosophical arguments can be effective in galvanizing public action, but the anthropocentric view, putting humans at the center of the narrative, can lead to more effective remedies. The protection of forests or fisheries is more likely achieved if the people in a position to use these resources have a stake in their protection. Ecotourism in nature preserves can give local residents an incentive to respect the preserve; using the dung of elephants and rhinos to create paper products for sale abroad gives people an incentive to protect animals that stray from their preserves. Elevating philosophical abstractions above people risks promoting inefficient policies.

In common usage, "capital" refers to human-made productive inputs, such as machinery, or the monetary value of those inputs. A broader definition treats capital as anything that yields a flow of services. Education augments our stock of human capital, making us more productive or otherwise enhancing our lives. Natural resources fall under this broader definition. A firm's decision to purchase machinery, or an individual's decision to acquire education, are "forward-looking" investment decisions; they depend on beliefs about their future consequences. These decisions are "dynamic" rather than "static," because their temporal aspect is central to the decision-making process. Resource management is a dynamic investment problem.

Like machinery, natural capital obeys physical laws: machines rust, trees age. The fact that the two types of capital inhabit the same physical universe connects resource economics to the broader field of economics. Market failures, particularly "externalities," are widespread in natural resource markets. An externality occurs when a person does not take into account nonmarket consequences of their action. Traffic congestion is a classic externality. Collectively, drivers create congestion, but individual drivers contribute negligibly to congestion; no driver has an incentive to take into account their effect on the congestion that others face. In the environmental and resource setting, firms may pollute, and fishers may harvest above socially optimal levels. These types of externalities, often associated with weak or nonexistent property rights, are central to the study of resource economics.

A natural resource without property rights cannot be bought and sold, and therefore does not have a market price reflecting its value. Informed policy decisions require a comparison of costs and benefits of alternatives (e.g., protecting the natural resource or allowing development). The lack of a price for a natural resource makes it difficult to value its services, complicating the policy problem (box 1.1).

The system of property rights affects the incentives that influence resource use. Regardless of the property rights system, extraction from a mine or harvest from a fishery alters the stock available for future use. Under private property, the owner has an incentive to take into account the effect of current decisions on the remaining stock, because the owner's future payoffs depend on that stock. In the absence of property rights, if each individual has negligible effect on aggregate decisions, no one has an incentive to take these stock effects into account. Farmers choose levels of pesticide and fertilizer to increase their profits. Some of these inputs enter waterways, where they damage the publicly owned ecosystem, as has occurred in the Everglades and in the Gulf of Mexico. Individual farms have negligible effect on the aggregate pollution, so it is rational for them to ignore these consequences. In the past few decades, society has established property rights for some fisheries, introduced regulations for some pollutants, and used public education campaigns to change behavior (e.g., littering). These kinds of changes usually require conscious political activity.

Box 1.1
Valuing Natural Capital

The cost of protecting watershed-based filtration systems for New York City's water supplies was estimated in 1996 to be $1–1.5 billion; the cost of building and operating a filtration system was estimated to be $6–8 billion. New York City protected the watershed.

The value of irrigation in a region of Nigeria was 4–17% of the losses to downstream floodplains arising from the diminished water flows caused by this irrigation.

Shrimp farming in Thailand causes the destruction of mangrove swamps, which provided nurseries for other fisheries and storm protection. The value of shrimp farming was about 10% of the lost value of ecosystem services.

The estimates for the Nigerian and Thai cases were made after the damage had occurred (the irrigation was put in place, and the shrimp farms developed). It may be costly or politically infeasible to undo these actions, for example, to reduce irrigation to increase water flows, or to restore the mangroves (Barbier 2011).

Rapid changes in resource stocks and the expected change of future stocks make resource economics an especially important field of study. The 2005 Millennium Ecosystem Assessment (United Nations 2005) reports that the recent speed and extent of human-induced change in ecosystems exceeds any in the historical record. Some changes, such as increased agricultural production, benefit people currently living but threaten future well-being by degrading resources. The past half-century saw a fifth of the world's coral reefs lost and another fifth degraded; a third of mangrove forests have been lost; water use from rivers and lakes has doubled; nitrogen flows entering ecosystems have doubled, and phosphorus flows have tripled. Human actions have increased the rate of species extinction as much as a thousandfold relative to rates found in the geological record (Kolbert 2014). Estimates of mammal, bird, and amphibian species threatened with extinction range from 10% to 30%. Tropical forests and many fisheries are in decline.

The Millennium Assessment evaluates 24 types of ecosystem services and concludes that 60% of these are degraded or threatened. The loss in natural capital may create abrupt changes (e.g., "flips" in water quality and the rapid emergence of new diseases). These changes tend to disproportionately harm the poor. Barring major policy changes or technological developments, ecosystems will likely face increasing pressure. Standard measures of wealth ignore these changes in natural capital. Attempts to account for natural capital show that almost half of countries in a World Bank (2014b) study are depleting their wealth by living off natural capital.

Climate change may pose the single greatest danger to future well-being. Climate change is likely to exacerbate current problems, such as those associated with species loss, the spread of diseases, and increased water shortages. It may also contribute to rising sea levels, increased frequency of severe weather events, and decreased agricultural productivity. The costs of these changes will depend on uncertain relations between stocks of greenhouse gases and changes in temperature, ocean acidity, and the sea level, and on the uncertain relation between these variables and economic and ecological consequences. The future stocks of greenhouse gases depend on future emissions, which depend on uncertain changes in policy and technology.

In recognition of human ability to fundamentally alter the earth's ecosystem, many scientists refer to the current geological period as the Epoch of the Anthropocene ("New Human Epoch"). Proposals for this epoch's starting date range from the early industrial age to the middle of the twentieth century.

The view that current resource use will create large costs to future generations leads to resource pessimism. Malthus, a nineteenth-century resource pessimist, claimed that population eventually outstrips food supplies, until starvation, war, or disease brings them back into balance. This description was quite accurate for most of human history but not for the past two centuries. Many countries have seen a demographic shift associated with higher income, leading to stabilization or decreases in population. In poor societies, children are an investment for old age. In rich societies, children do not provide the primary support for their aged parents, and the cost of raising children is high. These factors encourage smaller family sizes with rising income. Technological innovations have increased agricultural productivity and reduced the cost of transporting and storing food. Population and food security have both increased. Most recent famines were caused not by the absolute lack of food but by its unequal distribution.

In the nineteenth century, the British government was concerned that high consumption of coal would lead to future scarcity. William Jevons, a prominent economist, advised the government not to use policies that would lead to coal conservation, on the grounds that the market would resolve any future problem: if the price of coal did rise, businesses would reduce their demand, and innovators would develop substitutes for coal. In 1931 Harold Hotelling produced one of the cornerstones of the field of resource economics, responding to the pessimists of his time:

Contemplation of the world's disappearing supplies of . . . exhaustible assets has led to demands for regulation of their exploitation. The feeling that these products are now too cheap for the good of future generations, that they are being selfishly exploited at too rapid a rate, and that in consequence of their excessive cheapness they are being produced and consumed wastefully has given rise to the conservation movement. [Hotelling 1931, 137]

Hotelling studied the use of natural resources in an idealized market with perfect property rights, where a rational owner takes the finite resource supply into account. In this setting, prices signal scarcity, influencing decisions about extraction, exploration, and the development of alternate energy sources and new technologies. Price signals can also lead to fundamental changes in human behavior, such as family size.

Box 1.2
The (im)Possibility of Extinction

In the mid-1800s, driftnet herring fishermen asked for regulation to restrict the use of "longlines," which they claimed damaged fish stocks and reduced catches. Many scientists, believing that the self-correcting power of nature would take care of any temporary problems, resisted those requests. The scientific philosopher Thomas Henry Huxley, a member of British fishing commissions charged with investigating the complaints, explained in 1883 why the requests were unscientific and merely designed to impede technological progress: "Any tendency to over-fishing will meet with its natural check in the diminution of the supply, . . . this check will always come into operation long before anything like permanent exhaustion has occurred" (Kurlansky 1998, 122).

Others disagreed. Maine's fishery commissioner Edwin Gould stated in 1892: "It's the same old story. The buffalo is gone; the whale is disappearing; the seal fishery is threatened with destruction. Fish need protection" (Bolster 2015).

Barnett and Morse (1963) examined trends in resource prices, finding no evidence of increased scarcity. However, increased resource use led to a resurgence in resource pessimism, exemplified by Paul Ehrlich's *The Population Bomb*. Ehrlich, a biologist, observing rapid increases in the use of natural resources in the 1960s and accustomed to working with mechanistic models of insect populations, predicted imminent and catastrophic resource scarcity. Julian Simon, like Jevons almost a century earlier, thought that the market would take care of scarcity, as higher prices encouraged exploration, discovery, production and conservation. Simon proposed, and Ehrlich accepted, a bet that the inflation-adjusted price of a basket of five minerals would fall over a decade. This period of time seemed long enough to test Ehrlich's forecast of imminent scarcity. Simon won the bet; Ehrlich claimed that he had underestimated the rapacity of humanity's resource extraction, and that his prediction of scarcity was wrong only in the timing.

The resource pessimism of the 1960s led to renewed interest in resource economics during the 1970s and 1980s. The dominant strand of this literature extends Hotelling's earlier work, using the paradigm of rational agents operating with secure property rights. There has also been increased recognition of market failures, especially externalities associated with missing markets and weak property rights. Modern resource economics provides a powerful lens through which to study natural resources, precisely because it takes market failures seriously. The discipline provides a counterweight to pessimists' tendency to understate society's ability to respond to market signals while also providing a remedy to the excessively optimistic belief that markets, by themselves, will solve resource problems.

Agriculture and fisheries illustrate the power of markets and the problems arising from market imperfections. In both cases, markets have unleashed productivity gains leading to abundance. These gains occur in the presence of market failures, threatening (in the case of agriculture) or reversing (in the case of fisheries) the initial gains. Increases in agricultural productivity since the 1960s made it possible to feed twice the population with slightly more than a 10% increase in farmed land, reducing or eliminating the threat of starvation for hundreds of millions of people. Those changes were associated with increased pesticide and fertilizer use that threaten waterways, increased and likely unsustainable use of water, and increased loss of habitat. Increased demand for fish and the resulting higher prices induced fishers to adopt new technologies that raised their harvests. In many cases these gains were short lived, as the increased harvest degrades fish stocks, ultimately lowering harvest. Better regulation and the establishment of property rights can ameliorate these problems.

Markets respond by creating alternative sources of supply, such as aquaculture (farmed fish) instead of wild fish. From 1985 to 2014 annual world harvest from "capture" fisheries increased from 69 to 93 million tons, while aquaculture increased from 5 to 63 million tons. The World Bank (2014a) projects that aggregate supply of fish will increase 20% by 2030, when aquaculture will provide half of the fish consumed. Aquaculture can relieve the pressure on wild fisheries, but it also creates environmental damage (e.g., loss of mangrove swamps) and increases the demand from capture fisheries (e.g., fishmeal as a food source). New solutions create new problems.

Markets have been essential in "disproving" the resource pessimists thus far. Markets are powerful in part because they are self-organizing. They require a legal and institutional framework that respects private property and contracts; they often require regulation but not detailed governmental management. However, the beneficial short-run changes, such as increased agricultural production, coupled with market imperfections, may in the longer run validate the resource-pessimists.

Politics, in addition to technological limits and demography, creates obstacles to solving resource problems. Proposed remedies usually create winners and losers, with those who are harmed by the remedy often in a better position to defend their interests. Effective climate policy will reduce the wealth of fossil fuel owners, a politically powerful group. Some policies are driven by self-interest and are not explicitly linked to resource issues, while still having direct and harmful effects on resources. There is a near consensus (at least among economists) that several policies harm natural capital and are socially irrational: agricultural policies that promote environmentally damaging production along with commodity gluts, water policy that promotes excessive use and inefficient allocation across users, fossil fuel subsidies that exacerbate the problem of excessive greenhouse gas emissions, and fishing subsidies that worsen the problem of overharvest. Political power in the service of special interest groups explains these kinds of policy failure. Complex problems are hard to manage. Market failures require a policy response, but policy intervention sometimes is part of the problem, not part of the solution.

Clearer thinking will not dispel the technological, demographic, and political obstacles to socially rational resource use. However, clearer thinking and more precise language can help overturn prejudice and identify effective policy, and can provide a basis for negotiations. People might disagree on a conservation measure, but it is counterproductive to base the disagreement on identification with a political party or a disciplinary speciality (economics versus ecology). Resource economics can provide a common language and analytic framework, creating the possibility of moving beyond ideology. Resource economics also helps in understanding that institutional reform, such as the creation of property rights rather than the introduction of a new tax, is often an effective remedy to problems. Some people distrust property rights because they (correctly) see these as the basis for markets, and they (probably incorrectly) think that markets are responsible for the resource problem. Resource economics teaches that many problems are due not to markets, but to market *failures.*

Disagreements about resource-based problems tend to be easier to resolve when the problems are local or national rather than global, and when changes occur quickly (but not irreversibly) rather than unfolding slowly. The local or national context makes the horse-trading needed to compensate losers easier. The rapid speed of change makes the problem more obvious and increases the potential benefits of finding a solution. The most serious contemporary resource-based problems are global and unfold over long periods of time, relative to the political cycle.

A prominent international treaty, the Montreal Protocol, helped reverse the global problem of ozone depletion. The rapid increase in the ozone hole over the Southern Hemisphere made the problem hard to ignore, and the availability of low-cost alternatives to ozone-depleting substances made it fairly cheap to fix. International negotiations on other global problems—most prominently climate change—have been notably unsuccessful. It is difficult to summon the political will to make the international transfers needed to compensate nations that would be, or think they would be, better off without an agreement. The most serious effects of climate change will impact future generations, who have no direct representation in current negotiations.

Overview of the Book

Two points made above set the stage for the rest of this book. (i) Markets have the potential to ease environmental and resource constraints, contributing hugely to an increase in human welfare. (ii) Many problems arise from market failures, often associated with weak or nonexistent property rights; those market failures may diminish or even reverse the beneficial effects arising in other markets. Regulation that harnesses the power of markets, or the establishment of property rights, may make it easier to solve resource problems. Those regulations and institutional changes require political intervention; they do not arise spontaneously from market forces. The tools developed it this book can contribute to coherent analysis of these issues, making it possible to intelligently evaluate the facts of specific cases.

The pedagogic challenge arises because resources are a type of capital, requiring a dynamic setting in which agents are *forward looking*. In a static setting, firms' and regulators' decisions depend on current prices and, for example, pollution. In the dynamic resource setting, a firm's decision on how much of the resource to extract and sell in a period depends on the price in that period and the firm's beliefs about future prices. A regulator's (optimal) policy depends on beliefs about future actions, and these depend on future prices. This difference between the static and dynamic setting is central in the book's presentation of resource economics.

The first half of the book provides the foundation for studying nonrenewable resources, such as coal or oil. This foundation requires a review of some aspects of microeconomic theory and the development of methods needed to study dynamic markets. We apply these methods to the resource problem, emphasizing perfectly competitive markets with no externalities or other distortions. This material identifies incentives that are important in determining resource use and helps you understand the potential for markets, when they work well. The second half of the book applies these tools, emphasizing situations where market failures create a rationale for policy intervention. Policies can ameliorate the market failure, but poorly designed policy may cause unintended consequences. The book also moves from nonrenewable to *renewable* resources, making it possible to show how different systems of property rights and policies alter resource levels at different time scales.

Terms and Concepts

Epoch of the Anthropocene, renewable versus nonrenewable resource, market failure, externality, resource pessimist/optimist.

Sources

Notes at the end of each chapter include sources cited in the chapter. These notes also include uncited background material that indicates the provenance of ideas and provides suggestions for further reading.

Barnett and Morse (1963), observing that inflation-adjusted resource prices were not trending upward, concluded that there was no evidence of increased resource scarcity.

The United Nations' (2005) *Millennium Ecosystem Assessment* reports an international group of scholars' assessment of recent environmental changes, their consequences on human well-being, and likely scenarios for future changes.

Alix-Garcia et al. (2009) discuss the payment of environmental services in agriculture, an example of a market-based remedy to externalities.

Kolbert's (2014) *The Sixth Extinction: An Unnatural History* summarizes estimates of levels of species extinction.

Foley's (2006) *Adam's Fallacy* discusses Thomas Malthus and other important economists.

Barrett's (2003) *Environment and Statescraft* discusses the difficulty of creating effective global environmental agreements.

Clark's (2008) *A Farewell to Alms* provides a long run historical perspective on Mathus's ideas.

Sabin's (2013) *"The Bet"* examines the tension between resource optimists and pessimists, in particular between Ehrlich and Simon.

The World Bank's (2014b) *Little Green Data Book* provides statistics on green national accounting.

The World Bank's (2014a) *Fish to 2030* projects future fish supplies, emphasizing the role of aquaculture.

Hotelling (1931) is a classic paper in resource economics.

Solow (1974b) provides a review of resource economics.

Dasgupta's (2001) *Human Well-Being and the Natural Environment* develops the concept of natural resources as a type of capital.

Barbier's (2011) *Capitalizing on Nature* extends this concept to ecosystems, or ecological capital (e.g., wetlands, forests, and watersheds). The examples in Box 1.1 are taken from his book.

The quote by Huxley in Box 1.2 is from Kurlansky (1998), and the quote by Gould is from Bolster (2015).

2 Preliminaries

Objective
- Review the microeconomic foundation for the study of resource economics.

Information and Skills
- Understand the meaning of arbitrage, the distinction between exogenous and endogenous variables, and the use of comparative statics.
- Know the definition and purpose of elasticities and be able to calculate them.
- Understand the relation between competition and monopoly.
- Know the definitions and purposes of a discount rate and a discount factor; use them to calculate present values.
- Know the basics of welfare economics.

This chapter reviews and supplements the microeconomic foundation needed for natural resource economics. In the familiar "static" (one-period) setting, an equilibrium occurs when firms choose output to maximize profit, and individuals make purchases to maximize utility. Resource economics typically requires a "dynamic" (two-or-more-period) setting. Resource-owning firms begin with an initial stock of the natural resource and decide how much to supply in (typically) many periods; these firms solve dynamic problems. Equilibrium in a resource setting involves a time-path, or "trajectory" of prices and quantities, not a single price and quantity. For a nonrenewable resource such as coal or oil, the cumulative extraction over the firm's planning horizon cannot exceed the firm's initial stock level. For renewable resources such as fish, natural growth can offset harvest, causing the stock to either rise or fall over time.

A Road Map

"Arbitrage" is a trade (or a combined purchase and sale) that takes advantage of price differences between similar products across different markets. "Spatial arbitrage" occurs when an agent buys a commodity where the price is low and sells where the price is high (section 2.1). "Intertemporal arbitrage" occurs when an agent buys and sells a commodity at different points in time instead of different locations. A "no-arbitrage condition" holds once prices have adjusted, either across locations or across points in time, so that there are no remaining profitable trades. Intertemporal arbitrage is the basis for understanding equilibria in resource markets. Spatial arbitrage provides the foundation for understanding intertemporal arbitrage.

Models can clarify causal relations among variables. "Exogenous" variables are model inputs, and "endogenous" variables are model outputs. A technique known as "comparative statics" identifies the effect of a change in an exogenous variable on an endogenous variable (section 2.2). We frequently use elasticities to express the relation between variables (section 2.3).

We emphasize competitive equilibria. However, many important resource markets, including markets for petroleum, diamonds, and aluminium, are not, or have not always been competitive. We therefore also study monopoly. Many resource markets lie somewhere on the continuum between competition and monopoly. The relation between the equilibrium prices under these two markets depends on the elasticity of demand with respect to price (section 2.4). Numerical examples reinforce the difference between competition and monopoly, and show how to compute the different equilibria (section 2.5).

Discounting enables us to compare profits in different periods, and is key in framing the firms' optimization problems. Section 2.6 explains the relation between a discount factor and a discount rate and defines "present value." Section 2.7 provides three applications, showing how discounting is used and illustrating its importance. Welfare economics provides the foundation for the study of market failures (section 2.8).

2.1 Arbitrage

Objectives and skills: Understand arbitrage, and graphically represent and analyze the "no-arbitrage" condition.

Much of the intuition for later results rests on the idea of arbitrage over time. This idea is closely related to the more familiar idea of arbitrage over space. Suppose that there are 10 units of tea in China, where the inverse demand is $p^{China} = 20 - q^{China}$; p^{China} and q^{China} are price and quantity consumed in China, respectively. A "demand function" gives quantity as a function of price, and the "inverse demand function" gives price as a function of quantity. The inverse demand for tea in the United States is $p^{U.S.} = 18 - q^{U.S.} = 18 - (10 - q^{China})$. The first equality expresses U.S. price as a function of U.S. sales (as is standard); the second equality uses the constraint that total sales equal 10, $q^{U.S.} = 10 - q^{China}$, to express U.S. price as a function of sales in China.

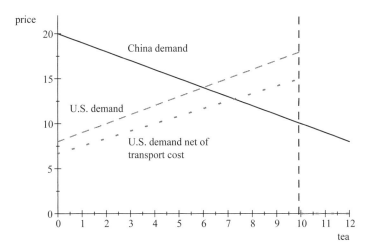

Figure 2.1
Horizontal axis shows tea sold in China. Solid line shows inverse demand for tea in China. Dashed line shows inverse demand for tea in the United States, as a function of sales in China. Dotted line shows price received by Chinese exporter with 30% transportation costs (discussed in section 2.2).

Figure 2.1 graphs inverse demand for both countries as functions of sales in China. The solid line is the inverse demand in China, and the dashed line is the inverse demand in the United States. Moving left to right on the horizontal axis increases sales in China and decreases U.S. sales, because total supply is fixed at 10. The U.S. demand function is therefore read right to left; the point 3 on the tea axis means that China consumes 3 units and the United States consumes 7 units. In this example, the equilibrium is "interior" : tea sales are positive in both countries.

If transportation is free, and sales are positive in both countries, then price in a competitive equilibrium must be equal in the two countries. This no-arbitrage condition is necessary for profit maximization: if it did not hold, a price-taking trader could buy a unit of tea in the cheap country and sell it in the expensive country, increasing profits. The no-arbitrage ($=$ profit-maximizing) condition, under zero transportation costs, holds where the solid and the dashed curves in Figure 2.1 intersect. At this point, China consumes 6 units, the United States consumes 4 units, and the equilibrium price, 14, is the same in both countries.

It is easy to become confused about causation in a competitive equilibrium. The trader in our tea example does not move tea from one location to another with the intention of causing the prices in the two locations to be the same. This competitive trader takes prices as given and continues to move tea from one location to another until no further trade is profitable. The cross-country equality of price is a consequence, not the purpose, of trade.

2.2   Comparative Statics

Objectives and skills: Understand the distinction between endogenous and exogenous variables and answer a comparative statics question.

Comparative statics questions ask how a small change in an exogenous variable alters an endogenous variable. The example using transportation cost illustrates comparative statics. The transportation cost is taken as given: it is exogenous. Price and quantity in China and the United States are determined by the model: they are endogenous. The comparative statics question is "How do transportation costs affect the equilibrium price and quantity in the two markets?" This question is simple enough to answer without a model: higher transportation costs decrease exports from China to the United States, increasing supply and decreasing the equilibrium price in China, and having the opposite effect in the United States. The simplicity enables you to focus on the method.

Transportation costs expressed as a percentage of value are called "iceberg transportation costs"; it is as if a certain fraction of the value melts in moving the good from one place to another. These costs include the shipping costs and ancillary costs of setting up distribution networks, acquiring information, and insurance. Denote the iceberg transportation cost as b (for "berg"); expressed as a percentage the cost is $b \times 100\%$. For $b = 0.3$, transportation cost equals 30% of the purchase price. An exporter who buys the good for p^{China} and spends bp^{China} to transport the good has a total unit cost of $(1+b)p^{\text{China}}$. In a competitive equilibrium with positive sales in both countries, the exporter's cost per unit must equal the revenue per unit: $(1+b)p^{\text{China}} = p^{\text{U.S.}}$, or

$$p^{\text{China}} = \frac{1}{(1+b)} p^{\text{U.S.}}. \tag{2.1}$$

Equation 2.1 is the no-arbitrage condition under iceberg transportation costs. For $b > 0$, equation 2.1 implies that the U.S. price exceeds the Chinese price.

The dotted line in figure 2.1 adjusts the U.S. inverse demand to account for 30% transportation costs. Each point on this dotted line shows the amount that an exporter receives per unit of sales, at a given level of U.S. consumption, after paying transportation costs. The equilibrium sales occurs at the intersection of the solid line and this dotted line, where the price in China equals the price, net of transportation costs, that an exporter receives for U.S. sales. At price 12.2, China consumes 7.8 units; the United States consumes the remaining 2.2 units. The U.S. transportation-inclusive price is $1.3 \times 12.2 = 15.9$.

Here "the law of one price" holds: the price, adjusted for transportation costs, is the same in both locations. This so-called law describes a tendency. Arbitrage requires that people have information about prices in different locations. If this information is imperfect, then arbitrage creates a tendency for prices to move together, but does not ensure price equality. The individual selling tea in China need not know the U.S. price. If each person in a chain of people in markets between China and the United States knows only the price in neighboring markets, they know whether it is profitable to move tea east or west. Markets aggregate information; the middlemen move the commodity from where the price is low to where it is high, in the process revealing information about and also reducing price differences. Technological advances make the flow of information cheaper and reduce transportation costs, assisting the forces of arbitrage. Apps make it possible to instantly compare prices in different stores. Farmers in developing countries use cell phones to learn about price differences in different markets.

Figure 2.1 illustrates the graphical approach to answering our comparative statics question. The figure shows how moving from zero to positive transportation costs shifts down a curve, changing the equilibrium. Mathematics helps for more complicated questions. The first step in addressing a comparative statics question is to be clear about which variables are exogenous and which are endogenous. In this case, the transportation parameter, b, is exogenous, and the prices and quantities in the two markets are endogenous.

The second step is to identify the equilibrium condition that determines the endogenous variables. In this case, the equilibrium condition is the no-arbitrage condition 2.1. The demand functions for the two countries, $p^{\text{China}} = 20 - q^{\text{China}}$ and $p^{\text{U.S.}} = 18 - q^{\text{U.S.}}$; the constraint, $q^{\text{U.S.}} = 10 - q^{\text{China}}$; and this equilibrium condition imply

$$20 - q^{\text{China}} = \frac{1}{1+b}\left(18 - \left[10 - q^{\text{China}}\right]\right). \tag{2.2}$$

Once we know q^{China}, it is straightforward to find $q^{\text{U.S.}}$ and the two prices.

Equation 2.2 gives q^{China} as an "implicit function" of b. Because of its linearity, this equation can be solved to yield the "explicit function":

$$q^{\text{China}} = \frac{20b + 12}{b + 2}.$$

Using the quotient rule, we obtain the derivative:

$$\frac{dq^{\text{China}}}{db} = \frac{28}{(b+2)^2} > 0. \tag{2.3}$$

An increase in transportation costs increases equilibrium sales in China.

2.3 Elasticities

Objectives and skills: Calculate elasticities and understand why they are unit free.

Economists frequently use elasticities instead of slopes (derivatives) to express the relation between two variables. The slope of the demand function equals the number of units

of change in quantity demanded for a one-unit change in price. The elasticity of demand
with respect to price equals the percentage change in quantity demanded for a 1% change
in price. Unless the meaning is clear from the context, we have to specify the elasticity
of something (here, quantity demanded) with respect to something else (here, price). In
general, the value of an elasticity depends on the price (or the "something else") at which
it is evaluated. Using q to denote quantity demanded and p to denote price, the demand
function is $D(p)$.

The symbol dq denotes the change in q, and the ratio $\frac{dq}{q}$ denotes the rate of change;
multiplying by 100 converts a rate to a percentage, so $\frac{dq}{q}100$ is the percentage change in q.
The percentage change in q for each 1% change in p is the ratio

$$\frac{\frac{dq}{q}100}{\frac{dp}{p}100} = \frac{\frac{dq}{q}}{\frac{dp}{p}} = \frac{dq}{dp}\frac{p}{q}.$$

The slope of the demand function (a derivative) is $\frac{dq}{dp} = \frac{dD(p)}{dp}$ which we also write as
$D'(p)$. The elasticity of q with respect to p, denoted η, is defined as[1]

$$\eta(p) = -\frac{dq}{dp}\frac{p}{q} = -D'(p)\frac{p}{D(p)}. \tag{2.4}$$

The convention of including the negative sign in the definition of the demand elasticity
makes the elasticity a positive value. If we want to evaluate this elasticity at a particular
price, say p_o, we express it as

$$\eta(p_o) = -D'(p_o)\frac{p_o}{D(p_o)}.$$

The magnitude of the elasticity of demand depends on characteristics of the good, income,
and prices of complements and substitutes. The elasticity of demand for necessities, such
as food staples, tends to be small, but the elasticity of demand for luxuries may be large.

Elasticities, unlike slopes, are unit free; this feature makes elasticities a less ambiguous
way to describe the response of one variable to a change in another.[2] Nothing fundamental
changes if we measure quantity in kilos rather than pounds, or prices in pesos rather than

---

1 Depending on the context, we write the price elasticity of demand as a function of the price, $\eta(p)$, or as a
function of quantity, $\eta(q)$. The elasticity is evaluated at a point on the demand function: the value of p determines
the value of q.

2 Units are important. Columbus underestimated the diameter of the earth partly as a consequence of confusion
over units. The common belief that Napoleon was quite short (the "little man complex") resulted from confusing
English with French units; in fact, he was slightly taller than the average man of his era. The 1999 Mars Climate
Orbiter was lost due to miscommunication about units between Lockheed Martin and NASA.

dollars. These changes alter the derivative but not the elasticity. A percentage of something does not depend on the units in which it is measured. Because the elasticity is the ratio of percentage changes, the elasticity is independent of units.

To illustrate the difference between a slope and an elasticity, suppose that if quantity is measured in pounds and price in dollars, the demand and inverse demand functions are:

demand: $q = 3 - 5p$ inverse demand: $p = \dfrac{3 - q}{5}$.

The elasticity of demand with respect to price, evaluated at $p = 0.5$ is

$$-\frac{dq}{dp}\frac{p}{q} = 5\frac{0.5}{3 - 5(0.5)} = 5. \tag{2.5}$$

If we measure price in cents ($\tilde{P}$) per pound instead of dollars per pound (p), then using $\tilde{P} = 100p$, the demand and inverse demand functions are

demand: $q = 3 - 0.05\tilde{P}$ inverse demand $\tilde{P} = 60.0 - \dfrac{1}{0.05}q$.

Changing units from dollars to cents changes both the vertical intercept and the slope of the inverse demand function, altering the demand function's appearance, but not the information it contains. The elasticity of demand evaluated at $\tilde{P} = 0.5 \times 100 = 50.0$ equals 5, as in equation 2.5. Changing the units of a variable changes the derivative but not the elasticity.

2.4   Competition and Monopoly

Objectives and skills: Understand the relation between competitive and monopoly equilibria.

The competitive firm takes the market price as given; the monopoly recognizes that price responds to sales. To compare competition and monopoly, it is important to hold everything else constant: the inverse demand function, $p(Q)$, and the industry cost function, $c(Q)$, are the same in the two types of markets, where Q is aggregate sales. We compare competitive and monopoly outcomes by comparing their necessary conditions for profit maximization.

The Industry and Firm Cost Functions
What does it mean to say that an industry, consisting of many firms, has a particular cost function? The simplest way to think of this is to imagine that the industry consists of a large number, n, of factories. Under monopoly, a single firm owns all factories; under the competitive structure, each firm own a single factory. Suppose that the cost of producing q in a single factory is $\tilde{c}(q)$. All firms in the competitive industry are identical, making it

reasonable to assume that they all produce the same quantity, $\frac{1}{n}$ of industry quantity, so $nq = Q$. If each factory produces $q = \frac{Q}{n}$, then the cost in each firm is $\tilde{c}(q) = \tilde{c}\left(\frac{Q}{n}\right)$ and the industry cost is $n\tilde{c}\left(\frac{Q}{n}\right)$. We *define* the industry cost as

$$c(Q) \equiv n\tilde{c}\left(\frac{Q}{n}\right). \tag{2.6}$$

(The symbol "$\equiv$" means "is defined as.") Taking the derivative of both sides of equation 2.6 with respect to Q and using the chain rule gives

$$\underbrace{\frac{dc}{dQ} = n\frac{d\tilde{c}}{d\frac{Q}{n}}\frac{d\frac{Q}{n}}{dQ}}_{\substack{\text{use eq 2.6 and}\\\text{chain rule}}} = n\frac{d\tilde{c}}{dq}\overbrace{\frac{1}{n}}^{\text{use defn of } q} = \frac{d\tilde{c}}{dq}. \tag{2.7}$$

Equation 2.7 states that the marginal cost of the industry (the expression on the left) equals the marginal cost of the firm (or factory), the last expression. This relation holds for any number of firms, n, provided that $q = \frac{Q}{n}$. A change in the market structure alters the equilibrium amount produced but not the technology and therefore not the relation between costs and output.

Competitive Equilibrium

A representative firm chooses output, q, to maximize profits $=$ revenue minus cost, $pq - \tilde{c}(q)$, taking price as given. The first-order condition is

$$\frac{d(pq - \tilde{c}(q))}{dq} = \underbrace{p - \tilde{c}'(q)}_{\text{MR} - \text{MC}} \overset{\text{set}}{=} 0 \quad \Rightarrow \quad p = \tilde{c}'(q). \tag{2.8}$$

"MR" denotes "marginal revenue" and "MC" denotes "marginal cost." The symbol "$\Rightarrow$" means "implies." The notation "$\overset{\text{set}}{=}$" emphasizes that a first-order condition is responsible for the equality. It is not true that "price minus marginal cost equals zero" for every price and quantity. However, that equality holds at the quantity that solves the firm's first-order condition.

Using the relation in equation 2.7, we replace $\tilde{c}'(q)$ with $c'(Q)$; recognizing that the price depends on aggregate sales, we replace p with the inverse demand function $p(Q)$ and then rewrite the optimality condition 2.8 as

$$\text{price} = \text{industry marginal cost: } p(Q) = c'(Q). \tag{2.9}$$

Monopoly Equilibrium

The monopoly, recognizing that the price depends on its sales, chooses output, Q, to maximize profits: $p(Q)Q - c(Q)$. We first write marginal revenue using the elasticity:

$$
MR(Q) \equiv \overbrace{\frac{d[p(Q)Q]}{dQ}}^{\text{defn of MR}} = \overbrace{\frac{dp}{dQ}Q + p}^{\text{use product rule}} = \overbrace{p\left(1 + \frac{dp}{dQ}\frac{Q}{p}\right)}^{\text{factor out } p}
$$

$$
= \underbrace{p\left(1 + \frac{1}{\frac{dQ}{dp}\frac{p}{Q}}\right)}_{\substack{\text{multiplying by a number} = \\ \text{dividing by its inverse}}} = \underbrace{p(Q)\left(1 - \frac{1}{\eta(Q)}\right).}_{\text{use defn of elasticity}}
\tag{2.10}
$$

The first-order condition for the monopoly is

$$
\frac{d(p(Q)Q - c(Q))}{dQ} = \overbrace{p'(Q)Q + p}^{\text{MR}} - \overbrace{c'(Q)}^{\text{MC}} \overset{\text{set}}{=} 0.
$$

Using the formula for marginal revenue gives the first-order condition

$$
\text{Marginal revenue} = \text{Marginal cost: } p(Q)\left(1 - \frac{1}{\eta(Q)}\right) = c'(Q).
\tag{2.11}
$$

Comparing the Two Equilibria

The equilibrium conditions for the competitive industry and the monopoly are

Competition: $p(Q) = c'(Q)$,

Monopoly: $p(Q)\left(1 - \frac{1}{\eta(Q)}\right) = c'(Q)$.

Both these equations involve the inverse demand function, $p(Q)$, and the industry marginal cost function, $c'(Q)$. The competitive equilibrium condition sets price equal to the industry marginal cost, and the monopoly condition sets marginal revenue equal to industry marginal cost. Using the necessary condition for a competitive equilibrium, we can (in many cases) obtain the monopoly necessary condition *merely by replacing p with* $p\left(1 - \frac{1}{\eta(Q)}\right)$.[3]

---

3 Early in the study of arithmetic, we learn that the order in which operations are performed matters: $(3 + 4) \times 7 = 49 \neq 3 + (4 \times 7) = 31$. The order of operations also matters in carrying out economic calculations. For the monopoly, we first replace price with the inverse demand function, and then we take the derivative of profit with respect to sales. For the competitive firm, we first take the derivative of profit with respect to sales, taking price as given, and then substitute the inverse demand function into the first-order condition to obtain an equation in quantity. *The order of these two steps is critical.*

The monopoly obtains a higher price ("exercises market power") by lowering sales. A given price increase requires a greater reduction in sales, the more elastic is demand. If demand is very elastic ($\eta(Q)$ is large), the monopoly has little ability to exercise market power. The formula for marginal revenue, equation 2.10, shows that as the market demand becomes infinitely elastic, that is, as $\eta(Q) \to \infty$ ("η goes to infinity"), marginal revenue equals price. If demand is very elastic at all prices, the monopoly has little market power and behaves like a competitive firm. The monopoly never produces where $\eta < 1$; at such a point, marginal revenue is negative.

Optimization and Equilibrium

At a competitive equilibrium, consumers maximize utility, resulting in a price-quantity combination on the demand function, and producers maximize profits, resulting in a price-quantity combination on the supply function. Markets clear, so supply equals demand. Optimization-based economic models are potentially useful only if people actually pursue their self-interest. Consistently irrational firms are not likely to survive. Shoppers may not buy food that is good for them, but they buy the food that they want, and in that respect they act in their self-interest. Competitive firms' optimal production level depends on the price they expect to receive, but their expectations may be wrong. If they have already committed a certain quantity to the market, but the price is lower than they expected, the price-quantity point is below the supply curve. Markets are unlikely to be exactly in equilibrium, but if people respond to their mistakes, those responses likely move a market toward equilibrium. If firms find that the price has repeatedly been lower than their marginal cost, they have an incentive to decrease quantity, causing price to rise and the outcome to move toward equilibrium.

Optimality and No-Arbitrage Conditions

We used only basic economic logic to obtain the no-arbitrage condition 2.1. We can also obtain this equation as the first order condition to an optimization problem. Using the constraint $q^{\text{U.S.}} = 10 - q^{\text{China}}$, profits for the price-taking tea seller (revenue in China plus revenue in the United States minus transportation costs) equal

$$\pi = p^{\text{China}} q^{\text{China}} + p^{\text{U.S}}(10 - q^{\text{China}}) - bp^{\text{China}}(10 - q^{\text{China}}).$$

The first-order condition (at an interior equilibrium) is

$$\frac{d\pi}{dq^{\text{China}}} = p^{\text{China}} - p^{\text{U.S}} + bp^{\text{China}} \stackrel{\text{set}}{=} 0.$$

Rearranging the last equation produces the no-arbitrage condition 2.1.

2.5 Examples: Competition and Monopoly*

Objectives and skills: Derive equilibrium conditions, use these to calculate equilibrium price and quantity, and show how the elasticity of demand affects monopoly power.

Examples show how to set up the objective functions for the competitive and monopoly industries, use the first-order conditions to find equilibrium price and quantity in the two cases, and examine the relation between the elasticity of demand and monopoly power. We use a "constant elasticity of demand function" $Q = \left(\frac{p}{A}\right)^{-\eta}$, with the inverse demand $p(Q) = AQ^{-\frac{1}{\eta}}$. For this demand function (but not in general), the elasticity η is a constant parameter, not a function of price. Assume that $\eta > 1$, so that marginal revenue is positive.

The industry cost function is $c(Q) = \frac{b}{2}Q^2$. Using equation 2.6, the individual-firm cost function consistent with this industry cost function is $\tilde{c}(q) = \frac{nb}{2}q^2$. If each firm produces $\frac{1}{n}$ of the industry total, Q, then industry cost equals

$$n\tilde{c}(q) = \overbrace{n\tilde{c}\left(\frac{Q}{n}\right)}^{\text{use defn of } \tilde{c}(q)} = n\frac{nb}{2}\left(\frac{Q}{n}\right)^2 = \underbrace{\frac{b}{2}Q^2}_{\text{simplify}} = c(Q).$$

$$\underbrace{\phantom{n\tilde{c}\left(\frac{Q}{n}\right)}}_{\text{use defn of } q}$$

The sum of individual firms' cost over all firms equals industry costs.

Competitive Industry

The firm's objective and first-order condition are

$$\text{objective: } \max_q \left[pq - \frac{nb}{2}q^2 \right],$$

$$\text{first-order condition: } p - bnq \overset{\text{set}}{=} 0.$$

The assumption that each firm produces $\frac{1}{n}$ of the industry total means $q = \frac{Q}{n}$, so $nq = Q$. Using this equality, and replacing p by the inverse demand function, $p = AQ^{-\frac{1}{\eta}}$, we obtain the equilibrium condition under competition:

$$AQ^{-\frac{1}{\eta}} - bQ = 0. \tag{2.12}$$

Solving this equation for quantity and then using the inverse demand function gives the equilibrium quantity and price:

$$Q = \left(\frac{A}{b}\right)^{\frac{\eta}{1+\eta}} \quad \Rightarrow \quad p = A\left(\frac{A}{b}\right)^{\frac{-1}{1+\eta}}.$$

The Monopoly

Using the inverse demand function, $p = A Q^{-\frac{1}{\eta}}$, the objective and first-order condition for the monopoly are

$$\text{objective: } \max_Q \left[\underbrace{A Q^{-\frac{1}{\eta}} \times Q}_{\text{revenue}} - \underbrace{\frac{b}{2} Q^2}_{\text{costs}} \right],$$

$$\text{first-order condition: } \left(1 - \frac{1}{\eta}\right) A Q^{-\frac{1}{\eta}} - b Q \overset{\text{set}}{=} 0.$$

Solving the first-order condition for Q and then using the inverse demand function to obtain price gives

$$Q = \left[\frac{A \left(1 - \frac{1}{\eta}\right)}{b} \right]^{\frac{\eta}{\eta+1}} \quad \Rightarrow \quad p = A \left[\frac{A \left(1 - \frac{1}{\eta}\right)}{b} \right]^{\frac{-1}{\eta+1}}.$$

Comparing the Competitive and Monopoly Prices

The ratio of the equilibrium monopoly to competitive price provides a measure of monopoly power. If the ratio equals one, the prices in the two markets are equal: there is no monopoly power. If the ratio is large, the monopoly price is much greater than the

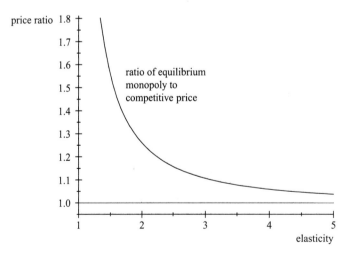

Figure 2.2
The ratio of monopoly to competitive price falls with η but is greater than 1 for finite η.

competitive price: monopoly power is significant. For our example, the ratio of equilibrium prices is

$$\text{price ratio} = \eta^{\frac{1}{\eta+1}} (\eta - 1)^{-\frac{1}{\eta+1}}.$$

Figure 2.2 shows that the monopoly price is much higher than the competitive price for low elasticity of demand but is close to the competitive price for high elasticity of demand.

2.6 Discounting

Objectives and skills: Understand the rationale for and the implementation of discounting.

A box of tea in China and a box of tea in the United States are not the same commodity if it is costly to move the box from one location to the other. Similarly, a dollar 10 years from now is not the same as a dollar today, because there is an opportunity cost, the forgone investment, of receiving the dollar later rather than earlier. Resource managers compare the value of extracting/harvesting at different points in time using discounting.

For a period of arbitrary length, say, 1 year, the discount rate, denoted r, equals the return on the most profitable riskless investment over that period. The discount rate is the price of using money; like most prices it is usually positive. The cost of a loan equals the amount the borrower must repay. A higher discount rate ($=$ interest rate) increases the cost, typically decreasing the demand for loans. People's willingness to lend money typically increases with the interest rate. The market forces of supply and demand, together with central bank policy, determine discount rates.[4] We treat the discount rate as an exogenous number.

If a person today invests z dollars for 1 year in an asset paying the rate r, at the end of the year the person has $z(1+r)$. This person is indifferent between receiving $1 at the beginning of the next year and $$z$ in the current period, if and only if $z(1+r)=1$, or $z = \frac{1}{1+r}$. We define $\rho \equiv \frac{1}{1+r}$ as the discount factor. This person is indifferent between receiving $43.60 at the beginning of next period, or $43.60 \times \rho$ at the beginning of the current period. Multiplying an amount received one year in the future by ρ, produces the "present value" of the future receipt. A person is indifferent between receiving $1 at the end of 2 years and $$z$ today if and only if $(1+r)(1+r)z=1$, or $z=\rho^2$. Thus, ρ^2 is the present value today of a dollar in 2 years; ρ^n is the present value of a dollar in n years.

---

4 People may prefer holding money in a bank instead of a mattress because the bank makes transfers more convenient. In extreme cases, people are willing to supply loans at a negative interest rate; they pay the bank to hold their money. Negative interest rates were adopted by some European Central Banks in 2014 and by Japan's Central Bank in 2016. However, episodes of negative interest rates are rare.

If a firm obtains profits π_t during periods $t = 0, 1, 2, \ldots, T$, then the present discounted stream of profits equals $\sum_{t=0}^{T} \rho^t \pi_t$. If $\pi_t = \pi$, a constant, and $T = \infty$ we have

$$\underbrace{\sum_{t=0}^{\infty} \pi \rho^t = \pi \overbrace{\sum_{t=0}^{\infty} \rho^t}}_{\substack{\text{factor out } \pi}} \overbrace{= \frac{\pi}{1-\rho}}^{\substack{\text{use formula for sum} \\ \text{of geometric series}}} = \underbrace{\frac{\pi}{1 - \frac{1}{1+r}}}_{\text{use defn of } \rho} = \underbrace{\frac{\pi}{r}(1+r)}_{\text{simplify denominator}} \underbrace{\approx \frac{\pi}{r}}_{\text{approx. equal to}} . \quad (2.13)$$

The first equality factors out the constant π; the second uses the formula for a geometric series; the third uses the definition of ρ, and the fourth simplifies the denominator. The approximation (indicated by "$\approx$") holds if r is much smaller than 1. (In the continuous time setting, where an integral replaces the sum, the approximation is exact.) The present value of a stream of profits, π, received in the current period and for the next T years equals

$$
\begin{aligned}
\sum_{t=0}^{T} \pi \rho^t &= \overbrace{\sum_{t=0}^{T} \pi \rho^t + \sum_{t=T+1}^{\infty} \pi \rho^t}^{\text{add and subtract 2nd and 3rd terms}} - \sum_{t=T+1}^{\infty} \pi \rho^t = \overbrace{\sum_{t=0}^{\infty} \pi \rho^t}^{\text{combine first two terms}} - \sum_{t=T+1}^{\infty} \pi \rho^t \\
&= \underbrace{\sum_{t=0}^{\infty} \pi \rho^t - \rho^{T+1} \sum_{t=0}^{\infty} \pi \rho^t}_{\text{factor out } \rho^{T+1} \text{ from second term}} = \underbrace{\frac{1 - \rho^{T+1}}{1 - \rho} \pi}_{\substack{\text{use formula for sum of} \\ \text{geometric series}}} .
\end{aligned}
\quad (2.14)
$$

Relation between the Discount Rate and the Length of a Period

The numerical value of the discount rate, and thus of the discount factor, depends on the length of the period of time. If a period lasts for 10 years, and an asset held for one 10-year period pays a return of $\tilde{r}$, then \$1 invested in this asset for three periods (30 years) returns $(1 + \tilde{r})^3$. This return is "compounded" every decade. We can convert this decadal return to an annual return by choosing the annual discount rate, r, to satisfy $(1 + r)^{10} = (1 + \tilde{r})$. Taking logs of both sides and then dividing by 10 gives $\ln(1 + r) = \frac{\ln(1 + \tilde{r})}{10}$. If $\tilde{r} = 0.8$, then $r = 0.061$; this asset pays an 80% return over a decade, or a 6.1% return compounded annually. We multiply by 100 to translate a rate into a percentage.

Discounting in Continuous Time*

In a few places later in the text we consider the situation where compounding occurs continuously; instead of a return being compounded every year, it is compounded every second, or every tenth of a second. If the discount rate under continuous compounding equals $\tilde{r}$, then the present value of \$1 t units of time in the future is $e^{-\tilde{r}t}$. If a unit of time equals 1 year, and the annual discount rate is r, then the continuous rate $\tilde{r}$ satisfies $e^{-\tilde{r}} = \frac{1}{1+r}$.

Table 2.1
Payment streams for two cases

Period	0	1	2	3	4	5
Payment (case 1)	2	6	3	4	9	16
Payment (case 2)	7	7	7	7	7	7

Taking logs of both sides gives $\tilde{r} = \ln(1 + r)$. For $r = 0.05$, $\tilde{r} = \ln(1.05) = 0.049$. A 5% return compounded annually is equivalent to a 4.9% return compounded continuously.

Numerical Examples

Table 2.1 shows two streams of payments (cases 1 and 2) over six periods, from period 0 through period 5. These values correspond to the π_t used above, with $t = 0, 1, 2, \ldots, 5$. The discount rate for a period is r, so the discount factor is $\rho = \frac{1}{1+r}$; a period lasts for 1 year, so r is the annual discount rate, and ρ equals the present value today, of a dollar received in 1 year. The present discounted value of the stream of payments in case 1 is

$$Z = \rho^0 2 + \rho^1 6 + \rho^2 3 + \rho^3 4 + \rho^4 9 + \rho^5 16. \tag{2.15}$$

If $r = 0.03$ (corresponding to a 3% annual discount rate), then $\rho = \frac{1}{1.03}$ and $Z = 36.11$. (The symbol Z has no special significance; we want to give the sum a name for ease of reference later.)

We can find the present discounted value of the stream of payments in case 2 using the same type of calculation; however, because the payment in each period is the same in case 2, it is faster to use the formula in equation 2.14. For this example, $\pi = 7$ and $T = 5$, so the present discounted value of the stream of payments is

$$\sum_{t=0}^{5} 7\rho^t = \frac{1 - \rho^{5+1}}{1 - \rho} 7.$$

For $\rho = \frac{1}{1.03} = 0.971$, this sum equals 39.06.

Now suppose that the person receives five "cycles" of the stream of payments shown in case 1. The first cycle begins in year 0, the second in year 6, the third in year 12, the fourth in year 18, and the fifth in year 24. We could calculate the present value of the stream of payments over these five cycles by extending the calculation shown in equation 2.15. A simpler method takes advantage of the fact that each cycle contains the same stream of payments. The present value, *at the beginning of each cycle*, of receiving the six payments in case 1 is Z (by definition). A person with discount rate r is indifferent between receiving this stream of payments over the 6 years beginning (for example) in year 18, and receiving the lump sum Z in year 18. The present value in year 0 of receiving either of these alternatives (the 6-year stream beginning in year 18 or the lump sum in year 18) is $\left(\rho^6\right)^3 Z = \rho^{18} Z$. The discount factor for each 6-year block is ρ^6, and there are three of these blocks before reaching year 18. Similarly, the present value, in year 0, of receiving the cycle of payments over years 12 through 17 is $\left(\rho^6\right)^2 Z$: there are two 6-year blocks of time before we reach year 12.

Merely to simplify notation, denote ρ^6 as $\tilde{\rho}$. Using the logic of the previous paragraph and the formula in equation 2.14, we can write the present discounted value of the stream of payments over the five cycles as

$$\sum_{t=0}^{4} Z \tilde{\rho}^t = \frac{1 - \tilde{\rho}^5}{1 - \tilde{\rho}} Z.$$

For our example, where $r = 0.03$, $\tilde{\rho} = \rho^6 = 0.837$, and $Z = 36.1$, we have

$$\sum_{t=0}^{4} Z \tilde{\rho}^t = \frac{1 - (0.837)^5}{1 - 0.837} 36.1 = 130.49.$$

2.7 Applications of Discounting

Objectives and skills: Be able to use discounting to study policy-relevant problems.

Three examples illustrate the role of discounting in policy-relevant problems. We show how discounting makes it possible to compare the costs of different methods of electricity production, affects the social cost of carbon emissions, and affects the implicit subsidy provided by a low-interest loan.

"Levelized Cost of Electricity"
Electricity can be produced using different production methods and different inputs, leading to different cost streams and producing different amounts of power. Nuclear-powered plants are expensive to build and require decommissioning, but they have low fuel costs. Fossil fuel plants have relatively low investment and decommissioning costs, but high fuel costs. The "levelized cost" of electricity (LCOE) provides a basis for comparing the cost of producing electricity using different methods. The data for this calculation include estimates of the year-t capital cost, C_t; variable cost, V_t (including fuel and maintenance); the amount of energy produced, E_t; and the lifetime (including construction and decommissioning time) of the project, $n + 1$ years. The formula for LCOE is

$$LCOE = \frac{\sum_{t=0}^{n} \rho^t (C_t + V_t)}{\sum_{t=0}^{n} \rho^t E_t}. \tag{2.16}$$

The numerator is the present discounted value of the stream of costs, and the denominator is the present discounted value of the stream of energy flows. The LCOE often excludes potentially important considerations: wind or solar may require significant network upgrades to bring the power to market; fossil fuels have health- and climate-related exter-nalities; nuclear power creates the risk of rare but catastrophic events. Incorporating these and other considerations requires additional data.

The example in Table 2.2 illustrates the calculation and shows the sensitivity of LCOEs to the discount rate. Type A generation method is expensive to construct but cheap to run and lasts a long time. Type B is cheap to build, expensive to run, and has a shorter lifetime. They both produce the same amount of energy per year (one unit).

For this example, the LCOE of the two power plants are

$$LCOE^A = \frac{\left(2 + \sum_{t=5}^{50} \rho^t (0.05)\right)}{\sum_{t=5}^{50} \rho^t 1}, \quad LCOE^B = \frac{\left(0.3 + \sum_{t=2}^{32} \rho^t (0.12)\right)}{\sum_{t=2}^{32} \rho^t 1}.$$

Figure 2.3 shows the ratio of the two levelized costs as a function of the discount rate. The costs are equal (the ratio is 1) for $r = 2.7\%$; Type A is 10% cheaper at $r = 2\%$ and 17% more expensive at $r = 4\%$. When "money is cheap" (the discount rate is low), it is

Table 2.2
Example: Two different types of power plants

	Capital Cost (billion $)	Annual Operating Cost (billion $)	Lifetime (years)	Construction Time (years)
Type A	2	0.05	45	5
Type B	0.3	0.12	30	2

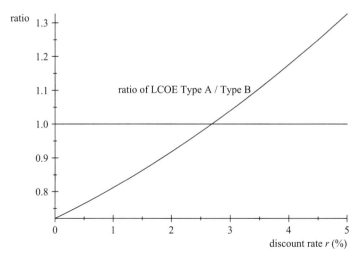

Figure 2.3
Ratio of LCOE $\frac{\text{Type A}}{\text{Type B}}$ increases with the discount rate r: expensive capital makes Type A relatively more expensive than Type B.

Table 2.3
Estimated LCOE (2012$/MWh) for plants entering service in 2019

Conventional coal $= 96$	IGCC $= 116$	Natural gas CCC $= 66$	Advanced nuclear $= 96$
Wind $= 80$	Wind offshore $= 204$	Solar PV2 $= 130$	Hydro $= 85$

Note: IGCC, Integrated Coal-Gasification Combined Cycle; CCC, Conventional Combined Cycle PV2, Photo-Voltaic 2. *Source*: U.S. Energy Information Administration (2014).

economical to use the method that has large up-front costs but lower costs overall (Type A). However, when the discount rate is high, it is economical to use Type B, which has lower initial costs but higher undiscounted total costs.

Table 2.3 shows U.S. LCOE estimates for several power sources.

Social Cost of Carbon

The social cost of carbon (SCC) is defined as the present discounted stream of damages due to a unit of carbon emissions today. It plays an important role in climate economics (chapter 19); the U.S. Environmental Protection Agency (EPA) Interagency Working Group (2013) uses the SCC in cost/benefit analyses of rules and legislation affecting greenhouse gas emissions. The SCC depends on the relation between a unit of emissions today and future carbon stocks, the relation between carbon stocks and temperature changes, the relation between temperature changes and economic damages, and the discount rate. Higher discount rates (lower discount factors) place less weight on future damages and therefore lead to a lower SCC. With a discount rate of 5%, the EPA estimates the SCC in 2015 at $11 per metric ton of CO_2, rising to $56 for a 2.5% discount rate; halving the discount rate increases the SCC by a factor of five.

These estimates involve complex models, but an example shows the role of discounting. Suppose that each metric ton of atmospheric CO_2 creates d dollars of annual economic damage, and that carbon leaves the atmosphere ("decays") at a constant rate δ.[5] With these assumptions, one unit of emissions today increases the carbon stock t periods from now by $(1 - \delta)^t$ and creates $d(1 - \delta)^t$ dollars of damage in period t. The present discounted value of the stream of damages due to this unit of emissions is

$$
\underbrace{SCC = \sum_{t=0}^{\infty} d(1 - \delta)^t \rho^t}_{\text{defn of SCC}} \quad \overbrace{= \frac{d}{1 - (1 - \delta)\rho}}^{\text{use formula for sum of geometric series}} \quad \underbrace{= \frac{d}{r + \delta}(r + 1)}_{\text{use defn of } \rho \text{ and simplify}} \; .
$$

The smaller is the discount rate (the larger is ρ), the larger is the SCC.

---

5 Carbon does not literally decay. CO_2 is emitted to the atmosphere, and over time some of it moves to different oceanic and terrestrial reservoirs. The model of constant decay is one of the simplest ways to approximate carbon leaving the atmosphere.

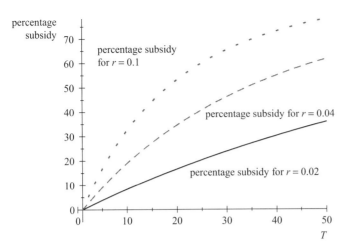

Figure 2.4
The subsidy, as a percentage of the loan, increases with the repayment period, T, and the discount factor, r.

Implicit Subsidies from Ignoring Discounting

The U.S. Reclamation Act of 1902 used receipts from the sale of federal lands to finance the Reclamation Fund, which paid for irrigation projects in Western states. The Fund was designed to be self-perpetuating, with the settlers who used the water repaying the cost of the project without interest. The settlers were thus given a no-interest loan. The repayment period was initially 10 years, but later projects were financed over 40–50 years. The implicit subsidy arising from these no-interest loans could be as high as 90% of the project's cost, depending on the length of the repayment period and the interest rate.

If users repay without interest the cost of a project, C, over a period of T years, their annual repayment is $\frac{C}{T}$. If the discount rate is r, the value of this stream of payments is (using equation 2.14) $\frac{C}{T}\frac{1-\rho^T}{1-\rho}$. The subsidy, as a percentage of the cost of the project, C, is

$$S = \frac{C - \frac{C}{T}\frac{1-\rho^T}{1-\rho}}{C}\,100 = \left(1 - \frac{1-\rho^T}{T(1-\rho)}\right)100.$$

Figure 2.4 shows the subsidy's sensitivity to the repayment period, T, and the interest rate. Low- or no-interest loans can result in large subsidies.

2.8 Welfare

Objectives and skills: Understand the meaning of "Pareto efficient," the two Fundamental Welfare Theorems, and the distinction between general and partial equilibrium.

Absent market failures, a competitive outcome is "Pareto efficient": there does not exist another allocation that makes at least one agent better off without making any agent worse off. Jiangfeng and Mary get utility only from their own consumption of a good with one unit of fixed supply; a feasible allocation gives Jiangfeng $z \geq 0$ and Mary $w \geq 0$ units of the good, with $z + w \leq 1$. A Pareto efficient allocation makes sure that all of the good is consumed; *any* outcome with $z + w = 1$ is Pareto efficient. People might prefer the equal but inefficient allocation, $z = w = 0.4999$ to the Pareto efficient (hereafter "efficient") but unequal allocation $w = 1$, $z = 0$. Efficiency means that none of the economic pie is being wasted, not that it is being divided fairly. "Fairness" is subjective, but "efficiency" has an objective meaning.

Two Fundamental Welfare Theorems describe welfare properties of competitive equilibria. The First Fundamental Welfare Theorem provides conditions under which a competitive equilibrium is efficient. The Second Fundamental Welfare Theorem provides conditions under which any efficient outcome can be "supported as a competitive equilibrium" by means of taxes and transfers. A transfer takes something away from one person and give it to another. A tax drives a wedge between the price that one person in a transaction pays and another person receives. Taxes and transfers "support outcome X as a competitive equilibrium" if, in the presence of these taxes and transfers, the competitive equilibrium equals X. For example, X might be a particular level of production, a particular level of pollution, or a particular distribution of income.

The conditions for the first theorem include the absence of externalities and the existence of "complete markets." Markets are complete if there is a market for every type of transaction that people would like to make. If someone would like to buy water and someone else is willing to sell water, then complete markets require that there exists a water market making this exchange possible. The conditions for the second theorem include that the economy is "convex": this requirement rules out increasing returns to scale (the situation where doubling all inputs more than doubles output).

Resource economics is an important field in large part because of the presence of market failures. These imply that the conditions of the First Fundamental Welfare Theorem are not satisfied, so there is no reason to think that competitive markets achieve an efficient outcome. However, the Second Fundamental Welfare Theorem means that competitive markets together with well-designed taxes and transfers potentially achieve efficiency. By pulling the correct levers (using the right taxes and transfers), it is possible to harness the power of markets to achieve socially desirable outcomes. Economists almost universally prefer market-based environmental policies, such as an emissions tax, rather than "command and control" regulations, which legislate details about production. Modern resource economics emphasizes institutional changes, such as the establishment of property rights, that potentially correct market failures, thereby making explicit regulation unnecessary for efficiency. Even if the conditions of the First Fundamental Welfare Theorem are satisfied, so that the competitive equilibrium is efficient, it might be ethically unattractive because of unequal distribution. The Second Fundamental Welfare Theorem implies that taxes and transfers can achieve a different, more socially acceptable, efficient outcome.

Partial versus General Equilibrium

The Fundamental Welfare Theorems are valid under general and partial equilibrium settings, deterministic and stochastic (= random) environments, and static and dynamic (one-period and many-period) economies. This book includes both static and dynamic models. With few exceptions, we consider only deterministic (no uncertainty) partial equilibrium models. Partial equilibrium models study a single market—in our case, the market for a natural resource. These models take as given all outside considerations that influence this market. For petroleum, the partial equilibrium model seeks to explain petroleum prices and quantities, over time, treating as exogenous all variables that influence supply and demand. Variables affecting supply include the discount rate, prices of factors of production (e.g., labor, machinery), and technology (e.g., drilling techniques). Variables affecting demand include levels of income, and prices of substitutes (e.g., natural gas) and complements (e.g., cars).

In a partial equilibrium setting, consumer and producer surplus measure consumer and producer welfare; the sum of consumer and producer surplus (= social surplus) measures social welfare.[6] In most dynamic partial equilibrium resource models, the criterion for aggregate social welfare equals the discounted stream of social surplus. (The "discounted stream of X" is shorthand for "the sum, over time, of the present discounted values of the single period values of X.") This criterion is known as "discounted utilitarianism"; section 11.4.3 and chapter 19 discuss some limitations of this criterion.

The First Fundamental Welfare Theorem implies that a competitive partial equilibrium resource market, without market failures, maximizes the discounted stream of social surplus. Under market failures, the competitive equilibrium is unlikely to achieve this goal, but with appropriate taxes and transfers it might do so.

2.9   Summary

A trade example illustrates the meaning of arbitrage over space. Many of the main ideas in this book are based on arbitrage over time: instead of selling the commodity in one country

---

6 Consumer surplus equals the area under the inverse demand function and above the horizontal line at the equilibrium price. It measures the difference between what consumers would be willing to pay and what they actually pay, and it thus provides a measure of consumer gains.

   Under competition, the supply curve equals industry marginal cost. The area under that curve, from zero to a positive quantity q, equals the variable cost of producing q. The area between the horizontal line at the market price and the supply function, defined as producer surplus, equals revenue minus variable cost; it thus provides a measure of producer gains.

rather than another, the firm sells it at one point in time rather than another. Understanding spatial arbitrage makes it easy to understand intertemporal arbitrage.

The method of comparative statics can help clarify the relation between exogenous parameters (model inputs) and endogenous outcomes (model outputs). Casual reasoning or graphical methods suffice to answer easy comparative statics questions, but more complicated questions require mathematics. Using an equilibrium condition (e.g., supply equals demand), we find a relation between exogenous and endogenous variables. We answer the comparative statics question by taking the derivative of the endogenous variable, with respect to an exogenous variable.

To compare competition and monopoly, we "hold everything else constant," apart from the market structure. We require that the demand and cost *functions* (not their *levels*) are the same for both market structures. Both the monopoly and the representative firm want to maximize profits. For the price-taking competitive firms, the equilibrium condition is "price equals marginal cost"; for the monopoly, the equilibrium condition is "marginal revenue equals marginal cost." The monopoly understands that its sales affect the price; the monopoly marginal revenue equals $p(1 - 1/\eta(p))$, where $\eta(p)$ is the elasticity of demand. If $\eta(p)$ is finite, the monopoly sells less than the competitive industry. Monopoly power decreases as demand becomes more elastic. It is important to be able to calculate an elasticity and to understand why it is unit free.

We use the discount factor to compare values (e.g., profits) received in different periods. The discount factor is $\rho = 1/(1 + r)$, where r is the discount rate, equal to the highest riskless return available to the agent. The discount factor converts future values into present values.

An outcome, such as the allocation of a product across individuals, geographical regions, or time, is Pareto efficient if there is no reallocation that makes some agent better off without making any agent worse off. The two Fundamental Welfare Theorems provide conditions under which a competitive equilibrium is efficient and under which any efficient outcome can be supported as a competitive equilibrium by means of taxes and transfers.

2.10   Terms and Concepts, Study Questions, Exercises, and Sources

Terms and Concepts

Demand function, inverse demand function, arbitrage, no-arbitrage condition, interior equilibrium, iceberg transportation costs, endogenous and exogenous variables, law of one price, implicit function, explicit function, comparative statics, first-order condition, marginal revenue, order of operations, discount function, discount factor, opportunity cost, compounding, capital cost, operating cost, decommissioning cost, levelized cost, partial and general equilibrium, externality, complete markets, efficient, Pareto efficient, consumer and producer surplus, feasible, discounted utilitarianism, taxes and transfers supporting an outcome.

Study Questions

1. Use the type of graph in figure 2.1 to illustrate the effect of a change on demand in one country, a change in available supply, or a change in transportation costs, on the equilibrium allocation of sales across countries.

2. Given inverse demand functions in two countries, available supply, and transportation costs, write down the equilibrium condition and write a comparative statics expression showing the effect of a change in an exogenous variable on an endogenous variable. Be clear about the distinction between exogenous and endogenous variables.

3. What is an elasticity? How does one calculate it? And what does it mean to say that the elasticity is unit free?

4. Given an industry cost function and an inverse demand, write down the equilibrium conditions that determine sales under competition and under monopoly.

5. What is the relation between a discount rate and a discount factor? What are they used for? Show how to calculate the present discounted stream of payoffs and how to work through the kinds of examples shown in section 2.7.

6. Summarize and explain the importance of the two Fundamental Welfare Theorems.

Exercises

1. When quantities are measured in pounds and prices in dollars, the demand function is $Q = 3 - 5P$.

    (a) What is the elasticity of demand evaluated at $P = 0.5$?

    (b) Express the same relation between demand and price using different units, q and p: q are in units of kilos, and p in pesos. (Which equation is correct: $q = 2.2Q$ or $q = \frac{Q}{2.2}$?) There are 3 pesos per dollar. (Which equation is correct: $p = 3P$ or $p = \frac{P}{3}$?)

    (c) Using the new units, q and p, express the elasticity of demand with respect to price, evaluated at the price of half a dollar.

    (d) What is the point of this exercise?

2. How does an increase in transportation costs affect the location of the dotted line in figure 2.1, and how does this change alter the equilibrium price and the allocation of tea between the two countries?

3. How does an increase in the available supply (e.g., from 10 units to 12 units of tea) change the appearance of figure 2.1, and how does this change in supply alter the equilibrium quantities and prices in the two countries?

4. Calculate $\eta(Q)$ for the demand function $Q = a - hp$ and then for the demand function $Q = ap^{-h}$, where h is a positive number. Graph the two elasticities as a function of Q for $a = 10$ and $h = 2$.

5. A monopoly owns 10 units of tea in China and has zero transportation costs ($b = 0$).

   (a) Using the inverse demand functions in section 2.1 and algebra, find monopoly sales in the two markets. How does the monopoly sales in China compare to sales by a competitive firm?

   (b) Redraw figure 2.1 without the dotted line but including the marginal revenue curves associated with the inverse demand functions in the two markets. Use this figure to compare sales levels under the monopoly and competition.

6. A monopoly owns 10 units of tea in China, faces the inverse demand functions in section 2.1, and has iceberg transportation costs, b. To simplify notation, denote sales in China as q (instead of q^{China}).

   (a) Find the expressions for revenue in China, revenue in the United States, and transportation costs, as functions of q. Use these expressions to write monopoly profits as a function of its sales in China.

   (b) Find the first-order condition for the problem of maximizing profits; solve the first-order condition to express q as a function of b. [Hint: For this problem, merely replacing "price" with "marginal revenue" in the equilibrium condition 2.1 does not give the correct monopoly first-order condition. It is necessary to begin with the monopoly's profit function and find the first-order condition by taking a derivative.]

   (c) Find the derivative of monopoly sales with respect to b. Are sales in China more sensitive to transportation costs under monopoly or competition?

7. Suppose that an industry has the cost function $c(Q) = 2Q + \frac{3}{2}Q^2$. This industry consists of n firms, each with cost function $\tilde{c}(q)$. Find $\tilde{c}(q)$. [Hint: "Guess" that the single firm's cost function is of the form $\tilde{c}(q) = aq + \frac{b}{2}q^2$. Then use the requirement that $c(Q) = n\tilde{c}\left(\frac{Q}{n}\right)$ to write

$$2Q + \frac{3}{2}Q^2 = n\left(a\frac{Q}{n} + \frac{b}{2}\left(\frac{Q}{n}\right)^2\right).$$

This relation must hold for all Q (not just a particular Q), so we can "equate coefficients" of Q and Q^2 to find the values of a and b.]

8. A plant that supplies 1 unit of electricity per year costs \$1 billion to build, lasts 25 years, and has an annual operating cost of \$0.2 billion; it costs \$0.1 billion to decommission the plant at the end of its lifetime (25 years). Assume that the construction costs and the operating costs are paid at the beginning of the period, and that the decommissioning cost

is paid at the end of the life of the plant. The annual discount rate is r, with discount factor $\rho = \frac{1}{1+r}$. Write the formula for the present value of the cost of providing 1 unit of electricity for 100 years, including the decommissioning costs. [Hint: First find the present value of providing 1 unit of electricity for 25 years. Denote this magnitude as Z. Then find the present value of incurring this cost, Z, four times: in periods 0, 25, 50, and 75.]

9. A monopoly faces the demand function $q = p^{-1.2}$ and has production costs $c(q) = \frac{b}{2}q^2$. Find the comparative statics of equilibrium sales with respect to the cost parameter, b. [Hint: Write the monopoly's first-order condition (marginal revenue equals marginal cost). Solve this expression for q as a function of b, and take the derivative of q with respect to b.]

10. A person plans to save \$1 for 20 years and can invest at an annual rate of 10% ($r = 0.1$). This investment opportunity compounds annually (meaning that they receive interest payments at the end of each year). A second investment opportunity pays a return of $\tilde{r} \times 100\%$, compounded every decade. (After one decade, the investment of \$1 yields $1 + \tilde{r}$.) For what value of $\tilde{r}$ is the investor indifferent between these two investments? (Assume that there is no chance that the person wants to cash in the investment before the 20-year period.) Explain the rationale behind your calculation.

Sources

The U.S. Energy Information Administration (2014) presents and explains estimates of the LCOE.

The Interagency Working Group (2013) presents estimates of the SCC.

Sen's *On Ethics and Economics* (1987) provides a background on welfare economics.

Aker (2010) provides evidence of the relation between cell phones and agricultural markets.

Glaeser and Kohlhase (2004) provide estimates of transportation costs, and discuss their role in international trade.

Prominent estimates of market power in resource markets include Hnyilicza and Pindyck (1976), Stollery (1985), Pindyck (1987), Ellis and Halvorsen (2002), Cerda (2007).

3 Nonrenewable Resources

Objective
• Use the two-period nonrenewable resource model to analyze competitive and monopoly equilibria.

Information and Skills
• Translate the techniques and intuition from the "trade in tea" model of chapter 2 to the nonrenewable resource setting.

• Derive and interpret an equilibrium condition and analyze it using graphical methods and calculus.

A two-period model provides much of the intuition needed to understand equilibrium in a nonrenewable resources market. We use graphical methods to analyze the equilibrium under competition or monopoly when firms are unable to save any resource beyond the second period. This chapter emphasizes the case where the initial stock is small enough, relative to demand, that firms want to exhaust the resource during this time. Arbitrage provides the basis for the intuition in resource models, but this chapter deals with arbitrage over time, instead of over space. A sales *trajectory* is the sequence of sales, and a price trajectory is the associated sequence of prices. In the two-period setting, each of these sequences contains only two elements.

A Road Map
Section 3.1 examines the competitive equilibrium; section 3.2 studies the monopoly outcome and compares prices under the two market structures. Section 3.3 uses calculus to determine the comparative statics of price with respect to extraction costs and the discount rate.

3.1 Competitive Equilibrium

Objectives and skills: Obtain and analyze the resource firm's "no-intertemporal arbitrage" condition, and understand the equilibrium effect of extraction costs.

Section 2.1 considered the allocation of a fixed quantity of tea over two countries, with iceberg transportation costs. Here, a fixed stock of the resource replaces tea, two periods replace the two countries, and the discount factor replaces the iceberg transportation costs. The method of analysis and the intuition are similar. The first period is denoted $t = 0$, and the second period by $t = 1$. A price-taking firm has discount factor ρ, faces prices p_0 and p_1 in periods 0 and 1, incurs extraction cost c for each unit extracted, and has a fixed stock of the resource, x units.

Let y be sales in period 0. Assuming that all of the resource is sold, $x - y$ equals period-1 sales. At an interior equilibrium, extraction is positive in both periods: $x > y > 0$. The firm wants to maximize the sum of present value profits in the two periods:

$$\pi^{\text{competitive}}(y; p_0, p_1) = \underbrace{(p_0 - c)y}_{\text{period-0 profit}} + \overbrace{\rho(p_1 - c)(x - y)}^{\text{PDV of period-1 profit}}. \tag{3.1}$$

("PDV" is the abbreviation for "present discounted value.") The derivative of profits, with respect to period-0 sales, is

$$\frac{d}{dy}\pi^{\text{competitive}} = (p_0 - c) - \rho(p_1 - c).$$

The firm prefers to sell all of its stock in period 0 if $(p_0 - c) > \rho(p_1 - c)$. It prefers to sell all of its stock in period 1 if $(p_0 - c) < \rho(p_1 - c)$. If the firm sells a positive quantity in both periods, as we assume, it must be *indifferent* about the timing of sales. This indifference requires that the present value of price minus marginal cost be the same in both periods:

$$\frac{d}{dy}\pi^{\text{competitive}} = 0 \text{ if and only if } \underbrace{(p_0 - c) = \rho(p_1 - c)}_{\text{no intertemporal arbitrage}}. \tag{3.2}$$

The "no-intertemporal arbitrage" condition states that the firm cannot increase its profits by moving sales from one period to another.

The competitive resource owner takes prices as given, but these prices respond to the quantity brought to market. Actions of an individual resource owner have negligible effect on the price, but all resource owners have the same costs and discount factor, so they have the same incentives. We model the industry as if a representative price-taking firm owns all of the stock.

Figure 3.1 shows the market when extraction costs are $c = 0$ and the inverse demand in both periods is $p = 20 - y$. Sales in period 0 equal y. With initial stock $x = 10$, period-1 sales equal $10 - y$. The solid line shows the inverse demand function in period 0: as y

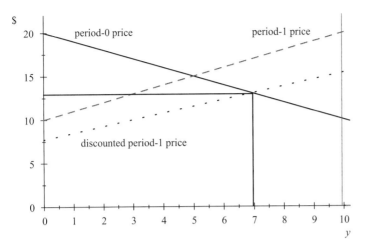

Figure 3.1
Demand in period 0 (solid line). Demand in period 1 (dashed line). Present value (i.e., discounted) of period 1 price (dotted line). Costs $= 0$.

increases, the equilibrium price falls. The dashed line shows the inverse demand function in period 1: as y increases, period 1 sales, $10 - y$, fall, so the price in that period rises. For a zero discount rate ($r = 0$) the discount factor, $\rho = \frac{1}{1+r}$, equals 1. In this case, firms allocate their stock evenly between the two periods, and the price in each period equals 15. With $r = 0$, the firm is indifferent between selling in periods 0 or 1 if and only if the prices in the two periods are equal.

The dotted line shows the time-0 present value of the period-1 price if the discount rate is $r = 0.3$, so $\rho = \frac{1}{1.3} = 0.77$. The equilibrium occurs where the *present value* of price is the same in both periods (where the solid and the dotted lines intersect). Equilibrium sales in period 0 equal 6.96, and the price is 13.04; period-1 sales equal 3.04, and the price is 16.96. Discounting the future makes future revenue less valuable to the firm in period 0, inducing the firm to sell more in period 0. This reallocation lowers the period-0 price and increases period-1 price.

The price-taking representative firm does not shift sales from one period to another with the *intention* of causing price to change. If, following an increase of r from 0 to 0.3, the firm did not reallocate sales, then the present value of a unit of sales in period 0 remains at $p_0 = 15$ and the present value of a unit of sales in period 1 falls from 15 to $15\frac{1}{1.3} = 11.5 < 15$. Here, the firm has an opportunity for intertemporal arbitrage. Prices adjust as the firm moves sales from period 1 to period 0, until, at equilibrium, there are no further opportunities for intertemporal arbitrage.

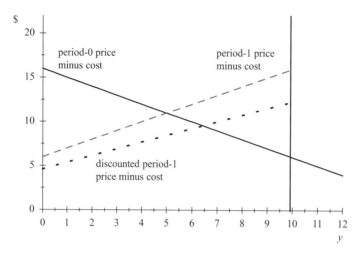

Figure 3.2
Demand − cost in period 0 (solid line). Demand − cost in period 1 (dashed line). Present value of period 1 price − cost (dotted line). For fixed costs, discounting increases period 0 sales.

Introducing Costs: $c > 0$

Figure 3.2 shows the outcome with constant average (= marginal) costs $c = 4$. The solid and dashed lines show price minus cost, instead of price, in the two periods. With zero discount rate, equilibrium sales are equal in the two periods, and the price in both periods is again $p = 15$, so price − cost = 11. In the absence of discounting, higher cost reduces the firm's profits, but it does not alter the sales (or price) trajectory and does not affect consumers.

The dotted line in Figure 3.2 shows the present value, at $t = 0$, of period-1 price minus extraction costs, for a discount factor $\rho = 0.77$. The equilibrium occurs where the present value of price minus extraction cost is equal in the two periods, at the intersection of the solid and the dotted lines. Here, period-0 sales equal 6.43 and the period-0 price is 13.57. *With discounting, higher extraction costs cause the firm to move production from period 0 to period 1.* Discounting, combined with higher extraction cost, raises the equilibrium period-0 price (lowering period-0 consumer surplus) and lowers period-1 price (raising period-1 consumer surplus). From the firm's period-0 perspective, a one unit increase in costs raises the period-0 average and marginal extraction cost by one unit, and raises the *present value* of cost in the next period costs by only ρ. For $\rho < 1$, the higher costs increase incentives to produce in the future instead of the present.

Intuition based on static supply and demand models may be misleading in nonrenewable resource markets. A cost increase in the static setting shifts up the supply curve, lowering equilibrium supply, raising the price, and reducing consumer surplus. For nonrenewable resources, the effect of a cost increase depends on the discount factor. With zero discounting, the extraction cost lowers firm profits but has no effect on prices and thus no effect on consumer surplus. With positive discounting, higher extraction costs shift supply from period 0 to period 1, raising period-0 price but lowering period-1 price.

3.2 Monopoly

Objectives and skills: Obtain the monopoly's equilibrium condition, and compare the monopoly and the competitive outcomes.

The monopoly, like the competitive firm, wants to maximize the present discounted value of profits, given by expression 3.1. However, the monopoly recognizes that its sales affect the price, whereas the competitive firm takes price as given. The present discounted stream of monopoly profits is

$$\pi^{\text{monopoly}}(y) = \underbrace{(p(y) - c)y}_{\text{period-0 profit}} + \underbrace{\rho(p(x - y) - c)(x - y)}_{\text{PDV of period-1 profit}}. \tag{3.3}$$

We can find the equilibrium condition for the monopoly by using the first order condition to the problem of maximizing $\pi^{\text{monopoly}}(y)$. A simpler approach, discussed in section 2.4, obtains this equilibrium condition by replacing price with marginal revenue in the competitive industry's equilibrium condition (the last part of equation 3.2). With $\eta(y)$ equal to the price elasticity of demand at sales y, marginal revenue, MR, is

$$MR(y) = p(y)\left(1 - \frac{1}{\eta(y)}\right), \text{ with } \eta(y) \equiv -\frac{dy}{dp}\frac{p}{y}.$$

The equilibrium condition for the monopoly is

$$\underbrace{MR(y) - c}_{\text{period 0 MR} - \text{MC}} = \underbrace{\rho[MR(x - y) - c]}_{\text{PDV of period-1 MR} - \text{MC}}. \tag{3.4}$$

The solid lines in Figure 3.3 show the period-0 and period-1 demand functions, $p_0 = 20 - y$ and $p_1 = 20 - (10 - y)$, minus marginal cost, $c = 4$, as a function of period-0 sales, y. The dashed lines show the marginal profit (i.e., marginal revenue minus marginal cost) corresponding to those two demand functions. Without discounting ($\rho = 1$), optimality for the monopoly requires that marginal profit in the two periods be equal. Here, the monopoly sells the same amount in both periods, so $y = 5$, as in the competitive equilibrium with no discounting. In this market, moving from a competitive market to a monopoly does not alter the outcome. This result is due to the fact that the stock of resource is fixed, together with the assumptions that the discount rate is 0 ($\rho = 1$) and that the world lasts only two periods. Neither the monopoly nor the competitive firm saves the resource beyond period 1.

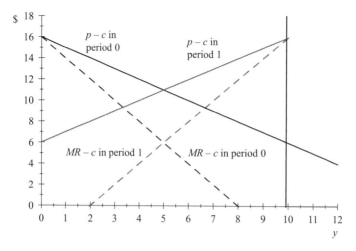

Figure 3.3
Without discounting ($\rho = 1$), the competive industry and the monopoly both sell half the quantity in each period. Solid curves show inverse demand minus marginal cost in the two periods, as a function of period-0 sales. Dashed curves show marginal revenue minus marginal cost.

Monopoly Is the Conservationist's Friend

With discounting, the monopoly and competitive equilibria are, in general, different. For the demand and cost functions used in this book (but not for all possible demand and cost combinations), the monopoly sells less in period 0, compared to the competitive industry. The monopoly therefore saves more of the resource for the future, compared to the competitive industry: "monopoly is the conservationists' friend." (However, see exercise 5.)

Figure 3.4 modifies figure 3.3, introducing discounting and illustrating that the monopoly is the conservationist's friend. Solid lines show the present value of price minus marginal cost, and dashed lines show the present value of marginal revenue minus marginal cost. The intersection of the solid lines identifies competitive period-0 sales, $y = 8.67$. The intersection of the dashed lines identifies monopoly period-0 sales, $y = 6$.

Reducing the discount factor from $\rho = 1$ to $\rho = 0.5$ increases period-0 sales under both market structures, but the increase is greater in the competitive market. Figure 3.5 uses the demand function $p = 20 - q$, $x = 10$, and the equilibrium conditions 3.2 (for competition) and 3.4 (for monopoly) to graph period-0 sales as a function of the discount factor, ρ. Raising extraction costs from $c = 0$ to $c = 4$ lowers period-0 competitive sales, except for two cases: (i) when the firm discounts the future so heavily that it wants to extract everything in period 0 ($\rho < 0.4$) or (ii) when the firm does not discount the future at all ($\rho = 1$), so that it extracts the same amount in both periods. (Compare the two solid curves in Figure 3.5.) The monopoly sells less in period 0 than competitive firms for $\rho < 1$. A higher valuation of the future (higher ρ) decreases period-0 sales for both types of firm.

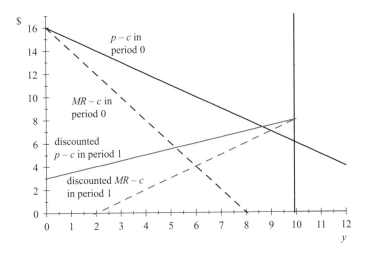

Figure 3.4
"Monopoly is the conservationist's friend." Discounting ($\rho < 1$) causes both the competitive industry and the monopoly to sell more in period 0. However, the monopoly sells less in period 0 compared to the competitive industry. Solid lines show the present value (with $\rho = 0.5$) inverse demand function minus $c = 4$ in the two periods; dashed lines show the present value marginal revenue functions minus $c = 4$.

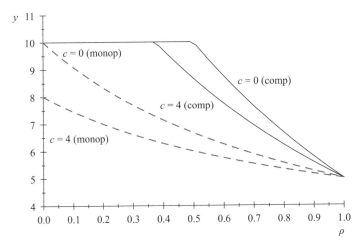

Figure 3.5
For $c = 0$ and $c = 4$, solid curves show period-0 competitive sales and dashed curves show monopoly sales, as functions of the discount factor, ρ.

3.3   Comparative Statics

Objectives and skills: Reinforce the distinction between exogenous and endogenous variables and answer a comparative statics question using calculus.

This section provides more practice in working through the comparative statics of a model. Following the procedure outlined in section 2.2, we express period-0 sales as a function of model parameters and take derivatives. The endogenous variables in this model are the prices and quantities in the two periods. Here we replace $p = 20 - y$ with $p = a - by$, and we replace the initial stock, 10, with a symbol, x. The exogenous variables are c, ρ, a, b, and x. The competitive equilibrium condition is

$$(a - by - c) = \rho(a - b(x - y) - c). \tag{3.5}$$

We can solve this equation to express period-0 sales as a function of the model parameters:

$$y = \frac{1}{b + b\rho}(a - c + \rho(c - a + bx)). \tag{3.6}$$

We can answer comparative statics questions by differentiating this expression with respect to model parameters:

$$\frac{dy}{dc} = \frac{\rho - 1}{b + b\rho} \leq 0, \quad \text{and} \quad \underbrace{\frac{dy}{db} = \frac{1}{b^2}\frac{\rho - 1}{\rho + 1}(a - c)}_{\text{use eq. 3.6 and quotient rule}} \leq 0. \tag{3.7}$$

The *choke price*, defined as the price at which demand falls to 0, equals a. If firms use the resource, it must be the case that $a > c$. Therefore, the two comparative statics inequalities are *strict* ($<$ instead of $=$) for $\rho < 1$. We have already showed graphically that (for $\rho < 1$) an increase in extraction costs lowers period-0 extraction. A larger value of b makes the inverse demand function steeper (i.e., it reduces demand at any price). The second comparative statics expression shows that this decrease in demand also reduces period-0 sales.

3.4   Summary

A competitive equilibrium with nonrenewable resources requires that firms have no incentive to reallocate sales across periods. This "no intertemporal arbitrage" condition states that the present value of the marginal return from selling a good is the same in both periods. Positive discounting ($r > 0$, $\rho < 1$) causes prices to differ across periods. With discounting, higher costs shift production from period 0 to period 1, raising the price and lowering consumer surplus in period 0 and creating the opposite changes in period 1. We performed comparative static by solving the equilibrium condition to express output as a function of model parameters and then taking derivatives.

We obtained the equilibrium condition for a monopoly by taking the equilibrium condition for a competitive firm and replacing price with marginal revenue. With constant marginal extraction costs and no discounting ($r = 0$, so $\rho = 1$), both types of firm sell the same amount, half of the available stock, in period 0. Under discounting ($\rho < 1$), the monopoly sells less in period-0 than the competitive firm. In this case, the monopoly is the conservationist's friend.

3.5   Terms and Concepts, Study Questions, Exercises, and Sources

Terms and Concepts
Extraction costs, intertemporal arbitrage, trajectory, "monopoly is the conservationist's friend," choke price.

Study Questions
For these questions, use the linear inverse demand function, $p = 10 - y$.

1. In a two-period setting with linear demand and constant average extraction costs c, use two figures to illustrate the equilibrium sales trajectory under competition and under monopoly for the two cases where (a) the discount factor is $\rho = 1$ and (b) the discount factor is less than 1. Explain the effect of discounting.

2. Answer questions 1 algebraically, using the equilibrium conditions under competition and monopoly.

Exercises
1. Figure 3.2 holds costs fixed at $c = 4$ and shows the effect of introducing discounting (moving from $\rho = 1$ to $\rho = 0.77$). This exercise asks you to create a figure showing the effect of changing costs, for a fixed discount factor.

(a) Using the the inverse demand function $p = 20 - y$, the initial stock $x = 10$, zero costs, $c = 0$, and the discount factor $\rho = 0.77$, create a figure showing the graphs of $20 - y$ and $\rho(20 - (10 - y))$; make these graphs solid lines, for ease of identification. Identify the equilibrium period-0 sales as point B.

(b) Now graph the relevant lines (needed to identify the equilibrium) when $c = 4$; make these graphs dashed lines for ease of identification. Identify the equilibrium period 0 sales as point A.

(c) How does an increase in marginal costs from 0 to 4 affect period-0 sales? Provide a brief economic explanation for this result.

2. Set the derivative of monopoly profit, $\pi^{\text{monopoly}}(y)$, defined in equation 3.3, equal to zero to obtain equation 3.4. The point of this exercise is to confirm that our method of obtaining equation 3.4 (by replacing "price" in the condition for the competitive industry,

with "marginal revenue") gives the correct result. We saved a step by not having to take the derivative of the monopoly's objective.

3. Consider the familiar static model (no resource constraint) where the inverse demand for a good is $p = 20 - y$, and the constant marginal production cost is $c = 5$.

(a) How much does a competitive industry supply in one period? How much does it supply in two periods?

(b) Now consider a resource setting where the resource can be extracted during only two periods. The demand and cost functions are as before and the initial stock is x. There is a "critical stock", denoted x^{crit} such that if $x > x^{crit}$, some of the resource stock remains unsold. What is the numerical value of x^{crit} for this problem? Explain.

4. In the two-period resource model, suppose that $p = 20 - y$, $c = 5$, and initial stock $x = 5$.

(a) By solving the equilibrium condition for y, write period-0 sales as a function of ρ.

(b) What is the sign of the derivative with respect to ρ of period-0 sales? In a sentence or two, provide the economic intuition for this sign.

(c) Find the critical numerical value of ρ, call it ρ^{crit}, such that period-1 extraction is 0 for $\rho \leq \rho^{crit}$. Explain why period-1 sales are 0 if this inequality holds.

5. Suppose that $c = 0$, the discount factor is ρ, and demand is constant elasticity, $y = p^{-\eta}$.

(a) Write the equilibrium conditions for the competitive firm and the monopoly in this case.

(b) For the monopoly equilibrium condition to be sensible, what restriction must be imposed on η? Provide the economic explanation for this restriction.

(c) Compare the level of period-0 sales under competition and under monopoly.

6. Consider the two-period model with inverse demand, $p = a - by$; constant average extraction cost, c; initial stock, x; and discount factor, ρ. Assume that in the competitive equilibrium extraction is positive in both periods, and the resource constraint is binding. Find $\frac{dy}{d\rho}$ and give the economic explanation for the sign of this derivative (one or two sentences). [Hint: Use equation 3.6, giving y as a function of ρ and other model parameters. No need to rederive this function. Take the derivative of this function with respect to ρ to find $\frac{dy}{d\rho}$. You will discover that the sign of this derivative depends on the sign of $(2c - 2a + bx)$. The trick is to determine the sign of this expression. Use the insight from question 3 to determine a condition on x implied by the assumption that the stock constraint is binding. This information enables you to determine the sign of $(2c - 2a + bx)$ and thereby determine the sign of $\frac{dy}{d\rho}$.]

4 Additional Tools

Objectives
- Work with a stock-dependent cost function; use the perturbation method to obtain equilibrium conditions; and express these conditions using rent.

Information and Skills
- Understand the rationale for using a stock-dependent extraction cost function and be able to work with a particular cost function.

- Derive and interpret the optimality condition to this problem for two cases: the resource constraint is binding or is not binding.

- Understand the logic of the perturbation method and apply it in the two-period setting.

- Understand the meaning of "rent" in the resource setting and use it to express the optimality (equilibrium) condition.

We build on the previous chapter, introducing (i) a more general cost function, (ii) the perturbation method, and (iii) the concept of rent. By considering the more general cost function at the outset, we avoid having to repeat derivations for each special case. The perturbation method provides a quick way to obtain the equilibrium condition in resource models. The concept of rent is important in resource economics. "Rent" is a common word, but it has a particular meaning in economics. This chapter considers only the competitive equilibrium. Rather than duplicate the analysis for the monopoly, we note that replacing "price" with "marginal revenue" in the competitive condition yields the equilibrium condition for monopoly.

A Road Map
Section 4.1 explains the difference between stocks and flows, and it introduces a cost function used throughout the book. The cost of extraction can depend both on the amount of resource in the ground (the stock) and the amount that is extracted (the flow).

Section 4.2 obtains the equilibrium (no arbitrage) condition using a familiar method; it then shows that an alternative, using perturbations, produces the same equilibrium condition. This duplication is valuable, because in multiperiod settings, the perturbation method provides an easier route to the equilibrium condition. The idea behind this method is intuitive. Imagine the firm beginning with a candidate for an optimal plan (e.g., selling 53% in period 0 and 47% in period 1). The firm can test whether this candidate is optimal by perturbing it: moving a small (infinitesimal) amount of sales from one period to the other. If this perturbation increases the firm's present discounted value of profits, the original candidate was not optimal. It the perturbation decreases the firm's profits, then using the opposite perturbation (e.g., moving sales from period 0 to period 1, instead of from period 1 to period 0) would increase profits. Thus, if the perturbation either increases or decreases profits, the candidate is not optimal. A necessary condition for optimality is that an infinitesimal perturbation does not change the payoff: *the derivative, with respect to the perturbation, of the payoff is zero.*

Section 4.3 explains the meaning and use of the term "rent" in resource economics. This concept provides a concise way of expressing an equilibrium condition and also helps with intuition. It is easier to understand a model if one knows how, at least in principle, to solve it. Section 4.4 provides an algorithm (a set of instructions), showing how to obtain the solution. Section 4.5 provides numerical examples.

4.1   A More General Cost Function

Objectives and skills: Understand the reasons for using a more general cost function and be able to work with an example.

The distinction between stock and flow variables is central to resource economics. A stock variable is measured in units of quantity (e.g., billions of barrels of oil, or tons of coal, or pounds of fish, or gigatons of carbon). The units of measurement do not depend on units of time. The number of tons of coal might change over time, but the statement that we have x tons of coal today does not depend on whether we measure time in months or years. The units of measurement of flow variables depend on units of time. The statement "This well produces 1,000 barrels of oil" is meaningless unless we know whether it produces this number of barrels per hour, day, or week. The variable x_t denotes the stock of a resource, with the subscript identifying time or the period number. The variable y_t is a flow variable, denoting extraction during period t. If a period lasts for 1 year, and quantity units are tons, then x_t is in units of tons and and y_t is in units of tons per year.

The constant average cost function used in chapter 3 assumes that marginal extraction costs do not depend on either the size of the remaining resource stock or on the rate of extraction. Here, we drop both of these assumptions. Marginal (and average) extraction costs typically increase as the size of the remaining stock falls. This relation likely holds at both the level of the individual mine or well and at the economy-wide level. At the individual level, shallow and relatively inexpensive wells are adequate to extract oil or water when the stock of oil or water in the ground is high. As stocks diminish, it becomes necessary to dig deeper and more expensive wells to continue extraction. At the economy-wide level, different deposits have different extraction costs. Because it is (generally) efficient to extract from the cheaper deposits first, extraction costs increase as the size of the remaining economy-wide stock falls. People began mining coal from seams that lay close to the ground; early oil deposits could be scooped up with little effort. As society exhausted these cheap deposits, it became economical to remove mountaintops to obtain coal and to exploit deep-water deposits to extract oil. Extraction costs rose as remaining economy-wide resource stocks fell.[1]

Average and marginal costs may increase with the rate of extraction. It might be necessary to pay workers overtime or to hire less qualified workers to increase extraction in a period. In this situation average and marginal extraction costs increase with the extraction rate. Costs might depend on both the stock (x) and the flow (y), so we write the total cost function as $c(x, y)$. The partial derivatives of this function have the following characteristics:

$$\frac{\partial c(x, y)}{\partial x} \leq 0, \quad \frac{\partial \left[\frac{c(x,y)}{y}\right]}{\partial y} \geq 0, \quad \frac{\partial^2 c(x, y)}{\partial y^2} \geq 0.$$

The first inequality states that a higher stock either lowers costs or (in the case of equality) leaves them unchanged. The second states that higher extraction either increases average costs or leaves them unchanged. The third states that higher extraction either increases marginal costs or leaves them unchanged.

A parametric example makes this cost function concrete:

$$c(x, y) = C(\sigma + x)^{-\alpha} y^{1+\beta}, \tag{4.1}$$

where C, α, σ, and β are non-negative parameters. Table 4.1 shows the relation between parameter values and marginal costs.

- Marginal extraction cost $\left(\frac{\partial c(x,y)}{\partial y}\right)$ is constant for $\beta = 0$ and increasing in y for $\beta > 0$.
- Marginal and average extraction costs are independent of the stock for $\alpha = 0$; a higher stock reduces these costs if $\alpha > 0$.
- If $\alpha > 0$ and $\sigma = 0$, extraction costs become infinite as x approaches 0; in this case, the resource is never physically exhausted (x remains strictly positive along an equilibrium trajectory). If $\alpha > 0$ and $\sigma > 0$, extraction costs remain finite as x approaches 0; in this case, the resource is physically exhausted if and only if $C\sigma^{-\alpha}$ is less than the choke price.

1 Many resource firms are vertically integrated, both extracting and processing natural resources. Some of the empirical literature (but not this book) distinguishes between extraction and processing costs.

Table 4.1
Relation between parameter values and marginal extraction costs

Parameter values	Cost function	Marginal cost	Marginal extraction costs
$C = 0$	0	0	Zero
$C > 0$, $\alpha > 0$, and $\beta > 0$	$C(x + \sigma)^{-\alpha} y^{1+\beta}$	$C(1 + \beta)(x + \sigma)^{-\alpha} y^{\beta}$	Increasing in extraction, decreasing in stock
$C > 0$, $\alpha = 0$, and $\beta = 0$	Cy	C	Independent of both extraction and stock
$C > 0$, $\alpha = 0$, and $\beta > 0$	$Cy^{1+\beta}$	$C(1 + \beta)y^{\beta}$	Increasing in extraction, independent of stock
$C > 0$, $\alpha > 0$, and $\beta = 0$	$C(x + \sigma)^{-\alpha} y$	$C(x + \sigma)^{-\alpha}$	Independent of extraction, decreasing in the stock

A Caveat

This model uses a single stock variable, x, and ignores the discovery and development of new stocks. Here, the resource stock falls over time, with extraction. In fact, new discoveries frequently occur, raising the size of "proven reserves" (known stocks) (see section 6.4). Stocks with cheaper extraction costs tend to be used first (see section 5.4), and newly discovered stocks are often more costly to extract. If we treated new discoveries as an increase in x, then our model of extraction costs would suggest (incorrectly) that these discoveries reduce extraction costs. However, the discovery of new stocks (e.g., in the Arctic region) does not alter the cost of extracting Saudi oil, except possibly via such effects as a change in the price of inputs.

4.2   The Perturbation Method

Objectives and skills: Understand how to obtain the firm's first order condition when the resource constraint is binding or slack, using both the substitution method and the perturbation method.

This section uses two approaches to derive the necessary condition for optimality (the *equilibrium condition*) in the two-period competitive market. The substitution approach begins by (i) using substitution to eliminate the constraint, (ii) then taking the derivative of the present discounted value of profits with respect to period-0 sales, and finally, (iii) replacing the price in each period (which the firm takes as exogenous) with the inverse demand function. The second approach uses the perturbation method. The perturbation method is useful for models with many periods, so we introduce it in a setting where it is easier to understand.

The initial stock of the resource, at the beginning of period 0, is x_0. A candidate consists of feasible extraction levels in the two periods, y_0 and y_1, that satisfy the resource constraint and the non-negativity constraints:

$$0 \le y_0 \le x_0, \quad 0 \le y_1 \le x_1 = x_0 - y_0.$$

Extraction cannot be negative and cannot exceed available stock; the available stock in period 1 equals the initial stock minus the amount that was extracted in period 0. The final inequality states that the ending stock, after period-1 extraction, must be non-negative. If extraction is positive in both periods and all of the resource is used, the constraints imply:

$$y_1 = x_1 = x_0 - y_0. \tag{4.2}$$

We consider two cases: (i) it is not optimal to use all of the resource, so $y_1 < x_1$; and (ii) it is optimal to use all of the resource, so $y_1 = x_1$.

   To understand these two cases, it helps to consider the firm's problem at period 1, after it has already made the period-0 extraction decision. In period 1, the firm has the remaining stock $x_1 = x_0 - y_0$. The firm can extract all the stock ($y_1 = x_1$) or leave some in the ground ($y_1 < x_1$). Equation 4.3 summarizes the second period extraction rule:

marginal profit if resource is exhausted

$$\overbrace{\left(p_1 - \frac{\partial c(x_1, y_1)}{\partial y_1} \right)}_{|y_1 = x_1} \quad \begin{cases} \geq 0 \Leftrightarrow y_1 = x_1 \\ < 0 \Leftrightarrow y_1 < x_1 \end{cases} \tag{4.3}$$

(The symbol "$\Leftrightarrow$" means "if and only if.") The left side of this relation shows the firm's marginal profit (price minus marginal cost) if the firm exhausts the resource (so $y_1 = x_1$, as the subscript indicates). The first line states that if extracting everything leads to a price greater than or equal to marginal cost, then the firm does indeed want to extract everything. The second line states that if extracting everything leads to price less than marginal cost, then the firm leaves some stock in the ground (so $y_1 < x_1$).

4.2.1 It Is Optimal to Use All of the Resource

Here we assume that in equilibrium $y_1 = x_1$; using the first line of equation 4.3, this assumption implies that period-1 marginal profit is greater than or equal to zero. The present discounted value of total profit for the price-taking firm is

$$\underbrace{p_0 y_0 - c(x_0, y_0)}_{\text{period-0 profit}} + \underbrace{\rho[p_1 y_1 - c(x_1, y_1)]}_{\text{PDV period-1 profit}}. \tag{4.4}$$

The Substitution Method of Obtaining the Equilibrium Condition

We can substitute the constraints 4.2 into the objective and so write the present discounted value of profits as

$$\pi(y_0) = p_0 y_0 - c(x_0, y_0) + \rho[p_1(x_0 - y_0) - c(x_0 - y_0, x_0 - y_0)].$$

The first order condition to the problem of maximizing $\pi(y_0)$ is

$$\frac{d\pi(y_0)}{dy_0} \stackrel{\text{set}}{=} 0.^2$$

This first order condition implies:

$$\underbrace{p_0 - \frac{\partial c(x_0, y_0)}{\partial y_0}}_{\substack{\text{increased profit due to} \\ \text{higher sales}}} = \rho \left[\overbrace{\left(p_1 - \frac{\partial c(x_1, y_1)}{\partial y_1} \right)}^{\text{reduced profit due to lower sales}} \quad \overbrace{- \frac{\partial c(x_1, y_1)}{\partial x_1}}^{\text{reduced profit due to higher costs}} \right]. \quad (4.5)$$

The optimal decision balances the gain from additional extraction in period 0 (the left side of equation 4.5) with the loss from lower extraction and higher costs in period 1 (the right side of the equation). The left side is the familiar "price minus marginal cost," the increase in period-0 profits from extracting one more unit in that period. The right side is the present value of two terms. The first term equals the reduction in period-1 profit due to having one less unit to sell. The second term is the cost increase due to a reduction in the stock at the beginning of period 1, resulting from the higher period-0 extraction. If costs are independent of the stock, then $\frac{\partial c(x_1, y_1)}{\partial x_1} = 0$; in this special case, the second term vanishes, and equation 4.5 then states that the present value of marginal profit is equal in periods 0 and 1.

Derivation of Equation 4.5*

The first order condition for the competitive firm's maximization problem is

$$\frac{d\pi(y_0)}{dy_0} = \left[p_0 - \frac{\partial c(x_0, y_0)}{\partial y_0} \right] + \rho \left[p_1 \frac{dy_1}{dy_0} - \frac{\partial c(x_1, y_1)}{\partial y_1} \frac{dy_1}{dy_0} - \frac{\partial c(x_1, y_1)}{\partial x_1} \frac{dx_1}{dy_0} \right] \stackrel{\text{set}}{=} 0. \quad (4.6)$$

The second bracketed expression uses the chain rule. A change in y_0 alters both y_1 and x_1, (potentially) changing period-1 costs. Using $\frac{dx_1}{dy_0} = -1$ and $\frac{dy_1}{dy_0} = -1$, we simplify the second bracketed expression of equation 4.6 to obtain

$$\frac{d\pi(y_0)}{dy_0} = \left[p_0 - \frac{\partial c(x_0, y_0)}{\partial y_0} \right] - \rho \left[p_1 - \frac{\partial c(x_1, y_1)}{\partial x_1} - \frac{\partial c(x_1, y_1)}{\partial y_1} \right] \stackrel{\text{set}}{=} 0.$$

Rearranging this condition gives equation 4.5.

The Perturbation Method

The approach used above to obtain equation 4.5 is cumbersome in the many-period problem. With that problem in mind, we consider the method of perturbation: a different route to the same goal. We begin with a candidate, y_0 and y_1, and the associated period-1 stock,

---

2 As in chapter 2, we use the notation $\stackrel{\text{set}}{=}$ to emphasize that the equality is a first order condition.

$x_1 = x_0 - y_0$. The assumption that it is optimal to consume all of the resource means that $y_1 = x_1$. Expression 4.4 shows the payoff associated with this candidate.

We can perturb this candidate by changing period-0 extraction by a small (positive or negative) amount, ε. Because (by assumption) it is optimal to consume all of the resource, a change in period-0 extraction of ε requires an offsetting change in period-1 extraction of $-\varepsilon$. The gain from a perturbation, $g(\varepsilon; y_0, x_1, y_1)$, equals the sum of the perturbed period-0 and discounted period-1 profits:

$$g(\varepsilon; \cdot) = \overbrace{p_0 \times (y_0 + \varepsilon) - c(x_0, y_0 + \varepsilon)}^{\text{period 0 profit if sales increase by } \varepsilon} + \rho \overbrace{\left[p_1 \times (y_1 - \varepsilon) - c(x_1 - \varepsilon, y_1 - \varepsilon) \right]}^{\text{period 1 profit if sales decrease by } \varepsilon}. \tag{4.7}$$

For an optimal candidate, the derivative of $g(\varepsilon; \cdot)$, with respect to ε (evaluated at $\varepsilon = 0$), is zero:

$$\frac{dg(\varepsilon; y_0, x_1, y_1)}{d\varepsilon} \bigg|_{\varepsilon=0} = 0. \tag{4.8}$$

Evaluating this derivative produces the same first order condition obtained above, equation 4.5.

Evaluating the Derivative in Equation 4.8*

Because ε appears in two places in the period-1 cost function, $c(x_1 - \varepsilon, y_1 - \varepsilon)$, we use the total derivative to evaluate the effect of ε on this function. Using the chain rule and

$$\frac{d(x_1 - \varepsilon)}{d\varepsilon} = \frac{d(y_1 - \varepsilon)}{d\varepsilon} = -1,$$

the total derivative of period-1 costs, with respect to ε, evaluated at $\varepsilon = 0$ is

$$\frac{dc(x_1 - \varepsilon, y_1 - \varepsilon)}{d\varepsilon} \bigg|_{\varepsilon=0} = -\left(\frac{\partial c(x_1, y_1)}{\partial y_1} + \frac{\partial c(x_1, y_1)}{\partial x_1} \right).$$

Using this equation, we have

$$\frac{dg(\varepsilon; y_0, x_1, y_1)}{d\varepsilon} \bigg|_{\varepsilon=0} = p_0 - \frac{\partial c(x_0, y_0)}{\partial y_0} - \rho \left[p_1 - \left(\frac{\partial c(x_1, y_1)}{\partial y_1} + \frac{\partial c(x_1, y_1)}{\partial x_1} \right) \right].$$

Set this derivative to 0 and rearrange to obtain condition 4.5.

Example: Comparing the Substitution Method and the Perturbation Method

An example (unrelated to resources) shows the relation between the substitution method and the perturbation method for constrained optimization. The objective and constraint are

$$\max_{x,y} 4xy - 3x^2,$$

subject to $3x + y = 2$.

The substitution method uses the constraint to write $y = 2 - 3x$, and then uses this equation to rewrite the objective as $4x(2 - 3x) - 3x^2$. The first order condition is

$$\frac{d(4x(2 - 3x) - 3x^2)}{dx} = 8 - 30x \overset{\text{set}}{=} 0 \Rightarrow x = \frac{4}{15}. \tag{4.9}$$

With the perturbation method, we begin with a candidate x, y that satisfies the constraint. If we increase our candidate x by ε, we must decrease the candidate y by 3ε, so that the constraint is satisfied after the perturbation. The payoff under the perturbation is

$$g(\varepsilon; x, y) = 4(x + \varepsilon)(y - 3\varepsilon) - 3(x + \varepsilon)^2.$$

If the candidate is optimal, then $g(\varepsilon; x, y)$ must be maximized at $\varepsilon = 0$. This condition requires

$$\frac{d\left(4(x + \varepsilon)(y - 3\varepsilon) - 3(x + \varepsilon)^2\right)}{d\varepsilon}\Bigg|_{\varepsilon=0} = (4y - 18x - 30\varepsilon)_{|\varepsilon=0} = 4y - 18x \overset{\text{set}}{=} 0.$$

Using the constraint, $y = 2 - 3x$, in the last equation, gives

$$4(2 - 3x) - 18x = 8 - 30x \overset{\text{set}}{=} 0 \Rightarrow x = \frac{4}{15}. \tag{4.10}$$

Comparison of the last parts of equations 4.9 and 4.10 show that the two approaches give the same answer. The advantage of the perturbation method becomes apparent only when we consider a resource problem with many periods, in Chapter 5.

4.2.2   It Is Optimal to Leave Some of the Resource Behind

If it is optimal to *not* exhaust the resource, then $y_1 < x_1$: the resource constraint is then referred to as "slack." The firm does not extract so much that marginal profit becomes negative. If the firm does not exhaust the resource, then it continues extracting up to the point that period-1 marginal profit is zero:

$$p_1 - \frac{\partial c(x_1, y_1)}{\partial y_1} = 0. \tag{4.11}$$

Using this equality in condition 4.5 (setting the first bracketed term equal to 0) yields the equilibrium condition when the resource constraint is slack:

$$p_0 - \frac{\partial c(x_0, y_0)}{\partial y_0} = -\rho \left[\frac{\partial c(x_1, y_1)}{\partial x_1}\right]. \tag{4.12}$$

The left side is the increase in profit due to extracting an additional unit in period 0; the right side is the present value of the cost increase due to the lower stock that results from an additional unit extracted in period 0.

4.3   Rent

Objectives and skills: Know the meaning of rent, use it to simplify the optimality condition, and understand the relation between rent in the two periods.

In common usage, "rent" refers to the payment to use something (e.g., land, a house, a car) for a fixed period of time; "price" refers the payment for owning this object. Economists use the term "rent" to denote the payment to a factor of production that exceeds the amount necessary to make that factor available. The classic example is rent to unimproved land. Because the land is in limited supply, it receives a payment. The payment is not needed to create the land—it already exists, regardless of the payment. However, the limited supply (= scarcity) means that other potential users are willing to bid for the land; the highest value use determines the rent in a competitive market (exercise 6). Natural resources command rent because of their scarcity.

Under competition, let us define *resource rent* as the difference between price and marginal extraction costs. Denoting rent in period t as R_t, we have

$$R_0 = p_0 - \frac{\partial c(x_0, y_0)}{\partial y_0}, \quad \text{and} \quad R_1 = p_1 - \frac{\partial c(x_1, y_1)}{\partial y_1}. \tag{4.13}$$

This definition corresponds to the economic meaning of "rent," not standard usage. Resource rent equals the difference between the amount obtained from selling a unit (its price) and the cost of bringing this unit to the market (the marginal cost).

Rent in the Static Setting

It is easier to understand the meaning of rent in the resource setting if you first understand its meaning in the simpler static setting. Figure 4.1 shows a supply function for land and three demand functions. There is a fixed stock of land, shown by point L on the quantity axis. Making land usable requires fencing it, and the marginal cost of fencing is constant at c. The "reversed L-shaped" curve through points c, d, and e shows the supply function for land. No land is supplied at a price less than c, the cost of fencing. At price c, any amount between 0 and L can be supplied. At a price above c, all available land, L, is supplied, but it is not possible to increase the supply. The supply function is therefore flat at c up to point d, and then vertical. The inverse demand function for an input, such as land, equals the value of marginal product of that input; figure 4.1 shows three inverse demand functions, the downward sloping lines through points A, B, and F.[3]

---

3 The marginal product of land, MP(land), equals the increase in output due to an additional unit of land. If the price of a unit of agricultural output is p^{ag}, the value of marginal product of land used for farming is $VMP(\text{land}) = p^{ag} \times MP(\text{land})$. Denote the price of land as p^{land}; farmers demand land up to the point where its value of marginal product equals its price: $p^{land} = VMP(\text{land})$. The inverse demand function for land is therefore VMP(land). The marginal product of land might fall with the amount of land, due (for example) to the presence of a fixed factor, such as managerial capacity. In this case, the slope of both VMP and MP falls with the amount of land: the demand function for land has a negative slope, as in figure 4.1.

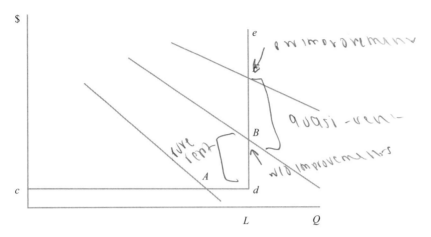

Figure 4.1
The supply function is the reversed "L" through points c, d, and e. Three different demand functions, through points A, B, and F, lead to three different equibrium prices and three values of rent. Q is the quantity of land, shown on the horizontal axis.

If the inverse demand is low (e.g., through point A), we have the familiar situation where the equilibrium price equals marginal cost. In this case there is unused land, shown by the horizontal distance between points A and d in figure 4.1. Land is not scarce, and rent is zero. If the demand function is higher (e.g., through point B), the equilibrium price equals the vertical coordinate of B and rent equals the distance between points B and d. Land is scarce, and rent is positive.

Rent in the Resource Setting
Let us use the definition of rent in equation 4.13 to write the optimality conditions in the two cases where the resource is exhausted or is not exhausted, using a single equation. If the resource is exhausted, then $R_1 \geq 0$; except for knife-edge cases, the inequality is strict. If the resource is not exhausted, then $R_1 = 0$. We can write the equilibrium conditions 4.5 and 4.12 as[4]

$$R_0 = \rho \left(R_1 - \frac{\partial c(x_1, y_1)}{\partial x_1} \right). \tag{4.14}$$

The resource rent is a measure of resource scarcity. Equation 4.14 states that the scarcity value in period 0 (R_0) equals the present value of the sum of two terms: the scarcity value in period 1 (R_1), plus the cost reduction due to having a larger period-1 stock. Either

---

4 Under monopoly, we define rent as marginal revenue (instead of price) minus marginal cost. With this modification, equation 4.14 gives the monopoly equilibrium condition.

or both of the terms on the right side, R_1 and $-\frac{\partial c(x_1, y_1)}{\partial x_1}$, could be zero or positive (but never negative). These two terms capture the two reasons that period-0 rent is (typically) positive:

1. Physical scarcity: We will run out of the resource. Extracting one more unit today means that we have one less unit to extract in the future. That extra unit of potential future extraction is valuable if and only if $R_1 > 0$. If, instead, $R_1 = 0$, then we will *not* run out of the resource (the resource is not scarce), thus eliminating one of the reasons that period-0 rent is positive.

2. Stock-dependent extraction costs: Extraction of an extra unit today makes future extraction more expensive. If, however $-\frac{\partial c(x_1, y_1)}{\partial x_1} = 0$, extraction cost does not depend on stock, and this reason for positive period-0 rent vanishes.

Rent versus Quasi-Rent

We return to the static setting, using land as an example, to explain the difference between rent and quasi-rent. The demand for land equals its value of marginal product, defined as the price of output (the agricultural product) times the marginal product of land. The marginal product of land, and thus the value of marginal product, depends on the quality (productivity) of the land. Very little productive land is unimproved. Previous investment that increases land productivity is "sunk," meaning that it cannot be undone. An owner who paid to remove rocks from a field cannot ask the workers to return their wage in exchange for putting the rocks back into the field. People are willing to pay more to use the more productive land, but the improvements continue to exist regardless of whether they command higher payments. Because the actual payments are not necessary for the continued existence of the improvements, they resemble rent. However, the improvements were made in the anticipation of payments, so the payments are not precisely rent. For this reason, payments resulting from a sunk investment are known as "quasi-rent." For emphasis, economists sometimes refer to the payment occurring in the absence of any improvement as "pure" rent.

Most natural resource stocks become available only after significant investments in exploration and development. Thus, payments in excess of marginal extraction costs, arising from the sale of resources, are the sum of pure rents and quasi-rents. Until chapter 11 we ignore this distinction, and refer to the resource rent merely as "rent."

Figure 4.1 illustrates the difference between rent and quasi-rent. In this example, the inverse demand function through point B shows the value of marginal product of unimproved land. Without improvements, the equilibrium price of this land is at B. An investment increases land's marginal productivity, shifting the inverse demand function up to the curve through F. With the investment, the equilibrium price equals the vertical coordinate of point F. The distance between points F and B equals the quasi-rent, the increase in price due to the prior investment. The distance between points B and d equals the pure rent.

4.4   Solving for the Equilibrium

Objectives and skills: Know how to use the optimality condition and the constraints to solve for the equilibrium prices and sales levels.

Given demand and cost functions, the initial stock, and the discount factor, the equilibrium conditions provide enough information to actually solve for the equilibrium. This model contains three endogenous variables, y_0, y_1, and x_1. We need three equations to find these three variables. The trick is to identify these three equations and then know how to use them. We describe the process here, and illustrate it in section 4.5 using examples.

We have to consider three cases: (i) the resource might be exhausted in period 0, leaving nothing to extract in period 1 ($y_0 = x_0$, so $y_1 = 0$); (ii) the resource might be exhausted in period 1, with positive extraction in both periods ($0 < y_0 < x_0$, and $y_1 = x_0 - y_0$); and (iii) the resource might not be exhausted ($y_0 + y_1 < x_0$). Let us proceed as follows. First, solve the model under the assumption that case (ii) holds. Second, determine whether the assumption is correct. The algorithm consists of the following steps:

- Step 1: In all these cases, the constraint $x_1 = x_0 - y_0$ provides one of the three equations; we need two more equations. We have (tentatively) assumed that case (ii) holds, so $y_1 = x_0 - y_0$; the equilibrium condition 4.5 is the third equation. We solve the equilibrium condition to obtain y_0, and then use the constraint and the assumption to obtain x_1 and y_1.

- Step 2: If the solution from step 1 gives $y_0 > x_0$, then $x_1 < 0$: our assumption that case (ii) holds then violates the non-negativity constraint, so the assumption is wrong. The non-negativity constraint is binding, so $y_0 = x_0$, implying that $y_1 = 0$. Here, all of the resource is used during period-0: case (i) holds.

- Step 3: If the proposed solution from step 1 satisfies $y_0 < x_0$, then we check whether rent in period 1 is non-negative. If $R_1 \geq 0$, our assumption that case (ii) holds, and the resulting solution, are correct. If, however, the proposed solution from step 1 implies that $R_1 < 0$, that solution is incorrect. We have now ruled out both cases (i) and (ii), so we conclude that case (iii) is correct. Our three equations consist of the constraint, $x_1 = x_0 - y_0$, the necessary condition 4.12, and equation 4.11. We solve these equations to find y_0 and y_1.

4.5   Examples*

Objectives and skills: Apply the methods developed above using examples.

Three examples provide practice using tools developed above. Example 1 shows how to use the algorithm in section 4.4 in a setting with constant marginal extraction costs.

Here we can solve for the equilibrium in closed form and use graphs to illustrate it. Example 2 shows how to use the perturbation methods to obtain the equilibrium condition in a case where extraction costs depend on stocks. Example 3 uses the algorithm in section 4.4, the results from example 2, and numerical methods to obtain the equilibrium as a function of the initial stock; it uses a graph to illustrate the equilibrium. Many of the examples and graphs in this book require numerical methods, a topic we do not cover. The goal is for you to follow the logic and derivations up to the point where numerical methods take over. There are many ways for interested readers to learn those methods. The numerical calculations and graphs in this book use MuPad, imbedded in the program Scientific Workplace, which has a tutorial. Many other excellent numerical packages are available.

Example 1: Use Rent and the Algorithm from Section 4.4
This example uses the definition of rent and the algorithm to obtain the equilibrium under linear demand and constant marginal extraction costs, $c(x, y) = Cy$, using $C = 4$, $\rho = 0.77$, and $x_0 = 10$. Here, equation 4.14 simplifies to $R_0 = \rho R_1$: the present value of rent is the same in both periods. In the interest of brevity, we ignore the possibility that all of the resource is consumed in period 0, leaving two remaining possibilities: the resource is exhausted over two periods, or it is not exhausted (cases (ii) and (iii) from section 4.4). I illustrate these two possibilities and show how to compute the equilibrium under high demand ($p = 20 - y$) and low demand ($p = 7 - y$).

We begin by using the equilibrium condition 4.14 under the assumption that the resource is exhausted (as step 1 of the algorithm instructs). Our three equations are: the optimality condition $R_0 = \rho R_1$; the constraint $x_1 = x_0 - y_0$; and the assumption that the resource is exhausted, $y_1 = x_1$. We use the last two equations to write $y_1 = x_0 - y_0$. Substituting this equation into $R_0 = \rho R_1$ gives, for the high-demand scenario:

$$20 - y_0 - 4 = 0.77(20 - (10 - y_0) - 4) \Rightarrow y_0 = 6.4 \Rightarrow R_0 = 20 - 6.4 - 4 = 9.6 > 0.$$

Because the present value of rent is the same in both periods, we know that $R_1 > 0$. For this problem, equilibrium extraction is $y_0 = 6.4$ and $y_1 = 10 - 6.4 = 3.6$.

In the low demand scenario, $R_0 = \rho R_1$ implies

$$7 - y_0 - 4 = 0.77(7 - (10 - y_0) - 4) \Rightarrow y_0 = 4.74 \Rightarrow R_0 = 7 - 4.74 - 4 = -1.74 < 0.$$

Here, the assumption that the resource is exhausted implies that rent is negative. Firms do not lose money, so the assumption must be false: the firm does not exhaust the resource, so its period-1 rent is zero. With stock-independent extraction costs, the present value of rent is the same in both periods. Therefore, period-0 rent is also 0. Thus, equilibrium requires $7 - y - 4 = 0$, or $y = 3$ in both periods.

Figure 4.2 illustrates these two possibilities; review figure 3.1 if figure 4.2 is unclear. The solid lines in this figure show the present discounted value of price minus marginal

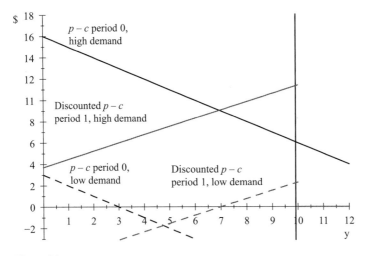

Figure 4.2
Solid lines shows price minus marginal cost with high demand, $p = 20 - y$, where the resource is exhausted.
Dashed lines show price minus marginal cost with low demand, $p = 7 - y$, where the resource is not exhausted.

cost with high demand, and the dashed lines show these relations with low demand. Under
the assumption that the resource is exhausted, the equilibrium occurs at the intersection of
the (solid or dashed) curves. In the high demand scenario, the intersection lies above the y-
axis, so it corresponds to positive rent = price–marginal cost. In this case, the intersection
gives the equilibrium. In the low demand scenario, the intersection lies below the y-axis, so
it corresponds to negative rent. In this case, the intersection does not give the equilibrium
(because rent is never negative). Consequently, the equilibrium occurs where the dashed
lines intersect the y-axis, where rent is zero: under low demand, the extraction y is 3 in
both periods.

Example 2: Using the Perturbation Method

This example uses $p = a - by$, initial stock x_0, discount factor ρ, and extraction cost
function $c(x, y) = \frac{y}{10+x}$. I show how the perturbation method leads to the equilibrium condition. First consider the case where the firm exhausts the resource ($y_1 = x_1$) and then
the case where the firm does not exhaust the resource ($y_1 < x_1$). The competitive firm's
objective and constraints are

$$\max_{y_0, y_1, x_1} p_0 y_0 - \frac{y_0}{10 + x_0} + \rho \left[p_1 y_1 - \frac{y_1}{10 + x_1} \right], \tag{4.15}$$

subject to: $x_1 = x_0 - y_0$ and $y_0 \geq 0$, $x_1 \geq 0$, $x_1 - y_1 \geq 0$.

We write the objective using the prices, p_0 and p_1 (not the inverse demand function), reflecting the fact that the competitive firm takes prices as given.[5]

A candidate solution consists of values of y_0, x_1, and y_1 that satisfy the constraints (i.e., are feasible). Under the assumption that the firm exhausts the resource ($y_1 = x_1$), a perturbation changes y_0 to $y_0 + \varepsilon$ and changes x_1 to $x_1 - \varepsilon$: if the firm extracts ε more units in period 0, the stock remaining at period 1 is reduced (relative to the candidate) by ε. The perturbation changes y_1 to $y_1 - \varepsilon$. The gain function is

$$g(\varepsilon; \cdot) = p_0 \times (y_0 + \varepsilon) - \frac{y_0 + \varepsilon}{10 + x_0} + \rho \left[p_1 \times (y_1 - \varepsilon) - \frac{y_1 - \varepsilon}{10 + x_1 - \varepsilon} \right], \tag{4.16}$$

and the necessary condition is

$$\frac{dg(\varepsilon; y_0, x_1, y_1)}{d\varepsilon} \bigg|_{\varepsilon=0} = \left[\underbrace{p_0 - \frac{1}{10 + x_0}}_{R_0} \right] - \rho \left[\underbrace{\left(p_1 - \frac{1}{10 + x_1} \right)}_{R_1} + \underbrace{\frac{y_1}{(10 + x_1)^2}}_{-\frac{\partial c(x_1, y_1)}{\partial x_1}} \right] \overset{\text{set}}{=} 0.$$

We rearrange the last equation to write the necessary condition as

$$\underbrace{p_0 - \frac{1}{10 + x_0}}_{R_0} = \rho \left[\underbrace{\left(p_1 - \frac{1}{10 + x_1} \right)}_{R_1} + \underbrace{\frac{y_1}{(10 + x_1)^2}}_{-\frac{\partial c(x_1, y_1)}{\partial x_1}} \right]. \tag{4.17}$$

Equation 4.17 specializes equation 4.5 to a particular cost function. We now replace the prices with the inverse demand function and replace x_1 and y_1 by $x_0 - y_0$ to obtain

$$a - by_0 - \frac{1}{10 + x_0} = \rho \left[\left(a - b(x_0 - y_0) - \frac{1}{10 + x_0 - y_0} \right) + \frac{x_0 - y_0}{(10 + x_0 - y_0)^2} \right]. \tag{4.18}$$

We can solve this equation numerically; in general, there are multiple roots. The correct root satisfies $0 < y_0 < x_0$.

Now we use the perturbation method to obtain the equilibrium under the assumption that the firm does not exhaust the resource. The gain function is

$$g(\varepsilon; \cdot) = p_0 \times (y_0 + \varepsilon) - \frac{y_0 + \varepsilon}{10 + x_0} + \rho \left[p_1 \times y_1 - \frac{y_1}{10 + x_1 - \varepsilon} \right]. \tag{4.19}$$

---

5 If we were studying the monopoly's problem, then we would use the inverse demand function, because the monopoly understands that its sales influence the price. See section 2.4.

The gain functions in equations 4.16 and 4.19 differ only in the term in square brackets. The former involves $y_1 - \varepsilon$ (reflecting the fact that the changed extraction in period 0 requires an offsetting change in period 1), and the latter involves y_1 (reflecting the fact that a change in period-0 extraction does not require an offsetting change in period 1). The necessary condition for optimality is

$$
\frac{dg(\varepsilon; y_0, x_1, y_1)}{d\varepsilon}\Big|_{\varepsilon=0} = \underbrace{\left[p_0 - \frac{1}{10 + x_0} \right]}_{R_0} - \rho \underbrace{\left[\frac{y_1}{(10 + x_1)^2} \right]}_{-\frac{\partial c(x_1, y_1)}{\partial x_1}} \stackrel{\text{set}}{=} 0.
$$

To find the equilibrium values, we replace the price by the inverse demand function and use the constraints to obtain an equation for y_0:

$$
a - by_0 - \frac{1}{10 + x_0} = \rho \left[\frac{y_1}{(10 + x_0 - y_0)^2} \right]. \tag{4.20}
$$

To solve this equation, we need to eliminate y_1. Because the stock is not exhausted, the firm produces to the point where price equals marginal cost in period 1, implying that

$$
a - by_1 - \frac{1}{10 + x_0 - y_0} = 0 \Rightarrow y_1 = \frac{1}{b}\left(a - \frac{1}{x_0 - y_0 + 10} \right). \tag{4.21}
$$

Substituting this value into equation 4.20 gives an equation in y_0. The correct root satisfies

$$
y_0 + y_1 = y_0 + \frac{1}{b}\left(a - \frac{1}{x_0 - y_0 + 10} \right) < x_0.
$$

Example 3: The Solution with Stock-Dependent Costs

Let us use the algorithm from section 4.4 and the results from Example 2 (and numerical methods) to obtain a solution. Set $a = 10$, $b = 1$, $\rho = 0.77$, leaving x_0 as a free parameter, to show how the solution depends on the initial stock. Following step 1 of the algorithm from section 4.4, we begin with the assumptions that extraction is positive in both periods and cumulative extraction exhausts the stock. We solve the equilibrium condition 4.18 to obtain y_0 as a function of x_0 and we write this function as $y_0 = Y_0(x_0)$. We do not have an analytic expression for this function; we rely on numerical methods. The solid curve in Figure 4.3 shows the graph of this function. The dashed line is the graph of $y_0 = x_0$, were everything is extracted in period 0. It is not possible to extract more than the total stock. The dashed and solid curves intersect at $x_0 = 2.3$, and the solid curve lies above the dashed line for lower values of x_0. The assumption that extraction is positive in both periods implies $y_0 > x_0$ if $x_0 < 2.3$. That plan is infeasible, implying that the assumption is

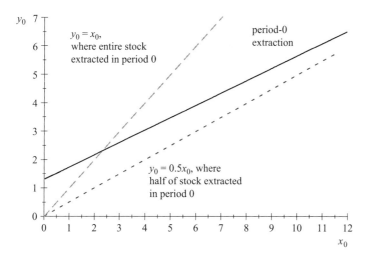

Figure 4.3
The solid line shows y_0 as a function of the initial stock, x_0, under the assumptions that extraction is positive in both periods and all of the resource is extracted. The dashed line shows the graph of $y_0 = x_0$, and the dotted line shows the graph of $y_0 = 0.5x_0$.

incorrect. Thus, for $x_0 \leq 2.3$, the firm extracts the entire stock in period 0. Figure 4.3 also shows a dotted curve, where $y_0 = 0.5x_0$. The solid curve lies above this line, so for this example, the firm extracts more in period 0 than in period 1.

We now know that for $x_0 > 2.3$, we are either in case (ii) (as our assumption asserts) or case (iii). We now proceed to step 3 of the algorithm. If the initial stock is extremely large, it is not optimal to exhaust the stock (in our two-period setting), because doing so causes price to be less than marginal costs. We can obtain the critical stock, above which the stock is not exhausted, by using the formula for period-1 rent under the assumption that the resource is exhausted:

$$R_1(x_0) = 10 - (x_0 - Y_0(x_0)) - \frac{1}{10 + x_0 - Y_0(x_0)}.$$

At the critical stock, above which the firm does not exhaust the resource, $R_1(x_0) = 0$. For our example, this critical stock is 19.92. For $x_0 > 19.92$, it is not optimal to exhaust the stock. For $x_0 > 19.92$, where period-1 rent is zero, we have

$$R_1(x_0, y_0, y_1) = 10 - y_1 - \frac{1}{10 + x_0 - y_0} \overset{\text{set}}{=} 0. \tag{4.22}$$

For $x_0 > 19.92$, we obtain y_0 and y_1 by solving equations 4.20 and 4.22.

In summary, for $x_0 \leq 2.3$, the firm extracts everything in period 0. For $2.3 < x_0 \leq 19.92$, period-0 extraction is given by the function $y_0 = Y_0(x_0)$; we do not have a closed form expression for this function, but we can graph it and evaluate it numerically for any value of x_0. Period-1 extraction equals $x_0 - Y_0(x_0)$, because the stock is exhausted. For $x_0 > 19.92$, extraction is positive in both periods, but the stock is not exhausted. We find the extraction levels in periods 0 and 1 by solving the pair of equations 4.20 and 4.22.

4.6 Summary

Extraction costs might depend on the remaining resource stock, and the marginal extraction costs might increase with the level of extraction. A parametric cost function allows for these possibilities. We used both the substitution method and the perturbation method to obtain the necessary condition for optimality in a two-period nonrenewable resource problem.

If demand is low relative to extraction costs, it might be optimal not to exhaust the resource. We therefore have to consider the possibilities that the resource is or is not exhausted. If the resource is exhausted, then the resource constraint means that extraction of an additional unit at $t = 0$ requires an offsetting reduction in extraction at $t = 1$. If the resource constraint is slack, it is not necessary to make this offsetting change at $t = 1$.

In competitive resource markets, rent is defined as price minus marginal cost. Under monopoly, rent is defined as marginal revenue minus marginal cost. Recognizing this difference in the definition of rent under a competitive firm and under a monopoly, we can express the equilibrium condition for both markets in the same manner: rent in period 0 (R_0) equals the present value of the rent in period 1 (R_1) plus the cost increase due to a marginal reduction in period-1 stock:

$$R_0 = \rho \left(R_1 - \frac{\partial c(x_1, y_1)}{\partial x_1} \right).$$

The firm never extracts when rent is negative; rent is either strictly positive or it is zero. We can use this fact, together with the equilibrium condition, to solve for the equilibrium, given specific functional forms and parameter values for costs and demand. We developed an algorithm that shows how to perform this computation.

4.7 Terms and Concepts, Study Questions, Exercises, and Sources

Terms and Concepts
Binding constraint, slack constraint, stock-dependent and stock-independent costs, perturbation, rent, quasi-rent.

Study Questions

1. An inverse demand function $p(y)$, an extraction cost function $c(x, y)$, a discount factor ρ, and an initial stock x_0 are given.

(a) Write down the competitive firm's objective (= payoff) and constraints for the two-period problem.

(b) What assumption does this firm make regarding price in the two periods?

(c) Write down and interpret the optimality condition (= first order condition) for the firm, under the assumption that sales are positive in both periods and the resource is exhausted. Explain what the various terms in the equation mean.

(d) Write down the definition of rent, and then restate the optimality condition in terms of rent in the two periods.

2. For the problem in question 1:

(a) What does it mean to say that the resource constraint is not binding?

(b) If the resource constraint is not binding, what is the value of period-1 rent?

(c) If the resource constraint is not binding, what is the value of period-0 rent?

(d) Describe the components of period-0 rent. (The answer to parts [c] and [d] should consider the two situations where extraction costs are independent of, or depend on, the stock.)

3. Using the objective (= payoff) for the firm in question 1, and the assumption that the resource constraint is binding, describe how you can derive the optimality condition, first by eliminating the constraint and second by using the perturbation method. It is not necessary to take derivatives or do any calculation; just describe the steps.

Exercises

1. This chapter considers only the competitive equilibrium.

(a) For a general inverse demand function, $p(y)$, and a general cost function, $c(x, y)$, write down the monopoly's optimization problem in the two-period setting.

(b) Under the assumption that the monopoly exhausts the resource and sells a positive amount in both periods, write down the equilibrium condition for the monopoly. [Hint: Review section 2.4, especially the last subsection.]

(c) Interpret this equilibrium condition.

2. Figure 4.4 graphs two cost functions of the form $C(\sigma + x)^{-\alpha} y^{1+\beta}$, with $C > 0$ and $\sigma > 0$; the graphs hold $x > 0$ fixed.

(a) What can you conclude about β, for both the dashed and the dotted graph? Explain your answers.

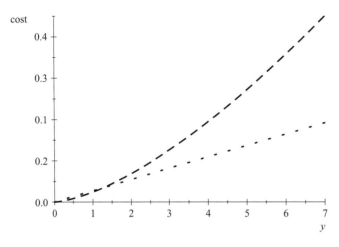

Figure 4.4
Graphs of two cost functions.

(b) What can you conclude about α, for both the dashed and the dotted graph? Explain your answers.

3. Replace the general cost function used in the first order condition 4.5 with the parametric example given in equation 4.1. Next, rewrite the equation, specializing by setting $\beta = 0$. Explain in words the meaning of this equation. (The point of this problem is to encourage students to spend a bit of time thinking about the optimality condition and working with the parametric cost function.)

4. Section 4.2.2 claims that the firm never extracts to a level at which marginal profit is negative. Explain, in a way that a noneconomist would understand, why this claim is true.

5. In our two-period setting, the gain function for a candidate at which the resource is exhausted is

$$g(\varepsilon; y_0, x_1, y_1) = p_0 \cdot (y_0 + \varepsilon) - c(x_0, y_0 + \varepsilon)$$
$$+ \rho[p_1 \cdot (y_1 - \varepsilon) - c(x_1 - \varepsilon, y_1 - \varepsilon)],$$

and the gain function for a candidate at which the resource is not exhausted ($y_1 < x_1$) is

$$g(\varepsilon; y_0, x_1, y_1) = p_0 \cdot (y_0 + \varepsilon) - c(x_0, y_0 + \varepsilon)$$
$$+ \rho[p_1 \cdot y_1 - c(x_1 - \varepsilon, y_1)].$$

Identify, by underlining, the difference between these two functions, and provide the economic explanation for this difference, using a couple of sentences.

6. This exercise adopts the common meaning of "rent," denoting the payment made to be able to use something (here, land) for a given amount of time (here, 1 year). The exercise illustrates (1) how rent is determined in a competitive market, (2) the relation between land rent and land price, and (3) the distinction between pure rent and quasi-rent.

There is a fixed stock of unimproved land, $L = 10$. The annual value of marginal product of land is $20 - q$, where q is the amount of land that is rented.

(a) Denote the annual rent for a unit of land as f. What is relation between the value of marginal product of land and the inverse demand for land rental? Using the answer to this question, and the fact that the equilibrium rent equates supply and demand, find the equilibrium value of f. (This number is the equilibrium rent when all of the land is rented out.)

(b) What price would someone with an annual discount rate of r be willing to pay to buy one unit of this land? Your answer gives the price as a function of the discount rate; recall equation 2.13. (The annual land rent is the amount a person pays to use a unit of land for 1 year; the price of a unit of land is the amount that someone pays to buy the land. By owning the land, a person can use it or rent it out every year. If they rent it out, they obtain the rent every year, from now until infinity. People have finite lives, but they can bequeath land to their successors.)

(c) If the land is improved, its value of marginal product increases by 2. If q units are improved, the value of marginal product increases from $20 - q$ to $22 - q$. What is the equilibrium annual rental rate, and what is the equilibrium price, if the entire stock of land is improved?

(d) Suppose that the per-acre cost of the improving the land is 15. What is the critical value of r at which the landowner is indifferent between leaving (all of) the land in its unimproved state, and improving all of it? (Your answers to part [b] and [c] enable you to determine how the improvement affects the price of land. A person is indifferent between making the improvement if the cost of the improvement equals the change in the price due to the improvement.)

(e) If the land is improved, what fraction of the rent (or the price) is pure rent, and what fraction is quasi-rent?

7. Consider a two-period problem. Demand in a period is $a - by$, and extraction costs are $c(y, x) = \frac{y}{10+x}$. A competitive firm has initial stock x_0 and discount factor ρ.

(a) Identify the endogenous variables. Assuming that it is optimal to extract all of the stock, write down the equations you would solve to obtain the values of these endogenous variables.

(b) Use these equations from part (a) to obtain a single equation giving y_0 as an implicit function of x_0.

(c) Now suppose that it is optimal not to exhaust the stock. Write the single equation that gives y_0 as an implicit function of x_0 in this case. [Hint: Review section 4.5.]

8. This problem asks you to apply the perturbation method to solve a problem similar to the example in section 4.2. Neither example is related to natural resources, but greater familiarity with the mathematical tools makes subsequent applications easier to understand. The problem is

$$\min_{x,y}(6xy - 2y^2),$$

subject to $4x - 2y = 5$.

(a) If the candidate x, y is feasible (meaning that it satisfies the contraint), and we increase x by ε units, what is the required change in y in order to satisfy the constraint?

(b) Use your answer to part (a) to write the gain function, $g(\varepsilon; x, y)$.

(c) Obtain the first and second derivatives of $g(\varepsilon; x, y)$ with respect to ε. Is this function concave or convex in ε? Does it reach a maximum or a minimum at $\varepsilon = 0$?

(d) Evaluate the first derivative from part (c) and $\varepsilon = 0$ to obtain the first order condition. Use this condition and the constraint to find the solution to the problem.

Sources
Pindyck (1978) develops a model of extraction costs linear in extraction and decreasing in stocks.

Livernois and Uhler (1987) develop the point raised in the Caveat subsection in section 4.1, showing empirically that extraction costs rise with aggregate stock; for individual wells, they find that costs fall with the remaining stock.

Livernois (1987) estimates the extraction cost function for oil, finding that marginal cost is constant in extraction and that the cost functions for different wells cannot be aggregated into an industry cost function

Chermak and Patrick (1995) estimate cost functions for natural gas, finding that costs fall with remaining reserves, but marginal costs fall with extraction.

Ellis and Halvorsen (2002) and Stollery (2008) provide empirical estimates of extraction costs.

5 The Hotelling Model

Objective
- Interpret and use the equilibrium condition for the T-period problem.

Information and Skills
- Understand the relation between two-period and T-period problems.
- Write down the objective, the constraints, and the Euler equation for the competitive firm in the T-period problem.
- Understand the relation between rent (and price) in any two periods.
- Understand the meaning of the "shadow value" of a resource.
- Show that firms exhaust cheaper deposits before beginning to extract from more expensive deposits.

The intuition developed in the two-period setting survives when the resource can be used an arbitrary number of periods. The perturbation method produces the optimality condition, known as the Euler equation in general settings and the Hotelling rule in the resource setting. The definition of rent leads to a concise statement of this rule. The two potential sources of rent (in our models) are limited supply and stock-dependent costs. We continue to assume that are no market failures, apart perhaps from monopoly. Subsequent chapters consider other market failures. We frequently refer to the resource as oil, but the model applies to any nonrenewable resource.

A Road Map
Section 5.1 presents the model in which extraction takes place during an arbitrary number of periods, explains how to obtain the equilibrium condition, and interprets that condition. This material requires little more than changing time subscripts in an equilibrium condition derived in chapter 4. Section 5.2 then uses the definition of rent to write this equilibrium condition concisely and to interpret it. Rent has several names with different interpretations (section 5.3).

Section 5.4 uses a special case to show that it is efficient to exhaust a low-cost deposit before extracting from a high-cost deposit. Section 5.5 explores the analogy between resource stocks and stocks in a publicly traded company; analogies can help improve intuition. Section 5.6 introduces the transversality condition and explains how to compute the equilibrium price and extraction trajectories. Section 5.7 reiterates that we can obtain the equilibrium conditions for a monopoly by beginning with the competitive equilibrium conditions and replacing price with marginal revenue.

5.1 The Euler Equation (Hotelling Rule)

Objectives and skills: Write the competitive firm's objective, constraints, and optimality condition (the Euler equation), and understand how the perturbation method is used.

The Hotelling model describes the equilibrium extraction of a nonrenewable resource. The Hotelling rule is the optimality condition for this problem. We first discuss the model taking the number of periods during which extraction is positive, $T + 1$, as given, leaving the determination of T to section 5.6. The representative competitive firm maximizes the present discounted sum of profits, subject to the resource constraint:

$$\max \left[\overbrace{(p_0 y_0 - c(x_0, y_0))}^{\text{period-0 profit}} + \overbrace{\rho(p_1 y_1 - c(x_1, y_1))}^{\text{PDV of period-1 profit}} \cdots \right.$$

$$\left. + \cdots \underbrace{\rho^t (p_t y_t - c(x_t, y_t))}_{\text{PDV of period-}t\text{ profit}} + \cdots + \underbrace{\rho^T (p_T y_T - c(x_T, y_T))}_{\text{PDV of period-}T\text{ profit}} \right] \tag{5.1}$$

$$= \max \sum_{t=0}^{T} \rho^t (p_t y_t - c(x_t, y_t)),$$

subject to

$x_{t+1} = x_t - y_t$, with x_0 given, $x_t \geq 0$, and $y_t \geq 0$ for all t.

For this type of dynamic problem, the first order (necessary) condition is known as the "Euler equation." In the nonrenewable resource setting, it is also called the Hotelling rule.[1]

---

1 In the nonrenewable resource setting, we use the terms "Hotelling rule" and "Euler equation" interchangeably, because the two terms refer to the same equation. In the renewable resource setting (chapter 15), the optimality condition is called the Euler equation but is not referred to as a Hotelling rule.

The equation is (appendix B.1)[2]

$$\underbrace{p_t - \frac{\partial c\,(x_t,\,y_t)}{\partial y_t}}_{\substack{\text{profit increase due to}\\\text{higher period-}t\text{ sales}}} = \rho \left[\underbrace{p_{t+1} - \frac{\partial c\,(x_{t+1},\,y_{t+1})}{\partial y_{t+1}}}_{\substack{\text{profit decrease due to}\\\text{lower period-}t+1\text{ sales}}} - \underbrace{\frac{\partial c\,(x_{t+1},\,y_{t+1})}{\partial x_{t+1}}}_{\substack{\text{cost increase due to}\\\text{lower stock}}} \right]. \tag{5.2}$$

Equations 4.5 (for the two-period problem, where $T = 1$) and 5.2 (for general T) are identical, except for the time subscripts. Equation 5.2 must hold for all pairs of adjacent periods when extraction is positive: $t = 0, 1, 2, \ldots, T - 1$.

Equations 4.5 and 5.2 have the same interpretation. If the firm sells one more unit in period t and makes an offsetting reduction of one unit in period $t + 1$, it receives a marginal gain in period t and incurs a marginal loss in period $t + 1$. The marginal gain in period t (the left side of equation 5.2) equals the increased profit, price minus marginal cost, due to the increase in sales. The marginal loss in period $t + 1$ is the sum of the two terms on the right side. The first term on the right side equals the reduced profit due to reduced sales, price minus marginal cost in period $t + 1$; the second term on the right side equals increased cost due to the lower stock in period $t + 1$.

5.2 Rent and Hotelling

Objectives and skills: Interpret the Euler equation using the definition of rent, and understand the relation between rent in any two periods.

Rent in competitive markets is defined as price minus marginal cost:

$$R_t = p_t - \frac{\partial c(x_t,\,y_t)}{\partial y_t}. \tag{5.3}$$

We are interested in the *equilibrium value* of rent: its value when the firm correctly solves its optimization problem. For brevity, we usually refer to this value merely as "rent." Rent can be interpreted as the *opportunity cost* of extracting the resource: the loss from extracting the marginal unit now rather than at some other time. Current extraction reduces future profits, creating an opportunity cost. Rearranging the definition of rent, we have

$$p_t = \frac{\partial c(x_t,\,y_t)}{\partial y_t} + R_t.$$

---

2 We sometimes show all subscripts, as in the derivative $\frac{\partial c(x_t,\,y_t)}{\partial y_t}$. Where there is no possibility of ambiguity, to conserve notation, we sometimes drop subscripts. For example, we write $\frac{\partial c(x_t,\,y_t)}{\partial y}$.

This equation states that in a competitive equilibrium, price equals full marginal extraction cost, where "full" means the sum of the standard marginal cost and the opportunity cost (= rent). We use the definition of rent to write the Euler equation (Hotelling rule) more compactly, as

$$R_t = \rho \left[R_{t+1} - \frac{\partial c(x_{t+1}, y_{t+1})}{\partial x_{t+1}} \right]. \tag{5.4}$$

Current rent depends on future rent and extraction costs: rent is a "forward-looking variable."

Constant Marginal Costs

If marginal costs are constant ($c(x, y) = Cy$), the Hotelling rule simplifies to

$$R_t = \rho R_{t+1}, \quad \text{or} \quad p_t - C = \rho(p_{t+1} - C). \tag{5.5}$$

The first equation states that the present value of rent is the same in any two adjacent periods with positive extraction. The constant cost model produces several important results.

• The present value of rent is the same in any two periods where extraction is positive:

$$R_t = \rho^j R_{t+j}. \tag{5.6}$$

(See exercises 5.2 for verification of equation 5.6.) The Hotelling rule states that the firm cannot increase its payoff by moving a unit of extraction between adjacent periods, t and $t + 1$. Equation 5.6 is more general: it states that the firm cannot increase its payoff by moving extraction between any two periods where extraction is positive (not merely between any two adjacent periods). The intuition is that a firm can sell the marginal unit in period t, invest the marginal profit (R_t) for j periods, and obtain the return $(1 + r)^j R_t$; alternatively, the firm can delay extraction of this marginal unit until period $t + j$, at which time it earns R_{t+j}. If there are no opportunities for intertemporal arbitrage, the firm must be indifferent between these two options, that is,[3]

$$(1 + r)^j R_t = R_{t+j} \quad \Rightarrow \quad R_t = \frac{1}{(1 + r)^j} R_{t+j} = \rho^j R_{t+j}. \tag{5.7}$$

• With constant marginal cost = average extraction cost, the value of the initial resource stock (equivalently, the value of the mine that contains that stock) equals the initial rent times the initial stock:

---

3 Recall the definition $\rho = \frac{1}{1+r}$ from section 2.6.

$$\overbrace{\underbrace{\sum_{t=0}^{T} \rho^t (p_t - C) y_t}_{\text{defn of value of mine}} = \overbrace{\sum_{t=0}^{T} \rho^t R_t y_t}^{\text{use defn of rent}}}^{} = \underbrace{R_0 \sum_{t=0}^{T} y_t}_{\text{use eq 5.6}} \overbrace{= R_0 x_0.}^{\text{use stock constraint}} \tag{5.8}$$

The value of the mine equals the present discounted stream of profits. The first equality uses the definition of rent, equation 5.3; the second uses equation 5.6 to replace $\rho^t R_t$ with R_0, and the third uses the stock constraint: aggregate extraction ($\sum_{t=0}^{T} y_t$) equals the initial stock (x_0).

- We can determine the rate of change of price or rent by (i) multiplying both sides of the two equations in 5.5 by $1 + r$, (ii) using $\rho = (1 + r)^{-1}$, and (iii) rearranging to obtain

$$\frac{R_{t+1} - R_t}{R_t} = r, \quad \text{or} \quad \frac{p_{t+1} - p_t}{p_t} = r - \frac{rC}{p_t}. \tag{5.9}$$

The first of these two equations says that *rent* rises at the rate of interest. The second says that *price* rises the rate of interest minus $\frac{rC}{p_t}$, that is, price rises at less than the rate of interest if $C > 0$. For $C = 0$, the second equation in 5.9 simplifies to

$$\frac{p_{t+1} - p_t}{p_t} = r, \tag{5.10}$$

which states that in a competitive equilibrium where extraction is costless, price rises at the rate of interest: the competitive firm is indifferent between selling in any two periods if and only if the present value of the price is the same in the two periods. For $C > 0$, equilibrium price rises more slowly than the interest rate. In chapter 3, we noted that constant extraction costs cause the firm to delay extraction, causing the initial price to be higher and the later price to be lower, thereby lowering $\frac{p_1 - p_0}{p_0}$ relative to the case where $C = 0$. Equation 5.9 shows that in the T-period setting, a positive C lowers the rate of change of price at every point in time.

Stock-Dependent Extraction Costs

When costs do not depend on the stock, current rent depends only on future rent. With stock-dependent extraction costs $\left(-\frac{\partial c(x_t, y_t)}{\partial x_t} > 0 \right)$, costs change over time as the stock is drawn down. In this case, the equilibrium value of current rent depends on both rent and extraction costs in future periods. The relation between (equilibrium) rent in periods t and $t + j$ is

$$R_t = \underbrace{\rho^j R_{t+j}}_{\text{scarcity: PDV of period } t+j \text{ rent}} \overbrace{- \sum_{i=1}^{j} \rho^i \frac{\partial c(x_{t+i}, y_{t+i})}{\partial x_{t+i}}}^{\text{costs: PDV of stream of higher costs}} . \tag{5.11}$$

(See exercise 3 for verification of equation 5.11.) Rent depends on scarcity and future extraction costs. If the firm extracts an extra unit today and makes an offsetting reduction j periods in the future, the present value of the future loss in profit, due to the lower future extraction, equals the first term on the right side of equation 5.11. The second term equals the present value of the stream of higher extraction costs from periods $t+1$ to $t+j$. Rent is a forward-looking variable.

Importance of Property Rights

The time trajectory of rents depends on the assumption that resource extractors have secure property rights. These firms understand that a change in extraction today implies an offsetting future change. Rent equals the value of having an additional unit to extract in the future, which equals the firm's opportunity cost of extracting the marginal unit today.

Without secure property rights, a firm risks losing stock that it keeps in the ground. Weaker property rights reduce a firm's incentive to conserve the resource, leading to lower rent. If firms have no property rights to the resource, they have no incentive to conserve and make zero rent. Many of society's resource-related problems arise from weak or nonexistent property rights, a topic we take up in chapters 9, 12, 14, and 17.

5.3   Shadow Prices

Objectives and skills: Understand the meaning of the shadow price of a resource.

The "shadow price" of a resource equals the amount that a firm is willing to pay to obtain an additional unit of stock in the ground (in situ). The modifier "shadow" recognizes that the actual market for such a transaction is hypothetical. The shadow price at time t equals the equilibrium rent at that time, R_t. This relation is general, but it is particularly obvious in the case of constant marginal extraction costs. Here, equation 5.8 shows that the value of the mine is $R_0 x_0$. The increase in this value due to the increase in the stock, x_0, is the rent, R_0. The mine owner would be willing to pay R_0 for one more unit of the resource at time 0. (The terms "shadow price" and "shadow value" mean the same thing.)[4]

In the absence of market failures, the owner's shadow price of the stock equals society's shadow price of the stock, even though the owner does not capture consumer surplus.

---

4 The method of Lagrange provides a different method of deriving the Euler equation. This method produces "Lagrange multipliers," which equal the value of having an additional unit of the stock at a point in time. The Lagrange multiplier in a period equals the shadow price of the resource, which equals the rent.

Both the owner and a social planner would pay the same amount for an additional unit of resource in the ground. In the presence of market failures, such as imperfect property rights and externalities, the private and social values diverge. The assertion that a resource owner is willing to pay exactly R_t for an additional unit of the stock in situ at time t is not self-evident: it might seem that an owner who receives one more unit of the resource would not simply extract that unit in the current period and thus earn R_t. Instead, the owner could extract some of the extra unit in the current period and some of it later. With that reasoning, it appears that the owner might pay more than R_t for the marginal unit. This conjecture is false because of the no-intertemporal-arbitrage condition: the owner has no desire to reallocate extraction over time. An owner who acquires one extra unit is indifferent between extracting it now and earning R_t, or extracting it later and earning the *present value* equal to R_t. The owner would therefore pay R_t for a marginal unit of the resource in situ.

5.4 The Order of Extraction of Deposits

Objectives and skills: Understand why a competitive industry exhausts a cheaper deposit before beginning to use a more expensive deposit.

We have assumed that there is a single deposit, with extraction costs $c(x, y)$. We can think of this model as approximating a more realistic situation where there are many different deposits with different extraction costs. In important cases, a competitive equilibrium exhausts the cheaper deposits before beginning to extract from more expensive ones. We confirm this claim for the case of constant marginal (= average) costs.

Suppose that there are three different deposits with different average extraction costs. Figure 5.1 illustrates an example, showing the relation, a step function, between average cost and the remaining stock in all mines. The average extraction costs are constant while a particular deposit is being mined and jump up once that deposit is exhausted, making it necessary to mine a more expensive deposit. If instead of there being only three mines, with significantly different costs, there were many mines, with only small cost differences between the most similar mines, then the figure would approach a smooth curve, showing average costs decreasing in remaining stock.

To show that firms exhaust cheaper deposits before using more expensive deposits, we consider the case where there are two competitive firms, a and b, owning deposits with constant extraction costs $C^a < C^b$. The high-cost firm, b, begins to extract only during or after the last period when the low-cost firm, a, extracts; possibly both firms operate during the last period when a extracts. We verify this claim using the fact that the Euler equation must hold for both firms: for any two adjacent periods, t and $t + 1$, during which a firm extracts, equation 5.9 holds, with C replaced by C^a or C^b (depending on which firm is extracting). Consider any two adjacent periods, t and $t + 1$, during which the low-cost firm is extracting. We need to show that the high-cost firm does not want to extract in t, the first of these two periods. (If the high-cost firm did want to extract in period t, then the claim

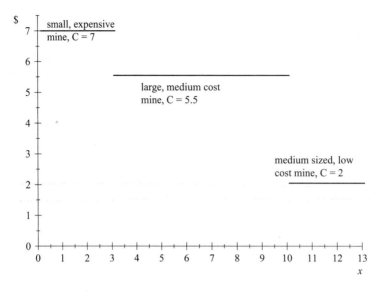

Figure 5.1
Average extraction costs as a function of remaining stock, when there are three deposits, with individual stocks 3, 7, and 2, and corresponding constant marginal = average extraction costs, 2, 5.5, and 7.

would not be true, because in that case extraction of high-cost deposits occurs in a period prior to the period when the low-cost deposits are exhausted.)

Because the low-cost firm extracts in both t and $t + 1$, equation 5.9 implies that

$$(p_t - C^a) = \rho(p_{t+1} - C^a). \tag{5.12}$$

Equation 5.12 and $C^a < C^b$ imply that (see exercise 2)

$$p_t - C^b < \rho(p_{t+1} - C^b). \tag{5.13}$$

This inequality implies that the high-cost firm strictly prefers to extract nothing in period t. If this firm were to extract a unit in period t, it would earn $p_t - C^b$. It could earn strictly higher present value profits by holding on to this unit and then selling it in period $t + 1$. Therefore, it is not optimal for the high-cost firm to sell anything in period t.

5.5   Resources and Asset Prices

Objectives and skills: Understand the relation between an asset pricing equation and the Hotelling rule.

Competitive equilibria eliminate opportunities for intertemporal arbitrage, both for natural resources and for other types of assets, such as shares in companies. We discuss the relation between the Hotelling rule and an asset pricing equation from financial economics. By multiplying both sides of equation 5.4 by $\rho^{-1} = 1 + r$ and rearranging the result, we can write the Hotelling rule as

$$r R_t = R_{t+1} - R_t - \frac{\partial c(x_{t+1}, y_{t+1})}{\partial x_{t+1}}. \tag{5.14}$$

Now consider the equilibrium price of an asset, such as a share in a company. There is no risk in our model, and a person can borrow a dollar for 1 year at the interest rate r. In this risk-free world, people know that next period, $t + 1$, the price of the asset will be P_{t+1}, and there will be a dividend on the stock, D_{t+1}. What is the equilibrium price of this asset today, in period t? If the price of the stock at the beginning of period t is P_t, a person who can borrow at annual rate r can borrow P_t at the beginning of the period and buy a unit of the stock. They must repay $(1 + r)P_t$ at the beginning of the next period (their costs). If they collect the dividend paid at the beginning of period $t + 1$, and sell the stock, they collect $P_{t+1} + D_{t+1}$, their revenue. Because the person has not used their own money or incurred any risk, the revenue from the transaction must equal the cost:

$$\underbrace{P_{t+1} + D_{t+1}}_{\text{revenue}} = \underbrace{(1 + r)P_t}_{\text{costs}}.$$

Rearranging this equality gives

$$\underbrace{r P_t}_{\text{cost of borrowing}} = \underbrace{P_{t+1} - P_t}_{\text{capital gains}} + \underbrace{D_{t+1}}_{\text{dividend}}. \tag{5.15}$$

Equation 5.15 is a no-arbitrage condition: it means that a person cannot earn profits by making riskless purchases and sales. The left side is the yearly cost of borrowing enough money to buy one unit of the stock. The right side is the sum of capital gains (the change in the price) and the dividend. To compare equations 5.14 and 5.15, recall that $-\frac{\partial c(y_{t+1}, x_{t+1})}{\partial x} \geq 0$, because a higher stock decreases or leaves unchanged extraction costs; this term equals the benefit that the resource owner obtains from lower future costs. It corresponds to the dividend, D_t, in equation 5.15. The asset price, P, corresponds to R, the resource rent.

In the asset price equation, if the dividend is 0, then the price of the stock must rise at the rate of interest in equilibrium: the capital gain due to the change in the asset price must equal the opportunity cost of holding the stock, $r P_t$. A positive dividend makes investors willing to hold the stock at lower capital gains. Similarly, in the resource setting, stock-dependent extraction costs cause the equilibrium rent to increase at less than the rate of interest. The stock-dependent extraction costs play the same role in the resource setting as the dividend does in the asset price equation.

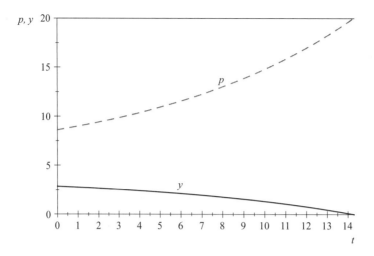

Figure 5.2
The dashed curve shows equilibrium price, and the solid curve shows equilibrium sales for the example with inverse demand $p = 20 - 4y$, constant marginal cost $C = 5$, discount rate $r = 0.1$, and initial stock $x_0 = 25$.

5.6   Completing the Solution

Objectives and skills: Understand the transversality condition, and be able to use the necessary conditions to obtain the equilibrium price and extraction trajectories.

A solution to the Hotelling model consists of a price and sales trajectory. Often we describe these trajectories using graphs. A change in extraction costs, an alternative source of energy, or some other exogenous change alters the equilibrium, changing the appearance of these graphs. By comparing the graphs under the different assumptions, we can see how exogenous changes alter the equilibrium price and sales trajectories. Figure 5.2 shows the price and sales trajectories for an example with constant marginal cost.

We obtain these trajectories using three necessary conditions. (i) The Hotelling rule determines the rate of change of price (or rent). (ii) The transversality condition, discussed below, determines the level of price (or rent) at T, the time when extraction ends. (iii) For the problem we consider here, where extraction costs do not depend on the stock, cumulative extraction from periods 0 to T equals the initial stock: leaving stock in the ground after extraction ceases is not part of an equilibrium. We refer to the condition that cumulative extraction equals the initial stock as the "exhaustion condition."[5]

---

5 If extraction costs depend on the stock, the cost of extracting the final unit of the stock may exceed the choke price (the maximum that people will pay for a unit). In this case, it is optimal to leave some stock in the ground. Stock-dependent costs also change the Hotelling rule.

Up to this point we have used a "discrete time" model, where the time indices are integers. This model enables us to derive the Hotelling rule using basic calculus, and it also leads to a clear interpretation of that equation using the idea of arbitrage. In a "continuous time" setting, the time variable, t, can take any non-negative value. The continuous time setting makes it easier to describe and explain the transversality condition, and to obtain and graph the solution to the model. We discuss the continuous time model here, under the assumption that the terminal time, T, is endogenous.[6]

For our example, inverse demand is linear, $p_t = a - by_t$. The transversality condition for this problem requires $p_T = a$: the price at the final time of extraction, p_T, equals the choke price, a. A moment after T, when sales are zero, the price equals a. The price never exceeds the choke price, so if the transversality condition were not satisfied, then $p_T < a$. In that case, during the moment of final extraction, rent is $R_T = p_T - C < a - C$. If this inequality holds, then the resource owner can perturb the candidate by reducing extraction by a small amount at instant T, reducing profits by $p_T - C$, and selling the marginal unit a moment later (when the price is a), earning $a - C > p_T - C$. Because this perturbation increases profits, any candidate that results in $p_T < a$ is not an equilibrium. Consequently, in equilibrium, $p_T = a$.

With constant marginal extraction costs, the Hotelling rule requires that rent ($=$ price minus marginal cost) rises at the rate of interest. Figure 5.3 shows the graphs of three price trajectories, corresponding to three arbitrary initial prices (p_0 equal to 7, 10, and 12). Each trajectory satisfies the Hotelling rule, but none of them are the equilibrium trajectory, because they are associated with arbitrary (nonequilibrium) initial prices. A higher initial price leads to a higher price trajectory, which reaches the choke price, $a = 20$, shown by the horizontal line in figure 5.3, at an earlier time. We define $T(p_0)$ as the time at which a price trajectory that begins at p_0 and satisfies the Hotelling rule reaches a. Figure 5.3 implies that $T(p_0)$ is a decreasing function of the initial price: the larger is p_0, the sooner the graph of price reaches the horizontal line at $a = 20$.

Given an arbitrary initial price, p_0, we can use $T(p_0)$ to calculate the corresponding terminal time. For this initial price, we can use the Hotelling rule to calculate the corresponding price trajectory, p_t, and then use the demand function to calculate the corresponding sales trajectory $y_t = \frac{a - p_t}{b}$. The equilibrium initial price leads to a sales trajectory that exhausts the initial stock, x_0. Figure 5.4 shows how we use this information to determine the equilibrium initial price. For any initial price, p_0, we can calculate $T(p_0)$, shown by the solid curve marked "T" in the figure. Given p_0 and the corresponding $T(p_0)$, we can calculate the cumulative sales, from time 0 to $T(p_0)$. The dashed curve shows this relation. For our example, the initial stock is $x_0 = 25$, shown by the horizontal

---

6 Appendix B.2 considers the discrete time setting with both endogenous and exogenous terminal time, and it also discusses the relation between the discrete and continuous time models.

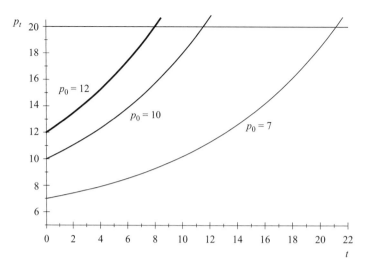

Figure 5.3
Three price trajectories, corresponding to different initial prices that satisfy the Euler equation. A higher initial price, p_0, causes the price trajectory to reach the choke price, $a = 20$, earlier.

line. The intersection of this line and the dashed curve occurs at point A, where $p_0 = 8.6$, the equilibrium initial price for this example. Drawing a vertical line (not shown) through A identifies this price. The vertical line intersects the graph of $T(p_0)$ at point B, where $T(8.6) = 14.3$.

Figure 5.2 uses this information to graph the equilibrium price and sales trajectories. The equilibrium price begins at 8.6, satisfies the Hotelling rule, and reaches the choke price $a = 20$ at $T = 14.3$. The equilibrium sales trajectory declines over this period, reaching zero sales at the terminal time. Cumulative sales equal the initial stock, $x_0 = 25$.

The Algorithm*
We solve this model using the following algorithm:

1. Use the Hotelling rule (rent rise at the rate of interest) to find the price at t as a function of the initial price:[7]

$$p_t = e^{rt}(p_0 - C) + C. \tag{5.16}$$

---

7 Subtracting C from both sides of equation 5.16 gives $p_t - C = R_t = e^{rt} R_0$. Taking the derivative with respect to time gives $\frac{dR_t}{dt} = re^{rt} R_0 = r R_t$, confirming that rent rises at the rate of interest. Thus, equation 5.16 satisfies the Euler equation.

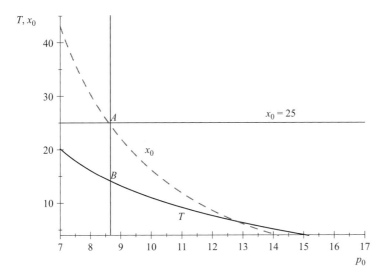

Figure 5.4
The solid curve labeled T shows $T(p_0)$, the time at which the price reaches the choke price $a = 20$, as a function of the initial price, p_0. The dashed curve shows cumulative extraction from 0 to $T(p_0)$ as a function of p_0. For an initial stock $x_0 = 25$, the equilibrium occurs at point A, implying $p_0 = 8.6$. Using the curve $T(p_0)$, we identify the terminal time using point B, where $T(8.6) = 14.3$.

2. Evaluate equation 5.16 at $t = T$ and use the transversality condition, $p_T = a$, to obtain

$$p_T = a = e^{rT}(p_0 - C) + C.$$

Solve the second equation to obtain T as an explicit function of p_0:

$$T(p_0) = \frac{1}{r} \ln \left[\frac{a - C}{(p_0 - C)} \right]. \tag{5.17}$$

The solid curve marked "T" in figure 5.4 shows the graph of the right side of equation 5.17.

3. Use equation 5.16 and the inverse demand function to obtain sales at t:

$$y(t) = \frac{1}{b} \left(a - \left(e^{rt}(p_0 - C) + C \right) \right). \tag{5.18}$$

4. Use equations 5.17 and 5.18 and the stock constraint to write cumulative extraction as a function of the initial price:

$$\text{cumulative sales} = x_0 = \int_0^{T(p_0)} \underbrace{\left[\frac{1}{b} \left(a - \left(e^{rt}(p_0 - C) + C \right) \right) \right.}_{\text{sales at } t, \ y_t} dt. \tag{5.19}$$

The dashed curve in Figure 5.4 shows the graph of the right side of equation 5.19. The solution to this equation (shown as the horizontal coordinate of point A in Figure 5.4) gives the equilibrium initial price, p_0. Once we know that value, we can use equations 5.16 and 5.18 to obtain the price and sales trajectory, graphed in Figure 5.2.

5.7 Monopoly

Objectives and skills: use previous results to write down and interpret the optimality condition for the monopoly.

We obtain the optimality condition under monopoly by using equation 5.2 and replacing price with marginal revenue, $MR_t = p_t(1 - 1/\eta(p_t))$, where $\eta(p_t)$ is the elasticity of demand. The monopoly's Euler equation is

$$
\overbrace{p_t\left(1 - \frac{1}{\eta(p_t)}\right)}^{MR} - \overbrace{\frac{\partial c(x_t, y_t)}{\partial y_t}}^{MC}
$$

increased profit due to extra unit extracted at t

$$
= \rho \left[\underbrace{p_{t+1}\left(1 - \frac{1}{\eta(p_{t+1})}\right) - \frac{\partial c(x_{t+1}, y_{t+1})}{\partial y_{t+1}}}_{\text{reduced profit due to reduction in extraction}} \quad \overbrace{- \frac{\partial c(x_{t+1}, y_{t+1})}{\partial x_{t+1}}}^{\text{higher cost due to lower stock}} \right]. \tag{5.20}
$$

For the special case where extraction is costless and the elasticity of demand is constant (inverse demand is $p = y^{-\frac{1}{\eta}}$, and η is a constant), equation 5.20 simplifies to equation 5.10.[8] Here, the monopoly and the competitive industry have the same price and sales path.

More generally, the monopoly and competitive outcomes differ. If extraction is costless but demand becomes more elastic with higher prices (as occurs for the linear demand function and many others), then monopoly price rises more slowly than the rate of interest. In this situation, the initial monopoly price exceeds the initial competitive price, so monopoly sales are initially lower than competitive sales. Here again, "the monopoly is the conservationist's friend."

---

8 With constant elasticity of demand and zero extraction costs, the monopoly Euler equation simplifies to $\left(1 - \frac{1}{\eta}\right)p_t = \rho\left(1 - \frac{1}{\eta}\right)p_{t+1}$, or $p_t = \rho p_{t+1}$, which is the same as the Euler equation for the competitive firm.

With constant elasticity of demand and nonzero extraction costs, the monopoly equilibrium approaches the competitive equilibrium as demand becomes more elastic (η increases). Section 2.5 makes a similar point in a simpler, one-period model. That section shows that the ratio of monopoly to competitive prices (in equilibrium) approaches 1 as $\eta \to \infty$. The more elastic is demand, the less market power the monopoly has, and the more similar are the monopoly and competitive outcomes.

Defining rent for the monopoly as marginal revenue (instead of price) minus marginal cost, we can write the monopoly's optimality condition as in equation 5.4. The interpretation of this equation is the same as under competition, provided that we keep in mind that the definition of rent under monopoly differs from that under competition.

5.8 Summary

The perturbation method is as easy to use for the T-period problem as for the two-period problem. It leads to a necessary condition for optimality (equivalently, an equilibrium condition) that expresses current price and costs as a function of next-period price and costs. This equation is known as the Euler equation; in the resource setting, it is also known as the Hotelling rule. We can express this equilibrium condition in terms of rent.

The current equilibrium market price and the rent depend on future prices and costs. Rent is a forward-looking variable. The Hotelling rule states that (equilibrium) rent in an arbitrary period equals the present value of rent in the next period plus the cost increase due to a marginal reduction in stock. For the special case where extraction costs are independent of the stock, the Hotelling rule states that the present value of rent is equal in any two periods where extraction is positive. If extraction costs are zero, the Hotelling rule states that price rises at the rate of interest. For positive constant average extraction costs, price rises more slowly than the rate of interest.

The Hotelling rule has a close analog in investment theory, where the asset pricing equation states that the opportunity cost of buying an asset must equal the capital gains plus the dividend from owning the asset. By relabeling the resource rent as the asset price, and the cost increase due to a lower stock as the dividend, the Hotelling rule becomes identical to this asset pricing equation.

We also discussed the following two points:

• Equilibrium rent in a period equals the amount that the resource owner would pay in that period for an extra unit of resource in the ground. Rent equals the shadow price for this hypothetical transaction, which equals the Lagrange multiplier associated with the resource constraint in this period.

• It is optimal to exhaust cheaper deposits before beginning to use more expensive deposits. We confirmed this result for the case of mines with different constant extraction costs.

We studied an example to introduce the transversality condition. We then showed how this condition and the Euler equation make it possible to find the initial price and the terminal time, and then obtained the graphs of the price and sales trajectory as functions of time.

5.9   Terms and Concepts, Study Questions, Exercises, and Sources

Terms and Concepts
Euler equation, Hotelling rule, transversality condition, asset price, capital gains, dividend, Lagrange multiplier, shadow price, in situ.

Study Questions
1. Consider a general inverse demand function $p(y)$ and the parametric cost function in equation 4.1. (a) Write down the competitive firm's objective and constraints. (b) Write down and interpret the Euler equation for this problem. (c) Without actually performing calculations, describe the steps of the perturbation method used to obtain this necessary condition.

2. What is the definition of "rent" in the nonrenewable resource problem for the competitive firm?

(a) Use this definition to rewrite the Euler equation for the problem described in question 1.

(b) Write down the relation between rent in period t and in period $t + j$ ($j \geq 1$), and interpret this equation.

(c) Explain the difference between the case where extraction costs depend on the stock and where extraction costs do not depend on the stock.

Exercises
1. Write the Euler equation for a monopoly facing the demand function $p = 20 - 7y$ with the cost function $c(x, y)$ and discount factor ρ. There is no need for a derivation.

2. Show that equation 5.12 and $C^b > C^a$ imply inequality 5.13. Proceed as follows. First add $C^a - C^b$ to both sides of equation 5.12. Then add and subtract ρC^b to/from the right side of this equation, and rearrange the right side to obtain

$$(p_t - C^b) = \rho(p_{t+1} - C^b) + (1 - \rho)(C^a - C^b). \tag{5.21}$$

Assuming that $r > 0$, use equation 5.21 to confirm equation 5.13.

3. (a) Use the Hotelling rule (equation 5.4) and an inductive proof (see appendix B.3) to establish equation 5.11.

(b) Provide the economic explanation of equation 5.11 in a couple of sentences.

4. Section 5.2 shows that with constant extraction costs, the value of the mine equals the initial rent times the initial stock. Suppose instead that extraction cost is strictly convex in extraction and is independent of the stock: cost equals $c(y_t)$, with $c'(y_t) > 0$ and $c''(y_t) > 0$. With convex costs, is the value of the mine greater or less than the initial rent times the initial stock? What is the economic meaning/explanation of your conclusion? [Hints: Use

equation 5.11 and the assumption that extraction costs do not depend on the stock to find a relation between rent in period 0 and the present value of rent in any future period. Then write the value of the mine as

$$\text{Value of mine} = \sum_{t=0}^{T} \rho^t \left(p_t y_t - c(y_t) \right)$$

$$= \sum_{t=0}^{T} \rho^t \left(p_t - \frac{c(y_t)}{y_t} - c'(y_t) + c'(y_t) \right) y_t$$

$$= \sum_{t=0}^{T} \rho^t \left(R_t + \left[c'(y_t) - \frac{c(y_t)}{y_t} \right] \right) y_t$$

The first equality gives the definition of the value of mine: the present value of revenue minus costs. The second equality factors out y_t and adds and subtracts marginal costs; the third equality uses the definition of rent. To complete your answer, think about the relation between marginal and average costs when costs are convex.

5. A competitive firm has constant marginal cost of extraction, C.

(a) Draw a dashed curve showing the equilibrium price trajectory (price as a function of time); list the conditions used to obtain this graph, and explain how each is used. (You do not have enough information to make this graph "accurate.") The exercise encourages you to review the material in section 5.6, in order to understand the conditions that the graph must satisfy.)

(b) On the same figure, draw a solid curve showing the equilibrium price trajectory under a slightly higher value of C. Justify your figure and provide an economic explanation. (This exercise encourages you to use logic, not calculus, to answer a comparative static question.) Before beginning, review Section 3.1, which shows how an increase in costs from zero to a positive level changes the equilibrium trajectory in the two-period setting. With this background, you are ready to begin answering the question. As a working hypothesis, assume that the change in C alters the initial price and the steepness of the curve. With this hypothesis, you need to consider only four possibilities: the solid curve (corresponding to the higher C) might begin at a lower or higher price and be flatter or steeper. The equilibrium conditions you listed in part (a) enable you to determine which of the four possibilities is correct. You can then confirm that your working hypothesis must be correct.

6. Extraction costs are zero and inverse demand is $p = a - bq$.

(a) Draw a dashed curve consistent with the equilibrium price trajectory under competition. (You do not have enough information to draw the exact graph, so you can only draw one that is "consistent with" the equilibrium trajectory; review section 5.6.)

(b) Write marginal revenue for this demand function as a function of price.

(c) Review material from the two-period model in section 3.2 before beginning this part of the exercise. Use the answer to part (b) and the material from section 5.7 to draw the monopoly equilibrium price trajectory (show this as a solid curve on the figure from [a].) You need to justify the relative position and shape of the solid and dashed curves; it is not enough to simply draw two curves.

Sources

Hotelling (1931) is the classic paper in the economics of nonrenewable resources.

Solow (1974b) and Gaudet (2007) provide time-lapse views of the role of the Hotelling model in resource economics.

Boyce (2013) provides an overview of oil and gas externalities and their regulation.

Pindyck (1978, 1980) made important contributions to analysis of the Hotelling model, including extensions to uncertainty.

Weitzman (1976b) studied the optimal order of extraction from mines with different costs.

Dasgupta and Heal (1979), Fisher (1981) and Conrad (2010) provide graduate-level treatment of the nonrenewable resource model.

Berck and Helfand (2010), Hartwick and Olewiler (1986), and Tietenberg (2006) provide undergraduate-level treatment of this material.

6 Empirics and the Hotelling Model

Objective

• Understand what it means to test the Hotelling model and the practical difficulties of performing such a test.

Information and Skills

• Understand the role of models in policy analysis.

• Summarize the main empirical implications of the Hotelling model.

• Have an overview of price patterns for several natural resources.

• Understand why data limitations complicate testing the Hotelling model.

Theories, to be useful, must generate hypotheses that can, at least in principle, be falsified by data. Models provide a means of stating a theory formally; like maps, they involve a trade-off between realism and tractability. A map of the world that consists of a circle is too abstract to be of any use; one containing all details of the world is equally useless.[1] Economic models help identify testable hypotheses, and they can be useful for studying policy questions. The neoclassical theory of the firm assumes that rational firms attempt to maximize profits. ("Rational" does not mean omniscient.) For natural resources, the theory implies that firms care about profits in current and future periods, not merely in a single period. The Hotelling model uses the profit-maximizing assumption and recognizes that resource stocks are finite. This model generates many hypotheses that can be tested in principle; lack of data makes it hard to test most of these in practice. The one hypothesis that is easily tested, based on constant extraction costs, is also easily rejected.

Resource pessimists worry that we will run out of essential resources. Resource optimists think that prices respond to impending shortages, creating incentives to conserve or to produce alternatives. This optimism rests on the belief that resource firms are rational

---

1 Jorge Luis Borges's (very) short story "On Exactitude in Science" tells the tale of an empire in which cartography becomes so precise that the empire creates a map of its territory on a 1:1 scale. Later generations decide that this map is useless, except as a source of clothing for beggars.

and maximize the expected discounted stream of profits. If the theory is correct (and if there are no market failures), then the First Fundamental Theorem of Welfare (section 2.8) implies that the competitive equilibrium is efficient. Here, the finite stock of nonrenewable natural resources is not a rationale for government intervention. (Concerns about equity or market failures might motivate policy intervention, just as in many other markets.) If, however, nonrenewable resource markets are inconsistent with even sophisticated versions of the Hotelling model, then prices might not signal impending scarcity, undercutting the basis for resource optimism.

The assumption of rational profit-maximizing firms is as plausible for natural resources as for other types of capital, where empirical testing has been more persuasive. We do not take literally the deterministic model in which agents perfectly forecast future prices, but it is unlikely that resource owners—or owners of other types of capital—ignore the future when deciding how to use their assets.

A Road Map
Section 6.1 discusses the relation between models and measurement (empirics), describes hypothesis testing, and sketches some practical difficulties in testing. The simplest version of the Hotelling model makes strong assumptions about costs and is inconsistent with data (section 6.2). We do not know whether this conclusion means that the strong assumptions are wrong or that the Hotelling theory itself is wrong. Section 6.3 uses an example to illustrate the difficulty of testing the Hotelling model under weaker assumptions. Section 6.4 discusses model extensions and additional empirical results.

6.1   Models and Empirics in Economics

Objectives and skills: Understand the uses of models and empirics in policy evaluation.

We begin by discussing the relation between models and empirics in policy evaluation. Chapter 8 uses a Hotelling model to explore the climate effects of a low-carbon alternative to fossil fuel. If the underlying model is incorrect, this "thought experiment" is not informative; therefore, the validity of the Hotelling model is important for policy evaluation.

Ideally, we would like to use actual experiments, of the type used in other disciplines, to determine the climate effects of a low-carbon alternative. Medical researchers can test the efficacy of a drug by randomly assigning people into a control group (receiving a placebo) or a treatment group (receiving the drug) and then comparing outcomes across the groups. The random assignment is essential to be able to draw conclusions about the drug, based on the comparison of outcomes. If the subjects self-select into the control or treatment group (i.e., if they decide on their own which group to join), then the assignment is not random. People's choices might depend on a characteristic that the statistician cannot observe. Perhaps the people most likely to benefit from the drug, or the sickest people, self-select into the treatment group. In that case, a comparison of outcomes across the two groups gives a biased estimate of the effect of the treatment on the population at large (see exercise 3).

The economist cannot give one group of worlds (the treatment group) the low-carbon alternative, and withhold it from another group (the control group), and then compare climates in the two groups of worlds. Model-based thought experiments provide an imperfect alternative to genuine experiments.

In the past several decades economics has increasingly relied on three empirical approaches to address policy questions. These use natural experiments, field experiments, and laboratory experiments, instead of the model-based thought experiments. In a "natural experiment," "nature" (or someone other than the researcher) determines whether a subject is assigned to the control or the treatment group. For example, if neighboring states have different minimum wage laws, comparing employment outcomes across similar cities on different sides of the border (and thus subject to different minimum wage laws) can provide information about the employment effect of these laws. It is often hard to find a natural experiment appropriate for a research question; nature seldom makes the group assignment randomly, as examples in sections 10.5 and 12.5 illustrate. In a "field experiment," the experimenter randomly assigns people to a control or a treatment group, and compares outcomes, as in medical research. For example, the treatment group of teachers receives a bonus, or some other incentive, for a good outcome, and the control group does not; or people in treatment villages receive training, and people in the control villages do not. A third approach uses laboratory experiments, often involving paid subjects, who answer questions or interact in controlled settings. These experiments test hypotheses related to risk aversion, discounting, cooperation, and other characteristics.

Empirical work uses statistical methods to test hypotheses. A test can "fail to reject" or reject a hypothesis, but it generally cannot "accept" a hypothesis. For example, a theory might imply that an elasticity is equal to 1, and a statistical test might imply that, with 95% confidence, the actual elasticity lies in the interval (0.98, 1.12). At a 5% significance level, we fail to reject the hypothesis. But we would also fail to reject the hypothesis that the elasticity equals 1.05. Both 1 and 1.05 lie in the interval (0.98, 1.12), but the elasticity cannot equal two different numbers, so it is meaningless to say that the test accepts our hypothesis. If the interval did not include our hypothesized value, then the test rejects the hypothesis.

6.2 Hotelling and Prices

Objectives and skills: Have an overview of the time trajectories of prices for major resources.

The simplest version of the Hotelling model, with zero extraction costs, implies that price rises at the rate of interest (equation 5.10). With constant average extraction cost,

$C > 0$, prices rise more slowly than the rate of interest (equation 5.9). Figure 6.1 shows the profiles of real prices (nominal prices adjusted for inflation) for six commodities. The dashed lines show the time trends fitted to this price data. The points of discontinuity in the dashed lines capture abrupt changes in the price trajectory. For most of these commodities, there are long periods during which the price falls, and at least one abrupt change in the price trajectory.

We need only price data to test the Hotelling model under the assumption of constant costs. In light of Figure 6.1, it is not surprising that research finds that this version of the Hotelling model is not consistent with data (Heal and Barrow 1980; Berck and Roberts 1996; Pindyck 1999; Lee, List, and Strazicich 2006). We therefore consider versions of the model with nonconstant costs and then consider other changes to the model or the testing procedure.

6.3   Nonconstant Costs

Objectives and skills: Understand why it is difficult to test the Hotelling model with nonconstant marginal extraction costs.

Lack of data makes it difficult to test the Hotelling model with nonconstant costs. Where costs depend on extraction level but not on remaining stocks, the Hotelling rule, equation 5.2, simplifies to

$$p_t - \frac{dc(y_t)}{dy} = \rho \left(p_{t+1} - \frac{dc(y_{t+1})}{dy} \right). \tag{6.1}$$

We do not observe marginal costs. If we assume that marginal costs equal $a + hy$, then we can write equation 6.1 as a function of prices and quantities and estimate the parameters ρ, a, and h. If the parameter estimates are implausible, the researcher concludes that the model does not fit the data. This procedure involves a joint hypothesis: equation 6.1 is a reasonable description of behavior, and $a + hy$ is a reasonable approximation of marginal cost. If the statistical tests reject our joint hypothesis, we do not know whether the rejection was due to the failure of one or both parts of the hypothesis.

If we had good data on costs, prices, and quantities, then we could estimate a flexible cost function and have a reasonable degree of confidence in the resulting estimate of marginal cost. We would then be closer to testing the hypothesis involving behavior. Low-quality cost data limits many fields of empirical economics. A common procedure in other fields uses a firm's optimality condition, together with information about input prices, to estimate marginal costs. Here, however, the empirical objective is to determine whether the optimality condition, the Hotelling rule, describes firms' behavior. It is not possible to both assume that the Hotelling rule holds and also to test whether it holds.

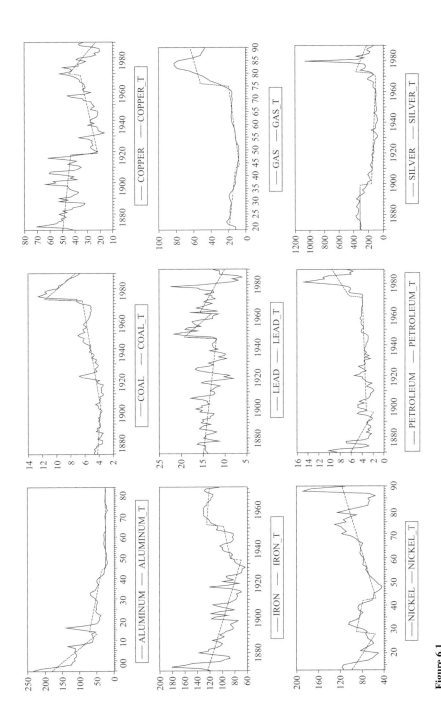

Figure 6.1
Real commodity prices. Source: Lee, List, and Strazicich (2006)

6.4   Testing Extensions of the Model

Objectives and skills: Recognize that extensions of the model lead to a better fit with data but increased difficulty of empirical testing; understand the use of proxies in estimation and the possibility of testing a Hotelling model applied to drilling instead of extraction.

The theory presented in chapter 5 omits many real-world features. Here we consider the empirical implications of (i) the discovery of new stocks, (ii) changes in demand due to changing macroeconomic conditions or the discovery of alternatives to the resource, (iii) changes in extraction costs due to changes in technology or regulation, (iv) general uncertainty, and (v) extraction constraints arising from the geology of oil fields.

Owners of stock in a company have a claim on future profits of the company; owners of a resource stock have a claim on future profits from selling the resource. Asset prices in general, and resource prices in particular, are forward-looking. Equilibrium asset prices (and resource rent) depend on expectations of future profits. Many firms (e.g., Amazon) had high stock valuations long before earning profits. The price of a company's stock depends on the market's perception of the company's future profitability. The equilibrium resource rent, and thus the current equilibrium resource price, depends on the resource firm's expectations of future prices and costs.

These expected future prices or events are "capitalized" into the asset price, meaning that the current asset price incorporates beliefs about them. Asset prices change in response to surprises. If the market has been expecting the Federal Reserve to increase interest rates, stock prices will likely not change much following the Fed's announcement of a rate increase; prices have already accounted for the possible rate increase. If the market had expected the Fed to maintain low interest rates, the surprising announcement of a rate increase may have a significant effect on the market. Changes in demand, technology, resource stocks, and policy (e.g., taxes) all affect incentives to extract and thus potentially affect resource prices. Anticipated and unanticipated changes have different equilibrium effects, just as with the Federal Reserve example. This feature complicates the estimation problem, because it requires that we take a stand on (or try to measure) the extent to which the market had anticipated important changes.

Stock Changes

The theory presented above ignores risk, including risk involving the discovery and development of new reserves. Firms invest in finding and developing new resource stocks, with uncertain success. Firms' attitudes toward risk influence their decisions about extracting known reserves and about searching for new reserves. Some extensions of the Hotelling model recognize that the exploration decision is endogenous. A simpler model takes the exploration decision as given, and treats the timing and magnitude of new discoveries as random variables. Rational firms factor this randomness into their extraction decisions. Large new discoveries create competition for previously existing deposits, lowering the value of those deposits. An unanticipated large new discovery therefore causes rent on existing deposits to fall. Because the new stocks do not alter extraction costs of previously existing deposits, the fall in rent requires a fall in price. In a model with random discoveries price rises between discoveries but falls at the time of a large new discovery. In this scenario, the price path is saw-toothed, rising for a while and then falling at times of new discoveries.

Royal Dutch Shell's Arctic drilling illustrates the complexity of oil exploration. In 2005 Shell announced that it had previously overstated its proven reserves (known stocks) by more than 20%. This "surprise" (to the market) resulted in an overnight drop of 10% in the value of company. In an effort to increase proven reserves, Shell ramped up its Arctic exploration, buying drilling leases and drilling equipment (Funk 2014). By the end of 2012 and a $6 billion investment, without having succeeded in drilling a well, much of its equipment was destroyed in a storm. Shell paused its exploration efforts in 2013; after receiving new permits, it resumed exploration, but it announced in September 2015 that it was abandoning these efforts. In August 2014, oil was $100/barrel, but the price had fallen to $27/barrel by early 2016. "Unconventional" sources of oil, such as in the Arctic, require a price of about $70/barrel to be economical.

Changes in Demand

Unanticipated and longlasting changes in demand can also change the price path. The Great Recession beginning in 2008 saw a reduction in aggregate demand, including a reduction in demand for many resources. Strong developing country growth from 1990 to 2008 increased resource demand. If a change in the economic environment causes firms to expect that future demand will be weaker than they had previously believed, then they revise downward their estimates of the value of their resource stocks. This downward revision in rent requires a reduction in price, just as occurs following discovery of a large new deposit. Thus, over a period when firms are revising downward their projections of future demand, and thus revising downward their belief about the current value of a marginal unit of the stock, the equilibrium price rises more slowly than the (simple) theory predicts, and might even be falling. The deterministic (perfect information, no surprises) model ignores unanticipated changes in demand, although those events could explain observed price falls.

Cost Changes

The simple Hotelling model ignores changes in costs, apart from those associated with changes in stock or extraction rates. The extraction cost function might shift up or down over time. Downward shifts lower price or lead to smaller price increases than the standard model predicts (Farzin 1995). Upward shifts lead to faster price rises. Technological advances lowered the cost of horizontal drilling and made hydraulic fracturing more effective, making it possible to develop previously inaccessible deposits. These cost reductions and the discovery of new deposits have similar equilibrium effects. Other changes, such as stricter environmental or labor rules, increase extraction costs. In projecting extraction costs for new reserves, Royal Dutch Shell in 2014 included a (still nonexistent) carbon tax of \$40/Mt CO_2 (Reuters 2014).

An example illustrates the effect of anticipated exogenously falling extraction costs. We replace the constant average cost C with

$$C(t) = C_0 + \frac{a}{1 + ft}, \tag{6.2}$$

where C_0, a, and f are positive. As in equation 5.6, the no-arbitrage condition (the Euler equation) requires that the present value of rent is constant:

$$p_t - \left(C_0 + \frac{a}{1 + ft} \right) = \rho \left[p_{t+1} - \left(C_0 + \frac{a}{1 + f(t+1)} \right) \right]. \tag{6.3}$$

Figure 6.2 shows the graphs of price, rent, and marginal cost under the cost function in equation 6.2.[2] Falling costs put downward pressure on the equilibrium price, just as with a standard good. Discounting promotes an increasing price trajectory, as in the model with constant costs, C. Initially, the cost effect is more powerful, so the equilibrium price falls. However, the cost decreases diminish over time, and costs never fall below C_0. Eventually, the effect of discounting becomes more powerful, and the equilibrium price rises. Rent (price minus marginal cost) rises at the constant rate, r, and marginal costs steadily decline to C_0. Adding frequent small shocks and occasional large discoveries causes the graph in Figure 6.2 to become saw-toothed and bumpy, making it more closely resemble the graphs of actual time series shown in Figure 6.1.

Uncertainty

A rich literature studies the role of uncertainty about new discoveries, changes in demand and extraction costs, and other features of nonrenewable resource markets (Pindyck 1980). Uncertainty alters the expected time path of rents, and thus of prices, complicating the already formidable empirical problem. Researchers use "proxies," observable variables closely related to the unobserved variable of interest: resource rents. In forestry the "stumpage price" is the price paid to a landowner for the right to harvest timber. Old-growth timber is a nonrenewable resource, and the stumpage price of this timber is a good proxy for rent. Researchers using this proxy find moderate support for the Hotelling model (Livernois, Thille, and Zhang 2006).

The stock price of a mining company is a proxy for the rent associated with the resource that the company mines. Both the observable stock price and the unobservable resource

---

2 Figure 6.2 corresponds to the continuous time version of the discrete time model, with $a = 30$, $C_0 = 10$, $f = 0.5$, and $r = 0.03$. The discrete time model leads to simpler derivations and more accessible intuition, but graphs in the continuous time model are smooth instead of step functions and are easier to construct and interpret.

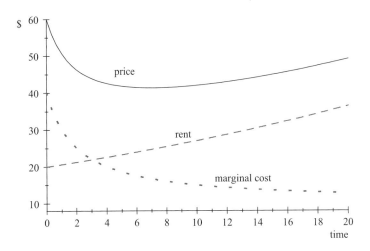

Figure 6.2
Equilibrium price, rent, and marginal cost.

rent are forward-looking variables that reflect the expected value of the stream of future profits from owning one more unit of an asset. The mining company is a composite of the resource and equipment that the company owns, and many other factors, including intangibles such as reputation. The resource stock and the mining company are not exactly the same, so the company stock price is not a perfect measure of the resource rent. However, because the resource is a large part of the company assets, the two are closely related. The previously mentioned 2005 fall in Shell's stock price, following the downward revision in its proven reserves, illustrates this relation.

Section 5.5 describes the change in asset prices under certainty. Under uncertainty, the Capital Asset Pricing Model (see below) shows that the equilibrium expected return to an asset depends on the asset's "beta"; the beta depends on correlation between the asset's return and the return to a diversified portfolio, and on the volatility of the asset relative to market volatility. If the beta is less than 1, including the asset in the portfolio reduces the variance of the portfolio. If the asset and the portfolio are negatively correlated, then the company tends to do well when the market does poorly, so owning stock in the company provides a hedge against market risk. (A hedge offsets the risk associated with a particular activity, e.g., investment in the market.) This hedge provides a benefit of owning the stock, and is analogous to the dividend discussed in section 5.5: it lowers the expected return needed to make investors willing to hold stock in the mining company.

Empirically, the stock price of companies owning copper mines is negatively correlated with the return on a market portfolio. This negative correlation provides a hedge against market risk, thereby lowering the equilibrium rate of increase of the mining company's stock price. If the observed stock price is a good proxy for the unobserved rent, then evidence that one variable is consistent with theory provides some evidence that the other is as well. Using data on copper mining companies, this research fails to reject the Hotelling model (Slade and Thille 1997). Other research finds mixed evidence for the Hotelling model.[3]

In general, the market return might have positive, negative, or zero correlation with resource prices. A disruption in oil supply due to war and political turmoil, as in the 1970s, can increase oil prices and lower the return to the market, leading to negative correlation between oil prices and market returns. Strong economic growth can increase both oil prices and market returns, leading to positive correlation. Certain kinds of shocks are associated with positive correlation, and other kinds with negative correlation (Kilian 2009). Empirical evidence finds zero correlation between oil prices and the market return but also finds that oil prices are negatively correlated with future economic growth. Large increases in oil prices preceded most of the post–World War II economic downturns (Hamilton 2011).

The Capital Asset Pricing Model (CAPM)*

Investors can buy (i) a risk-free asset (e.g., government bonds) that pays a safe return r_f; (ii) a risky market portfolio with random return $\tilde{r}_m$ having expectation $E\tilde{r}_m = \bar{r}_m$; or (iii) stock in a company that owns a nonrenewable resource, with a risky return of $\tilde{r}_c$ and an expected return $\bar{r}_c$. The market premium from investing in the stock market instead of the risk-free asset is $\bar{r}_m - r_f > 0$. The beta of the mining company is

$$\beta = \frac{\text{covariance}(\tilde{r}_m, \tilde{r}_c)}{\text{variance}(\tilde{r}_m)} = \text{correlation}(\tilde{r}_m, \tilde{r}_c) \frac{\text{s.d.}(\tilde{r}_c)}{\text{s.d.}(\tilde{r}_m)},$$

where "s.d." denotes standard deviation. A company's beta is less than 1 if its correlation with the market is small and/or its volatility (as measured by its standard deviation) is small relative to the market's. If the beta is less than 1, then adding the mining stock to the market portfolio decreases the variance of the portfolio. If the mining asset is negatively correlated with the market (its beta is negative), then the mining asset provides a hedge against market uncertainty. If all investors are rational and risk averse, have the same information, and have no borrowing or lending constraints, the CAPM shows that the equilibrium expected return to the mining asset is $\bar{r}_c = r_f + \beta(\bar{r}_m - r_f)$ (Fama and French 2004). For $\beta < 1$, the equilibrium expected return to the mining asset is less than the equilibrium expected return to the market portfolio.

---

3 In addition to the papers cited above, the empirical literature includes Miller and Upton (1985), Halvorson and Smith (1991), Chermak and Patrick (2001, 2002), Lin and Wagner (2007), and Malischek and Todle (2015).

Hotelling Applied to the Drilling Decision

The standard Hotelling model considers the extraction decision, taking as given the initial level of the stock. A variation, applied to oil, emphasizes the decision to drill new wells (Anderson, Kellog, and Salant 2016). Oil production requires first drilling a well, leading to a recoverable stock, and then extracting the oil. The remaining stock in the well determines the well pressure, which determines the amount that can be extracted during any interval (the "maximum flow"). As the stock remaining in the well falls over time, the pressure in the well also falls, reducing the maximum flow.

The average cost function in equation 6.4, graphed in Figure 6.3, illustrates this situation:

$$\text{average cost} = \frac{c(y, x)}{y} = \begin{cases} c_0, & \text{for } y \leq \alpha x \\ c_0 + \beta(y - \alpha x), & \text{for } y > \alpha x. \end{cases} \tag{6.4}$$

Average extraction cost in a well is constant until the flow reaches a critical level, αx, beyond which more rapid extraction ($y > \alpha x$) is very expensive. The parameter α determines the relation between the stock and the critical flow, and the parameter β determines how quickly costs increase beyond the critical level. Suppose that β is sufficiently large (perhaps infinite), so that it is never economical to extract at a rate greater than αx; in this case, αx is the maximum flow from the well with stock x; the maximum flow from this well falls as the stock falls. There are many wells with the same cost function but possibly different stock levels. Because no well extracts at a rate greater than its maximum flow, all wells have the same level of average costs, c_0. The upper limit on aggregate extraction from a field with multiple wells equals α times the amount of oil in all of the wells.[4]

All wells have the same level of average extraction costs making this model similar to the simplest Hotelling model, where the equilibrium condition requires that price minus c_0 rises at the rate of interest (equation 5.5). However, under the flow constraint ($y \leq \alpha x$), forward-looking profit-maximizing behavior is consistent with price minus marginal cost trajectories that rise either more slowly or more quickly than the rate of interest. To understand why the flow constraint has this effect, we review the logic of the Hotelling rule in the standard case (without the flow constraint) and show how the flow constraint overturns that logic.

• In the standard model, the price minus c_0 could not rise more slowly than the rate of interest: if it were to do so, producers would want to reallocate sales from the future to the present, reducing the current price and increasing the future price, until the equilibrium

---

4 If a company drills a new well too close to an existing one, the new well decreases pressure in the existing well, creating a negative externality. Many oil fields are managed using "compulsory unitization," which requires companies operating in the same field to coordinate, limiting these kinds of negative externalities.

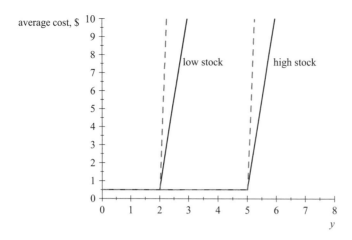

Figure 6.3
Average cost (equation 6.4) for $c_0 = 0.5$, $\alpha = 1$, and $\beta = 10$ (solid line) or $\beta = 40$ (dashed line), and $x = 2$ (low stocks) or $x = 5$ (high stocks).

condition is restored. The flow constraint may make it impossible to increase current production by enough to bring about this change in relative prices. Therefore, in the presence of the flow constraint, the price minus marginal cost might rise more slowly than the rate of interest.

• In the standard model, price minus marginal cost could not rise more quickly than the rate of interest: if it were to do so, producers would prefer to delay sales, increasing the current price and reducing future prices, until the equilibrium is restored. The flow constraint does not prevent producers from reducing current sales, but it might prevent them from increasing their future sales, thus making it impossible to achieve the reallocation that would restore the Hotelling rule.

In summary, under the flow constraint, price minus marginal cost could rise more slowly or more quickly than the rate of interest, even if all forward-looking profit-maximizing firms have the same average costs. This possibility is a special case of the general result that with stock-dependent extraction costs, equilibrium does not require price minus marginal cost to rise at the rate of interest.[5]

Absent flow constraints, firms would not incur the cost of sinking a new well until they had exhausted their current well. However, with the flow constraint, firms might want to sink multiple wells. If a firm has one well with stock x_t, and each new well starts with stock x_0, then opening a new well enables the firm to increase the flow of production from αx_t to $\alpha(x_t + x_0)$: the new well "relaxes a constraint." The firm has to decide when to

---

5 This example has a kink in the cost function at the maximum flow, so marginal cost is not defined at that point.

sink new wells. Suppose that the cost of drilling a well increases with the number of other wells being drilled at that time; for example, increased drilling requires paying overtime or hiring less productive workers or using less efficient drilling rigs. Then, there is an upward-sloping supply function for drilling services. The equilibrium drilling decision results in a modified Hotelling rule, but one applied to drilling instead of extraction. Texas oil data is consistent with this modified Hotelling model (Anderson, Kellog, and Salant 2016).

6.5   Summary

The Hotelling model can produce many hypotheses that can be tested in principle. Data reject the simplest (and least plausible) of these hypotheses; the lack of reliable cost data makes it difficult to test more plausible versions. With constant marginal and average extraction costs, the Hotelling model implies that price minus marginal cost rises at the rate of interest. This implication is a joint hypothesis; it is based on a theory of firm behavior (forward-looking profit maximization) and an assumption about costs. Statistical tests reject this joint hypothesis, but because the cost assumption is implausible, rejection provides little information about the validity of the behavioral theory.

Adding real-world features, including nonconstant marginal extraction costs, exploration, random shocks to stock, demand or cost, or systematic time-varying changes to costs, can generate simulated price paths that resemble observed price paths. Lack of data makes it difficult to test models with these features. Because we cannot observe rents, they have to be constructed using estimates of marginal costs. Empirical tests of the Hotelling model using such constructed data thus involve a joint hypothesis concerning the theory of profit maximization and assumptions about marginal costs. A few studies, using such proxies as stumpage fees for timber or the stock price of companies that mine resources, provide modest support for the behavioral theory underlying the Hotelling model. A recent study of the oil industry provides support for a variation of the Hotelling model that emphasizes the drilling instead of the extraction decision.

The forward-looking profit-maximizing assumption means that the effect on resource prices of changes (e.g., in technology, policy, or demand) depends on the extent to which markets anticipated those changes. It is difficult to measure the degree of anticipation, further complicating the problem of testing the Hotelling model.

Policy analysis often relies on simple models. The Hotelling model, despite its empirical limitations (and its inability to help predict short-term price changes), is widely used to analyze resource policy.

6.6   Terms and Concepts, Study Questions, Exercises, and Sources

Terms and Concepts
Natural versus field experiments, real versus nominal prices, joint hypothesis, control group, treated group, self selection, anticipated versus unanticipated changes, proven reserves, proxies, hedge, market portfolio, market return, CAPM, stumpage.

Study Questions
1. (a) Describe the simplest version of the Hotelling model's predictions about change in prices over time.

   (b) Describe important features of price series for actual nonrenewable resources, and contrast these to the predictions of the simplest Hotelling model.

2. What does it mean to empirically "test" the Hotelling model? Discuss some of the difficulties in conducting such a test. (Your answer should develop the idea that there are many versions of the Hotelling model, not just the simplest one. Your answer should also discuss the fact that a test of the Hotelling model is almost certainly a test of a joint hypothesis and should explain why this matters.)

Exercises
1. Extraction costs are $C(t)y$ with

$$C(t) = C_0 + \frac{a}{1+ft},$$

where $a > 0$ and $f > 0$.

   (a) State in words what this cost function states in symbols.

   (b) For $C_0 = 5$ and $a = 1 = f$, graph $C(t)$ as a function of t.

   (c) Explain how to derive the Euler equation 6.3. (It is not necessary to perform calculations.)

2. Consider the following inverse demand function:

$$p_t = \frac{a}{a_0 + a_1 t} - y_t.$$

   (a) On the same figure, draw two graphs of this inverse demand function, showing p_t as a function of y_t, for two values of t. For these graphs, select positive values of the parameters a_0, a_1, and a (e.g., $a = a_0 = a_1 = 1$). How does t affect the inverse demand function?

   (b) Consider a competitive industry with constant marginal $=$ average extraction costs, C, facing this demand function. Using the results presented in chapter 5, write the Euler equation for this model (no derivation needed).

Table 6.1
Probability of getting better for the different types of people, depending on their group

	Advice only	Advice + drug
Type A	0.4	0.4
Type B	0.4	0.7

(c) Explain what this equilibrium condition implies about the rate of change in prices. Provide an economic explanation.

3. This question illustrates the self-selection problem and clarifies the importance of random assignment to groups in an experiment. Half of a population with a particular health condition is type A and the remaining half is type B. A medical researcher wants to test the efficacy of a drug for this population. With health advice only, 40% of both types get better. The drug does not help type A people but increases the percentage of type B people who recover to 70% (see table 6.1). The researcher does not know this information and conducts an experiment to attempt to uncover it.

(a) Given the information in table 6.1, what fraction of people with the health condition is expected to recover if no one receives the drug? What fraction is expected to recover if everyone with the condition receives the drug? What is the percentage increase in the probability of recovery due to the drug for the population at large?

(b) The researcher has a sample of 1,000 people with the condition; 500 are randomly assigned to the treatment group (those who get the drug and the health advice) and 500 to the control group (those who get only the health advice). Based on the actual recovery probabilities in table 6.1, what fraction of each group in the sample is expected to get better? Using these estimates, what is the expected percentage increase in the probability of recovery due to the drug? [Hint: If half the people in the treatment group have a 0.7 probability of recovery, and half have a 0.4 probability of recovery, what is the expected probability of recovery for a person randomly drawn from the treatment group? Then ask the same question of someone randomly drawn from the control group and compare the two probabilities.]

(c) Suppose that instead of random assignment, type B people tend to self-select into the treatment group, resulting in 70% of the treatment group being type B. The control group ends up with 30% of type B people. The researcher is unaware of this self-selection, and proceeds as if group assignment had been random. What is the expected estimate of the increase in the probability of recovery due to the drug, based on this sample, when the researcher ignores self-selection? How does the failure to correct for self-selection bias the estimate of the efficacy of the drug? [Hint: Under the assumptions, 70% of people in the treatment group have a 0.7 probability of recovery, and 30% have a 0.4 probability of recovery. What is the probability that someone randomly drawn from the treatment group recovers? Then ask the same question of someone randomly drawn from the control group and compare the recovery probabilities of the two groups.]

Sources

This chapter relies heavily on the surveys by Livernois (2009) and Slade and Thille (2009). Krautkraemer (1998) and Kronenberg (2008) also provide useful surveys.

Heal and Barrow (1980), Berck and Roberts (1996), Pindyck (1999), and Lee, List, and Strazicich (2006) test the Hotelling model using price data.

Miller and Upton (1985) for oil and gas; Slade and Thille (1997) for copper; and Livernois, Thille, and Zhang (2006) for old-growth timber use proxies to test the Hotelling model.

Halvorsen and Smith (1991) use a restricted cost function to estimate shadow prices in the Canadian metal mining industry, rejecting the implications of the Hotelling model.

Chermak and Patrick (2001) use a model similar to Halvorsen and Smith, and fail to reject the Hotelling model. Chermak and Patrick (2002) subject the same data to four specifications, two of which reject and two of which fail to reject the Hotelling model.

Lin and Wagner (2007) find support for the Hotelling model for 8 of 14 minerals.

Malischek and Todle (2015), using uranium mining data, reject an extension of the Hotelling model that includes market power and exploration.

Pindyck (1980) pioneered the large literature on uncertainty and nonrenewable resources.

Farzin (1995) discusses the impact of technological change on resource scarcity.

Hamilton (2011) studies the relation between oil prices and economic activity.

Kilian (2009) discusses the distinction between oil demand and supply shocks.

Fama and French (2004) explain the CAPM and discuss its empirical significance.

Reuters (2014) reports Shell's assumption of carbon tax in projecting future extraction costs.

Funk (2014) describes Shell's experience drilling in the Arctic.

Anderson, Kellog, and Salant (2016) construct a variation of the Hotelling model, apply to drilling, and test it using Texas data.

7 Backstop Technology

Objective
- Examine the effect of a backstop technology on nonrenewable resource extraction.

Information and Skills
- Know the meaning and the empirical importance of backstop technologies.
- Understand why the backstop lowers prices even before it is used.
- Understand the effect of extraction costs on the timing of backstop use.

A "backstop" technology provides an alternative to the nonrenewable resource. Solar power, wind power, and other methods of generating electricity are backstops for fossil fuels. We assume that the backstop, available to all firms, is a perfect substitute for the resource; can be produced at a constant average cost, b; and can be supplied without limit. In contrast, the natural resource has a finite potential supply, and only resource owners can extract it. We also assume that the availability of the backstop is widely known; its eventual use therefore comes as no surprise.

The eventual use of the backstop lowers equilibrium price and increases extraction even before the backstop begins to be used. The equilibrium level of resource extraction and thus the resource price depend on firms' expectations of *future* prices. The backstop lowers the market price once is used, and via expectations, it also lowers price before it is used. This insight is true generally. Anything that changes future resource prices—or, in an uncertain world, people's beliefs about these future prices—changes current extraction decisions. In the static model, competitive supply in a period depends on the price in that period. In the nonrenewable resource setting, however, current supply depends on current and (beliefs about) future prices.

A Road Map
Section 7.1 describes the backstop technology. Section 7.2 introduces the residual demand function and shows how the backstop affects the residual demand facing fossil fuel producers. A two-period example illustrates the effect of a backstop technology on the equilibrium in a nonrenewable resource market; the existence of the backstop lowers the resource price

even in the period before the backstop is used. Section 7.3 incorporates the backstop model into the T-period Hotelling model, under the assumption of constant marginal extraction costs. As in the two-period setting, the backstop lowers price and increases extraction, even before the economy begins to use it. The constant extraction cost structure makes the main result easy to understand, but it obscures important aspects of the interaction between resources and backstops. Section 7.4 therefore considers more general extraction cost functions.

7.1 The Backstop Model

Objectives and skills: Understand the simplest model of a backstop technology.

We use y_t to denote resource use and z_t to denote the amount of the alternative produced using the backstop in period t; $w_t = y_t + z_t$ is supply of the resource plus the backstop good. Fossil fuels and renewable power can be expressed in common units of energy, so we can interpret w as energy. The assumption that the resource (e.g., oil) and the alternative produced using the backstop technology (e.g., solar power) are perfect substitutes means that the price in any period depends only on the sum of the resource and the backstop good brought to market, w_t. If both are produced during a period, they have the same price. Consumers pay $p(w)$ for the quantity $w = y + z$.

This model of the backstop technology misses important real-world features. Just as coal is not a perfect substitute for oil, a low-carbon alternative, such as solar power, is not a perfect substitute for a fossil fuel. Solar power, unlike natural- gas and coal-powered generation, creates an "intermittency" problem: the power goes off when the sun goes down. We would need a model with different prices for each product to take into account the products' imperfect substitutability. The assumption of a constant marginal backstop cost $(= b)$ is also restrictive. In fact, costs might either rise or fall with production levels or with cumulative production. Producing solar power uses land, and the most economical locations are likely to be used first. Therefore, subsequent solar farms may be more expensive than earlier units, leading to decreasing returns to scale. There may also be economies of scale, learning by doing, and technological advances that offset those cost increases. The history of new technologies shows that learning by doing and technological progress cause costs to fall over time. The cost of solar power is estimated to have fallen by a factor of 50 between 1976 and 2010 (Timilsinia, Kurdgelashvili, and Narbel 2011). We overlook the products' imperfect substitutability and many of the complications associated with backstop costs to retain a simple description of the resource and backstop interaction.

In a competitive equilibrium, during periods when the backstop is used, price = marginal cost = b. We state this observation as

$$z > 0 \implies p(w) = b. \tag{7.1}$$

7.2 A Two-Period Example

Objectives and skills: Use the residual demand function to study the effect of a backstop technology in a two-period setting.

We introduce the concept of "residual demand" in a static (one-period) model and then use the residual demand to study a two-period resource model. In the static model, suppose that there are two sources of energy supply: fossil fuels, with the marginal cost = supply function $S^f(p)$, and solar power, with the marginal cost = supply function $S^s(p)$. By assumption, the two types of energy are perfect substitutes, so they receive the same price. Aggregate supply equals the sum of supply from the two sources, $S^f(p) + S^s(p)$. Demand is $D(p)$. Equilibrium requires that aggregate supply equals demand:

$$\underbrace{S^f(p) + S^s(p)}_{\text{aggregate supply}} = D(p), \quad \text{or} \quad S^f(p) = \underbrace{D(p) - S^s(p)}_{\text{residual demand}}.$$

We obtain the second equation by subtracting the solar supply function from both sides of the first equation. The function $D(p) - S^s(p)$ is the residual demand facing the fossil fuel sector: the demand for fossil fuels, after subtracting the supply of solar power. The "residual *inverse* demand" facing the fossil fuel sector gives the price this sector receives for a given level of sales.

We assume that the marginal cost of solar power (= the solar power sector's supply function) is constant at b, leading to a simple expression and graph of the residual demand for fossil fuels. Figure 7.1 shows an aggregate demand function, $p = 20 - y$ (through points $a, d,$ and e) and the solar supply function (at the constant $b = 15$). The market price never exceeds b, because the solar sector can supply an unlimited amount at $p = b$. The solar sector supplies nothing at lower prices. The residual (inverse) demand function facing the fossil fuel sector is the kinked solid curve through points $b, d,$ and e. The residual inverse demand is flat at the backstop price and equals the aggregate demand function at lower prices. The availability of the backstop at price b cuts the top off of the inverse demand function that the fossil fuel sector faces. We can write the residual inverse demand function as

$$p(y) = \min[b, 20 - y]. \tag{7.2}$$

If the fossil fuel sector supplies $y = 3$, it would have received the price $20 - 3 = 17$ in the absence of the backstop. With the backstop, and given that $b = 15$, the fossil fuel sector receives the price 15 when it supplies $y = 3$. The backstop supplies the residual quantity, $5 - 3 = 2$, so the market clears at the price $p = b = 15$.

Now we consider a two-period resource model, as in chapter 3. The world lasts for two periods; the fossil fuel sector has constant average = marginal extraction cost, C, initial stock x, and discount factor, ρ. We assume that the parameters are such that in equilibrium,

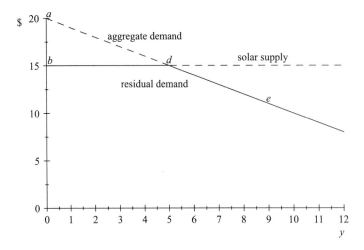

Figure 7.1
Aggregate demand is the curve through points a, d, and e. The backstop supply function is horizontal line at point $b = 15$. The residual demand is the kinked curve through points b, d, and e. The backstop cuts the top off the residual demand function facing the fossil fuel sector.

the fossil fuel firm sells a positive amount in each period and exhausts its stock over the two periods.

The equilibrium condition for this price-taking competitive fossil fuel sector is exactly as in chapter 3:

$$p_0 - C = \rho(p_1 - C). \tag{7.3}$$

The present value of price minus marginal cost (= rent) is the same in the two periods (under the assumption that sales are positive in both periods). Denoting y as sales in period 0 and $x - y$ as sales in period 1, and using the residual inverse demand function in equation 7.2, we can write the equilibrium condition 7.3 as

$$\min[b, 20 - y] - C = \rho(\min[b, 20 - (x - y)] - C). \tag{7.4}$$

Figure 7.2 shows the graphs of the left and right sides of equation 7.4 for the parameter values $b = 15$, $C = 5$, $x = 10$, and $\rho = 0.7$. The dashed portion of the two curves show price minus marginal cost in period 0, and the discounted price minus marginal cost in period 1, in the absence of the backstop. (Review figure 3.2.) Without the backstop, equation 7.3 is satisfied at point A, where period-0 sales equal 6.8 and $p_0 = 13.2$. The backstop cuts the top off the curves that show price minus cost and discounted price minus cost. With the backstop, the equilibrium occurs at point D, where sales in period 0 equal 8 and $p_0 = 12$.

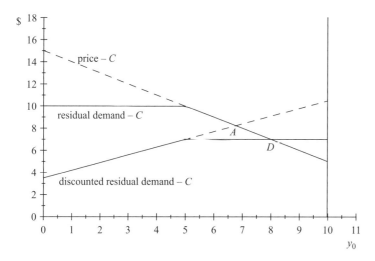

Figure 7.2
The backstop cuts the top off the (discounted) price minus marginal cost curves, leading to the kinked curves. C is the marginal cost. The backstop moves the equilibrium from point A to point D, increasing period-0 sales and reducing period-0 price.

This example shows that the availability of the backstop increases sales and lowers the price even before the backstop is used. The fact that the resource stock is limited links the markets in the two periods, in much the same way as the fixed supply of tea ties together the markets in the two countries of our trade example in section 2.1.

7.3 The T-period Problem

Objectives and skills: Combine the backstop model and the Hotelling model to determine the effect of a backstop on the resource price and extraction trajectories.

We continue to assume constant average extraction costs, $c(x, y) = Cy$, with $C < b$ (otherwise, the resource is worthless) and b is less than the choke price (otherwise, the backstop is worthless). This problem is almost the same as the problem discussed in section 5.4, where mines were assumed to have different extraction costs. There we denoted the costs as C^a and C^b, and here we denote them as C and b. Here, instead of the expensive mine with finite stock, there is a backstop that can produce unlimited quantities. Section 5.4 shows that either the cheaper mine is exhausted before extraction begins from the more expensive mine, or there is a single transitional period during which both mines are used. The same pattern occurs here, if we replace "the more expensive mine" with "the backstop technology."

A "phase" is an interval of time during which particular sources supply the market. In this case there are two phases: the resource supplies the market during the first phase, and the backstop supplies the market during the second. There may be a single transitional period, during which both are used, when the two phases overlap. The last period with positive resource extraction is T. For $t < T$ (the first phase), resource extraction is positive and backstop production is zero. For $t > T$, the backstop supplies the entire market.

Because $C < b <$ the choke price, the mine owner eventually exhausts the stock: the sum of extraction from $t = 0$ to T equals the initial stock. The owner's objective, optimality condition (Hotelling rule), and exhaustion condition are

$$\text{objective: } \max \sum_{t=0}^{T} \rho^t [p_t y_t - C y_t],$$

$$\text{Hotelling rule } p_t - C = \rho(p_{t+1} - C) \quad \text{for } t = 0, 1, 2, \ldots, T - 1, \tag{7.5}$$

$$\text{exhaustion condition: } \sum_{t=0}^{T} y_t = x_0.$$

We use graphs of the equilibrium price and sales trajectory to describe the equilibrium to this model (see section 5.6). We want to show how the backstop alters the equilibrium. The backstop does not alter the firm's objective or the Hotelling condition, which constrains the rate of change of price (or rent); it also does not change the exhaustion condition, which requires that cumulative sales equal the initial stock of resource. However, the backstop does alter the transversality condition, thus altering prices and sales along the entire path.

Our example here uses a constant elasticity of demand function, $y = p^{-\eta}$; demand approaches zero only as the price becomes infinite, so here the choke price is infinite. (With linear demand, the choke price equals the vertical intercept of the demand function.) Absent the backstop, for the demand function $y = p^{-\eta}$, extraction approaches zero over time but never reaches zero in finite time: $T = \infty$.[1] The dashed curves in Figures 7.3 and 7.4 graph the equilibrium price and sales trajectories without the backstop. These figures use inverse demand $y = 10p^{-2}$, $C = 2$, $x_0 = 42$, and $r = 0.05$.

The solid curves in these figures graph the equilibrium price and sales trajectories with the backstop. Here, the resource price never exceeds $b = 5$, because the backstop can supply an unlimited amount at that price. The resource price rises over time, obeying

---

1 If the stock were exhausted in finite time, $T < \infty$, then the resource firm could perturb the candidate by reducing extraction by a small amount, $\varepsilon > 0$, a moment before T, when extraction is positive and the price is finite. The loss from this perturbation is finite. The gain from selling this stock a moment after T, when sales under the candidate are zero and the price is infinite, is $\infty \times \varepsilon = \infty$. Because the gain of the perturbation exceeds the loss, a candidate that ends extraction at a finite time is not an equilibrium for this demand function.

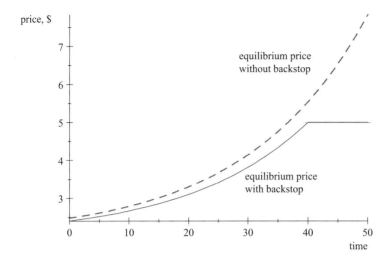

Figure 7.3
The solid curve shows the equilibrium price under the backstop. The dashed curve shows the equilibrium price without the backstop. Demand is $y = 10p^{-2}$, $C = 2$, $b = 5$, $x_0 = 42$, and $r = 0.05$.

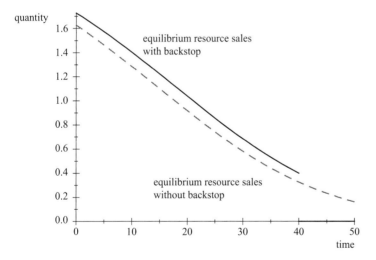

Figure 7.4
The solid curve shows the equilibrium quantity of resource sales under the backstop. The dashed curve shows the equilibrium quantity without the backstop.

the Hotelling condition, and reaches the backstop price at a finite time, $T = 40$ for this example.

These figures illustrate that the backstop lowers the equilibrium price path, shifting up the equilibrium sales path, even before the backstop is used. The future use of the backstop lowers future prices, which also lowers the current price, because the Hotelling rule connects current to future prices.

7.4   More General Cost Functions

Objectives and skills: Understand how the backstop changes the price and extraction trajectory when average extraction costs depend on either the level of extraction or on the resource stock.

The constant average (= marginal) cost function in the previous section illustrates the basic features of backstops, but it has two empirically false implications. (i) The model implies that, with the possible exception of a single transitional period, the resource and the backstop are not used in same period. However, when marginal costs increase with extraction rates, the resource and the backstop might be used simultaneously in many periods. (ii) The constant-cost model implies that the resource is physically exhausted before the backstop starts being used. However, when costs increase as the stock of resource falls, it may not be economical to physically exhaust the resource. We consider these two features separately.

7.4.1   Costs Depend on Extraction but Not on Stock

Here we assume that marginal costs depend on the rate of extraction but not on the stock: $c = c(y)$, with $c'(y) > 0$, $c''(y) > 0$, and $c'(0) < b;$[2] for example, $c(y) = Cy^{1+\beta}$, with $\beta > 0$. The resource is used during an initial phase, and only the backstop is used during the final phase; there may be a phase when both the resource and the backstop are used simultaneously. We can think of the energy industry as consisting of a single representative firm, able to use either or both the natural resource and the backstop.[3] This firm's objective is to maximize

$$\sum_{t=0}^{\infty} \rho^t [p_t \times (y_t + z_t) - c(y_t) - bz_t].$$

2 The first two inequalities state that marginal costs are positive and increasing in extraction (i.e., costs are convex). The third inequality states that for sufficiently small extraction (y close to zero), extraction is cheaper than production from the backstop. Without the third assumption, the resource is worthless.

3 Section 5.4 uses a slightly different assumption, under which different firms own the two mines. When firms are price takers, the two approaches (having one representative firm maximize the sum of profits from both mines, or having two representative firms, each maximizing the profits from a single mine) lead to the same equilibrium outcome.

The Hotelling rule holds during a phase when the resource is being used:

$$p_t - c'(y_t) = \rho(p_{t+1} - c'(y_{t+1})).\tag{7.6}$$

Here, the present value of rent (= price − marginal cost) is constant.

During a phase when the backstop is sold ($z > 0$), price equals marginal cost: $p_t = b$ (by equation 7.1). During a phase when both the resource and the backstop are being used, $p_t = b$, and the Hotelling rule both hold:

$$b - c'(y_t) = \rho[b - c'(y_{t+1})].\tag{7.7}$$

Interpretation

Rent can rise because price rises, marginal extraction cost falls, or a combination of the two. During a phase when both the resource and the backstop are sold, price is constant. Because rent is rising during this phase, marginal extraction cost must be falling. Consequently, resource extraction must be falling (because marginal cost increases with extraction). The price is constant during this phase, so total sales are also constant; consequently, backstop sales are rising. During this phase, the backstop supplies an increasing share of a constant level of output.

To interpret equation 7.7, suppose that the industry is in a phase when both the resource and the backstop are being sold. Consider a perturbation in which the representative firm extracts one more unit of the resource in period t and makes an offsetting reduction in extraction in period $t + 1$. Because the price is constant at b during this phase, the perturbation does not alter total (resource + backstop) sales or revenue. In period t, the unit increase in resource sales is offset by a unit decrease in backstop sales (thus maintaining the constant price b); similarly, in period $t + 1$, the unit decrease is resource sales is offset by a unit increase in backstop sales.

The perturbation alters costs but not revenue. In period t, the perturbation decreases costs from backstop production by b and increases costs from resource extraction by $c'(y_t)$, leading to a net decrease in costs of $b - c'(y_t)$, the left side of equation 7.7. In period $t + 1$, the perturbation increases costs from backstop production by b and decreases costs from resource extraction by $c'(y_t)$, leading to a present value net cost increase costs of $\rho[b - c'(y_{t+1})]$, the right side of this equation. The no-arbitrage condition states that the current cost decrease equals the present value of the future cost increase. Along an optimal extraction path, the firm has no desire to reallocate resource sales: there are no opportunities for intertemporal arbitrage.

7.4.2 Stock-Dependent Costs

We now consider the case where the firm's extraction cost is $c(x, y) = C(\sigma + x)^{-\alpha} y$. Average extraction cost depends on the resource stock but not on the rate of extraction: costs are lower when the resource stock is higher. We assume that $b < C(\sigma + 0)^{-\alpha}$, so

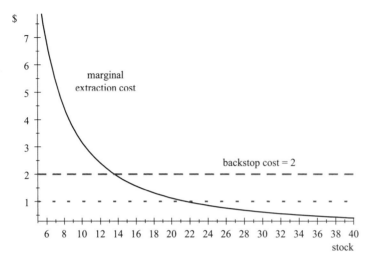

Figure 7.5
Extraction stops once the resource stock reaches the critical threshold at the intersection of the marginal extraction cost curve and the backstop cost. Cumulative extraction equals the initial stock minus this critical threshold. A reduction in the backstop cost, from the dashed to the dotted line, increases the critical threshold, thus reducing cumulative extraction.

it is not optimal to physically exhaust the resource. A critical threshold, x_{min}, solves $C(\sigma + x_{min})^{-\alpha} = b$; at $x = x_{min}$, average (= marginal) extraction costs equal the backstop costs. For stocks below this level, the backstop is cheaper than the resource, so the backstop supplies the entire market. If the initial stock of the resource is x_0, then the "economically viable stock," defined as the amount that it is economical to extract, is approximately $x_0 - x_{min}$.[4]

In this case, the resource is not physically exhausted. Coal is one of the many examples of such a resource. Even apart from issues related to climate change, we will not use all of the coal on the planet, simply because at some point extraction costs exceed the cost of an alternative. Figure 7.5 shows a graph of stock-dependent average costs (solid curve) and a backstop cost of 2 (dashed line). Extraction stops once the stock is at or below $x_{min} = 13$, the intersection of the solid and the dashed curves. The cost of extracting stocks below this level exceeds the backstop cost. It is optimal to drive the resource to the critical level x_{min}; stopping extraction when the stock is above this level leaves valuable resource in the ground. If the backstop cost falls from $b = 2$ to $b = 1$, the dashed line shifts to the dotted

---

4 Why "approximately" instead of "exactly"? We assumed that extraction costs depend on the stock at the beginning of the period. Thus, for example, if the stock is slightly above x_{min}, it might be optimal to extract to a level slightly below x_{min}. However, if the current stock is below x_{min}, further extraction is uneconomical. This complication does not arise in a continuous time model, where the economically viable stock is exactly $x_0 - x_{min}$. The discrete and continuous time models are similar if the length of each period in the discrete model is small.

line, leading to an increase in the intersection, x_{min}, and a decrease in the economically viable stock, $x_0 - x_{min}$.

As with constant average extraction cost, the trajectory consists of two phases: an initial phase, during which extraction is positive and the backstop is not used; followed by an infinitely long phase, during which only the backstop is used. There is at most a single period when both the resource and the backstop are used.

7.5 Summary

The anticipated backstop lowers the trajectory of the resource price even before the backstop is used. This dependence reflects the fact that a firm's resource extraction decision is an investment problem. Extraction in a period depends on the relation between price in that period and in all subsequent periods. The backstop model drives home an important point: the resource supply in a period depends on the entire trajectory of anticipated future prices. In contrast, in the familiar static model, supply is a function of current but not future prices. If the average extraction cost is independent of the extraction level, the trajectory consists of two phases. In the first phase, only the resource is used; in the second, only the backstop is used. If the marginal extraction cost increases with extraction, there may be a phase during which society simultaneously uses both sources of energy.

7.6 Terms and Concepts, Study Questions, Exercises, and Sources

Terms and Concepts
Backstop technology, residual demand, transitional period, decreasing and increasing returns to scale, phase, learning by doing, economically viable stock.

Study Questions
1. Explain why the backstop technology lowers the competitive equilibrium price and raises extraction even before the backstop is actually used.

2. Different assumptions about extraction costs have different implications concerning the simultaneous use of the natural resource and the backstop.

   (a) Suppose that average (and marginal) extraction costs are constant. Is there ever a phase during which both sources of energy supply the market? Explain.

   (b) Suppose that extraction costs are increasing with the rate of extraction but do not depend on the remaining stock. Describe the possible combination of phases.

   (c) Explain the source of the difference in parts (a) and (b).

3. Suppose that average (and marginal) extraction costs depend on the remaining resource stock but not on the level of extraction. How does the magnitude of the backstop cost affect cumulative extraction?

Exercises

1. In the constant cost model, explain why the resource is worthless if $C \geq b$. What is the resource rent in this case?

2. Section 7.3 assumes that the trajectory begins with a phase during which the resource supplies the entire market. Using a simple argument (involving no calculations), explain why the equilibrium conditions are inconsistent with the existence of either (1) an initial phase containing more than a single period during which both the backstop and the resource supply the market, or (2) an initial phase during which the backstop supplies the entire market.

3. The text assumes that the availability of the backstop is common knowledge. Suppose instead that no one knows anything about the backstop until the resource price reaches the level b, where it is economical to use the backstop. At that time and thereafter, the existence of the backstop with constant marginal cost is common knowledge. Referring to Figure 7.3, provide a verbal description of what the equilibrium price trajectory looks like in this alternative scenario. (You can supplement your verbal description with a graph if this helps.) Think about what the equilibrium price trajectory must look like before the price hits b, and what it must be like after that time.

4. Figures 7.3 and 7.4 represent a case where the backstop marginal (= average) cost is constant at $b = 5$; in this case, the backstop begins to be used at $t = 40$. Consider a scenario where everything else is the same as in these figures, except that now the backstop cost falls exogenously over time. The marginal (= average) cost of the backstop at t is $b(t) = 3 + \frac{10}{1+gt}$.

   (a) For what value of g does the backstop cost reach 5 at $t = 40$?

   (b) Suppose that g is slightly lower than the value you identified in part (a). How, if at all does this alter the equilibrium price trajectory (the solid curve) in Figure 7.3? Explain your reasoning.

5. Figures 7.3 and 7.4 represent a case where the backstop (marginal = average) production cost is a constant, b. For this exercise suppose instead that the backstop cost equals $\frac{1}{2}bz^2$, so the marginal cost of the backstop equals bz (instead of being constant at b). As before, average extraction costs are constant at C.

   (a) What is the backstop supply function, and what is the backstop inverse supply function in this case?

   (b) Denote the inverse demand for energy ($w = y + z$) as $p = D(w)$. Draw a linear demand function, and set $C = 5$. Include in this figure the backstop supply function, assuming that b is such that the resource is not worthless. (Depending on the magnitude of b, the resource is or is not worthless; this question encourages you to think about the relation between b and the value of the resource.) Explain your figure.

(c) Under the assumptions of part (b), might there be an initial phase during which the resource supplies the entire market (as is the case when the backstop marginal cost is constant)? Explain.

(d) Describe the evolution over time of the backstop market share. (Refer to section 7.4.1.)

Sources

Timilsina, Kurdgelashvili, and Narbel (2011) review the evolution of solar power costs.

Heal (1976) is an early paper on natural resources and a backstop.

Dasgupta and Heal (1974) study the case where the backstop becomes available at a random time.

Tsur and Zemel (2003) consider research and development investment that lowers the cost of the backstop.

8 The Green Paradox

Objective
• Use the Hotelling model to study the climate effects of a policy that promotes a low-carbon fuel.

Information and Skills
• Understand how a lower backstop cost affects cumulative extraction, the extraction profile, or both.

• Explain why both of these changes might have climate-related consequences.

• Be able to synthesize this information to describe and then evaluate the Green Paradox.

We discuss the "Green Paradox" for three reasons. First, the topic is intrinsically important because of its relevance to climate policy. Second, it provides an example of a situation where well-intentioned policies can backfire, a possibility that arises in many other contexts. Chapter 9 provides a more general perspective on this issue; the current chapter sets the stage for the general discussion by considering a specific example in detail. Third, the material shows how the Hotelling model can be used to illuminate a policy question. Models make it easier to understand real-world concerns.

Burning fossil fuels increases atmospheric stocks of greenhouse gases (GHGs). Scientific evidence shows that these higher stocks will affect the world's climate, possibly leading to rising sea level; increased frequency and severity of epidemics, storms and droughts; rapid and large-scale extinction of species, with unpredictable consequences; and temperature and precipitation changes that might decrease agricultural productivity, worsening food insecurity and increasing human migration. These risks have spurred interest in the development of low-carbon "green" alternative energy sources, such as solar and wind power. People debate the use of policy that encourages the development of these alternatives.

We consider a research and development (R&D) subsidy to decrease the cost, b, of a green backstop energy source. A cheaper backstop provides economic benefits when it is used, and if anticipated, also reduces the fossil fuel price and increases consumption before the backstop is used (chapter 7). The lower current prices benefit energy consumers, but if fossil fuel consumption was already socially excessive due to a pollution externality, the increased consumption potentially lowers welfare. The possibility that an apparently beneficial change (the lower-cost backstop) harms society is known as the "Green Paradox." The key to the paradox is that firms change their behavior today in response to anticipated future changes. A carbon tax that begins in the future can also generate the Paradox.

Absent market failures, cheaper energy increases welfare by increasing the sum of producer and consumer surplus. The lower backstop cost benefits society in this perfect world, but the First Fundamental Welfare Theorem (chapter 2) implies that there is no need to subsidize green alternatives here. We do not subsidize competitive computer manufacturers, even though their innovations benefit consumers; the market rewards innovators by the amount needed to induce them to undertake the socially optimal level of innovation.

We are interested in public policy where market failures are important. GHG emissions are a long-lasting global pollutant; the damage arising from their stock does not depend on which country emitted the GHGs. Fossil fuels also generate local pollutants, such as SO_2 and total suspended particles (TSP). The reduction in these local pollutants generates local health benefits that are important in many countries; China and India suffer from severe coal-related health problems, and the Obama administration used the co-benefits of emissions reductions as an economic justification for environmental rules to reduce carbon emissions. Countries capture all of the health benefits from reducing local pollutants but only a fraction of those from reducing a global pollutant. Absent an international agreement, countries therefore internalize only a fraction of the cost of their GHG emissions, leading to excessive emissions.

A Road Map

Section 8.1 notes that green industrial policy might affect the climate by altering cumulative extraction and/or by changing the shape of the extraction trajectory. Section 8.2 builds on Chapter 7, describing the effect of a lower backstop cost on cumulative extraction and on the extraction profile. Most proponents of green industrial policy emphasize the first effect, and the Green Paradox literature emphasizes the second. Section 8.3 gives example where the changed extraction profile increases climate-related damages. Section 8.4 provides a broader perspective and assessment of the Green Paradox.

8.1   The Approach

Objectives and skills: Understand the distinction between the climate effect of changes in cumulative extraction and in the shape of the extraction profile.

Does a seemingly beneficial policy, such as a subsidy that lowers the cost of the backstop, help correct the climate externality? The subsidy has two types of effects on the externality. First, it tends to reduce cumulative extraction of fossil fuels over the life of the resource, improving the climate problem. Second, it alters the extraction path, increasing extraction early on and decreasing extraction later. This tilting of the extraction path can worsen the climate problem. Either effect might dominate, so we cannot presume that the lower backstop price benefits the climate. We consider the two effects separately, using the backstop model from Chapter 7. A model that combines the two effects is more complex but not more insightful. An improvement in technology corresponds to a reduction in b, to $b' < b$.

Proponents of green subsidies argue that the social benefits arising from reduced climate-related damages justify the R&D costs of green technology. To focus on the Green Paradox, we ignore the investment costs. Even in the absence of R&D costs, does society want the lower backstop costs? A large literature discusses the merits of "industrial policy," governmental attempts to promote specific industries. All the arguments for and against this type of government intervention also apply to green industrial policy.[1] The Green Paradox is specific to green industrial policy, raising the possibility that society might not want the better technology even if it were free.[2]

Change in the Stock

By choice of units, we can set one unit of extraction equal to one unit of emissions, so reducing cumulative extraction creates an equal reduction of cumulative emissions. One short ton of subbituminous coal contains about 3,700 pounds of CO_2. Defining a "unit of coal" to equal a short ton and a "unit of CO_2" to equal 3,700 pounds, one unit of coal equals one unit of CO_2.

Historical emissions determine the initial stock of atmospheric carbon. Some carbon in the atmosphere migrates to other reservoirs, including the ocean and biomass. The simplest way to approximate this movement uses a constant decay rate for the stock of atmospheric GHGs, $S(t)$:

$$\frac{dS(t)}{dt} = y(t) - \delta S(t), \tag{8.1}$$

---

1 A frequent criticism of industrial policy is that the government does a poor job of picking winners. Subsidies to Solyndra, a manufacturer of components to solar panels that went bankrupt in 2011, cost U.S. taxpayers $500 million. Businesses also sometimes make unsuccessful investments: consider Shell's investment in Arctic drilling (section 6.4).

2 The Green Paradox concerns policies that directly affect markets in the future and only indirectly affect current markets. Some green policies have direct effects on current markets. For example, renewable fuel portfolio standards require a minimum fraction of energy produced using fossil fuel substitutes. Current solar and wind subsidies increase the demand for green energy sources today, not merely in the future. These sources are substitutes for fossil fuels, so the portfolio standards and the subsidies decrease the current consumption of fossil fuels, and do not lead to a Green Paradox.

where $y(t)$ is emissions (= extraction, a flow) at time t, and $\delta > 0$ is the decay rate. The stock rises if $y(t) > \delta S(t)$ and falls if $y(t) < \delta S(t)$. The half-life of the stock equals the amount of time it takes half of a given stock to decay. With constant decay rate δ, if the half-life is between 100 and 200 years, and if we pick the unit of time to equal 1 year, then $0.0035 < \delta < 0.007.$[3]

The model in equation 8.1 makes it possible to make a number of points simply. However, the process that actually governs changes in atmospheric GHG stocks is much more complicated. Moreover, GHG stocks cause damages indirectly (e.g., via their effect on temperature or precipitation) instead of directly. In addition, the inertia in the climate system causes global average temperature and other climate variables to respond to changed GHG stocks with a delay. Therefore, the climate impact of current emissions might increase over decades before eventually diminishing.[4] There is also a risk of positive feedbacks arising if temperature crosses a threshold. For example, higher temperatures caused by higher stocks of GHGs might melt permafrost, releasing additional GHGs.

8.2   Cumulative Extraction and the Extraction Profile

Objectives and skills: Understand how the backstop affects cumulative extraction and the extraction profile.

Section 7.4.2 considers extraction costs $= C(\sigma + x)^{-\alpha} y$; for this model, costs increase as the remaining resource stock falls. Society stops extracting when the resource stock reaches the threshold $x_{\min}$, the solution to $C(\sigma + x_{\min})^{-\alpha} = b$; cumulative extraction, over the life of the resource, is $x_0 - x_{\min}$. A lower backstop price, $b' < b$, increases the threshold, lowering cumulative extraction (see figure 7.5). To the extent that climate-related damages arise because of cumulative emissions, the lower backstop cost reduces climate-related damages, as proponents of green industrial policy hope.

If extraction costs are independent of the stock, the reduction in backstop costs does not affect cumulative emissions, but it still changes the extraction profile. The lower backstop cost reduces future prices, reducing the rent in earlier periods and decreasing the firm's opportunity cost of selling the resource. The lower opportunity cost increases sales early in the program. Because the resource stock is finite, sales cannot increase at every point in time, so the lower backstop costs lead to earlier exhaustion of the resource.

---

3 With constant decay rate δ, $e^{-\delta t}$ of a unit of the stock present at time 0 remains at time t. Setting $e^{-\delta t} = 0.5$ and solving for t produces the half-life of the stock, $\frac{-\ln 0.5}{\delta}$. If the half-life equals 100 years, then solving $100 = \frac{-\ln 0.5}{\delta}$ implies $\delta \approx 0.007$.

4 Prominent climate-economics models (e.g., DICE, due to Nordhaus, 2008) use climate components in which the major effect on temperature occurs five or six decades after the release of emissions. Ricke and Caldeira (2014) provide evidence that major effects occur much sooner.

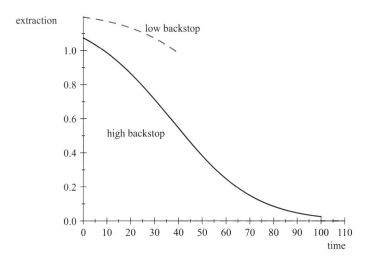

Figure 8.1
The low backstop cost increases extraction early in the program; it tilts the extraction trajectory to the present.

Figure 8.1 shows extraction profiles under high and low backstop costs for constant extraction costs, $C < b' < b$.[5] The lower backstop cost increases extraction early in the program and causes exhaustion to occur sooner. Exhaustion occurs at $t = 40$ under the low cost and at $t = 100$ under the high cost. The lower backstop cost tilts the extraction trajectory toward the present (small t). In this example, provided that the improvement is anticipated, it does not matter whether it is available right away, at $t = 0$, or at $t = 39$; in either case, it is not used until $t = 40$.

8.3 Why Does the Extraction Profile Matter?

Objectives and skills: Understand three reasons why a tilt in extraction profile might increase climate-related damages.

This section considers three reasons why a tilt to the present in the extraction profile potentially worsens climate change. (i) The tilt might make it more likely that we cross a threshold that triggers a catastrophe, such as rapid melting of the Antarctic ice sheet. (ii)

5 Figure 7.4 can be interpreted as comparing extraction profiles under an infinitely costly backstop and under a backstop with a finite cost. Figure 8.1 compares extraction profiles under backstops with a high and a low cost. The two figures have the same message: lowering the cost of the backstop increases resource production before the backstop is used.
   All figures in this chapter use a continuous time model with constant average extraction costs, $C = 5$, $\rho = 0.95$ (a discount rate of 5%), demand $D = 10p^{-1.3}$, and an initial stock of $x_0 = 46$. The high backstop cost is $b = 100$, and the low cost is $b' = 6$.

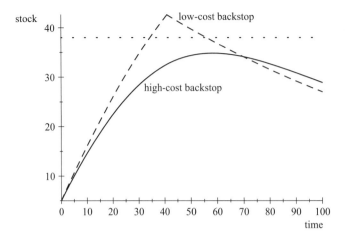

Figure 8.2
Stock of GHGs under the two extraction paths in Figure 8.1. The low backstop cost leads to higher extraction early in the program and so a higher maximum value of the stock of GHGs.

The tilt increases the rate of change in the stock of GHGs, and society might be worse off when change occurs more quickly. (iii) The tilt leads to a higher stock trajectory in the near term. If costs are convex (meaning that marginal damages increase with the stock) the higher stock leads to a much higher level of damages, at least in the near term.

Catastrophic Changes

There may be a tipping point: a critical level of GHG stocks (or temperature) above which the system abruptly changes or serious damages occur. Figure 8.2 shows why the tilted extraction path can increase the risk of crossing such a threshold. The two extraction profiles in Figure 8.1 have different effects on the stock of atmospheric carbon.

The (historically determined) initial stock level at time $t = 0$ is the same for both extraction paths. For $t > 0$, the stock trajectory depends on the extraction (= emissions) trajectory. Because extraction is initially higher under the low backstop-cost, the stock grows more quickly in that scenario, relative to the high backstop-cost scenario. Figure 8.2 shows the GHG stock trajectories corresponding to the two extraction profiles taken from figure 8.1; we obtain these graphs by solving equation 8.1, using the extraction profiles in figure 8.1 and the initial condition $S(0) = 0$. For the first 70 years, the stock trajectory under the extraction path corresponding to the low backstop cost lies above the trajectory corresponding to the high backstop cost.

Figure 8.2 has a horizontal dotted line at a stock of 38. If a stock above 38 triggers a catastrophe, then it occurs in about 40 years under the low-backstop-cost trajectory, but it never occurs under the high-backstop-cost trajectory. If the catastrophe is sufficiently severe, then the future economic benefits arising from the low-cost backstop do not compensate society for the catastrophe. The lower-cost backstop does not cause the catastrophe: the accumulation of GHG stocks does that. But the lower-cost back-stop changes the competitive equilibrium extraction trajectory, changing the GHG stock trajectory and thereby triggering the catastrophe.

Figure 8.2 illustrates a possibility, but it does not establish that a particular outcome is likely. Its key feature is that the maximum stock level under the low-cost backstop is above the maximum stock level under the high-cost backstop. Provided that the probability of catastrophe increases with the maximum stock level, this model (together with parameter assumptions) implies that the lower backstop cost increases the probability of catastrophe. This result happens because the initial emissions profile is higher under the low-cost backstop.

Rapid Changes

The more rapid change in GHG stocks, associated with the lower backstop costs, might increase social costs. Society eventually replaces infrastructure, but climate-related change might accelerate the process. If we know that rising sea levels will make some highways and bridges obsolete in 150 years, then we can divert investment from maintaining them and build more resilient substitutes. If we have to replace this infrastructure within the next 50 years, we may be forced to write off much of the current infrastructure that would, absent rising sea levels, still be useful for decades.

As a simple way of modeling this dependence of climate-related costs on the speed of change, denote the stock at time t as $S(t)$ and the speed of change in the stock, the time derivative, as $\frac{dS(t)}{dt}$. Suppose that marginal damage is constant in the stock but increasing in the speed of change:

$$\text{damage} = S(t) + 10 \left(\frac{dS(t)}{dt} \right)^2.$$

From figure 8.2, it is evident that the stock initially increases more rapidly under low back-stop costs: its slope—the time derivative—is greater than that of the high-cost backstop. The initial stock level is fixed by historical emissions. During the early part of the program, the stock levels are similar, so the damages related directly to the stock are also similar in the two scenarios. However, because the stock rises much more quickly in the low-backstop-cost scenario, the damages related to the speed of change of stocks is higher there. Therefore, early in the program, total damages are higher under low backstop costs. Figure 8.3 graphs of damages under the two backstops. Damages corresponding to the low-cost backstop (dashed curve) are higher early in the program.

Convex Damages

If damages are convex in the stock, then *marginal* damages are higher, the higher is the stock. The simplest case of convex damages uses $D(S_t) = \frac{1}{2} S_t^2$, so marginal damages equal

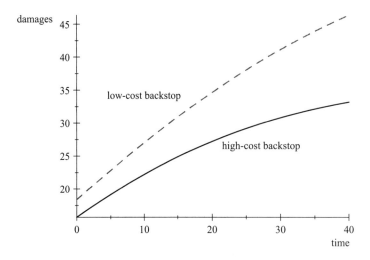

Figure 8.3
Marginal damages are constant in the stock and increasing in the speed of change of the stock. Damages early in the program are higher under the low-cost backstop.

$D'(S_t) = S_t$. With this functional form, the graphs in figure 8.2 can be interpreted both as the stock and as the marginal damage (because the two are equal). The ratio of damages under two arbitrary stock levels, S^A and S^B, equals $(S^A/S^B)^2$. For our example, the stock under the low backstop cost is higher than that under the high backstop cost early in the program; damages early on are higher under the low backstop cost. With discounting, damages early in the program receive more weight in the welfare calculation compared to later damages. Therefore, the tilt in the extraction profile, arising from a decrease in the backstop cost, can lead to a large increase in the present discounted value of the stream of damages, when damages are convex in the stock.

8.4   Discussion of the Paradox

Objectives and skills: Understand the merits and limitations of the Green Paradox.

We presented the Green Paradox in the context of industrial policies that lower backstop costs. The same logic applies to (anticipated) carbon taxes that begin low and rise over time, or other policies that lower future producer prices of fossil fuels. These policies tend to lower current prices, increasing current extraction. Green subsidies and future carbon taxes are politically more palatable than policies that discourage current fossil fuel use. Their greater political appeal, resulting in higher likelihood of implementation, makes it is worth asking whether such policies have unintended consequences.

Theory and Empirics

The literature on the Green Paradox emphasizes the potential for unintended consequences. Due to its speculative nature, most of this literature uses analytic or simulation-based models. Van der Werf and Di Maria (2012) survey the literature, and Pittel, van der Ploeg, and Withagen (2014) bring together recent contributions. The Green Paradox illustrates the constructive role that theory can play in informing policy. Theory works best when it is simple enough to communicate easily. That simplification usually requires focusing on a small set of issues to the exclusion of others, creating the risk of missing important countervailing forces.

The dearth of natural experiments makes it difficult to assess whether the Green Paradox is empirically important; the U.S. Acid Rain Program and the legislative history of the Waxman-Markey bill (section 9.6) provide some evidence. The U.S. Acid Rain program was phased in over a decade, making both coal producers and consumers aware of future sulfur emissions constraints (Ellerman and Montero 1998). The anticipation of these constraints potentially has both a supply and a demand effect. Green Paradox models emphasize the former, usually neglecting the latter. Notification of future constraints reduced the estimated rent on high-sulfur coal, as the Green Paradox predicts. Power plants, the major consumers, recognized that the policy would make future emissions expensive. Businesses replace capital as it wears out, taking into account their expectation of future market conditions. The future sulfur emissions constraints gave power plants an incentive to replace aging capital stock with cleaner technology, reducing demand for high-sulfur coal before the constraints came into force. The supply and demand effects nearly balanced each other, leading to statistically insignificant effects on equilibrium consumption (Di Maria et al. 2013). The Waxman-Markey bill would have capped carbon emissions from some sources, reducing the value of coal. The Green Paradox predicts that the abrupt collapse of efforts to pass this bill, and the resulting altered expectations of future prices, would increase the value of coal deposits and lower incentives for current extraction. The collapse of the legislation increased the value of stored coal but had no detectable effect on extraction (Lemoine 2016).

Importance of Rent

The Paradox is relevant only for resources that have a substantial component of rent in their price. Rent is a significant component of the price of oil but is a much smaller component of the price of coal. Resource-based commodities with low rent are similar to standard commodities. The Green Paradox has only slight relevance for such commodities, but so does the theory of nonrenewable resources.

Importance of Elasticities

The significance of the Green Paradox depends on the price elasticities of supply and demand for fossil fuels. At least in the short run, demand is quite inelastic. With a low elasticity of demand, a lower current price transfers income from fossil fuel owners to fuel consumers, having modest effects on current consumption.

The Green Paradox is based on the assumption that a downward revision of beliefs about future energy prices would lead to a significant increase in current supply. Technical constraints may limit the supply response, at least in the short run. Many resource firms operate at or near capacity, and therefore have limited ability to quickly increase their supply. It may also be costly for them to shut down operations, lowering their flexibility to reduce supply. These considerations tend to reduce short-run supply elasticities, reducing the significance of the Green Paradox.

Political Opposition to Fossil Fuel Use

Climate change activists encourage universities and pension and other investment funds to divest from fossil fuel companies, largely on the grounds of social responsibility. These activists draw parallels with the divestment from South Africa during the apartheid regime. By 2015, several universities (including the University of Massachusetts and Stanford) and cities (including Seattle, San Francisco, and Portland) had begun to divest from coal companies. Proponents recognize that divestment by a single fund has negligible effect on markets, but they hope that the publicity surrounding divestment debates will raise climate awareness.

Some people claim that there is also a narrow economic rationale for divestment, arising from the regulatory risk that fossil fuel companies face. Partly based on this rationale, in 2015 Norway's parliament instructed the Government Pension Fund Global (GPFG), the world's largest sovereign fund, to divest from 114 companies, including 32 coal companies and several oil sands producers (Schwartz 2015). (Ironically, shortly thereafter, Norway's parliament voted to subsidize a national coal producer.) Fossil fuel companies might be overvalued, and therefore poor investments, if the market does not properly account for regulatory risk (e.g., future carbon taxes). This economic argument raises the question why a political body is better than investment fund managers at assessing a company's value. In addition, we noted (see section 6.4) that at least one large oil company explicitly accounts for regulatory risk when assessing investment opportunities.

Whatever its justification, if the divestment movement becomes powerful enough to lower the value of fossil fuel companies, it could have the perverse effect of increasing current emissions. The mechanism is the same as described in the Green Paradox. In the simplest Hotelling model, we saw (equation 5.8) that the value of the firm equals the initial rent times the initial resource stock. A decrease in the firm's value requires that the resource rent fall. A fall in resource rent—whatever its cause—increases current supply of fossil fuels. Possibly offsetting this effect, the fall in resource rent lowers incentives to find and develop new stocks, thus reducing cumulative supply. These two effects, greater current extraction but lower cumulative extraction, mirror the two effects described in section 8.2.

Strategic Behavior

The Paradox depends on the behavior of oil exporters. The Organization of Petroleum Exporting Countries (OPEC) recognizes that its aggregate sales affect the market price, so it is not a price-taker. OPEC faces a competitive fringe and is riven with internal dissension, but it (likely) understands that the demand function is predetermined by past events, including past OPEC behavior. Some past investments in infrastructure (e.g., highways) increase the current demand for fossil fuels, and other investments (e.g., development of fuel-efficient cars) decrease that demand. OPEC observed that its oil embargo of the early 1970s led to investment changes that potentially shifted the oil import demand function. (Our description of the Green Parodox, in contrast, assumes that the demand function is exogenous.) OPEC profits are likely to be higher if it maintains a reliable and "reasonably priced" source of petroleum, discouraging investments that reduce future import demand, instead of trying to extract every cent of consumer surplus available in the near term.

Green policies that reduce future fossil fuel demand have ambiguous effects on OPEC's strategic incentives. (i) OPEC might decide that lower current fossil fuel prices would discourage the development of green technologies. Acting on that belief, OPEC's strategic response increases current sales even more than the standard Green Paradox suggests. (ii) OPEC might think that maintaining a large stock of reserves (to ensure future supply) discourages green investment. Acting on that belief, OPEC's strategic response is to conserve stocks, thus working against the Green Paradox. (iii) OPEC might decide that efforts to discourage green substitutes for fossil fuel are doomed. If OPEC decides that there is no point in maintaining "reasonably low" prices, it becomes rational to exercise market power to the fullest extent possible, without worrying about the effect that high prices have on the future demand function, working against the Green Paradox.

8.5   Summary

The Green Paradox illustrates the possibility that well-intentioned policies can backfire. The paradox potentially applies to policies that directly affect future energy markets (e.g., anticipated carbon taxes that begin in the future, or subsidy-induced reductions in the costs of backstop technologies that will be used in the future). These policies directly affect future demand for fossil fuels. Because of the dynamic linkages in resource markets, those future prices affect resource owners' current supply decisions.

Policies that reduce future demand decrease owners' incentive to hold on to their stock, tilting the extraction trajectory toward the present, increasing current extraction, and reducing extraction in some future periods. This tilt may harm the climate. The higher earlier extraction may increase the peak stock of atmospheric carbon, raising the probability of a catastrophe. The tilted extraction profile also increases the rate of change of atmospheric stock. Society may be worse off, the more rapidly this change occurs. The tilted extraction profile is likely to increase damages if marginal damages are increasing in the level of the stock.

If extraction costs depend on the remaining resource stock, green policies reduce cumulative extraction. Lower cumulative extraction, and the associated reduction in cumulative carbon emissions, benefit the climate. The net effect of green policies that lower future demand for fossil fuels therefore depends on the balance between the effects of lower cumulative extraction and of higher earlier extraction. The Green Paradox is valuable as a cautionary tale, but its practical importance is still being debated.

8.6   Terms and Concepts, Study Questions, Exercises, and Sources

Terms and Concepts
Research spillovers, business as usual, green industrial policy, the Green Paradox, climate threshold, catastrophic change, stock and flow variables, decay rate, half-life of a stock, convex damages, predetermined versus exogenous.

Study Questions
1. State the meaning of the Green Paradox in the context considered in this chapter (where green industrial policy reduces the cost of a low-carbon renewable alternative to fossil fuels).

2. Discuss some of the reasons that the Green Paradox might occur in the case where fossil fuel marginal extraction costs are constant. Your answer should include both a description of how, and an explanation of why, the industrial policy changes the extraction profile. It should also include a discussion of how and why this change in extraction profile might change climate-related damage.

3. Suppose now that extraction costs increase as the remaining resource stock falls. How and why does this different assumption about extraction costs affect the likelihood that the Green Paradox occurs?

Exercises
1. In Scenario A, the damage caused by a stock S is fS (with $f > 0$ a constant). In Scenario B, the damage caused by a stock is FS^2 (with $F > 0$ a constant).

   (a) Graph damage and marginal damage in these two scenarios (as functions of S).

   (b) In which scenario are damages convex?

   (c) Explain in a sentence or two the meaning of convex damages.

2. Scenarios A and B are identical in every respect (e.g., demand function, initial resource stock, and extraction cost function), except for the following: in Scenario A, a backstop

with constant marginal cost b is available at time $t = 0$; in Scenario B, it is known at time $t = 0$ that the backstop will not become available until $t = 49$.

(a) Suppose that in Scenario A, the backstop begins to be used at time $t = 50$. What, if any, is the difference in extraction trajectories in the two scenarios? Explain your answer briefly.

(b) Scenario C involves uncertainty; the time at which the backstop will become available is a random variable with expected value $t = 50$. The time of availability might be smaller or larger than $t = 50$. Compare the equilibrium in Scenario C with those in Scenarios A and B, and justify your conjectures.

Sources

The DICE model due to Nordhaus (2008) is probably the most widely used model that integrates models of the economy and the climate.

Ricke and Caldeira (2014) provide evidence showing that major effects of emissions occur within the first decade of emissions release.

Sinn (2008) is an early study of the Green Paradox.

Hoel (2008, 2012) studies the role of extraction costs and demand characteristics.

Gerlagh (2011) distinguishes between a "weak" and "strong" Green Paradox.

Van der Ploeg and Withagen (2012) provide an in-depth analysis of the Paradox.

Van der Werf and Di Maria (2012) survey the literature.

Pittel, Van der Ploeg, and Withagen's (2014) edited volume brings together recent contributions.

Winter (2014) studies the Green Paradox in the presence of climate feedbacks.

Ellerman and Montero (1998) examine the effect of future emissions constraints on earlier sulfur emissions.

Di Maria et al. (2013) discuss the Green Paradox in the context of the U.S. Acid Rain Program.

Alberini et al. (2011) provide estimates of the elasticity of demand for electricity.

Karp and Stevenson (2012) discuss green industrial policy.

Lemoine (2016) empirically tests the responsiveness of current coal price to expectations of future policy.

Schwartz (2015) describes Norway's divestment decision.

9 Policy in a Second-Best World

Objective
- Be familiar with policy complications under multiple market failures.

Information and Skills
- Understand the Theory of the Second Best and the Principle of Targeting.
- Calculate and graphically illustrate the Pigouvian tax.
- Compare the optimal tax under monopoly and competition.
- Understand the difference between policy complements and substitutes.
- Understand how policies' interactions alter their welfare consequences.

Economists use the term "distortion" to mean any departure from an efficient allocation, or anything that causes such a departure. Examples include (1) the gap between price and marginal cost arising from the exercise of market power, (2) the gap between the private and social marginal production costs arising from a pollution externality, and (3) the gap between workers' incentive to supply labor (their after-tax wage) and firms' cost of labor. Economists often emphasize efficient competitive markets (i.e., without distortions) relegating market imperfections to a second tier of importance. We can make general statements about perfectly competitive markets, but not about markets with imperfections. To paraphrase Tolstoy: perfect markets are all alike; every imperfect market is imperfect in its own way.

The focus on perfect markets yields valuable insights. For example, the Hotelling model explains why scarcity per se is not a rationale for government intervention. The theory of comparative advantage explains why trade potentially raises national income in all trading partners, even if they have very different levels of development. The perfectly competitive paradigm is reasonably accurate for many markets. However, the emphasis on perfectly competitive markets sometimes seems like a rationalization of Dr. Pangloss's claim that "Everything is for the best in this best of all possible worlds." Market failures are important, especially in natural resource settings.

The "Theory of the Second Best" (TOSB) provides an organizing principle, making it easier to identify common elements in different situations. A "first-best" policy corrects a distortion (e.g., a pollution externality) or achieves an objective (e.g., raises government revenue) as efficiently as possible. It is difficult to rank, or even identify, all conceivable policies; we might know that a particular policy is not first best, but not whether it is fourth or seventeenth best. We say a policy is "second best" whenever it is not first best. The TOSB warns that intuition developed in studying perfect markets or markets with a single imperfection (e.g., a pollution externality) may be unreliable when there are multiple distortions. A policy intervention that seems likely to improve welfare might make matters worse, or in less extreme circumstances, it might create unnecessary collateral damage. We also discuss a closely related idea: the Principle of Targeting. To emphasize intuition about second-best settings, we consider only simple policies, primarily taxes and subsidies. The policy landscape contains many other types of policy.

A Road Map

Welfare analysis with market imperfections requires a definition of social surplus that includes such components as environmental costs and tax burden, in addition to consumer and producer surplus (section 9.1). We give two examples of the TOSB, one showing its relevance to a widely debated policy issue and the other showing that the basic idea is already familiar, although previously described using different language.

We then study an example of the TOSB, where a monopoly creates an environmental externality (section 9.2). A policy that seeks to correct the environmental externality, while ignoring the monopoly distortion, can lower welfare. We introduce the idea of a Pigouvian tax.

A tax on pollution and a subsidy on abatement (= the reduction of pollution) have the same effect on a firm's incentives to pollute, and in that respect appear equally efficient. However, these two policies have different effects on the distortions stemming from a government's need to raise revenue (section 9.3). The TOSB reminds us to consider such distortions.

The TOSB is important because superficially unrelated distortions may interact, magnifying or reducing each other. The underpricing of natural resources causes environmental and resource problems, many associated with agriculture. Agricultural price supports likely magnify the resource-related distortion. The resulting welfare loss can be large enough that the social value of production in a sector is less than the social value of inputs used in the sector, lowering national income, creating negative value-added. Producers in the sector might nevertheless obtain profits because of the wedge between social and private values (section 9.4).

Policy interactions are central to the TOSB. Borrowing from consumer demand theory, we can classify a pair of interacting policies as substitutes or complements. Section 9.5

notes that green industrial policies and carbon taxes are sometimes discussed as if they were substitutes, when in fact they are likely to be complements. Green industrial policies might increase the optimal level of the carbon tax instead of making that tax unimportant.

There would be no role in economics for the TOSB if society used only efficient policies. Inefficient policies sometimes arise when a group with narrow interests prevails over broader social interests. The model of the collective action problem provides a succinct way to think about political outcomes, including the political success of inefficient policies (section 9.6). U.S. subsidies for the ethanol industry illustrate the power of special interest groups.

9.1 Welfare and Second-Best Policies

Objectives and skills: Understand a welfare measure in the presence of market failure, and have a basic understanding of the TOSB.

Comparing the welfare effect of policies requires consideration of such factors as environmental cost or the government's need to raise revenue. Here we introduce a welfare function, used elsewhere in this chapter, and then consider two examples of the TOSB. These examples help develop intuition about the meaning and the generality of the TOSB. This section also introduces a closely related idea, the Principle of Targeting.

Social Welfare

In the partial equilibrium setting, we measure consumer and producer welfare by using consumer and producer surplus. Absent market failures, a competitive equilibrium maximizes the sum of producer + consumer surplus and is efficient. With market failures, we need a broader definition of welfare. For concreteness, assume that the market failure arises from pollution, a negative externality. We can imagine four types of agents in the economy: producers, consumers, those who suffer from pollution, and the general taxpayers subject to taxes outside the polluting sector; in reality, of course, people often play two or more of these roles. We consider just two policies: a tax on pollution and a subsidy on abatement. Taxing pollution generates tax revenue, making it possible to decrease other taxes, benefitting taxpayers. An abatement subsidy requires raising other taxes to finance the subsidy, imposing a cost on taxpayers but benefiting the recipients of the subsidy. Initially we assume that taxes outside the polluting sector are nondistortionary, so one dollar in tax revenue or subsidy cost in the polluting sector creates a one dollar benefit (under the tax) or a one dollar cost (under the subsidy) to taxpayers. Social welfare is

$$\text{consumer surplus} + \text{producer surplus} - \text{pollution costs} + \text{tax revenue.} \quad (9.1)$$

Tax revenue from the polluting sector is positive under an emissions tax and negative under an abatement subsidy.

Examples

The Green Paradox describes the consequence of using a poorly targeted policy. The policy goal is to reduce carbon emissions. Low-carbon alternatives to fossil fuels might help achieve that goal, but green industrial policy potentially changes the extraction profile in a way that harms the climate system. First-best policies, such as emissions taxes or cap and trade, directly target the objective of reducing carbon emissions.

Some activists promote trade restrictions to achieve environmental objectives. Trade may increase environmentally destructive production, as occurred with shrimp harvesting that kills turtles. In the 1990s the United States imposed a trade restriction to redirect U.S. shrimp imports away from fisheries that resulted in high turtle mortality. A trade restriction might benefit the environment, but it is seldom the optimal policy to achieve this goal. Turtle mortality was a consequence (but not the goal) of shrimp harvesting. The policy objective was to decrease turtle mortality, not to reallocate trade from one supplier to another. An efficient policy targets the environmental/resource objective. The U.S. trade restriction led to an international dispute that was resolved by the World Trade Organization (WTO). The WTO accepted that the United States had the right to use policies for the purpose of protecting international resources, such as turtles, but it found that U.S. policy contravened WTO law, because it restricted trade unnecessarily. The United States dropped its trade restriction but required exporting countries to use shrimping nets that kept turtles from getting caught.

The Principle of Targeting

These examples illustrate both the TOSB and the "Principle of Targeting" (POT), which states that a market failure (a "distortion") should be targeted as closely as possible. Many policies inflict collateral damage when correcting a distortion. The Principle of Targeting reminds us to align policies with objectives. In many cases, the application of the Principle is straightforward. It is necessary to clearly identify the problem or objective, and to distinguish between features that cause the problem and those that are associated with it. In the Green Paradox example, the problem is carbon emissions, not an excessively high backstop cost. In the trade example, the problem is not trade, but that turtles are killed when shrimp are caught. The Principle tells us that the efficient policy reduces carbon emission in the first case and alters fishers' harvesting techniques in the second. Because efficiency requires matching policies with targets, it typically requires that a regulator have the same number of policies as targets.

9.2   Monopoly + Pollution

Objectives and skills: Use graphs and algebra to compare output under a social planner, a competitive firm, and a monopoly, in the presence of an externality.

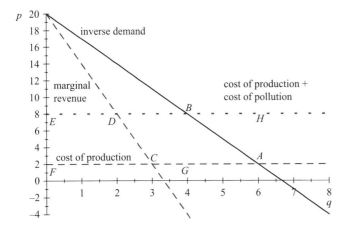

Figure 9.1
Point A is the competitive equilibrium with no pollution tax. Point B is the competitive equilibrium with the optimal (Pigouvian) tax $v = 6$. Point C is the monopoly equilibrium with no pollution tax. Point D is the monopoly equilibrium with the non optimal tax $v = 6$.

A graphical/algebraic example illustrates the TOSB and introduces the Pigouvian tax, an important idea in environmental and resource economics. This example, involving a polluting monopoly, shows that a policy intended to alleviate one problem (pollution) might exacerbate another (market power).

Figure 9.1 shows the inverse demand function, $p = 20 - 3q$, and the corresponding marginal revenue curve, $MR = 20 - 6q$. Average and marginal costs are constant at 2. The "pollution intensity" (the number of units of pollution per unit of output) in this example is constant, equal to 1 by choice of units. Often it is possible to reduce pollution intensity by using a more expensive production method, so the assumption of constant pollution intensity is unrealistic. A caveat at the end of this section explains why we make this assumption and the cost of doing so. Finally, we assume that each unit of production creates \$6 of environmental damages; social costs are proportional to pollution (section 9.5 relaxes this proportionality assumption). Under these assumptions, the private cost of production is 2, and the social cost, which includes environmental damages, is $2 + 6 = 8$.

An untaxed competitive industry produces where price equals marginal cost (point A in the figure). The monopoly sets marginal revenue equal to marginal cost, (point C). The symbol v represents a tax; if $v < 0$, the policy is a subsidy: a negative tax is a subsidy. The optimal tax for the competitive industry, known as the "Pigouvian tax," is $v = 6$. The socially optimal level of production and the price occur at point B. The tax $v = 6$ supports the socially optimal outcome: competitive firms facing this tax produce at the socially optimal level. The optimal tax causes firms to face the social cost of production, inducing them to internalize the pollution cost.

If the monopoly is charged the tax $v = 6$, its tax-inclusive cost of production also equals the social cost. The monopoly facing $v = 6$ produces at point D. Absent the tax, the monopoly produces too little, relative to the socially optimal level: point C lies to the left of point B. The tax causes the monopoly to reduce output, lowering social welfare: the optimal tax under competition ($v = 6$) lowers social welfare under monopoly. For this example, the optimal policy under monopoly is a subsidy, $v < 0$.

We can use figure 9.1 to identify the components in expression 9.1. Absent a tax, under competition, consumer surplus equals the area under the inverse demand function, above the price ($p = 2$); the pollution cost equals the area of the rectangle $AFEH$, the amount of production times the environmental cost per unit; the tax revenue is zero; and with constant marginal costs, producer surplus is zero. Under the optimal tax, consumer surplus falls by $AFEB$ (a loss in social welfare); the environmental cost falls by $AGBH$ (a gain in social welfare); and tax revenue increases from zero to $GFEB$ (a gain in social welfare). The net gain in welfare is the triangle ABH. This triangle equals the distortionary cost of the externality in the absence of policy. The first-best policy eliminates the distortion without creating collateral damage.

Aggregate social welfare under monopoly and the optimal subsidy is the same as under competition and the optimal tax, but the distribution of welfare differs in the two scenarios. Output, and therefore environmental damage and consumer surplus, are the same in the two cases. However, under competition and the optimal tax, taxpayers obtain the tax revenue $GFEB$. Under monopoly, taxpayers subsidize the monopoly (by the amount 6×4, the per-unit subsidy times the level of output for this example) instead of receiving tax revenue; in addition, the monopoly receives profits of $GFEB$ (price minus marginal cost times output).

The Algebra

The socially optimal level of production equates the marginal benefit of consumption (the consumer price) to the full social marginal cost of production (the private marginal cost plus the externality), resulting in $20 - 3q = 2 + 6$. The socially optimal level of production is $q^* = 4$. A competitive firm facing the tax v produces where price equals private marginal cost plus the tax, $20 - 3q = 2 + v$, implying the production level $q^{\text{compet}} = 6 - \frac{1}{3}v$. The optimal tax for the competitive firm causes the competitive level of production to equal the socially optimal level ($q^{\text{compet}} = q^*$), which requires the tax $v = 6$, equal to the externality.

The monopoly facing a tax v produces where marginal revenue equals production cost plus the tax, $20 - 6q = 2 + v$, implying $q^{\text{monop}} = 3 - \frac{1}{6}v$. The monopoly produces at the socially optimal level if $q^{\text{monop}} = q^*$, or $3 - \frac{1}{6}v = 4$, implying that $v = -6$, a subsidy.

A Caveat: The Constant Pollution Intensity Assumption

The assumption of constant pollution intensity makes this example simple, but it also obscures an important point. With constant pollution intensity, output moves in lockstep with pollution. In this case, there is a single distortion, and thus a single target, under both monopoly and competition. There is too much output and too much pollution under competition; for our choice of parameter values (but not in general), there is too little output and too little pollution under monopoly. Under both market structures, the existence of a single target enables the planner to achieve the optimal level of output and pollution using a single instrument, a tax or subsidy.

Matters are different when pollution intensity changes with production methods. Under competition, there is a single distortion: too much pollution for the given level of output. The Pigouvian pollution tax induces the competitive industry to choose the optimal pollution intensity; because this industry produces where marginal cost equals price, it chooses the optimal level of output *if* it faces the optimal pollution tax.

In contrast, there are two distortions under monopoly: the pollution externality and the exercise of market power. In general, the planner needs the same number of policy instruments as there are targets (distortions that the policymaker seeks to correct). Under monopoly with variable pollution intensity, the policymaker needs two policies to achieve the first best. A pollution tax targets pollution, and an output subsidy targets the output level. Even under the more plausible assumption of variable pollution intensity, the main point of this section remains: a policy that is optimal in one setting may inflict collateral damage and even lower social welfare in another setting.

9.3 Distortionary Taxes

Objectives and skills: Understand why a tax and a subsidy have the same effect on a polluter's incentives but have different fiscal effects.

The TOSB reminds us that distortions interact, even when they arise in different sectors of the economy: the toe bone is connected to the shoulder bone. To develop intuition about the connections among different policies and distortions, we examine the relation between a pollution tax and distortions arising from government revenue collection outside the polluting sector.

A producer group might be able to block a socially beneficial pollution tax. A subsidy to abate can be equally effective in altering polluters' incentives and would likely attract producers' political support. However, the pollution tax and abatement subsidies have different welfare effects once we recognize that raising government revenue usually creates an economic distortion. We therefore drop the (unrealistic) assumption made in section 9.1 that tax policies outside the polluting sector are nondistortionary. In this case, a pollution tax is more efficient than an abatement subsidy. In a partial equilibrium setting, pollution taxes create a "double dividend," causing the optimal pollution tax to exceed the Pigouvian level. A general equilibrium perspective can overturn that conclusion.

Subsidizing Abatement

Instead of taxing firms that create pollution, society can subsidize them to abate (= reduce pollution). A firm has the same incentive to reduce pollution if it is taxed $1 for each unit of pollution, or given a subsidy of $1 for each unit that it abates. Under the tax, pollution increases the firm's tax payments. Under the subsidy, pollution reduces the firm's revenue from abatement. These two costs have the same effect on the firm's incentives, so they tend to lead to the same level of pollution. Income effects or behavioral anomalies may cause the actual effects to differ.[1]

There are both political and economic obstacles to using the subsidy instead of the tax. The subsidy imposes a cost on taxpayers, requiring a transfer from general tax revenue to a specific group of firms. Even if the pollution reduction is worth this cost, it may be hard to convince voters to tax themselves to pay firms for stopping a socially harmful practice. Raising revenue to finance subsidies creates a deadweight loss in addition to the direct distributional effect of taking income away from a group to give to another. (Chapter 10 discusses deadweight loss.) The distinction between a transfer and a deadweight loss is important. Taking $1 from Mary to give to Jiangfeng is a transfer, not a cost to the economy. However, if the government has to take $1.25 from Mary to give $1 to Jiangfeng, there is a $0.25 deadweight loss to the economy. The government makes transfers using a "leaky bucket."

The pollution tax corrects a distortion and does not create deadweight loss in the polluting sector. However, taxing other sectors to finance a subsidy for the polluting sector typically does create a deadweight loss. If the deadweight loss associated with general taxes is 25% of revenue raised by a tax, then financing a $1 subsidy to this polluting industry creates a deadweight loss of $0.25. If, instead, the polluting industry is taxed $1, and that tax revenue is transferred to general funds, then other taxes can be reduced by $1.00, saving society the deadweight loss of $0.25. Replacing a $1 pollution tax with a $1 abatement subsidy increases social costs by $0.50. Taxing pollution is likely more efficient than subsidizing abatement.

The Pigouvian tax equals the social marginal cost of pollution. Taking into account only the polluting sector, the Pigouvian tax is optimal. The previous example suggests that when we take into account the distortions associated with taxes in other sectors, the optimal pollution tax might be higher than the Pigouvian level. This possibility is known as the "double dividend hypothesis." A pollution tax lowers pollution (the first dividend) and by raising revenue, it allows the reduction of taxes in other sectors, lowering deadweight loss there (the second dividend). The Pigouvian tax addresses the goal of lowering pollution,

---

1 Taxes and subsidies change groups' income levels, possibly causing them to respond differently to the same price; a rich person consumes more first class airline tickets than does a poor person. The partial equilibrium model takes income as given and therefore excludes income effects. Section 10.3 takes up this point.

Behavioral economics studies show that people's reservation price for selling an item (their "willingness to accept") frequently exceeds their reservation price for buying the same item (their "willingness to pay"). People who run firms may exhibit similar asymmetry in preference, a type of "loss aversion," causing them to respond differently to pollution taxes and abatement subsidies. However, the logic of the marketplace encourages businesses to respond in the same way to the two policies.

but not the second dividend. Because the second dividend apparently increases the value of a pollution tax, the optimal tax may exceed the Pigouvian level. The double dividend hypothesis is closely related to the TOSB: distortions outside the targeted sector can change the optimal policy in the targeted sector.

A General Equilibrium Perspective*

A careful examination of the double dividend hypothesis requires taking into account multiple markets, using a general equilibrium setting. Research shows that the optimal pollution tax might be either higher or lower than the Pigouvian level, depending on modeling and parameter assumptions (Bovenberg and van der Ploeg 1994; Goulder 1995; and Bovenberg 1999). One piece of intuition suggests that the optimal pollution tax is less than the Pigouvian level, contrary to the double dividend hypothesis. The basis for the intuition is that a labor tax tends to be a less distortionary means of raising revenue than a commodity tax. Both types of taxes create distortions, but the labor tax is more diluted, because it affects production in many sectors, instead of only a few sectors, as with commodity taxes. A pollution tax is similar to a commodity tax (or equivalent to a commodity tax if pollution intensity is a constant) and commodity taxes are relatively inefficient means of raising revenue. Therefore, raising a pollution tax above the Pigouvian level (implicitly taxing the polluting commodity) may lower efficiency. In this case, the optimal pollution tax is less than the Pigouvian level.

9.4 Output and Input Subsidies

Objectives and skills: Understand why the optimal level of a policy depends on other policies, and why a sector might create negative value-added, even if profits in the sector are positive.

Subsidies create transfers and distortions. The transfers have equity implications, but only the distortions matter from the standpoint of efficiency. Using the leaky bucket metaphor, the distortion corresponds to leaks in the bucket, the distortionary cost is the amount of water that leaks out, and the transfer is the amount of water that reaches the recipient.

The TOSB reminds us that apparently unrelated policies might interact. The joint welfare consequence of policies can be greater or less than the sum of the welfare consequence of each policy in isolation. Many counties use both output and input subsidies, particularly in their agricultural sectors, so this combination of policies is empirically important. The output subsidy increases output, raising the use of most inputs. An input subsidy favors the use of the subsidized input. An output subsidy can magnify the distortionary cost of an input subsidy.

Subsidies can be explicit or implicit. Producers likely prefer implicit subsidies, because their lower visibility makes them easier to defend in the political arena. An explicit subsidy pays producers a subsidy per unit of output produced or input purchased, creating obvious transfers from taxpayers to producers. In contrast, a trade restriction raises domestic price by limiting cheaper imports, providing an implicit output subsidy and creating a transfer from consumers and/or taxpayers to domestic producers. Underpricing natural resource creates an implicit input subsidy. The full social marginal cost of water equals the cost of extracting and transporting the water plus its opportunity cost (see chapter 17). If the price farmers pay does not include water's opportunity cost, farmers receive an implicit water subsidy, creating a transfer from taxpayers and future water users to farmers. U.S. sugar producers receive implicit output subsidies in the form of import restrictions, and they receive implicit input subsidies in the form of underpriced water or unpriced pollution related to their water use.

A tax or subsidy drives a wedge between private and social marginal values (or prices). When a country can buy and sell a good at the world price = 1 (for simplicity) the social marginal value of domestic production of this good is 1: the amount saved by producing a unit domestically instead of buying it on the world market. If domestic producers receive a per-unit subsidy of s, the private value (to domestic producers) of a marginal unit of output of the good is $1 + s$. If the social marginal value (= social opportunity cost) of an input is p and producers receive a per-unit input subsidy ϕ, producers' private value of the input is $p - \phi$.

Suppose that sugar is produced using a fixed factor (land) and variable inputs (labor and water). The sector's "value-added" equals the social value of the sugar it produces minus the social cost of the water and labor it uses. The sector's profit (equivalently, the returns to the fixed factor, land) equals the private value of its output minus the private cost of the land and water it uses. When private and social costs are not equal, the social value-added and the private profits need not be equal. If the social value of inputs exceeds the social value of output, a sector creates negative value-added. A sector might create negative value-added even if private profits in the sector are positive.

Example

An example illustrates the interaction between output and input subsidies. A country can buy sugar at the world price, 1, and it can produce domestic sugar, S, using labor, L; water, W; and a fixed stock of land, F (having no other uses). The production function is $S = F^{1-\alpha-\beta} L^\alpha W^\beta$. There is free trade, so consumers pay the fixed world price, 1. Farmers receive an output subsidy, s, so they receive the price $1 + s$ per unit of output. The output subsidy creates an inefficiency, because it causes expensive domestic sugar to replace cheap foreign sugar. However, it does not affect consumer welfare, because the consumer price is fixed at 1 due to the assumption of free trade. The market for labor is efficient, with the price of labor equal to ω, its opportunity cost. The full social marginal cost of water is p, but producers receive a subsidy, ϕ, so their cost for a unit of water is $p - \phi$.

Price-taking farmers hire labor and buy water to maximize profits, π, equal to the difference between revenue and the payment for labor and water:

$$\pi(s,\phi) \equiv \max_{L,W} \left[\underbrace{(1+s)F^{1-\alpha-\beta}L^{\alpha}W^{\beta}}_{\text{farmer's revenue}} - \overbrace{(\omega L + (p-\phi)W)}^{\text{payments for labor and water}} \right]. \tag{9.2}$$

Profit equals the rent earned by owners of the fixed factor, F. The value-added, λ, from domestic sugar production is

$$\lambda(s,\phi) \equiv \left[\underbrace{F^{1-\alpha-\beta}L^{\alpha}W^{\beta}}_{\text{social value of production}} - \overbrace{(\omega L + pW)}^{\text{social cost of labor and water}} \right]. \tag{9.3}$$

The expressions for farmer profits and value-added differ, because (i) the farmer values a unit of output at $1+s$, whereas the value to society is 1, the cost of obtaining this unit from imports; and (ii) the farmer values a unit of water at $p-\phi$, whereas the cost of this unit to society is p. The difference between farmer profits and value-added equals the transfers from society to farmers:

$$\pi(s,\phi) - \lambda(s,\phi) \equiv \underbrace{sF^{1-\alpha-\beta}L^{\alpha}W^{\beta}}_{\text{transfer due to output subsidy}} + \underbrace{\phi W}_{\text{transfer due to input subsidy}}. \tag{9.4}$$

The output subsidy, s, encourages farmers to produce too much sugar, causing them to buy too much labor and water relative to the socially optimal level. The water subsidy causes farmers to buy too much water per unit of output. A higher output or water subsidy increases social loss, and the two subsidies reinforce each other: the distortion caused by the water subsidy is worse, the larger is the output subsidy. If both subsidies are zero, then the farmer faces the social prices, 1 and p. The farmer facing $s=0=\phi$, who chooses labor and water to maximize profits (equation 9.2) also maximizes value-added (= social surplus). Therefore, $\pi(0,0) = \lambda(0,0)$ is the socially optimal level of surplus for this sector. The subsidies benefit farmers and also change their input decisions, lowering social surplus: for positive s and/or positive ϕ:

$$\pi(s,\phi) > \pi(0,0) = \lambda(0,0) > \lambda(s,\phi).$$

The loss in social surplus, as a percentage of the optimal level, equals

$$\frac{\lambda(0,0) - \lambda(s,\phi)}{\lambda(0,0)} 100. \tag{9.5}$$

If value-added under the subsidies is negative ($\lambda(s,\phi) < 0$), then the loss in social surplus exceeds 100%; this sector creates negative value-added to society, even though farm profits are positive.

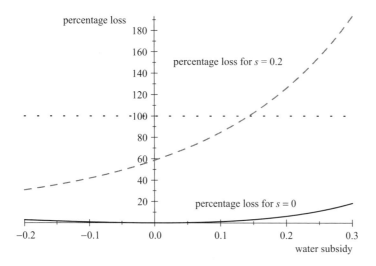

Figure 9.2
The percentage loss in surplus associated with the water subsidy, under a 20% ($s = 0.2$) and a 0% ($s = 0$) output subsidy. For water subsidy levels higher than the intersection of the loss curve and the flat line at 100%, the sector has negative value-added. The optimal water subsidy is 0 for $s = 0$ and negative (a tax) for $s = 0.2$. The figure uses parameter values $\alpha = 0.6$, $\beta = 0.2$, and $p = 1 = \omega$.

Figure 9.2 graphs the percent loss in surplus as a function of the water subsidy, for two values of the output subsidy, $s = 0$ and $s = 0.2$.[2] For combinations of s and ϕ resulting in a percentage loss above the dotted line (at 100%), the sugar sector creates negative value-added to society, although farmer profits are positive.

• For $s = 0$, the welfare cost (= loss in surplus) of the water subsidy is minimized at $\phi = 0$, where there are no distortions. The welfare cost rises slowly with the water subsidy: small subsidies create small losses.

• For $s = 0.2$, it is optimal to tax water; negative values of ϕ reduce the total welfare loss. For this example, the optimal water policy under $s = 0.2$ equals $\phi = -0.73$, a 73% tax. The welfare cost rises rapidly with the water subsidy; even a small water subsidy creates a large additional welfare loss.

• The welfare loss exceeds 100% if $\phi > 0.14$ and $s = 0.2$, or if $\phi > 0.5$ and $s = 0$. Water subsidies above these thresholds cause the sector to have negative value-added: the social value of inputs exceeds the social value of output.

2 Denote by $W(s, \phi)$ and $L(s, \phi)$ the equilibrium value of farm purchases of water and labor as functions of the two subsidies. We find these functions by solving (numerically) the first order conditions to the problem in equation 9.2. Substituting these functions into equation 9.3 gives the value of $\lambda(s, \phi)$. Evaluating this function at $s = 0 = \phi$ gives $\lambda(0, 0)$, a number. Using the function $\lambda(s, \phi)$ and the number $\lambda(0, 0)$ in expression 9.5, we obtain the percentage loss in social surplus, graphed in figure 9.2.

Figure 9.2 illustrates many of this chapter's themes. In the absence of an output subsidy, the optimal water subsidy is zero. However, if the output subsidy is fixed at a positive level, it is optimal to tax water use. That tax partly offsets the inefficiently high demand for inputs caused by the output subsidy. A small water subsidy creates only a small and slowly increasing (with ϕ) welfare loss if $s = 0$, but it create a large and rapidly increasing welfare loss if $s = 0.2$. Distortions can cause a sector to have negative value-added, even if the sector makes profits. In this case, profits consist entirely of transfers; because of the leaky bucket, producers receive less than the value lost to other agents in the economy. In this case, sugar production lowers social welfare: with $s = 0.2$ and $\phi > 0.14$, shutting down the industry raises social welfare, even though it idles cropland.

9.5   Policy Complements

Objectives and skills: Determine the socially optimal pollution tax when marginal costs increase with the level of pollution, and understand the distinction between policy complements and substitutes.

The TOSB reminds us that policies may have unexpected effects; the interactions among policies might also be surprising. Borrowing from demand analysis, we say that two policies are "substitutes" if the implementation of one makes the other less valuable to society; they are "complements" if the implementation of one makes the other more important. We look at an example where two policies that are often discussed as substitutes may in fact be complements. The setting uses increasing marginal pollution cost, thus relaxing one of the assumptions in section 9.2.

Policy Substitutes or Complements

Positive research spillovers arise if research conducted by one firm helps other firms. With positive spillovers, firms undertake less than the socially optimal level of research, creating a rationale for green industrial policy. Green subsidies are also often supported as a second-best alternative to politically infeasible carbon taxes. The American Enterprise Institute and the Brookings Institution, a conservative and a liberal think tank, respectively, both endorsed R&D subsidies for green technology as a substitute (or alternative) for taxes (Leonhardt 2012). These green policies subsidize firms for doing something socially useful (developing new technologies) instead of for refraining from doing something socially harmful (polluting); the policies therefore likely encounter less political resistance than an abatement subsidy. Chapter 8 shows that green industrial policies might aggravate the pollution problem. We use this result to show that instead of being a substitute for a carbon tax, green industrial policy might increase the social importance of a carbon tax: the policies may be complements (Winter 2014).

In a competitive fossil fuel sector (see equation 5.3), we have

$$p - \frac{\partial c(x, y)}{\partial y} = R, \text{ or } p = \underbrace{\frac{\partial c(x, y)}{\partial y} + R}_{\text{full private MC}}. \tag{9.6}$$

(Here we suppress time subscripts.) The second equality states that the equilibrium resource price equals the sum of marginal extraction cost and the opportunity cost ($= \text{rent} = R$) of extraction. Chapter 8 explains why green industrial policy might reduce rent, R.

Increasing Marginal Costs of Pollution

As with the example in section 9.2, we assume that 1 unit of production (here, extraction) creates 1 unit of pollution: reducing pollution requires a corresponding reduction in output. In the previous example, we took the marginal damage resulting from pollution to be a constant, but here we assume that marginal damage increases with the level of extraction. Extraction ($=$ emissions, by choice of units) of y creates damages equal to y^2, so marginal damages equal $2y$. To find the Pigouvian tax, we first identify the socially optimal level of extraction, denoted y_t^*; we achieve this by equating price to social marginal costs ($=$ marginal extraction costs plus the opportunity cost, R, plus marginal damage, $2y$), and solving for y. We then set the Pigouvian tax equal to the marginal damage, evaluated at socially optimal extraction: $2y^*$.

The Effect of Rent on the Pigouvian Tax

Figure 9.3 illustrates the case where the firm has constant marginal extraction costs, $\frac{\partial c(x, y)}{\partial y} = C$. Suppose that at some point in time the private combined marginal cost is $C + R = 10$, shown by the solid horizontal line in the figure. For our example, the social marginal cost equals the private marginal cost plus the (external) environmental marginal damage, $10 + 2y$. If a green industrial policy lowers resource rent by 5 units, the private combined marginal cost, and also the social marginal cost, falls by 5 units.

The upwardly sloping solid curve in figure 9.3 is the graph of $2y + C + R$, the full social marginal cost, equal to marginal damage plus the private cost. A 5-unit reduction in rent causes this combined social marginal cost to shift from the positively sloped solid line to the positively sloped dashed line. This reduction in social cost increases the socially optimal level of production from the intersection at point A to that at point B.

The reduction in rent decreases the combined social cost of extraction, thereby increasing the socially optimal level of extraction, thereby increasing marginal damages, which then increases the optimal tax. This result is general: where marginal damages increase with the level of extraction (or production), a decrease in firms' marginal cost leads to an increase in the optimal tax. With lower marginal cost, competitive firms produce more, and the higher production leads to higher marginal damages and a higher optimal tax.

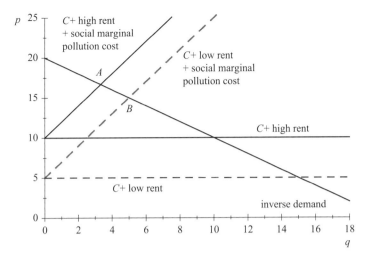

Figure 9.3
Socially optimal production occurs at A under high resource rent, and at B under low rent. The optimal tax equals the vertical distance from the production point to the private marginal cost plus rent. A fall in resource rent increases the optimal tax.

The Pigouvian tax causes firms to face the social cost of production, inducing firms to produce at the socially optimal level. If a firm faces a constant tax v and has private costs (inclusive of opportunity cost, its rent) equal to 10, its private cost equals social costs if and only if the tax equals the vertical distance from point A to 10. The Pigouvian tax equals this distance, which we denote v^A. If the firm's rent falls so that its rent-inclusive private cost now equals 5, the Pigouvian tax equals the vertical distance from point B to the horizontal dashed line; we denote this tax as v^B. It is apparent from the figure that $v^B > v^A$. The decrease in rent increases the optimal tax. In this case, an emissions tax and a rent-reducing green industrial policy are complements, not substitutes: the green industrial policy leads to a higher optimal tax.

The Algebra

Figure 9.3 uses the inverse demand (equal to the marginal benefit of consumption), $p = 20 - y$. The socially optimal level of production, y^*, equates the marginal benefit of consumption (the market price) to the full social cost of production, equal to the private cost, $C + R$, plus the externality cost, $2y$. This equality requires $20 - y = C + R + 2y$, or $y^* = \frac{20 - R - C}{3}$. A competitive firm facing the tax v produces where the price equals its private cost plus the tax, implying $20 - y = C + R + v$, or $y^{compet} = 20 - R - v - C$. The Pigouvian tax causes the competitive firm to produce at the socially optimal level, requiring $y^{compet} = y^*$, or $\frac{20 - R - C}{3} = 20 - R - v - C$, implying $v^{Pigouvian} = \frac{40}{3} - \frac{2}{3}R - \frac{2}{3}C$. A reduction in rent (leading to an outward shift in the firm's supply function) increases the

Pigouvian tax. In this example, green industrial policy lowers the resource rent, increasing the Pigouvian tax: the green industrial policy and the carbon tax are policy complements.

9.6 Politics and Lobbying

Objectives and skills: Understand the meaning of the collective action problem and illustrate the power of lobbying.

The TOSB is important because governments often use inefficient policies. The U.S. ethanol subsidy illustrates the role of lobbying. Policies emerge from a political process, sometimes influenced by lobbying or corruption. Lobbying does not imply corruption, but it influences outcomes. The Sunlight Foundation estimates that in the United States between 2007 and 2012, 200 companies spent $5.8 billion on lobbying and campaign contributions, and they received $4.4 trillion in federal support or contracts: $760 for each dollar contributed. Changes in U.S. law, notably the Supreme Court ruling in "Citizens United," make it easier to use money to influence outcomes. In 2014, Transparency International (www.transparency.org) ranked the United States as the seventeenth least-corrupt out of 175 countries.

The concept of a "collective action problem" helps in understanding political outcomes. A collective action is a costly action taken by a group for the benefit of that group. People prefer other members of their group to incur the costs, while they share the benefits. Society may impose a solution to this problem by forcing group members to contribute, provided that a sufficiently large fraction of the group has voted to do so. U.S. marketing orders, labor laws, and compulsory unitization of oil fields illustrate these procedures.

• The U.S. Agricultural Marketing Agreement Act of 1937 obliges producers to participate in marketing orders, which might require minimal quality levels (to maintain reputation), limited production (to maintain high prices), or fees (to pay for generic advertising).

• About half of U.S. states have laws requiring workers to pay union dues to a legally recognized union, on the ground that all workers benefit from union representation in their workplace.

• "Compulsory unitization" in the oil and gas industry enables a majority of producers extracting from a reservoir to require all producers in the reservoir to manage it for the common good (as if they were a single firm). This enforced agreement keeps firms from creating negative externalities for other producers in the field (e.g., by extracting too rapidly or sinking wells too closely together).

The constitutionality of both marketing orders and of mandatory union dues has been challenged in U.S. courts. Plaintiffs object, for example, that they do not share the goals of the marketing order or the union, and that their enforced participation deprives them of their property or their right of self-expression. What seems to one person to be a solution to the problem of collective action appears to another as an infringement on liberty.

Successful lobbying requires that groups sharing a common interest contribute to the lobbying effort. Producer groups are allowed to represent the industry's interests to legislators and can coordinate the individual firm's lobbying contributions. A narrowly defined group with strong mutual interests (e.g., firms in a sector threatened by pollution regulation) are in a better position to solve their collective action problem and be effective at lobbying compared to a larger group with more diffuse interests (e.g., citizens who might benefit from the regulation).

Renewable Fuel Standard and Waxman-Markey

In 2005 the U.S. introduced a Renewable Fuel Standard (RFS), requiring annual minimum consumption levels of different biofuels. The EPA implements the policy by estimating gasoline demand in the next year and dividing annual targets of the different biofuels by the estimated gasoline consumption to obtain a ratio, σ_i, for biofuel i. Gasoline producers are required to use σ_i gallons of biofuel i for each gallon of gasoline they produce. These producers face a "blending constraint" that increases their cost of production; biofuels are more expensive than gasoline.

Proponents of the RFS justify it using an "infant industry" argument, claiming that biofuels will eventually be important both as low-carbon alternatives to fossil fuels and as alternatives to foreign sources of petroleum. Because the current state of technology and infrastructure would not enable this industry to survive under market conditions, government policy is needed to protect this "infant" until it grows into a mature industry. Infant industry arguments go back at least to the early 1800s, when they were used to justify trade restrictions. Many opponents of the RFS begin as skeptics of the infant industry argument, because infants often fail to mature. The applicability of the infant industry argument is questionable here, because the RFS has promoted the production of corn-based ethanol, for which the technology was already mature (National Research Council 2011).[3]

The RFS emphasis on corn-based ethanol has three disadvantages in addition to having low potential to encourage new technology. First, it leads to a small (and by some estimates nonexistent) reduction in carbon emissions. Second, it diverts a major food crop from food to fuel, increasing food prices and worsening food insecurity in some parts of the world. Third, the policy encourages farmers to cultivate marginal land that would otherwise have been left fallow under a conservation program. The RFS creates large transfers from the general public (in the form of higher fuel prices) to corn growers, likely with little environmental or technological benefit. The RFS was estimated to increase U.S. fuel costs by $10 billion per year (Bryce 2015).

---

3 After 2015, ethanol produced using cellulosic material, including the inedible part of corn and special crops such as switchgrass, is scheduled to become more important in the RFS. Cellulosic biofuels rely on an immature technology, where government support can potentially lead to large improvements. However, the RFS's support for corn-based ethanol is unlikely to promote the development of cellulosic biofuels.

The (never-passed) Waxman-Markey bill (2009) would have imposed a cap on carbon emissions and required that fuels eligible for the RFS produce greater carbon reduction than had been achieved at the time. Thus, Waxman-Markey would have reduced the transfers that corn producers receive under the RFS. Representatives tend to vote their constituents' interest. Representatives from districts that benefit under the RFS were more likely to oppose Waxman-Markey, and they also received greater campaign contributions from groups opposing the bill. The cap and trade policy under Waxman-Markey would have reduced emissions more efficiently than the RFS does. The gains under the RFS are concentrated in a small number of districts, whereas the benefits of Waxman-Markey would have been widely dispersed. Lobbying opposed to Waxman-Markey received more financial support than did lobbying favoring the bill (Holland et al. 2015).

9.7   Summary

This chapter introduces the notion of a second-best policy or outcome: one that is not optimal, or first best. The Principle of Targeting (POT) recognizes the importance of carefully matching policies and objectives. A Pigouvian tax causes competitive firms to internalize an externality (e.g., to take into account the social cost of pollution) when making production decisions.

The Theory of the Second Best (TOSB) and the POT are deceptively simple ideas, with important economic implications. The TOSB reminds us that markets connect apparently unconnected outcomes or policies. A policy that reduces one market failure may, in the presence of a second market failure, actually lower welfare. We illustrated this result using an example of a monopoly that produces pollution; moving from the zero emissions tax to the Pigouvian tax might decrease social welfare. A policy that is optimal under perfect competition might be harmful under monopoly. In general, a change in market structure or in some (apparently) extraneous policy or distortion alters the effect of a pollution tax, altering the optimal level of that policy. The POT reminds us to beware of collateral damage and to attempt to match policies with targets (objectives). For example, a trade restriction is unlikely to be an optimal response to an environmental problem.

We provided different perspectives on the TOSB by means of three examples, in addition to the monopoly + pollution model.

• In the first example, raising government revenue by means of taxes outside the polluting sector creates a welfare loss, also known as a deadweight loss. A pollution tax or an abatement subsidy have (approximately) the same effect on incentives to pollute, but they have opposite effects on the amount of revenue that must be raised outside the polluting sector. When we take into account the distortions associated with taxes outside the polluting sector, the pollution tax is likely to be more efficient than an abatement subsidy, and the optimal pollution tax differs from the Pigouvian tax.

• The second example examined the relation between an output subsidy and an input subsidy arising from an underpriced natural resource input, such as water. An output subsidy can significantly increase the welfare cost of an input subsidy. If the output subsidy is fixed, but the input subsidy can be varied, it is (in our example) optimal to tax the input. The output subsidy encourages production, causing the sector to use too many resources; an input tax can partly offset that tendency, thereby improving welfare. In the presence of distortionary policies, a sector's social value-added can be negative, even though the sector generates profits for farmers; in this case, closing down the sector increases welfare.

• Our final example showed that a green R&D subsidy might increase the optimal pollution tax. In that circumstance, the R&D subsidy and the pollution tax are complements. Policy discussions sometimes treat the two policies as if they were substitutes.

9.8 Terms and Concepts, Study Questions, Exercises, and Sources

Terms and Concepts
Theory of the Second Best, Principle of Targeting, distortion, Pigouvian tax, a tax supports or induces an outcome, internalize an externality, collective action problem, value-added, Renewable Fuels Standard (RFS), deadweight loss, abatement, double dividend, increasing marginal pollution costs, policy complements and substitutes.

Study Questions
1. Use a graphical example (and a static model) to show that the Pigouvian tax that corrects a production-related externality (e.g., pollution) in a competitive setting might lower social welfare if applied to a monopoly.

2. You are in a conversation with someone who states that, in a particular market, international trade increases production in poorer countries with weaker environmental standards, thereby increasing a global pollutant (one that causes worldwide damage, not just damage in the location where production occurs). The person claims that a trade ban is a good remedy for this problem. Regardless of your actual views, use concepts from this chapter to discuss this person's proposal.

3. (a) Explain why a tax on pollution and a subsidy on abatement have the same effect on firms' incentives to pollute.

(b) Summarize the political and the economic reasons why in practice, an abatement subsidy and a pollution tax are likely to have different consequences for society.

4. Describe (in a few sentences) the double dividend hypothesis and the rationale for the hypothesis.

5. Explain the distinction between policy complements and substitutes. Discuss green industrial policy and carbon taxes as policy complements or substitutes.

6. Explain why an input subsidy causes a distortion. Explain why an output subsidy exacerbates the welfare loss due to the input subsidy.

7. Explain what it means to say that a sector has negative value-added. Explain why, in the presence of subsidies or other distortions, a sector might generate profits but have negative value-added.

Exercises

1. Inverse demand is $p = b(20 - q)$ (with $b > 0.4$), private average = marginal cost is $C = 2$, and environmental damage per unit of output is 6. Consumer welfare equals consumer surplus. Taxpayers benefit from tax revenue, and they do not like having to pay the cost of subsidies.

   (a) Write the price elasticity of demand, and describe the relation between b and this elasticity.

   (b) Find the optimal pollution tax for the competitive firm as a function of b. Why did we assume $b > 0.4$?

   (c) Find the optimal pollution tax under the monopoly as a function of b.

   (d) Graph the optimal taxes under competition and monopoly as functions of b. Describe these graphs in a few words. Provide an economic explanation for the relations between the optimal tax and the slope of the inverse demand function, under both a competitive firm and a monopoly.

2. Inverse demand is $10 - q$, firms are competitive with constant average = marginal costs C, and pollution-related damages (arising from output) are $q + \frac{1}{2}\beta q^2$, with $\beta > 0$. Assume $C < 9$.

   (a) What is marginal damage?

   (b) Find the socially optimal level of production and the Pigouvian tax under competition as functions of C and β. Why did we assume $C < 9$?

   (c) Determine the comparative statics of the Pigouvian tax with respect to both C and β

   (d) Provide the economic explanation for these comparative statics expressions.

3. Suppose that (private) constant marginal costs is C, each unit of pollution creates d dollars of social cost (external to the firm), and the inverse demand function is $p(q)$.

   (a) What is the optimal pollution tax for the competitive industry, and what is the socially optimal consumer price, p^*?

   (b) Express marginal revenue as a function of price and the elasticity of demand; use this formula to obtain the monopoly's first order condition when facing an arbitrary tax/subsidy.

(c) Evaluate the monopoly's first order condition at the socially optimal price, p^*, identified in part (a). From this equation, subtract the equation that determines the socially optimal price (price = full social marginal cost). Use the result to obtain a formula for the optimal tax under the monopoly. This formula is a function of the socially optimal price and the elasticity of demand at that price. This tax "supports" the socially optimal level of production, leading to the socially optimal consumer price.

(d) Now suppose that $p = q^{-1/\eta}$ with $\eta > 1$. Use your formula from part (c) to find the optimal tax/subsidy under the monopoly, as a function of the parameter η.

(e) Write the difference between the Pigouvian tax, ν^{compet}, and the tax/subsidy that suppors the optimal level of production under the monopoly. Provide an economic explanation for the role of η in this difference.

4. Assume the following: inverse demand in the polluting sector is $p = 20 - 3q$, private average = marginal cost is $C = 2$ in that sector, and environmental damage per unit of output is 6. In Scenario A, the government is able to raise revenue using nondistortionary taxes outside the polluting sector (e.g., by means of a lump-sum tax). In Scenario B, taxes outside the polluting sector are distortionary; every \$1 of tax revenue creates an aggregate loss to consumers and producers of \$1.10.

(a) Using the concepts developed in this chapter, describe (without math) the social incentives to tax production in the two scenarios, and explain how these differing incentives affect the relative magnitudes of the tax in the polluting sector in the two scenarios.

(b) Find the optimal tax for a competitive industry in Scenario A and in Scenario B. Scenario A should be familiar, but Scenario B is a bit different. For this scenario, proceed as follows. (1) Find the level of production, under competition, as a function of an arbitrary tax; denote this function as $q(\nu)$. (2) Recall that consumer surplus equals the area below the inverse demand function and above the price. Given the tax, ν, the price is $2 + \nu$ and the quantity sold is $q(\nu)$ (from step [1]). Use the formula for the area of a triangle to compute consumer surplus. (3) The tax revenue is $\nu \times q$, and you are told that the social value of the tax revenue is $1.1\nu \times q$. (4) Find the expression for environmental damage, using step (1). (5) Social surplus, $S(\nu)$, equals consumer surplus minus environmental damage plus the social value of tax revenue. (For this problem, where marginal cost is constant, producer surplus is always zero.) Using the previous steps, write the expression for social welfare, and maximize it with respect to ν. Check that the $S(\nu)$ is concave, so the first order condition gives a maximum, not a minimum.

Sources
Lipsey and Lancaster (1956) is the classic article on the TOSB.
  Okum (1975) is credited with the "leaky bucket" metaphor.

Fowlie (2009) and Holland (2012) provide recent applications of the TOSB related to environmental regulation.

Tritch (2015) discusses the statistics on U.S. lobbying provided by the Sunlight Foundation.

Auerbach and Hines (2002) survey the literature on taxation and efficiency.

Prakash and Potoski (2007) provide examples of collective action in environmental contexts.

Bovenberg and van der Ploeg (1994), Goulder (1995), and Bovenberg (1999) discuss the double dividend hypothesis.

Winter (2014) shows that carbon taxes and green industrial policy are likely to be policy complements.

Leonhardt (2012) describes the political popularity of green industrial policy.

Holland et al. (2015) study the political economy connections between the RFS and the Waxman-Markey bill.

The book written by a committee convened by the National Research Council (2011) discusses U.S. biofuels policy.

Bryce (2015) provides the estimated cost to motorists ($10 billion/year) of the RFS.

The USDA (2016) describes U.S. sugar policy.

10 Taxes: An Introduction

Objective
• Understand the principles of taxation.

Information and Skills
• Understand the meaning of tax incidence and of tax equivalence.
• Understand the relation between tax incidence and elasticities.
• Identify the welfare effects of taxes.
• Understand the relation between "cap and trade" and a pollution tax.

This chapter puts aside the reasons for government intervention to focus on some of the consequences of intervention. Governments use many policies other than taxes and their mirror image, subsidies. However, taxes are important in the policy landscape, and they are relatively easy to analyze. A few facts about the effects of taxes provide a background for studying other kinds of policy. We use a static (one-period) partial equilibrium supply and demand framework. Chapter 11 adapts these tools to study taxes applied to natural resources, where we need a dynamic (multiperiod) framework. We consider competitive "closed" markets: those without international trade in the taxed commodity, so domestic production equals domestic consumption. The model has three types of agents: consumers, producers, and taxpayers; many people belong to two or all three of these groups. Consumer surplus, producer surplus, and tax revenue measure these agents' surplus, and social welfare equals the sum of the three measures. Where we consider the reason for taxes, it is important to have a fourth component, such as pollution costs (as in equation 9.1).

A Road Map
Section 10.1 defines the terms "tax incidence" and "tax equivalence." The cost of a tax is borne not just by the person with the statutory obligation to pay it but also by people who buy from or sell to that person. The misconception that the economic cost of a tax can be limited to those with statutory obligation to pay for it is partly responsible for the popularity of the Polluter Pays Principle. Section 10.2 uses graphs and an algebraic example for a more formal discussion of tax incidence and equivalence.

Section 10.3 introduces a measure of the distortionary cost of a tax, the deadweight loss, already alluded to in section 9.3. The relations between the price elasticities of supply and demand, the tax incidence, and deadweight loss lead to rules of thumb for optimal tax policy. Section 10.4 discusses limitations of the static partial equilibrium model. A general equilibrium analysis shows how income effects and interactions with other markets modify insights from the partial equilibrium setting. A dynamic setting recognizes that short- and long-run elasticities can differ, complicating one of the rules of thumb.

Section 10.5 discusses cap and trade, and its relation to an emissions tax. Cap and trade is important in its own right, and it fits into a chapter on taxes for two reasons. First, under perfect competition and certainty, a cap and trade policy is equivalent to an emissions tax. Other types of policies can also be described by comparing them to taxes, although few other policies have the same tax equivalence. Second, the concept of tax incidence provides a means of estimating the fraction of pollution permits (under cap and trade) that would have to be given instead of sold to firms, so that regulation does not reduce producer surplus.

10.1   Tax Incidence and Equivalence

Objectives and skills: Understand the meaning of tax incidence and tax equivalence.

Most taxes are calculated on a unit or an ad valorem basis. Under a "unit tax," v, if the producer price is $\$p$, then the consumer price is $\$p + v$; the difference between these prices equals the unit tax. Under an "ad valorem tax," τ, if the producer price is $\$p$, then the consumer price is $\$(1 + \tau)p$; the ratio of these prices equals 1 plus the ad valorem tax. The two taxes have a simple relation. If producers receive the price p and one group of consumers pays a unit tax, v, while another group of consumers pays an ad valorem tax, τ, the two groups pay the same price if $p + v = (1 + \tau)p$, or $v = \tau p$. We can work with either type of tax; hereafter, we use a unit tax.

We assume that people are rational in the sense that their willingness to buy a commodity depends on the price they pay, not on how the price is calculated. A rational consumer is as likely to buy a commodity priced at $1.10 "out the door" as a commodity marked at $1.00 that requires payment of a 10% sales tax at the cash register. In both cases, the final price equals $1.10. People sometimes react differently in these two settings, possibly because the extra 10 cent cost is more salient (noticeable) in the first case (Chetty, Looney, and Kraft 2009).

Tax Incidence and Tax Equivalence

In a "closed economy" (no international trade) it does not matter whether consumers or producers have the statutory obligation to pay the tax. The equilibrium price and quantity, and thus the consumer and producer surplus and the tax revenue, are the same regardless of whether the tax is levied on consumers or producers: consumer and producer taxes are "equivalent." The concept of "tax incidence" clarifies the reason for tax equivalence. Suppose that without a tax, the equilibrium price is $12. Does a $2 tax levied on consumers mean that their tax-inclusive price rises to $12 + $2 = $14? In general, the answer is "no." The tax increases the price consumers pay, thereby (typically) reducing the quantity they purchase. The reduction in sales moves producers down their supply curve, reducing the price they receive. The consumer tax incidence equals the increase in the price consumers pay, as a percentage (or fraction) of the tax; the producer tax incidence equals the decrease in price producers receive, as a percentage (or fraction) of the tax.

If the $2 tax causes the tax-inclusive price that consumers face to rise from $12 to $13.50, then the price that producers receive equals $13.5 − $2 = $11.5, because the difference between consumer and producer price equals the unit tax. Consumers pay the share

$$\frac{\$13.5 - \$12}{\text{tax}} = \frac{\$1.5}{2} = \$0.75,$$

and producers pay the remaining share, $0.25. Consumers' tax incidence is 75%, and the producers' tax incidence is 25%. The tax incidence does not depend on which agent has the statutory obligation to pay the tax, because in a closed economy, domestic production equals domestic consumption; it is not possible to change one without an equal change in the other. (Appendix C.1 shows that this equivalence does not hold in an open economy.)

The Polluter Pays Principle

The "Polluter Pays Principle" states that polluters, instead of those who suffer from pollution (the "pollutees") should pay the cost of pollution. If production causes pollution, the Principle implies that tax should be levied on production, not consumption. The equivalence of producer and consumer taxes (in a closed economy) undercuts this Principle. The special case where the pollution intensity is fixed and marginal pollution damage is a constant (as in section 9.2) makes this point obvious. If a unit of production creates $2 worth of environmental damage, external to the firm, the optimal tax is $2. In view of the equivalence of a producer and consumer tax, it does not matter whether this tax is levied on producers or consumers. The levels of producer and consumer surplus, environmental damage, and tax revenue are the same under either form of the tax. It also does not matter which agent is responsible for the environmental damage; in this case, the polluter-pollutee distinction is meaningless. If pollution arises from consumption of a good or service, instead of production, a tax equal to marginal social environmental damage, levied on either production or consumption, achieves efficiency. The larger point is that an environmental (or any other) policy that raises costs affects many agents, not only those directly responsible for paying the higher costs.

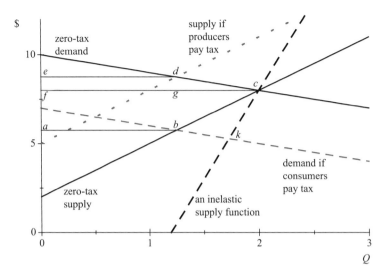

Figure 10.1
Zero-tax supply and demand functions and the (dashed and dotted) supply and demand functions (through points b and d) when consumers or producers have the statutory obligation to pay the tax. The two taxes are equivalent. The steep supply function through k is discussed in section 10.3.

10.2   A Graphical and Algebraic Perspective

Objectives and skills: Identify the effect of a tax on price and output, and confirm the equivalence of consumer and producer taxes.

For rational agents, consumer and producer taxes are equivalent in a closed economy. Figure 10.1 shows demand and (marginal cost =) supply curves without taxes; the equilibrium price and quantity is at point c, where consumers and producers face the same price. Once we introduce a tax, the consumer and producer prices are different, so we can no longer use the same axis to measure both prices. We have to be clear about what the vertical axis now measures. Suppose that we introduce a consumer unit tax of v. We continue to let the vertical axis be the price that producers receive and to denote the producer price by p. Therefore, the tax does not alter the location of the supply curve. The tax causes the consumer price to be $p + v$. The original demand function shows the relation between quantity demanded and the price that consumers pay. However, the vertical axis now represents the price that producers receive.

Because the price that consumers pay and the price that producers receive are not the same when a tax is imposed, we cannot use the original demand function to read off the quantity demanded for an arbitrary producer price. Supply is a function of p and demand is a function of $p + v$, and we cannot let one axis represent both these values. This difficulty is easily resolved. The demand function when consumers pay the tax v equals the original demand function, shifted down by the magnitude v, leading to the dashed demand function in figure 10.1. The vertical distance between the original demand function and the demand function under the tax is v. This "new" demand function shows demand as a function of producer instead of consumer price.

The intersection of the original supply function and the new demand function occurs at point b, showing the equilibrium quantity and producer price under the tax. The equilibrium consumer price (at point d) equals the producer price plus v. Denote the distance between any two points x and y as $\|xy\|$. The tax increases the consumer price by $\|gd\|$ and decreases the producer price by $\|bg\|$. The sum of these two changes is $\|bd\| = v$. The consumer and producer taxes incidences are $\frac{\|gd\|}{v} \times 100\%$ and $\frac{\|bg\|}{v} \times 100\%$.

If producers instead of consumers bear the statutory obligation for the tax, then the vertical axis represents the price consumers pay. Now the tax does not change the demand function, but it causes the supply function to shift up by v units to the dotted supply function. It is apparent from figure 10.1 that the equilibrium quantity and the tax-inclusive consumer and producer prices are the same, regardless of which agent has the statutory obligation to pay the tax: the taxes are equivalent (see appendix C.2).

Algebraic Example

Inverse demand is $p = 10 - Q$, and marginal cost (= inverse supply) is $MC = 2 + 3Q$. With no tax, supply = demand implies the equilibrium price $p^* = 8$ and the equilibrium quantity $Q^* = 2$. If consumers have the statutory obligation to pay a unit tax $v = 3$, inverse demand, written as a function of the producer price, p, shifts to $10 - Q - 3$ (because consumers have to pay $p + 3$); the supply function is unchanged, so equilibrium occurs where $10 - Q - 3 = 2 + 3Q$, implying the equilibrium quantity $Q = 1.25$, the producer price $2 + 3(1.25) = 5.75$, and the consumer tax-inclusive price $10 - 1.25 = 8.75$. The consumer tax incidence is $\frac{8.75-8}{3}100 = 25\%$, and the producer tax incidence is $\frac{8-5.75}{3}100 = 75\%$.

If producers have the statutory obligation to pay the tax, inverse demand (as a function of the consumer price) remains at $p = 10 - Q$, but the supply curve shifts to $S = 2 + 3Q + 3$ (because producers deduct the tax from the payment they receive from consumers). Setting demand equal to supply gives $10 - Q = 2 + 3Q + 3$, or $Q = 1.25$, as above. The consumer and producer prices, and therefore the tax incidences, are also the same.

10.3   Tax Incidence and Deadweight Loss

Objectives and skills: Understand the relation between tax incidence and welfare, and the effect of supply and demand elasticities on tax incidence and deadweight loss.

In figure 10.1, the loss in producer surplus due to the tax equals the rectangle *abgf* plus the triangle *bcg*; the loss in consumer surplus equals the rectangle *fgde* plus the triangle *dcg*. Tax revenue equals the rectangle *abde*. The producer's rectangle, *abgf*, as a share of the larger rectangle, *abde*, equals the ratio of the sides of the rectangles, $\frac{\|bg\|}{v}$, which equals the producer incidence; the producer's triangle, bcg, as a share of the larger triangle bcd also equals this ratio. Therefore, the reduction in producer surplus, as a share of the reduction in consumer + producer surplus, equals the producer's tax incidence. If the demand or supply function is not linear, then the "triangles" are only approximately triangular, and the incidences are only approximations of the producer and consumer share of combined loss.

To calculate the tax incidence, we need to know the price with and without the tax. We can use supply and demand price elasticities to approximate the tax incidence for small taxes. The price elasticity of supply, θ, and of demand, η, evaluated at the equilibrium price in the absence of a tax, are

$$\theta = \frac{dS(p)}{dp}\frac{p}{S}, \quad \text{and} \quad \eta = -\frac{dD(p)}{dp^c}\frac{p}{D}. \tag{10.1}$$

The change in equilibrium producer price (a decrease) due to a small tax is

$$\frac{dp}{dv} = -\frac{1}{\frac{\theta}{\eta}+1}. \tag{10.2}$$

(See appendix C.3.) Equation 10.2 is a comparative static expression (section 2.2). The change in the equilibrium consumer price, $p + v$, is

$$\frac{d(p+v)}{dv} = \frac{1}{\frac{\eta}{\theta}+1}. \tag{10.3}$$

Equations 10.2 and 10.3 show that the tax's effect on the producer and consumer prices depends on the ratio of elasticity of supply and demand. If demand is relatively elastic compared to supply ($\frac{\eta}{\theta}$ is very large, and $\frac{\theta}{\eta}$ very small), then the tax has negligible effect on the consumer price, but a large effect on producer price. In this case, producers bear most of the tax incidence. If the elasticity of supply is large relative to demand, the effect is reversed. The formulae for tax incidence are

$$\text{producers' approx. tax incidence} = \frac{1}{\frac{\theta}{\eta}+1}100, \text{ and}$$

$$\text{consumers' approx. tax incidence} = \frac{1}{\frac{\eta}{\theta}+1}100. \tag{10.4}$$

A lower elasticity of supply corresponds to a steeper supply function and a larger producer tax incidence. Figure 10.1 shows a less elastic supply curve through point k, intersecting the original equilibrium, at point c: absent a tax, the equilibrium is the same for both supply functions. You should identify the equilibrium quantity and the consumer and producer prices under the tax, to show that the less elastic supply curve increases the producer incidence of the tax. Similarly, smaller values of η mean that demand is less elastic, implying a steeper inverse demand function and a higher consumer tax incidence. By rotating the demand function around point c, you can visualize the effect of making demand less elastic.

In the model discussed here, social welfare is the sum of producer and consumer surplus and tax revenues. The reduction in social welfare, due to moving from a zero tax to a positive tax, equals the reduction in consumer and producer surplus, minus the increase in the tax revenue. In figure 10.1, this net loss equals the triangle bcd, society's deadweight loss (DWL) of the tax. For small taxes, the distortionary cost of the tax is small relative to the transfer from consumers and producers to taxpayers. (Triangles are small relative to rectangles.) In the case of linear supply and demand functions, the DWL is literally a triangle (known as the "Harberger triangle"). For general supply and demand functions, the approximate DWL is (see appendix C.4)

$$DWL \approx \left(\frac{1}{2 \left(\frac{1}{\theta} + \frac{1}{\eta} \right)} \frac{Q}{P} \right) v^2. \tag{10.5}$$

Formula 10.5 shows the following results:

Result (1). The approximate DWL is proportional to the square of the tax.

Result (2). The deadweight loss is lower, the smaller is the elasticity of supply or demand.

Not surprisingly, the DWL is zero for a zero tax and increases with the magnitude of the tax; the important point is that the DWL increases faster than the tax (Result [1]). Figure 10.2 illustrates the convex relation between the DWL and the tax.[1] Result (1) implies that it is efficient to use a broad tax basis. For example, we may be able to raise the same amount of revenue by using a tax $\frac{v}{2}$ in each of two markets, instead of a tax of v in a single market. Denote the term in parenthesis in equation 10.5 as X. If X is the same for both markets in our example, then the deadweight loss of using the tax v in one market is approximately Xv^2, whereas the deadweight loss of using $\frac{v}{2}$ in the two markets is approximately $2 \times X \left(\frac{v}{2} \right)^2 = \frac{X}{2} v^2$. For this example, doubling the tax base reduces the deadweight loss by 50%.

Result (2) implies that, other things equal, the deadweight loss of a tax is lower, the smaller is either the elasticity of supply or demand. Where there are no market failures, the zero-tax competitive equilibrium is efficient, maximizing the sum of consumer surplus, producer surplus, and tax revenue ($= 0$ under a zero tax). A positive tax increases tax

1 A negative tax is a subsidy. Figure 10.2 shows that the DWL is symmetric around $v = 0$. Both taxes and subsidies create inefficiencies.

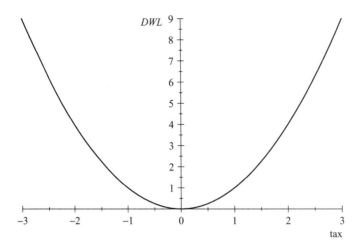

Figure 10.2
Graph of the approximation of deadweight loss.

revenue (from zero) but leads to a larger reduction in the sum of producer and consumer surplus, lowering social surplus. The efficiency loss occurs because the tax reduces the equilibrium quantity of supply and demand. The less elastic is supply and/or demand, the smaller is this reduction in equilibrium quantity, and the smaller is the loss in social surplus. If the elasticity of either supply or demand is zero, the tax has no effect on equilibrium quantity, and no effect on social surplus, so the deadweight loss is zero. In this case, the tax merely distributes surplus from consumers or producers to taxpayers: the tax creates a transfer, but not an efficiency cost.

The two results above imply the two rules of thumb:

Rule 1. It is better to have a broad tax base (i.e., tax many instead of few goods).

Rule 2. It is better to tax goods that have lower elasticity of supply or demand.

A third rule states: It is better to tax "bads," such as pollution, rather than "goods," such as labor or investment. Many taxes ignore these rules.

10.4   A Closer Look at Welfare

Objectives and skills: Understand some of the complications arising when we consider the reasons for the tax, general equilibrium effects, and the difference between short- and long-run elasticities.

A static partial equilibrium static setting that ignores the reasons for the tax simplifies the presentation but obscures some important issues. We discuss some of those issues here.

The Importance of General Equilibrium

The partial equilibrium setting uses three agents—consumers, producers, and tax payers—and it uses the loss in producer surplus to measure the tax's effect on producers. However, owners of the firm typically bear only a fraction of the reduction in producer surplus. When the firm reduces supply, it also reduces demand for inputs, including labor. If the fall in demand reduces the wage or aggregate employment, then the tax also reduces workers' welfare; if it reduces the price or aggregate demand for other inputs, producers of those inputs may also be harmed. Factors of supply bear some of the cost of commodity taxes. The general equilibrium setting recognizes these and many other indirect effects, which the partial equilibrium framework ignores.

Some taxes are directly levied on commodities, and others on factors of supply, such as labor. The partial equilibrium framework implies that if the elasticity of supply (of the commodity or the factor directly taxed) is zero, then producers or factor owners bear the entire tax incidence, and the deadweight loss is zero. In this case, the tax shifts welfare from producers or factor owners to taxpayers but causes no efficiency loss. Unimproved land is the classic example of a factor with zero elasticity of supply. Henry George, a nineteenth-century political economist, proposed a single tax on unimproved land; partial equilibrium reasoning suggests that this tax causes no efficiency loss.

A general equilibrium setting recognizes that this conclusion is likely too optimistic, because markets for different products or factors are linked. If landowners also supply farm labor, the land tax lowers their income and wealth. If the tax-induced reduction in income causes farmers to work harder (to make up for lost income), the change in labor supply alters the level and equilibrium price of the output. The tax-induced reduction in farmers' wealth might also induce them to rebuild their wealth by accumulating more capital. The higher stock of capital increases labor's marginal productivity, increasing the equilibrium wage and lowering the return to capital. The changes in these factor prices shift the tax incidence to factor owners (benefiting workers and harming capitalists in this scenario). If the revenue from the land tax is given to workers, their higher income might cause them to supply less labor, increasing the equilibrium wage (Feldstein 1977).

Using consumer surplus to measure the change in consumer welfare is also problematic. Consumer theory recognizes that a change in the price of a commodity causes both a substitution and an income effect. Consumer surplus ignores these complications and provides an exact measure of consumer welfare only under restrictive assumptions.

Reasons for the Tax

Our discussion in this chapter ignores the reason for the tax and also assumes that the welfare gain arising from the tax equals the tax revenue. Chapter 9 notes that the Pigouvian tax corrects an externality, increasing welfare. If consumers benefit from lower pollution, that benefit offsets their lower consumer surplus. Here, using the change in consumer surplus to measure the change in consumer welfare overstates the cost of the tax to consumers.

Table 10.1
U.S. estimates of marginal excess burden

Income tax	Payroll tax	Consumer sales tax	Property tax	Capital tax	Output tax
50%	38%	26%	18%	68%	21%

Source: Based on Conover (2010).

The tax collected in a particular sector makes it possible to reduce taxes in other sectors without reducing government expenditures. By setting the welfare benefit of the tax in a particular sector equal to the tax revenue collected there (the rectangle *abde* in figure 10.1), we implicitly assume that the taxes in other sectors have no distortionary cost. If, as is more likely, taxes raised in other sectors create a welfare cost, then reducing taxes there creates an additional welfare gain (see section 9.3); here, the welfare gain of the tax we analyze exceeds the rectangle *abde*.

General Equilibrium Estimates of Welfare Loss
The general equilibrium efficiency costs cannot be described by a simple formula, but they can be estimated using numerical "computable general equilibrium" (CGE) models. These models have one or more utility-maximizing representative consumers, and two or more sectors in which representative firms maximize profits. CGE models avoid the simplifying assumptions of partial equilibrium models, but they are complex, and they require other assumptions that may be hard to understand. This lack of transparency is important, because the model results can be used to promote a political agenda. Despite this caveat, CGE estimates of the effects of taxes provide a useful perspective.

Table 10.1 shows CGE-based estimates, for several U.S. taxes, of the "marginal excess burden," defined as the additional loss in welfare (measured in dollars), as a percentage of additional tax revenue.[2] The property tax has the lowest excess burden, consistent with the low elasticity of supply of land.

The large number of disparate CGE efficiency estimates, and the difficulty of understanding exactly why a particular model yields a particular estimate, makes it hard to assess the efficiency cost of taxes for the economy as a whole.

Time Consistency
Putting aside the general equilibrium complications, the partial equilibrium analysis has a simple and powerful policy message: the deadweight loss associated with taxes is lower, the lower is the elasticity of supply or demand associated with the taxed product or factor. The difference between short- and long-run elasticities complicates this message.

---

2 The marginal excess burden exceeds the "average excess burden" (defined as the welfare cost per unit of tax revenue) if the percentage increase in deadweight cost, due to a higher tax, exceeds the percentage increase in tax revenue. This condition likely holds.

To illustrate, suppose that the government can use a combination of capital and labor taxes. The government wants to minimize the deadweight loss associated with the taxes, while raising a certain amount of tax revenue in each period. Investment takes time; the current stock of capital depends on previous, not on current, investment, so the supply of capital is quite inelastic in the short run; current capital taxes create little deadweight loss. This observation implies that most of the revenue in the current period should be raised using a capital tax. However, the future stock of capital depends on current investment, which depends on beliefs about future capital taxes. This fact causes the future stock of capital to be sensitive to expectations of future capital taxes.

If the policymaker today can make a binding commitment to the time profile of taxes, she would like to raise most of current revenue using a capital tax but promise to use a low future capital tax (Judd 1985; Straub and Werning 2015). The current labor tax can therefore be low, but the future labor tax must be high to raise the required amount of revenue in each period. The time consistency problem is that "once the future arrives, it has become the present." The policymaker in the future has the same incentives as the policymaker today. She would like to raise the required amount of revenue with little deadweight loss and therefore does not want to implement the program announced earlier. If today's planner cannot bind planners in the future to carry out the program that she wants to use, that program is not credible; investors would not believe that they will face low capital taxes in the future, reducing their incentive to invest and creating an additional distortion.

10.5   Taxes and Cap and Trade

Objectives and skills: Understand the ingredients of a cap and trade policy, its relation to an emissions tax, and how to estimate the fraction of permits that have to be grandfathered to compensate firms.

Emissions taxes and cap and trade are market-based environmental policies. "Command and control" policies, in contrast, reduce emissions by mandating certain types of technology or production methods. Market-based policies likely reduce emissions more cheaply compared to command and control policies (Fowlie, Holland, and Mansur 2012). By the end of 2014, there were almost 50 carbon markets worldwide, the largest being the European Union's Emissions Trading Scheme (EU ETS) (World Bank 2014c). Southern California's trading scheme for NO_x, RECLAIM, has operated since 1994. The (never passed) 2009 Waxman-Markey bill envisioned setting up a U.S. market for carbon emissions. Environmental reform requires people to change their behavior, usually imposing a cost.

Under cap and trade, the government announces a pollution ceiling (the cap), and requires that firms have one "pollution permit" for each unit of emissions; the aggregate number of permits equals the cap. The permits might be given (grandfathered) to firms, or firms might be required to purchase them from the government.[3] Firms are allowed to trade permits, causing permit *use* (= emissions, determined via the market) to differ from permit *allocation* (determined by grandfathering). The market price for permits depends on magnitude of the cap (= supply of permits) and on firms' cost of reducing emissions (= demand for permits). Higher abatement costs make firms willing to pay more for an emissions certificate, shifting out the demand and increasing the equilibrium price. A higher cap shifts out the supply, reducing the equilibrium price.

In equilibrium, firms are indifferent between buying an additional permit certificate, which allows them to produce another unit of emissions, or incurring the marginal abatement cost to reduce emissions by one unit. This indifference does not depend on whether firms are given or must buy permits. Consequently, the equilibrium permit price does not depend on whether permits are given away or sold. (Appendix C.5 explains these claims more thoroughly.) Because all firms face the same permit price, and all reduce emissions to the point where marginal abatement costs equal the permit price, all firms have the same equilibrium level of marginal abatement costs; therefore, a cap and trade policy leads to an efficient allocation across firms of the allowed level of pollution.[4] The market minimizes the aggregate cost of achieving a given level of abatement.

Giving (instead of selling) firms pollution permits lowers their cost of complying with the regulation. Firms facing the prospect of cap and trade want to persuade legislators to grandfather a large share of permits. Politicians may be generous, to mute firms' opposition to the environmental regulation. The Waxman-Markey bill proposed giving businesses a declining (over time) share of the permit allowance; economists discussed whether that plan would hand firms a windfall. Generous grandfathering in the EU ETS may have increased polluting firms' profits (Sijm, Neuhoff, and Chen 2006; Hintermann 2015). When does grandfathering merely cushion businesses from a loss of profits due to regulation, and when is it a windfall? Let us first answer a different, simpler question and then explain why that answer also answers the first question.

The simpler question is "Under a tax v, what fraction of tax revenue would the government have to return to firms, to make firms approximately as well off under the tax as they were before the tax?" The discussion in section 10.3 notes that the reduction in producer surplus in figure 10.1 equals the tax revenue times the producer incidence, plus the triangle bcg. Therefore, if firms are given the share of tax revenue equal to the producer

---

3 Grandfathering refers to the practice of exempting certain groups from a new rule or law. The term originated during the late nineteenth century when Southern states created voting obstacles (such as literacy tests) to disenfranchise black citizens. White voters were exempt from these obstacles if their grandfather had voted.

4 If firms' future permit allocations are positively related to their current emissions, then firms have a strategic incentive to increase their emissions in order to increase future allocations. With this strategic incentive, the market does not achieve the efficient allocation across firms of the aggregate level of emissions. Regulators are aware of this possibility and try to design allocation schemes to reduce or avoid strategic behavior.

tax incidence, plus a bit more to make up for the triangle, then firms are as well off as they were without the tax.

To apply this answer to our original question, we use the fact that taxes and quotas are equivalent, in a particular sense. A cap establishes a limit on pollution; trade in permits leads to a price for permits. There is a quota-equivalent tax that results in the same level of pollution as does the cap. This quota-equivalent tax equals the equilibrium price of permits under cap and trade. For example, suppose that if regulators set a cap of 1.25 units of emissions, the equilibrium price of an emissions permit is $3.00. The quota-equivalent tax is $3.00; if regulators impose this tax instead of using a cap, firms respond by emitting 1.25 units. This result implies that the value of quota rents (= number of quotas × price per quota, $1.25 \times 3.00 = 3.75$ for our example) equals the value of tax revenue (= amount of pollution × tax level).[5] Grandfathering the (arbitrary) fraction s of permits is equivalent to giving firms the fraction s of quota rents, which in turn is equivalent to giving them the fraction s of tax revenue under the quota-equivalent tax.

We showed above that giving firms the fraction of tax revenue equal to the producer tax incidence makes them almost as well off under the tax as they were without the tax. We then showed that grandfathering firms the (arbitrary) fraction s of quotas is equivalent to giving firms the fraction s of tax revenue, under the quota-equivalent tax. Putting together these two observations, we conclude that grandfathering firms the fraction of quotas equal to the producer tax incidence (under the quota-equivalent tax), makes firms almost as well off as they would be without regulation. If firms are grandfathered a slightly higher share of quotas (to make up the triangle bcg), then the regulation does not reduce their surplus.

It is worth repeating two assumptions that underlie this analysis. First, the economy is closed. To the extent that the policy affects electricity generators, the closed economy assumption is reasonable for both the United States and the European Union, where there is little external trade in electricity. To the extent that the policy affects producers of carbon-intensive traded goods, the closed-economy assumption is inappropriate. Domestic regulation may have little effect on the price at which the country can buy or sell carbon-intensive traded goods. In this case, producers face a very elastic excess demand function, defined as the horizontal difference between the domestic demand function and the rest-of-world supply function. Domestic producers therefore bear nearly the entire incidence of the regulation. Regulation harms these firms, even if the regulator grandfathers all

---

5 Using figure 10.1 and the assumption that one unit of output creates one unit of pollution, a pollution cap of 1.25 (the horizontal coordinate of point b) leads to output 1.25. If this level of pollution (= output) is enforced by the cap 1.25, the resulting quota price equals $\|bd\|$, the distance between firms' marginal production cost (at $Q = 1.25$) and the market price. Firms would pay $\|bd\|$ to obtain an additional pollution permit, because that permit enables them to produce an additional unit. The profit made on that additional unit is the difference between the output price (at point d) and marginal cost (at point b). The tax that supports output (= pollution) at 1.25 equals $v = \|bd\|$. Thus, $\|bd\|$ is the quota-equivalent tax for the quota 1.25.

permits.[6] The second assumption is that pollution is proportional to output. More realistically, taxes change the pollution intensity, so there a difference between an output tax and a pollution tax. The analysis is more complicated in this case, but the insights obtained here are still relevant.

Testing Efficiency by Using a Natural Experiment

Earlier in the section, it was asserted that rationality implies that firms' equilibrium level of emissions depends on the permit price but not on the number (possibly zero) of permits that the firm receives for free (their permit allocation). Consequently, in a well-functioning market, the permit price does not depend on this allocation. Therefore, cap and trade leads to equality across firms' marginal abatement costs, independently of the permit allocation: cap and trade is an efficient means of reducing pollution.

How might we test whether this efficiency hypothesis is correct? We can imagine randomly assigning firms different allocations of permits. If the hypothesis is correct, then a firm's allocation of permits has no effect on its pollution: firms' pollution levels should be uncorrelated with their allocations. If, in our experiment, the correlation between allocations and emissions is not significantly different from zero, we fail to reject the efficiency hypothesis; if the correlation is significantly different from zero, we reject the efficiency hypothesis.

If all firms had the same allocation of permits, it would be impossible to learn anything about the effect of that allocation on their emissions decisions. However, in practice firms often receive different levels of permit allocations. It might be tempting to test our hypothesis by computing the correlation between observed allocations and firms' pollution levels, and then testing whether that correlation is significantly different than zero. However, that procedure is not valid, because in the real world, permit allocation is not random. (See exercise 6.3 for an example of problems arising when the sample is not random.) Firms that emitted more in the past typically receive higher allowances. Moreover, the characteristics (e.g., old technology) that caused firms to be high emitters in the past also tend to make them high emitters in the future. Therefore, the assignment of allowances on the basis of historical emissions creates a positive correlation between allowances and emissions. That correlation sheds no light on the efficiency hypothesis.

A "natural experiment" (section 6.1) uses a setting with a degree of randomness that makes it possible to treat real-world data (almost) as if it were experimental data.

---

6 If the regulation shifts supply from domestic (regulated) sources to foreign (unregulated) sources without altering price (and therefore without affecting aggregate supply), regulation shifts production, and pollution, from the domestic economy to the rest of the world. In this case, some of the domestic pollution reduction achieved by the regulation "leaks" outside the country's borders. This pollution shift is known as "leakage" in general, and as "carbon leakage" in the case of climate regulation. If foreign production methods are more carbon-intensive than domestic methods, the shift in supply might increase the aggregate amount of pollution. In this case, regulation can increase global pollution: leakage can exceed 100%.

California's RECLAIM emissions trading program randomly assigned firms to different "permit allocation cycles," which allocated allowances at different times during the year; these two cycles tended to have different size allocations. Similar firms randomly assigned to different groups therefore tended to receive different levels of allowances. By controlling for observed firm characteristics, the (limited) randomness in assignment of allowances, arising from genuine randomness in assignment to an allocation cycle, makes it possible to statistically test the efficiency hypothesis. These tests fail to reject the efficiency hypothesis (Fowlie and Perloff 2013).

10.6 Summary

Environmental and resource economists are usually interested in taxes or subsidies as a means of correcting a market failure. This chapter puts aside those considerations in order to examine taxes' price and welfare effects. Taxes typically change equilibrium price and quantity, creating a deadweight loss to society. The partial equilibrium measure of a tax's deadweight loss equals the reduction in the sum of consumer and producer surplus, minus the tax revenue. The consumer incidence of the tax equals the increase in the price that consumers pay, expressed as a percentage of the tax. The producer incidence equals the reduction in the price that producers receive, expressed as a percentage of the tax. These incidences approximately equal producers' and consumers' share of the combined reduction in producer + consumer welfare. In a closed economy (no international trade), it does not matter whether the tax is imposed on consumers or on producers; the two taxes are equivalent. In some settings, it does not matter whether the polluter or the pollutee directly pays the tax; their actual cost is the same. Producers and consumers typically share the burden of a regulation that increases production costs.

A higher demand elasticity lowers the consumer incidence. A higher supply elasticity lowers the producer incidence. The deadweight loss of a tax is approximately proportional to the square of the tax. Therefore, a given tax increase, beginning with a low tax, causes a small increase in deadweight loss; the same magnitude of tax increase, beginning with a large tax, causes a large increase in deadweight loss. The deadweight loss might be a significant fraction of tax revenue and can therefore significantly reduce the potential social benefit arising from a program that requires additional tax revenue. A smaller elasticity of supply or a smaller elasticity of demand both reduce a tax's deadweight loss.

Three rules of thumb of optimal taxation are: (1) it is better to tax commodities or factors for which the elasticity of supply or demand is small (so that the deadweight loss is small), (2) it is better to have a broad tax base (so that a given amount of revenue can be raised using small taxes in each sector), and (3) it is better to tax bads than goods. General equilibrium relations can shift the tax incidence in subtle ways. In a dynamic setting involving investment, the short-run elasticities of supply and demand typically differ from their long-run analogs, complicating the problem of designing tax policy and potentially leading to a time inconsistency problem.

Under cap and trade, the equilibrium permit price depends on the level of the cap but not on the whether the permits are given or auctioned to firms. A pollution tax equal to the equilibrium price of emissions permits leads to the same level of emissions as under a cap. If firms are given (rather than having to buy) the fraction of permits slightly greater than their tax incidence under the quota-equivalent tax, the cap and trade policy may have little effect on industry profits.

10.7   Terms and Concepts, Study Questions, Exercises, and Sources

Terms and Concepts
Unit tax, ad valorem tax, consumer and producer tax incidence, rational buyers, behavioral economics, approximation of tax incidence, closed and open economies, Polluter Pays Principle, tax equivalence, Harberger triangle, deadweight loss (or cost) of taxes, approximation of deadweight loss, approximation of tax revenue, factor prices, general equilibrium effects, computable general equilibrium (CGE) model, time consistency, cap and trade, equivalence of a cap and trade and a tax policy, grandfathering, carbon leakage.

Study Questions
1. (a) What does it mean to say that a producer and a consumer tax are "equivalent" in a closed economy? (The answer should include a definition of the term "incidence.")

   (b) Use either a graphical or a numerical example to illustrate this equivalence in a closed economy.

2. (a) Use a graphical example to show how the consumer and producer tax incidences (in a closed economy) depend on the relative steepness of the supply and the demand functions at the equilibrium price.

   (b) Using this example, explain how the approximation of consumer tax incidence depends on the demand elasticity relative to the supply elasticity, evaluated at the no-tax equilibrium.

3. An opponent of government programs might argue that the true economic cost of financing these programs exceeds the nominal cost of the programs. Advocates of some government programs or taxes argue that they correct market failures. Using the concepts from chapter 9 and this chapter, explain these two positions.

4. Suppose that a regulator imposes a producer tax in a closed economy.

   (a) Use the concept of producer tax incidence to approximate the fraction of the tax revenue that would have to be turned over to producers to make them almost as well off under the tax + transfer as they were before the tax.

(b) Use the concept of consumer tax incidence to approximate the fraction of the tax revenue that would have to be turned over to consumers to make them almost as well off under the tax + transfer as they were before the tax.

(c) Is it possible, by means of transferring the tax revenue (associated only with this particular tax), to make both producers and consumers exactly as well off under the tax + transfer as they were before the tax? Explain.

5. (a) Describe a cap and trade policy. (Explain how it works.)

(b) Explain what it means to auction permits.

(c) Explain why firms' equilibrium levels of pollution does not depend on whether permits are given to the firm or auctioned.

6. (a) What is meant by the claim that a pollution tax and a cap and trade policy are equivalent?

(b) Explain why the claim is true in the particular setting we used.

Exercises

Assume for all questions that the economy is closed.

1. Draw a linear demand function and a linear marginal cost function.

(a) Use this figure to identify (graphically) consumer and producer incidence of a unit consumer tax, v, in a competitive equilibrium.

(b) Now rotate the original supply function around the zero-tax equilibrium, making the supply function less elastic. Identify the consumer and producer tax incidence and compare these to your answer in part (a).

(c) Explain the relation between your answer to part (b) and equation 10.4. (This exercise requires reproducing material in the textbook, with no additional analysis. The point of the exercise is to encourage you to think carefully about the material.)

2. Using the approximation of deadweight loss in equation 10.5, show that deadweight loss increases with either the elasticity of demand or the elasticity of supply. [Hint: Take a derivative.] For this exercise, you are holding the tax and the zero-tax equilibrium quantity and price constant, and considering the effect of making either the demand or the supply function flatter (more elastic) at this equilibrium. Provide an economic explanation for the relation you just showed.

3. Suppose that instead of using a cap and trade, a regulator uses a "cap and no trade" policy, in which firms are allocated pollution permits but are not allowed to trade them. Is a pollution tax equivalent to a cap and no trade policy? Explain your answer.

4. A profit tax is usually expressed as a percentage or fraction of profits. For this exercise, ignore fixed (or sunk) costs, so producer surplus (revenue minus variable costs) equals profits. A competitive industry has variable costs $c(q)$. Marginal costs increase with sales

$(c'(q) > 0)$, so the competitive supply function has a positive slope; in this case, producer surplus in a competitive equilibrium is positive. The inverse demand function is $p(q)$. At quantity q, industry profit (here equal to producer surplus) is $p(q)q - c(q)$. Firms pay a profit tax ϕ, so their after-tax profit is $(1 - \phi)[pq - c(q)]$.

(a) How, if at all, does this profit tax affect the equilibrium price in a competitive equilibrium?

(b) What, if anything, does a profit tax affect in a competitive equilibrium? (Make a list of the features of the competitive equilibrium that are relevant, and ask which, if any, of those features are altered by the profits tax.

Sources

Chetty, Looney, and Kraft (2009) conduct an experiment in a grocery store that shows that people respond to the salience of a tax.

Hines's (2008) concise discussion of the welfare effects of taxes provides background for the material in section 10.4.

Goolsbee (2006) estimates an excess burden of 5–10% for corporate income tax but a burden of more than 100% for a tax on broadband.

Gentry (2007) reviews evidence that labor bears a significant share of the incidence of corporate taxes.

Feldstein (1977) discusses the general equilibrium effects of a land tax.

Diewert, Lawrence, and Thomson (1998) and Conover (2010) review estimates of tax incidence; Table 10.1 is based on Conover.

Judd (1985) discusses the time path of capital taxes; Straub and Werning (2015) show the sensitivity of steady state taxes to the intertemporal elasticity of substitution; Karp and Lee (2003) discuss the time inconsistency of the optimal program.

World Bank (2014c) surveys carbon markets across the world.

Fowlie, Holland, and Mansur (2012) document the success of the RECLAIM market for NO_x.

Fowlie and Perloff (2013) use data from the RECLAIM market to test the efficiency hypothesis, as described in section 10.5.

McAusland (2003, 2008) compares environmental taxes in open and closed economies.

Sijm, Neuhoff, and Chen (2006) and Hintermann (2015) provide evidence that grandfathering in the EU ETS might have given firms windfall profits.

11 Taxes: Nonrenewable Resources

Objective
- Use the Hotelling model to analyze taxes for nonrenewable resources.

Information and Skills
- Have an overview of actual fossil fuel taxes.
- Understand the time consistency problem associated with quasi-rent.
- Understand how taxes alter a firm's extraction incentives.
- Understand the effect of the time profile of a tax on the consumer and producer tax incidence trajectories.

Some results from static tax analysis carry over to the dynamic setting: in a closed economy, the incidence of the tax is the same regardless of whether it is levied on consumers or producers, and for every unit tax, there is an equivalent ad valorem tax. In this setting, there is no loss in generality in assuming that producers have the statutory obligation to pay a unit tax. In other respects, taxes might have qualitatively different effects in a static setting and in a dynamic setting with natural resources. In a static setting, taxes reduce equilibrium quantity. In the resource setting, a tax reallocates sales across periods but possibly has no effect on cumulative supply. The tax-induced change in the timing of sales can affect welfare. Supply in natural resource markets depends on firms' expectations of future taxes.

A Road Map

Section 11.1 reviews current fossil fuel policies used throughout the world. The combined explicit and implicit subsidies arising from tax breaks and the failure to impose externality costs are large and create substantial distortions. Removing the bulk of these distortions, even without taking into account the global externality associated with climate change, would significantly reduce GHG emissions. Resource taxes can be understood using the Hotelling rule (section 11.2).

Up to this point, we have taken the initial resource stocks as given. However, these stocks require previous investment in exploration and development. Once made, these investments are sunk, creating the incentive for governments to behave opportunistically, including by using taxes (section 11.3). This incentive is more important in the international setting. Investment treaties with investor-to-state provisions potentially remove this incentive, benefiting both investors and host countries (those receiving the investments) but also limiting the host's sovereignty. These treaties are controversial.

A numerical example illustrates many features of resource taxes (section 11.4). This example compares the effects of taxes with different "profiles," those that increase slowly or rapidly over time. A tax's profile affects the time trajectory of consumer and producer tax incidence and welfare. We also use this example to compare the effects of a tax that is anticipated before it goes into effect and a tax that comes as a surprise. That material reinforces the point that the current resource price depends on beliefs about what will happen in the future.

11.1   Current Fossil Fuel Policies

Objectives and skills: Know the basics of fossil fuel policies and understand the rationale for reforming them.

Natural resources, particularly fossil fuels, are important in the world economy, and governments derive substantial revenue from their taxation. Between 2005 and 2010, the (mostly rich) 24 countries in the Organization for Economic Cooperation and Development (OECD) raised about $850 billion per year in petroleum taxes, including goods and services taxes and value-added taxes. For large oil producing countries, government receipts from the hydrocarbon sector were a large fraction of total government revenue (2000–2007 data): 72% for Saudi Arabia, 48% for Venezuela, and 22% for Russia. (Except where noted otherwise, statistics are taken from IEA et al. 2011.)

The oil sector in many rich countries receives significant implicit subsidies in the form of tax deductions. These indirect producer subsidies implicitly subsidize consumption, in the same manner that a producer tax indirectly taxes consumption (see chapter 10). Middle-income and developing countries that export fossil fuel directly subsidize domestic fuel consumption by maintaining a domestic price lower than the world price. For both groups of countries, these policies subsidize fuel consumption, creating significant distortions. The failure to include externality costs also creates a large fossil fuel implicit subsidy.[1]

In 2009, leaders of the G20 (a group of wealthy countries) committed to rationalizing and phasing out inefficient fossil fuel subsidies that encourage wasteful consumption. A group of international organizations estimated the scope of energy subsidies and made suggestions for their reduction. Their report identified 250 individual mechanisms that support fossil fuel production in the OECD countries, having an aggregate value of US$ 45–75 billion per year over 2005–2010; 54% of this subsidy went to petroleum,

---

1 A tax deduction and an explicit subsidy are not literally the same. A tax below the marginal social cost of pollution and an explicit subsidy are also not literally the same. However, these policies have similar economic consequences. They result in inefficiently high production, and they transfer income from taxpayers to producers.

24% to coal, and 22% to natural gas (IEA et al. 2011). In the United States tax breaks provide fossil fuel subsidies of about \$4 billion per year (Aldy 2013). These tax breaks include write-offs for some drilling costs, a domestic manufacturing tax deduction, and a percentage depletion allowance for oil and gas wells. These subsidies transfer income from taxpayers to resource owners. Underpriced leases for mines and wells on federally owned land also transfer income from taxpayers to producers.

A group of 37 emerging and developing countries subsidize domestic fuel consumption, maintaining domestic prices below international prices. This group accounted for more than half of world fossil fuel consumption in 2010. With a domestic price of p^d and a world price of p^w, the per-unit subsidy is $p^w - p^d$. The nation loses $p^w - p^d$ times the amount of subsidized consumption from selling fuel at the low domestic price instead of the higher world price. Most of the countries maintained a stable domestic price, while the world price fluctuated, causing the per-unit subsidy also to fluctuate. The cost of the subsidies to their domestic treasuries amounted to \$409 billion in 2010 and \$300 billion in 2009. Oil received 47% of the total, and the average subsidy was 23% of the world price. The subsidy rates were highest among oil and gas exporters in the Middle East, North Africa, and Central Asia.

A common justification for fuel subsidies is that they benefit the poor, providing them with access to energy services. However, only 8% of the \$409 billion subsidy in 2010 went to poorest 20% of the population. If the subsidy had been eliminated, the fuel sold at world price, and each person then given an equal share of the proceeds, the poorest 20% would have received approximately twice as much as they did under the subsidy. Fuel subsidies—like most commodity subsidies—are an inefficient way to help the poor. This observation is another example of the Principle of Targeting: giving the poor income transfers is a more efficient way of increasing their welfare compared to subsidizing the cost of a commodity for everyone. Absent reforms, 2011 estimates project that these fossil fuel subsidies will reach \$660 billion per year by 2020. Eliminating consumption subsidies would reduce 2020 fuel demand by an estimated 4.1% and CO_2 emissions by 4.7%.

An International Monetary Fund (IMF) study estimates the economic cost of fossil fuel subsidies, including unpriced externalities (Coady et al. 2015). The study finds that the implicit subsidy arising from unpriced externalities is larger than other subsidies. Local health effects, not climate change, account for the bulk of this externality cost. The estimated global energy subsidies (including the externality cost) was a substantial fraction of world gross domestic product (GDP); their removal would have significantly raised global GDP and raised substantial government revenue. Estimates of the increase in global GDP due to major trade liberalization proposals are typically much smaller. By this measure, removing energy subsidies would increase global income by more than would trade liberalization. The IMF estimates that eliminating explicit subsidies and imposing externality costs would reduce carbon emissions by 23% and reduce deaths related to fossil fuel air pollution by 63%.

Fossil fuel subsidies violate the three rules of thumb for optimal taxes (section 10.3). The first rule states that the tax base should be broad so taxes on each sector can be low. Subsidizing rather than taxing the fossil fuel sector narrows the tax base, and it requires higher taxes in other sectors to finance the fossil fuel subsidies. The second rule states that it is efficient to raise revenue by taxing goods with low supply and demand elasticities. Fossil fuels have inelastic short-run supply and demand, but they are subsidized. The third rule notes that a commodity that creates a negative externality (pollution in the case of fossil fuels) should be taxed, not subsidized. In addition, commodity subsidies are an inefficient means of making transfers to the poor. Political power, not economic logic, explains the tax and subsidy policies used in a wide range of fossil fuel markets, for both importers and exporters countries, and for rich and developing nations.

The dollar value of subsidies to renewable energy sources (e.g., solar and wind power) is much smaller than the value of direct fossil fuel subsidies (i.e., excluding the unpriced externalities), but renewables account for a small part of the energy market. The direct subsidy per unit of energy is 2–3 times larger for renewables than for fossil fuels. However, subsidies in the renewables sector have been variable, while fossil fuel subsidies have been comparatively stable. When subsidies are variable, it is risky for investors to count on their continuance, blunting the encouragement such subsidies offer to investment.

11.2   The Logic of Resource Taxes

Objectives and skills: Understand the effects of taxes on resource extraction.

A tax sequence creates a deadweight loss if and only if it alters the timing of extraction. We use a model with constant marginal extraction costs, C, to explain the effect of output taxes on the timing of extraction. Using a more general cost function, we then discuss the possibility that the tax affects cumulative extraction. This section concludes by discussing an ad valorem profits tax.

A price-taking firm with constant marginal extraction costs, facing the output tax sequence $v_0, v_1, v_2, \ldots$, wants to maximize the present discounted stream of profits, which is equal to revenue minus extraction costs minus tax payments. The firm takes the tax as given but understands that its extraction trajectory possibly affects the present discounted stream of its tax payments. Its objective is

$$\max \left(\underbrace{\sum_{t=0}^{T} \rho^t p_t y_t}_{\text{revenue}} - \underbrace{\sum_{t=0}^{T} \rho^t C y_t}_{\text{extraction cost}} - \underbrace{\sum_{t=0}^{T} \rho^t v_t y_t}_{\text{tax payments}} \right).$$

The constant tax and the tax that increases at the rate of interest are easy to analyze.

A Constant Tax

If the tax is constant ($v_t = v$, a constant), the present-value sum of extraction costs plus tax payments can be written as

$$\text{extraction cost} + \text{tax payments} = \sum_{t=0}^{T} \rho^t (C + v) y_t.$$

From the standpoint of the firm, increasing the tax from 0 to the positive constant v has the same effect as increasing costs from C to $C' = C + v$. Section 3.3 shows that a higher extraction cost causes firms to shift production from the current period to future periods, because discounting reduces the present value of costs incurred in the future. For the same reason, a constant tax shifts extraction from the present to the future, raising the consumer price early in the program and lowering it in the future.

A Tax That Increases at the Rate of Interest

The tax $v_t = v_0(1+r)^t$ increases at the rate of interest. We assume that v_0 is small enough that $C + v_0(1+r)^T$ is less than the choke price, where T is the date of final extraction in the absence of a tax. With this assumption, the tax does not alter the consumer price trajectory and creates no deadweight loss. It shifts rent from mine owners to the treasury; producers bear the entire tax incidence. For this tax, we have

$$\overbrace{\rho^t v_t = \rho^t v_0(1+r)^t}^{\text{use defn. of the tax}} = \overbrace{\left(\frac{1}{1+r}\right)^t (1+r)^t v_0}^{\text{use defn. of } \rho} \overbrace{= v_0}^{\text{simplify}}. \tag{11.1}$$

The first equality repeats the definition of the tax, the second uses the definition of ρ, and the third follows from simplification. Equation 11.1 states that the present value of the tax is constant. Using this equation in the expression for tax payments gives

$$\text{tax payments} = \sum_{t=0}^{T} \rho^t v_t y_t = \overbrace{\sum_{t=0}^{T} v_0 y_t}^{\text{use eq 11.1}} = \overbrace{v_0 \sum_{t=0}^{T} y_t}^{\text{factor out } v_0} \overbrace{= v_0 x_0}^{\substack{\text{use stock} \\ \text{constraint}}}. \tag{11.2}$$

The last equality uses the fact that the sum of extraction over all periods equals the initial stock. Equation 11.2 shows that for a tax that grows at the rate of interest, the extraction trajectory does not affect the present discounted value of the stream of tax payments. Therefore, this tax does not alter the firm's extraction incentives, creating zero deadweight loss and zero consumer incidence; the producer incidence is 100%. This tax transfers $v_0 x_0$ from producers to taxpayers, creating no distortion. Equation 5.8 shows that under constant extraction costs and zero tax, the value of the firm is $R_0^{NT} x_0$, where R_0^{NT} is the no-tax initial rent. Therefore, under the tax that grows at the rate of interest, the after-tax value of the firm is $(R_0^{\mathrm{NT}} - v_0)x_0$. By setting the initial tax, v_0, slightly below R_0^{NT}, the government extracts nearly all of the rent from the resource owner.[2]

Stock-Dependent Extraction Costs

Taxes might reduce cumulative extraction when costs are stock dependent. Suppose that without taxes firms do not physically exhaust the stock, as in the example from section 7.4.2. Positive taxes reduce the after-tax producer price and therefore reduce the expense that firms are willing to incur to bring a unit of resource to market. These taxes increase the stock threshold, below which firms find it unprofitable to extract. The taxes therefore reduce cumulative extraction, creating a deadweight loss and consumer and producer tax incidence.

An Ad Valorem Profits Tax

A constant ad valorem profits tax, τ, reduces profits in each period by $\tau \times 100\%$. A firm with gross profit π_t, subject to this tax, has after-tax profit $(1 - \tau)\pi_t$. The tax scales down profits proportionally in every period without altering the firm's extraction incentives, and therefore it does not alter the price trajectory or create a deadweight loss. A time-varying profits tax, in contrast, alters the firm's incentives, affecting both consumers and firms and creating a deadweight loss.

11.3 Investment

Objectives and skills: Understand how taxes affect incentives to develop resource stocks, and understand the resulting hold-up problem.

Rent is the return to a factor of production in fixed supply; quasi-rent is the return to a sunk investment. Most natural resource stocks require significant sunk investment in exploration and development. The difference between the price that a competitive firm receives and its marginal cost of extracting the resource is the sum of rent and quasi-rent. Earlier chapters referred to this sum as "rent" merely in the interest of simplicity. For the purpose of studying tax policy, the distinction is important. Suppose that the initial rent + quasi-rent for a mine with constant extraction costs is $R_0 = 10$, and the initial stock is $x_0 = 10$, so the value of this mine (using equation 5.8) is 100. Each mine costs 5 to develop, and on average, a firm must develop five mines to find one that is successful; the average development cost of a successful mine is 25, so the rent is 75, and the quasi-rent is 25.

Prior to the exploration and development, the government might announce a tax that begins, at the time of initial extraction, at 7.5, and rises at the rate of interest. With this

---

2 If $v_0 > R_0^{\mathrm{NT}}$, the tax causes the firm to reduce cumulative extraction, driving the firm's rent to zero and creating a positive deadweight loss and consumer tax incidence.

tax, the government captures all rent but leaves firms with the quasi-rent. In this case, firms break even. Once a successful mine is in operation, the government might be tempted to renege on its announcement and impose an initial tax of $v_0 = 10$, which increases at the rate of interest. This tax transfers all rent + quasi-rent from the firm to taxpayers. The firm in this case loses all its sunk investment costs, and it suffers a net loss of 25. This temptation to renege illustrates the potential time inconsistency of optimal plans. The situation where one agent (here the government) takes advantage of a second agent's (here the resource firm) sunk investment is known as a "hold-up problem."[3]

The real-world importance of the hold-up problem varies with the setting. If there are many cycles of investment and extraction, then the government has an incentive to adhere to its promises to maintain its reputation. By behaving opportunistically, this government obtains the short-run benefit of higher tax revenue, but it discourages future investment. Hold-up tends to be more important for a single large project (e.g., a one-time development of offshore oil deposits). These considerations also apply to non-resource-related infrastructure projects, such as developing a harbor or a transportation network. The government's temptation to renege may be greater if the major investors are foreigners, because domestic investors might be better able to defend their interests in the political arena (Bohn and Deacon 2000). For large one-off foreign-sourced investment projects, hold-up can be a major issue. Without protection against opportunistic behavior, foreign investors are unwilling to undertake the project or they require a risk premium.

The OECD and other international organizations attempted, during the 1980s and 1990s, to negotiate a Multilateral Agreement on Investment to resolve this hold-up problem. This agreement was promoted as a means of encouraging international investment, much as the World Trade Organization promotes international trade. The Multilateral Agreement on Investment was never completed, but there are currently hundreds of bilateral investment treaties that have provisions similar to the Multilateral agreement. Most of these bilateral agreements involve one rich and one developing country; the United States is party to over 40 of them. The investment chapter in the North American Free Trade Agreement (NAFTA) was a major source of opposition to that agreement. Similarly, much of the opposition to the Trans-Pacific Partnership, negotiated in 2015, focuses on the investment chapter.

The investor-to-state provision in these agreements is particularly controversial. The parties to these treaties are countries, not private firms, but the investor-to-state provision permits a private investor originating in one signatory (usually the rich country) to sue, in an international court, the government of the other signatory (usually the developing country) for violation of the treaty. The stated purpose of this provision is to protect investors

---

3 "Hold-up" has two possible meanings here, either as a robbery or as a delay (because the government's incentive to behave opportunistically may delay—perhaps indefinitely—the investment).

against confiscation of their investment; some treaties also provide protection against measures that are "tantamount to expropriation," such as confiscatory taxes (like the example at the beginning of this section) or post-investment changes to environmental rules.

Business interests regard the investor-to-state provision as important, because they lack confidence that their own government would defend their interests. Foreign policy considerations might make the U.S. government reluctant to invoke a treaty in protection of a U.S. investor. The investor has no such qualms about exercising the treaty rights. The treaty provides an avenue for redressing a host's opportunistic behavior. Treaty supporters expect that this mechanism will promote foreign investment. Opponents object that the treaties transfer sovereignty from countries to corporations, limiting a country's ability to exercise its "police powers" (e.g., environmental regulation) and to respond to contingencies (e.g., a recession) not foreseen at the time of investment.

By signing bilateral agreements many developing countries have already agreed to investor-to-state provisions. These countries, as in our example of the government tempted to extract quasi-rent, face either a real or perceived time inconsistency problem. The investment treaty, with its restrictions on sovereignty, is a type of commitment device, encouraging foreign investment by making it harder for the government of the host country to behave opportunistically. The cost to the host of this commitment device is the potential loss in sovereignty (Aisbett et al. 2010).

11.4   An Example

Objectives and skills: Understand: the effect of the time profile of the tax trajectory on equilibrium price trajectories, and the resulting trajectories of tax incidence; the welfare changes associated with a tax trajectory; and the difference between anticipated and unanticipated taxes.

Apart from the constant tax and the tax that increases at the rate of interest, it is difficult to obtain analytic results for nonrenewable resource taxes. This section therefore uses graphs to present results for a numerical example. The time profile of the tax trajectory (e.g., whether it increases rapidly or slowly) determines its effect on the extraction and price trajectories. If the tax changes slowly, then we are close to the situation of a constant tax, where we saw that the tax shifts production from early to late periods, causing early consumer prices to rise and later prices to fall (relative to the no-tax scenario). Here, the consumer incidence is positive early in the program and becomes negative later; the producer incidence is less than 100% early in the program and exceeds 100% late in the program. If the tax increases very rapidly (relative to the discount rate), firms have an incentive to extract early so that they reduce the present discounted stream of tax payments: they prefer to extract when the tax is low instead of high. In this case, the consumer incidence of the tax is negative early in the program but becomes positive later; the producer

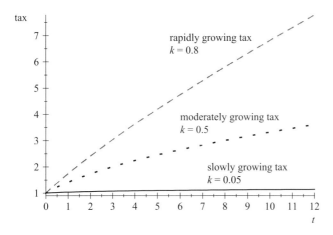

Figure 11.1
Three tax profiles.

incidence exceeds 100% early in the program and is less than 100% later. We also quantify the welfare effects of a tax.

We can then compare the effects of a future tax that is anticipated versus one that comes as a surprise, reinforcing a central theme of this book: rational resource owners base their current decisions on their beliefs about future circumstances (e.g., prices, taxes). An unanticipated future tax does not alter owners' beliefs and therefore does not alter their behavior prior to the tax. In contrast, an anticipated future tax does alter behavior before the tax is imposed. Both the anticipated and unanticipated taxes change behavior after the tax comes into effect.

The numerical example uses the time-varying tax, $v(t) = (t+1)^\kappa$, with $v(0) = 1$. Figure 11.1 shows that larger values of κ lead to a faster increase in the tax. If κ is close to 0, the tax grows slowly, and the situation is similar to the constant tax case discussed in section 11.2; this tax shifts extraction toward the future, decreasing the firm's present-value stream of tax payments. If κ is large, the tax grows quickly; this tax shifts extraction toward the present, reducing the quantity of sales that incur the relatively high future taxes, and thereby reducing the firm's present-value stream of tax payments.

11.4.1   The Price Trajectories

We use the steps discussed in section 5.6 to calculate the equilibrium consumer and producer price trajectories under a particular tax trajectory, with demand $= 10 - p$, constant extraction costs $C = 1$, initial stock $x_0 = 20$, and discount rate $r = 0.04$. For the zero tax, $v = 0$, the resource is exhausted at $T = 11.3$. For the slowly growing tax, the terminal time is only slightly greater, $T = 12$. The rapidly growing tax gives producers a strong incentive

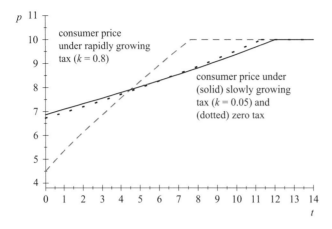

Figure 11.2
The consumer price trajectory under rapidly growing tax (dashed curve), under slowly growing tax (solid curve) and under zero tax (dotted curve).

to extract early, while the tax is still relatively low, leading to a much earlier exhaustion time, $T = 7.6$. Figure 11.2 shows the equilibrium price trajectories under these three tax profiles. Each trajectory reaches the choke price, $p = 10$, at the time of exhaustion.

The equilibrium price trajectories under the zero tax (dotted curve) and under the slowly increasing tax (solid curve) are almost indistinguishable. The positive tax encourages firms to delay extraction, increasing the initial price; the increasing tax profile encourages firms to move extraction forward in time, reducing the initial price. These two effects almost cancel. In contrast, the steeply rising tax trajectory gives firms a much stronger incentive to extract early, while the tax is still relatively low. The steeply rising tax therefore leads to a substantially lower initial price and earlier exhaustion.

11.4.2   Tax Incidence

The consumer incidence equals the difference in the consumer price with and without the tax, divided by the tax, times 100 (to convert to a percentage). The producer incidence equals 100 minus the consumer incidence. Unless the tax increases at the rate of interest, it causes a reallocation of supply over time; it does not change cumulative supply, which is equal to the initial stock. Thus, for some periods, the tax (unless it increases at the rate of interest) lowers the equilibrium consumer price, leading to negative consumer tax incidence, and producer tax incidence above 100%. In a static competitive model, both the consumer and producer tax incidences lie between 0 and 100%.

Figure 11.3 graphs the producer and the consumer tax incidences under the slowly increasing tax. The consumer incidence begins at about 15% and becomes negative at the time when the dotted and solid curves in figure 11.2 cross, $t = 6.5$. At later dates, the

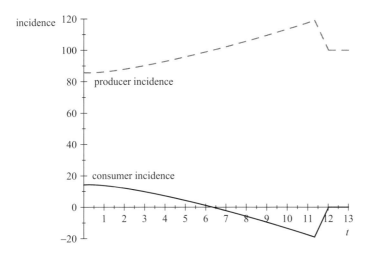

Figure 11.3
Consumer and producer tax incidence under the slowly increasing tax.

tax reduces the equilibrium consumer price, so the consumer incidence is negative there, and the producer incidence exceeds 100%.

The resource is exhausted at $t = 11.3$ with no tax and at $t = 12$ under the slowly growing tax. For $11.3 < t < 12$ the consumer price is lower under the tax, so the consumer incidence is negative. However, the consumer price rises over time under the tax, whereas it is constant (at the choke price) with no tax. Therefore, the consumer incidence increases toward zero. For $t \geq 12$ the resource is exhausted in both cases, so the consumer price equals the choke price and the consumer tax incidence is zero.

Figure 11.4 graphs the consumer and producer tax incidence over time under the rapidly growing tax. This tax lowers the equilibrium consumer price for $t < 4.5$, so over this region, the consumer incidence is negative, and the producer incidence exceeds 100%; at later dates, the tax incidence for both consumers and producers lies between 0 and 100%.

11.4.3 Welfare Changes

Here we consider the resource tax's welfare cost. If the consumer price in period t is $p(t)$, consumer surplus, $CS(t)$, producer profit, $PS(t)$, and tax revenue, $G(t)$ (G for "government"), are

$$CS(t) = \int_{p(t)}^{10} (10 - q)dq = 50 - 10p(t) + \frac{1}{2}p(t)^2,$$

$$PS(t) = (p(t) - v(t) - 1)(10 - p(t)),$$

and $G(t) = v(t)(10 - p(t)).$

(11.3)

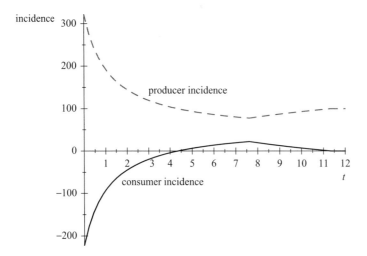

Figure 11.4
Consumer and producer tax incidence under the rapidly increasing tax.

Table 11.1
Agents' welfare and percentage change in welfare under the zero tax, the slow tax, $v(t) = (t + 1)^{0.05}$; and the fast tax, $v(t) = (t + 1)^{0.8}$

	Consumer welfare	Producer welfare	Taxpayer welfare	Social welfare	$\frac{DWL}{\text{tax rev}} \times 100\%$
Zero tax	20.2	114.4	0	134.6	
Slow tax	19	97.2	18.3	134.5	0.55%
Percentage change	−5.9%	−15%	NA	−0.07%	
Fast tax	33.1	50.1	47	130.2	9.4%
Percentage change	+64%	−56.2%	NA	−3.3%	

Note: Percentage change is relative to $v = 0$. NA indicates not applicable.

A consumer's, producer's, or taxpayer's welfare equals the present discounted value of their stream of single-period payoffs (consumer or producer surplus or tax revenue). This discussion abstracts from the reason for the tax. If the tax is used to finance a socially useful program, a full accounting of welfare has to include that social benefit. Table 11.1 shows welfare for consumers, producers, and taxpayers, and the sum of these three measures (= social welfare) under the zero tax and for both the slowly and the rapidly growing tax. The last column shows the discounted stream of social loss as a percentage of the discounted stream of tax revenue; for the slowly growing tax, the loss is about half a percent of tax revenue, and for the rapidly growing tax it is about 9% of tax revenue.

For our numerical example, the deadweight loss is $\frac{3.3}{.07} = 47$ times higher under the rapidly growing tax compared to the slowly growing tax. The no-tax trajectory is efficient. The tax reduces efficiency to the extent that it changes the extraction profile. Figure 11.2

shows that the slowly growing tax has negligible effect on the consumer price trajectory; therefore it has negligible effect on the sales trajectory, leading to a very small welfare loss. In contrast, the rapidly growing tax causes a large change in the consumer price and thus a large change in the extraction trajectory, resulting in a relatively large loss in efficiency. In the static setting, the DWL depends on the magnitude of the tax (equation 10.5). In the dynamic setting, the DWL depends on the *shape* (= time profile) of the tax. For our example, the rapidly growing tax leads to higher DWL, but this result is incidental. Suppose that Tax A starts out large and increases at the rate of interest, while Tax B is relatively small and constant. From section 11.2, we know that Tax A does not change the extraction trajectory and therefore creates no distortion, while Tax B does change the extraction trajectory and therefore creates a welfare loss. Tax A can be larger at every point in time than Tax B, but the welfare cost is zero under Tax A and positive under Tax B.

In the static setting, the tax increases the consumer price, lowering consumer welfare. In the nonrenewable resource setting, the tax increases price in some periods and lowers it in other periods. Depending on the magnitude and the timing of the changes, consumer welfare might either increase or decrease. The slowly growing tax increases consumer price (relative to the no-tax scenario) early in the trajectory and reduces the price late in the trajectory; the rapidly growing tax creates the opposite changes. Discounting makes the early changes in welfare more important than later changes, explaining why the slowly growing tax reduces consumer welfare and the rapidly growing tax increases consumer welfare. The producer incidence of both taxes is always positive, so both taxes reduce producer welfare.

Welfare: A Closer Look
We measured consumer welfare using the present discounted stream of consumer surplus. This procedure is standard, but it has a shortcoming that we mention here and revisit in chapter 19. The consumers alive today are not the same people who will be alive in 100 years. What does it mean to say that "consumer welfare" increases, when one group of consumers is better off and another worse off? Discounting privileges those currently living at the expense of future consumers, raising ethical issues.

Our measure of social surplus at a point in time also adds up the surplus of possibly different people, consumers and producers. That aggregation is ethically less problematic for two reasons. First, consumers and producers may or may not be different people, whereas individuals living today and in 100 years are almost certainly different people. Second, consumers and producers currently living have at least the potential to influence current government policy that affects their well-being. People living in the future have no direct voice in the current political process.

11.4.4 Anticipated versus Unanticipated Taxes

In the examples above, the tax is announced at the beginning of the problem, at time 0. Here we compare the no-tax case with two scenarios where a constant tax, $v = 3$, begins at

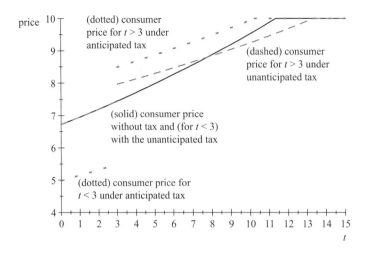

Figure 11.5
Solid curve shows the trajectory of consumer price in the absence of a tax. The dashed trajectory shows consumer price when the tax imposed at $t = 3$ is unanticipated. The dotted trajectory shows consumer price when the tax at $t = 3$ is anticipated at $t = 0$. For $t < 3$ the solid and dashed curves are identical, so the dashed curve is obscured.

a future time, $t = 3$. In one scenario, producers anticipate the tax and adjust their sales even before the tax begins. In the second scenario, with the unanticipated tax, producers can make no provision for it before it begins. Our example uses the demand function $q = 10 - p$, with constant costs $C = 1$ and discount rate $r = 0.03$. Figure 11.5 shows the trajectories of consumer (tax-inclusive) price in the three scenarios. Figure 11.6 shows the trajectories of rent (price–marginal cost–tax) in the three scenarios. Chapter 8 notes that an anticipated future carbon tax increases current emissions. The example here illustrates this effect.

An unanticipated tax changes nothing before the tax begins. The price and rent trajectories under the unanticipated tax are the same as the zero-tax trajectories prior to $t = 3$. (The solid curves cover the dashed curves for $t < 3$.) At $t = 3$ producers discover that they now face the tax, so the tax-inclusive cost of providing the commodity suddenly increases, causing producers to lower sales relative to the no-tax scenario. The equilibrium consumer price jumps up, and the rent jumps down.

With an anticipated tax (dotted curves), producers sell more (relative to the no-tax scenario) early in the program, before the tax begins, to reduce their tax liabilities. These high sales lead to a low initial price trajectory. The price jumps up at $t = 3$, when the tax begins. The trajectory for rent is continuous (dotted curve in figure 11.6) under the anticipated tax, rising at the rate r. In the absence of surprises, the equilibrium rent takes into account ("capitalizes") future changes (in this case, the tax change). For the same reason, an anticipated backstop technology alters the sales and price path before the backstop comes into use (chapter 7).

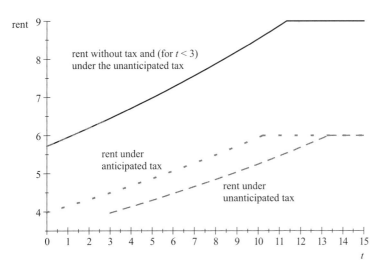

Figure 11.6
Solid curve shows the trajectory of rent in the absence of a tax. The dashed trajectory shows rent when the tax imposed at $t = 3$ is unanticipated. The dotted trajectory shows rent when the tax at $t = 3$ is anticipated at $t = 0$.

Denote the equilibrium consumer price in the instant before the tax increase as p^-, and the price immediately after the tax as p^+; the tax causes the price to jump at t by $\Delta \equiv p^+ - p^-$. The anticipated tax leads to a larger value of p^+ and a smaller value of p^-, and thus a larger jump, Δ, relative to the unanticipated tax: compare the dotted and the dashed curves in figure 11.5. The lower pre-tax price under the anticipated tax leads to higher extraction, leaving less stock in that scenario. At $t = 3$, producers in both scenarios know they face the tax. However, the producer in the anticipated tax scenario has (at $t = 3$) a smaller stock, causing subsequent sales to be lower and price to be higher.

11.5   Summary

The theory of optimal taxation suggests that fossil fuels should be relatively heavily taxed, to offset the negative externality associated with their consumption and to take advantage of their relatively low elasticities of supply and demand. However, both rich and developing nations, and both importers and exporters, subsidize consumption of fossil fuels. Political constraints impede international attempts to move toward more rational resource policies.

The effect of taxes in nonrenewable resource markets depends on the shape of the tax trajectory. A constant tax encourages producers to delay extraction, so they can reduce the present value of their tax liability. A rapidly growing tax encourages producers to advance extraction, so that more of their sales is taxed at the lower rate; this strategy also reduces the present value of producers' tax liability. Therefore, a flat or slowly growing tax tends to delay extraction, and a rapidly growing tax tends to advance extraction. If the tax grows at the rate of interest, it has no effect on the extraction trajectory. Apart from this special case, taxes reallocate supply over time, changing the price trajectory and creating deadweight loss. In some periods the tax increases supply, creating a negative consumer incidence and a producer incidence exceeding 100%. The zero-tax competitive equilibrium maximizes social surplus, so any tax that changes the extraction profile reduces social surplus. In the static competitive setting, both consumers and producers bear some of the incidence of the tax: the tax decreases both agents' welfare. In the resource setting, when the tax shifts production from one period to another, it increases consumer surplus in some periods. The tax might either increase or decrease the present discounted value of the stream of consumer surplus. However, the tax reduces the producer price in every period, lowering the present discounted stream of producer profit.

The resource price capitalizes an anticipated tax even before the tax is implemented. This tax alters the equilibrium even before the tax is imposed. An unanticipated tax cannot affect anything before it begins. With an anticipated tax, rent changes smoothly over time. An unanticipated tax causes a sudden drop in rent when the tax begins. Both taxes cause an upward jump in price when the tax begins; the jump is larger under an anticipated tax.

We emphasize the relation between taxes and extraction decisions, usually keeping the investment decision in the background. However, investment is important in resource markets, creating quasi-rents—the return to a sunk investment. Price minus marginal costs, which we usually refer to as "resource rent," is in fact the sum of genuine rent and quasi-rent. The fact that investment is sunk at the time of extraction creates a time consistency or hold-up problem. This problem is likely most severe in the case of large, one-off foreign investments. International investment treaties, with an investor-to-state provision, attempt to ameliorate this hold-up problem by "tying the hands" of a government, reducing its sovereignty.

11.6   Terms and Concepts, Study Questions, Exercises, and Sources

Terms and Concepts
Tax trajectories, hold-up problem, bilateral and multilateral investment treaties, investor-to-state provisions, commitment device, rate of change of a tax (or of anything else), shape or time profile of a tax trajectory, trajectories of producer and consumer tax incidence, intertemporal welfare (the integral, or the sum, of the discounted stream of consumer or producer welfare), anticipated versus unanticipated taxes.

Study Questions
For all these questions, assume that extraction costs equal Cy, with $C \geq 0$ (C a constant), and assume that the tax plus C is less than the choke price in every period.

1. (a) Explain how a constant tax alters the competitive nonrenewable resource owner's incentives to extract, and how the tax affects the equilibrium price trajectory.

   (b) Now explain how an increasing tax trajectory alters the competitive resource owner's incentives and thereby alters the equilibrium price trajectory. (Your answer to both parts should make clear how the taxes affect the relative advantage of extracting at one point instead of another.)

   (c) Use your answers to parts (a) and (b) to explain why the three tax profiles shown in figure 11.1 give rise to the three price profiles shown in figure 11.2.

2. Using figure 11.2, sketch the consumer and producer tax incidence over time for the slowly growing and the rapidly growing taxes. (Figures in the text contain those graphs. You should attempt to produce the sketches using only figure 11.2 and then compare their answers with the other figures in the text. Their sketches should correctly show the intervals of time where an incidence is negative, positive and less than 100%, or greater than 100%.)

3. (a) Explain why, if the elasticity of supply is positive, a tax reduces consumer surplus in the static setting.

   (b) Explain why, in the resource setting, the tax must increase consumer surplus at some points in time.

   (c) Explain why the answer to part (b) implies that a tax might either increase of decrease the present discount stream of consumer surplus.

   (d) What is the ethical objection to using the present discounted stream of consumer surplus as a measure of consumer welfare?

Exercises

1. A profit tax is levied on profits (instead of on sales quantity). If the profit tax is $\phi(t)$ and before-tax profits equal $(p(t) - C)y(t)$, after-tax profits equal $(1 - \phi(t))(p(t) - C)y(t)$. Compare the effects, on a mine owner's incentive to extract, of a constant profit tax ϕ and a profit tax $\phi(t)$ that increases over time.

Sources

Sinclair (1992) points out the effect of a rising carbon tax on the incentive to extract fossil fuels.

Boadway and Keen (2010) survey the theory of resource taxation.

Section 11.1 is based largely on the International Energy Agency (2011).

Coady et al. (2015) provide estimates of the cost (including environmental costs) of resource subsidies.

Parry et al. (2014) illustrate the design of efficient energy taxes for 150 countries.

Aldy (2013) discusses the fiscal implications of eliminating U.S. fossil fuel subsidies.

Daubanes and Andrade de Sa (2014) consider the role of resource taxation when the discovery and development of new deposits is costly.

Lund (2009) reviews the literature on resource taxation under uncertainty.

Bohn and Deacon (2000) discuss investment risk with natural resources.

The website https://ustr.gov/sites/default/files/TPP-Chapter-Summary-Investment.pdf summarizes the investment chapter in the Trans-Pacific Partnership. Public Citizen, at https://www.citizen.org/documents/analysis-tpp-investment-chapter-november-2015.pdf explains the opposition to this part of the agreement.

Aisbett et al. (2010) discuss investment risk and bilateral investment treaties.

12 Property Rights and Regulation

Objective
• Understand how property rights alter second-best regulation.

Information and Skills
• Have an overview of the evolution of property rights and the relation between property rights and resource policy.
• Be familiar with the Coase Theorem, and understand its relevance to policy in the presence of externalities.
• Have an overview of fishery regulation and subsidies, and understand how these can lead to overcapitalized fisheries.
• Be familiar with the use of property rights–based regulation in fisheries.

Previous chapters emphasize competitive equilibria in nonrenewable resource markets (e.g., oil, coal) with perfect property rights. This chapter extends the analysis in two ways, discussing imperfect property rights and also providing a foundation for the study of renewable resources (e.g., fish, groundwater, forests, the climate). Many natural resource problems arise from weak or nonexistent property rights, although this relation is not always evident. Section 9.2 discusses the pollution problem without mentioning property rights, but this problem can framed as arising from nonexistent property rights. If individuals do not own the right to a clean environment, they cannot restrict pollution. If firms do not own the right to pollute, they cannot extract a fee from individuals in exchange for lowering their pollution; they therefore have no incentive to abate. Absent property rights, the government can use the Pigouvian tax to achieve the optimal level of pollution. Property rights sometimes make government regulation unnecessary.

We discuss property rights in the context of fisheries, which are economically important and plagued by imperfect property rights. A large body of research studies fisheries, providing insight that is applicable to many other resource problems. Due to overfishing, loss of habitat, and climate change, 30% of the world's fisheries are at risk of population collapse. Fisheries support nations' well-being through direct employment in fishing, processing, and services, accounting for hundreds of billions of dollars annually. More than 55 million people were directly employed in fisheries, including aquaculture, in 2010. Fish provide nearly 3 billion people with 15% of their animal protein needs, helping support nearly 8% of the world's population (United Nations 2005; Dyck and Sumaila 2010; Sumaila et al. 2011).

A Road Map
Section 12.1 defines different types of property rights, noting that these evolve and that the boundaries between them often blur. We then discuss the Coase Theorem, which shows that the creation of property rights can lead to an efficient outcome (section 12.2). Instead of using explicit regulations, such as taxes or command and control policies, it might be more efficient to foster strong property rights and then let self-interested individuals determine the outcome. Efficiency depends on the existence but not on the allocation of property rights (i.e., who possesses the rights).

Section 12.3 introduces fishery economics. As with most natural resources, fishery regulation occurs in a second-best world: the regulator cannot perfectly match policy "instruments" (rules, taxes) to "targets" (levels of catch, number of boats, amount of fishing gear). Therefore, regulation typically creates collateral damage, which in fisheries often manifests as overcapitalization (too many boats and too much gear). Section 12.4 uses an analytic model to illustrate the second-best nature of regulation. Overcapitalization and other forms of collateral damage limit the efficacy of standard regulation. Property rights–based regulation has become increasingly important during the past three decades. Section 12.5 describes this approach and explains how it avoids some of the problems of standard regulation. Many governments subsidize their fishery sectors, aggravating market failures (section 12.6), as is also the case in the fossil fuels sector (see section 11.1).

12.1   Overview of Property Rights

Objectives and skills: Identify the leading modes of property rights; recognize that the boundaries between them are blurred and that property rights evolve.

A spectrum of social arrangements govern natural resource use. The leading modes are private property, common property, open access, and state/public property. With private property, an individual or a corporation owns the asset and determines how it is used. Common property limits the use of the asset to a certain group (e.g., those living in a village); community members, pursuing their individual self-interest, decide how to use the asset. Anyone is free to use an open access resource. Governments make decisions about state-owned property. A field owned by a person or corporation is private property. A field on which anyone in the village can graze their cows, but from which those outside the village are excluded, is "common property." A field that anyone can use is "open access."

The boundaries between types of ownership structure often blur, both as a consequence of explicit regulation and informal behavior. Labor, health, and environmental laws govern working conditions and pesticide use on privately owned land, limiting the exercise of private property rights. Custom, sometimes codified into law, also limits private property rights. In Britain, anyone can use paths across privately owned farmland, provided that they do not create a nuisance; in Norway, people are allowed to enter uncultivated private property to pick berries. Common property dilutes property rights, but social norms and regulation often limit community members' actions. Everyone in the village may be allowed to graze one cow, but not ten, on the village common. Open access resources are often heavily regulated. An open access fishery is open to all boats, but the entrants may be subject to size restrictions and season limits. A group using a nominally open access resource might also exert pressure to restrict outsiders' access. State ownership runs the gamut from control of the economy, as in the pre-1991 Soviet Union to federally owned land in the western United States, much of which is leased to ranchers or miners at below-market rates.

Actual property rights sometimes differ from legal rights. "De jure" rights describe the legal status of property, and "de facto" rights describe the actual property rights. As the costs and benefits of protecting traditional rights or establishing new rights change, the form of property rights may also change. For example, California beaches are open to the public, so their de jure status is open access. However, local surfers at some beaches make it uncomfortable or dangerous for outsiders to surf, a practice known as "localism." Localism shifts de facto rights from open access toward common property. Surfing etiquette imposes rules on surfers' use of the finite supply of waves, and localism influences who surfs. A higher quality of the surf increases locals' incentive to discourage outsiders, but it also increases outsiders' demand, making it harder for locals to exclude them (Kaffine 2009). The extent of de facto property rights may respond to changes in these incentives.

Social upheaval or changes in trade and migration might be either causes or effects of changes in resource property rights.

• The enclosure movement in the United Kingdom, converting village commons to private property, was formalized by acts of parliament in the eighteenth and nineteenth centuries, but it began centuries earlier. Owners of the newly enclosed land changed agricultural practices, leading to higher yield and labor productivity. The enclosures dispossessed rural populations, creating a landless class of workers and promoting urban migration.

• In the late nineteenth- and early twentieth-century, Igbo groups in Nigeria converted palm trees from private to common property in response to increased palm oil trade. Trade increased the value of the palm trees, increasing the need to protect them from overharvesting (Fenske 2012). In this case (but not in general), monitoring and enforcement costs needed to protect the resource were likely lower under common property.

• Prior to the 1920s, Alaskan aboriginal communities owned salmon fisheries as common property. The 1924 White Act, later incorporated into the state's constitution, abrogated those aboriginal rights, ceding them to the state and forbidding private resource ownership, thus preventing nonresidents from controlling the fishery (Johnson and Libecap 1982). The Act replaced effective common property management with open access, leading to resource degradation and requiring formal regulation.

• The U.S. government owns almost half the land in the 11 Western states. Groups promoting a transfer to state ownership think that the states would be more responsive to local interests, although administrative costs would likely increase. In Utah, where federal agencies manage 65% of the land, a study concludes that the state could cover these costs, but with some strain to state finances (Strambro et al. 2014).

• The introduction of land titles in Mexico enabled people to maintain their property rights without continuous personal use of the land. This strengthening of de jure property rights encouraged migration (de Janvry et al. 2015).

• A long-running dispute in the United States tests the limits of private property rights. The "Doctrine of Regulatory Taking" seeks to define zoning and environmental rules that diminish the value of property as "takings," requiring compensation under the Fifth Amendment to the U.S. Constitution. The doctrine proposes strengthening private property rights by weakening governments' police powers (e.g., the ability to protect the environment).[1]

The collapse of the Soviet Union and the liberation of its satellites in the 1990s led to widespread transformation of property rights. Reformers agreed on the goal of converting state ownership to private property, both to increase economic efficiency and to provide a foundation for democracy, but people debated the right pace of privatization. Those supporting rapid privatization feared that a slower pace would perpetuate inefficiencies and make it possible to reverse reforms. Others were concerned that rapid privatization without a supporting institutional framework would be unsuccessful. Countries in the Soviet bloc followed different paths and had widely different results. In Russia, the transformation created a class of oligarchs and an entrenched system of corruption, while in other parts of the bloc it led to systems of private property similar to those in Western democracies. Without well-functioning institutions, including strong support for the rule of law, private property may not promote either economic efficiency or democracy. The system of property rights can be changed by legislative action or revolution, but institutions usually evolve slowly.

Private property diminishes or eliminates some common property or open access externalities. Grazing an additional cow on a field creates benefits for the cow's owner. A cow

---

1 U.S. Supreme Court rulings have largely reaffirmed these police powers, undermining the Doctrine of Regulatory Taking. Investment treaties' investor-to-state provisions (section 11.2), requiring compensation for regulation that is "tantamount to expropriation," strengthen the Doctrine in the sphere of international law.

that competes with other animals for fodder creates a negative externality for other users, much as an additional driver contributes to road congestion. The overgrazing can also lead to erosion, damaging the field and lowering future productivity. This situation, where negative externalities harm a natural resource, is an example of the "tragedy of the commons" (Hardin 1968). Private owners internalize the congestion created by the additional cow and are less likely to overgraze the field.

Many societies have successfully managed common property natural resources, avoiding the tragedy of the commons (Ostrom 1990, 2007; Dietz, Ostrom, and Stern 2003). Common property management requires widespread agreement on the rules of use and mechanisms for monitoring and enforcing the rules. Stable conditions and homogenous users increase the success of common property management. A rapid change that increases the demand for the resource, such as migration or opening to trade, can undermine common property management.

Following political upheaval, local elites might capture resources previously owned by the community (in the case of developing countries) or the state (in the case of the Soviet Union). This transfer of property rights destroys traditional monitoring and enforcement mechanisms. In a politically unstable environment without institutions to protect property rights, the new owners recognize that the next political upheaval might replace them with another group of elites. The combination of current absolute but insecure property rights is particularly likely to lead to overuse of the resource. The current owners can use the resource to enrich themselves; the risk of losing control causes them to attach too little weight to the resource's future use and encourages violence to either protect or transfer property rights.

Many situations, regardless of the property rights, require some form of regulation, involving monitoring and enforcement. Regulation is particularly necessary under open access, which is especially vulnerable to the tragedy of the commons. Common property management in small communities has often avoided this tragedy. As communities integrate into wider markets, the management practices frequently break down, requiring different kinds of regulation. Converting the village commons to a privately owned farm gives farmers the incentive to avoid erosion, but not to correct off-farm externalities, such as pollution runoff. It might be possible to correct this externality by creating property rights to the waterways that absorb the pollution. If that remedy is impractical or politically unacceptable, the policy prescription is to regulate pollution.

12.2   The Coase Theorem

Objectives and skills: Understand the meaning and implication of the Coase Theorem.

"Transactions costs" include the costs of reaching and enforcing an agreement. The Coase Theorem states that if these costs are negligible, and property rights are well defined, agents can reach the efficient outcome regardless of the distribution of property rights. In this case, there is no need for a regulator, because private agents reach an efficient outcome by bargaining; they do not leave money on the table. The government's only role is to ensure that agents honor their contracts (and possibly to make transfers to promote fairness); efficiency does not require those transfers. In many situations where we observe regulation instead of a bargained outcome, transactions costs are large, making it impractical for agents, bargaining among themselves, to achieve an efficient outcome. In other situations, the property rights are not well defined, leaving agents uncertain about the payoffs of reaching a bargain, which makes an agreement harder to achieve.

To illustrate the Coase Theorem, suppose that the total profit of a fishery depends on the number of boats operating there. With one boat, the profit is 1, with two boats, the aggregate profit is 4, and with three boats, the aggregate profit is 3. Initially, three individually owned boats operate in the fishery. The surplus obtained from inducing one boat to exit equals $4 - 3 = 1$. A person with exclusive property rights to the fishery insists that the other two fishers leave the sector and buys an additional boat, reaching the efficient outcome. If all three fishers have the right to fish, and if the transactions costs are small, they can reach an agreement in which one of them sells her right to fish to the other two and leaves the sector. There are many routes to achieving a bargain, and many different splits of the surplus.

Three equally productive fishers can create a lottery that determines who leaves the sector.[2] The person who leaves receives a payment of $1 + x$, their initial profit plus the compensation x for leaving. The two remaining fishers split the higher profit, each receiving 2, and share the cost of buying out the departing fisher, for a net benefit of $2 - \frac{1+x}{2}$. The expected payoff to an agent participating in a fair lottery (where the chance of leaving the sector is 1/3) is $\frac{1}{3}(1 + x) + \frac{2}{3}\left(2 - \frac{1+x}{2}\right) = \frac{4}{3}$, which is greater than their payoff under the status quo and is independent of x. All agents receive the same expected payoff before the lottery. If $x > \frac{1}{3}$, the person who leaves is a winner, and if the inequality is reversed, this person is a loser; setting $x = \frac{1}{3}$ ensures that all agents receive the same actual (not merely the same expected) payoff. Other procedures (e.g., arm wrestling) could also determine who leaves.

The Coase Theorem states that rational agents achieve an efficient outcome if transactions costs are small and property rights well defined. It does not predict how the outcome is obtained or the surplus shared. Differences in bargaining power, perhaps due to differences in outside options (a fisher's best alternative to remaining in the sector) or levels of bargaining skill lead to different distributions but not different aggregate bargaining surplus.

---

2 If the fishers are not equally productive, then an efficient procedure must choose the two most productive to remain in the fishery.

12.3   Fisheries: The Basics

Objectives and skills: Have an overview of the recent history of fishery regulation, and of the difficulties associated with regulating and evaluating regulation.

Prior to the twentieth century, the doctrine of "freedom of the seas" limited nations' sovereignty to 3 miles from their coastline, permitting other nations to operate outside that area. In the twentieth century, countries began to claim sovereignty over larger areas, often to protect their fisheries. The United Nations Convention on the Law of the Sea, concluded in 1982, replaced earlier agreements, giving nations an "exclusive economic zone," for example, to harvest fish or extract oil, 200 miles beyond their coastline. (The United States signed but has not ratified this agreement.)

U.S. fisheries are regulated under the 1976 Magnuson-Stevens Fishery Conservation and Management Act and its ammendments. Regulatory goals include conserving fishery resources, enforcing international fishing agreements, developing underused fisheries, protecting fish habitat, and limiting "bycatch" (fish caught unintentionally). The law establishes Regional Fishery Management Councils, charged with developing Fishery Management Plans that identify overfished stocks and propose plans to restore and protect them. For each fishery, a scientific panel determines the "acceptable biological catch," and the managers then set an "annual catch limit," not to exceed the acceptable biological catch. The Councils can limit access to specific boats or operators, restrict fishing to certain times of the year or certain locations, regulate fishing gear, and require on-board observers to ensure that boats obey regulations. National Oceanic and Atmospheric Administration (NOAA) Fisheries publishers an annual report on the status of U.S. Fisheries. In 2014 and 2015 the annual catch rate was too high in about 8% of these, the stock was too small in about 37%, and 38% of previously overfished stocks were classified as "rebuilt" (NOAA 2016).

Regulation promulgated under the Magnuson-Stevens Act, like most fishery regulation, is based on stock and catch "biomass," the number of tons of fish. Biomass does not capture the age and size distribution of the stock or the catch: 20 half-pound fish and 10 1-pound fish both contribute 10 pounds of biomass. Larger fish are easier to catch but also contribute more, via breeding, to the species' success. Most regulation also targets individual species or stocks, ignoring the interactions among them. It is difficult to regulate individual stocks using biomass. Taking into account age and size distributions and the interactions among multiple stocks would, in principle, increase efficiency, but it would also increase regulatory complexity. Regulation strikes a balance between the ideal and the practical.

Most of the world's important fisheries are concentrated in countries' exclusive economic zones and are regulated. Many fisheries are "regulated open access": fishers are free to enter the industry, but they face constraints on fishing gear and on the length of the season. Regulation has protected fish stocks in many but not all cases. Political and institutional constraints and scientific limitations sometimes lead to overfished stocks. Identifying

Box 12.1
The U.S. Northwest Atlantic Scallop Fishery: A Success Story

> Fishers catch scallops by dragging dredges along the seabed. In 1994, the U.S. government closed three areas; scallopers moved to and subsequently exhausted stocks in other areas. University of Massachusetts biologists, funded by fishers, concluded that the population in the closed areas had rebounded. The industry began to commit a fraction of its profits to conduct surveys. Using this data, the National Marine Fisheries Service (NMFS) closes over-fished seabeds long enough to allow the population to recover (about 3–5 years), a system resembling field rotation in agriculture (Wittenberg 2014). The program relies on good data and cooperation between fishers and NMFS. Fishers have a common interest in preserving the stock, and they trust the data, because they supply it.

the actual stock is a difficult measurement problem. Box 12.1 illustrates the importance of reliable data. Random stock changes, perhaps due to changes in ocean conditions or stocks of predators and prey, make it difficult to determine safe stock levels. Managers may ignore scientific evidence if they distrust it or are swayed by lobbying from fishers or processors. "Regulatory capture" occurs when regulators substitute society's goals with the narrower interests of the groups they are charged with regulating.

Even if regulation is successful in protecting a stock, it often leads to overcapitalized fisheries (too many boats or too much gear), resulting in financial distress for fishers. Estimates of overcapitalization range from 30% to more than 200%. Overcapitalization reduces industry profits, increasing the cost, decreasing revenue from harvesting a given catch, or both. Overcapitalization arises from the mismatch between targets (or "margins") and "instruments" (or policies) (Smith 2012). A target is anything that a regulator would, ideally, like to control. The payoff from a fishery depends on many variables other than the catch and the stock, including nets, engines, and other boat equipment. The Regional Fishery Management Councils have the authority to regulate most of these potential targets, but regulation of every business decision is impractical. Most regulation involves simple policies (e.g., restricting the length of the season or limiting the number of boats). When the regulator restricts one margin (e.g., by limiting the season length), fishers respond on another margin (e.g., by changing the gear they use). Regulators cannot control all margins, so regulation is second best. Fishers acting in their self-interest inflict externalities on others, leading to inefficient outcomes.

Management outcomes must be measured against objectives: to speak of an optimal resource tax or an optimal catch limit, we must decide what the policy is intended to optimize. Neoclassical resource economics uses the present value of the stream of social surplus, a special case of discounted utilitarianism (DU), as the criterion for evaluating fishery and other resource management. Chapters 15 and 16 adopt this criterion in studying fisheries, Chapter 17 applies it to water resources, and Chapter 19 notes both its uses and limitations in climate economics. DU has a precise definition and a well developed (but not universally accepted) theoretical basis. It provides a foundation for policy analysis, enabling us to evaluate taxes, catch limits, and other resource policies. The standard DU criterion does not attach intrinsic importance to the ecological health of a fishery. Depending on circumstances, that criterion might recommend maintaining a large stock, or harvesting a stock to extinction. It does not attach importance to community objectives, such as stable employment.

These limitations motivate economists to develop other ways to measure welfare and thus to assess regulation. Chapter 18 explains how economists think about sustainability and describes indices used to evaluate resource use. Some of these indices include a broad range of resources, and some focus on a specific class, such as fisheries. The Fishery Performance Indicator evaluates fisheries on the basis of a triple bottom line involving ecological, economic, and community criteria (Anderson et al. 2015). The ecological component depends on the health of the stock. The economic component includes fishing costs and revenue, and their volatility. Community-based criteria include crew and processor employment, wages, health, education, and social standing. Some fisheries have high scores on some indicators and low scores on others. The Alaskan salmon and Oregon Dungeness crab have ecologically healthy stocks but poor economic performance, with excess capacity, short harvest seasons, supply gluts, and low prices. The Kenyan octopus and Seychellois sea cucumber fisheries do a poor job of managing stocks but currently provide substantial economic benefit.

Measurements of stock size, employment, and many other ingredients of the Fishery Performance Indicator are apples and oranges. Any index that summarizes disparate categories must take a stand on how to weigh or, more generally, how to aggregate them. DU is a particular means of aggregation.

12.4   A Model of Overcapitalization*

Objectives and skills: Understand why second-best regulation often causes overcapitalization.

We illustrate overcapitalization and the loss in industry profits using a model with four targets (or margins): annual allowable catch, A; the number of boats, N; the number of days of the season, D; and the amount of "effort" per boat per day, E. Effort is an amalgam of all of the decisions the fisher makes (e.g., boat size, crew, gear characteristics). Each unit of effort costs w per day; E units of effort enable a boat to catch $E^{0.5}$ fish per day.

In the first-best setting, the regulator has four policies (or instruments) that make it possible to control all four margins. To examine the scenario when regulators cannot control every margin, we consider a second-best setting where the regulator chooses the annual catch, A, and enforces that choice by selecting the length of the season, D. Fishers choose effort, E, to maximize their profits. We first consider the case where N is fixed, and then the case where N is endogenous.

Exogenous N

Individual fishers, each with a boat, choose effort to maximize profit (revenue minus cost). If the price of a unit of fish is p, the fisher chooses E to maximize profits per day:

$$\max_E (pE^{0.5} - wE) \Rightarrow \frac{d(pE^{0.5} - wE)}{dE} \overset{\text{set}}{=} 0 \Rightarrow E = \left(0.5\frac{p}{w}\right)^2. \tag{12.1}$$

Given that the N fishers choose this level of effort, the manager who wants to set annual catch equal to A must choose the number of days of the season, D, so that the exogenous number of fishers (N), times the catch per day per fisher ($E^{0.5}$), times the number of days, equals A:

$$NE^{0.5}D = N\left(\left(0.5\frac{p}{w}\right)^2\right)^{0.5} D \overset{\text{set}}{=} A \Rightarrow D = 2\frac{Aw}{Np}. \tag{12.2}$$

The potential fishing season has S days; $\delta = \frac{D}{S}$ equals the fraction of the potential season that fishing is allowed, and we assume that $\frac{D}{S} < 1$:

$$\text{Assumption: } \delta = \frac{2Aw}{NSp} < 1. \tag{12.3}$$

The inequality states that, given fishers' individually optimal choice of effort per day, the annual allowance, A, constrains the length of the season. If inequality 12.3 were reversed, then fishers could work the entire season without exceeding the ceiling, making regulation unnecessary.

In this second-best setting, total industry profit equals

$$\text{profit}^{\text{second best}} = DN(pE^{0.5} - wE)$$

$$= \underbrace{2\frac{A}{N}\frac{w}{p}N\left(p\left(\left(0.5\frac{p}{w}\right)^2\right)^{0.5} - w\left(0.5\frac{p}{w}\right)^2\right)}_{\text{use eq 12.1 and 12.2 to eliminate } E \text{ and } D} = \underbrace{\frac{Ap}{2}}_{\text{simplify}}.$$

In the first-best setting (conditional on N), the regulator chooses both effort and the number of days. The harvest limit, A, fixes revenue at pA, so profit maximization requires minimizing the cost of harvesting A. Cost minimization requires setting $D = S$, the maximum feasible season (see exercise 3). The increase in D, relative to the second-best setting, requires reducing effort per day, so that the catch limit is not exceeded. The first-best level of effort is $E = \left(\frac{A}{NS}\right)^2$. Substituting this level of effort, and $D = S$, into the expression for industry profits, gives

$$\text{profit}^{\text{first best}} = DN(pE^{0.5} - wE) = SN\left(p\left(\frac{A}{NS}\right) - w\left(\frac{A}{NS}\right)^2\right) = pA - \frac{A^2w}{NS}.$$

First-best regulation increases industry profit by

$$\frac{\text{profit}^{\text{first best}} - \text{profit}^{\text{second best}}}{\text{profit}^{\text{second best}}}100\% = \frac{\frac{1}{2}Ap\left(1 - \frac{2Aw}{NSp}\right)}{\frac{Ap}{2}}100\% = (1 - \delta)100\%.$$

Fishers act in their self-interest in choosing effort, but they inflict a negative externality on the industry: as effort increases, catch per day also increases, requiring that the regulator shorten the season to maintain the annual catch limit. Self-interested behavior leads to excessive effort and too-short a season. This static model does not distinguish between a durable input, such as a boat, and a variable input, such as crew size. In this context, "overcapitalization" means that there are too many productive assets in the sector. Overcapitalization decreases industry profits.

Endogenous N

If the number of boats, N, responds to profits, it is another target, or margin. Suppose that initially the fishery is unregulated, leading to depleted stocks, high costs, and low profits. In equilibrium, boats earn their opportunity cost; no one wants to enter or leave the sector. If a restriction on annual catch succeeds in rebuilding the stock, lowering costs and increasing profits, additional boats want to enter.

The opportunity cost (e.g., rental) of a boat is F/year. Under second-best regulation, where the length of the season adjusts to maintain the catch limit, we saw above that industry profit (exclusive of boat rental cost) is $\frac{Ap}{2}$, or $\frac{Ap}{2N}$ per boat. Under free entry, boats enter until the profit per boat, inclusive of rental cost, equals zero: $\frac{Ap}{2N} - F = 0$, or $N = \frac{Ap}{2F}$ (ignoring the fact that the number of boats must be an integer). For smaller values of N, additional boats have an incentive to enter the fishery, to obtain positive profits, and for larger values of N, existing boats have an incentive to leave the fishery, to avoid losses.

Consider the case where the regulator controls only season length, and the number of boats is in equilibrium $\left(N = \frac{Ap}{2F}\right)$. A change enables the regulator to control effort (in addition to season length). We showed above that this change, at the initial level of N, increases industry profit, also increasing the profit per boat and encouraging additional boats to enter. The original number of boats $\left(N = \frac{Ap}{2F}\right)$ is already excessive from the standpoint of society (see exercise 4). Reducing effort per boat allows a longer season and increases profits per boat, but it also attracts additional boats. Getting one margin right (reducing effort per boat) causes another margin (the number of boats) to move further from the social optimum. This kind of problem is endemic to a second-best setting: fixing one problem can make another worse. A regulator who can determine the number of boats, the level of effort per boat, and the length of the season, can achieve the (unconditional) first best; that degree of regulation is seldom practical.

This situation is empirically important. The race to catch fish (and the resulting overcapitalization) leads to shorter seasons and lower industry profit in many fisheries. In the early twentieth century, the North Pacific halibut fishery operated throughout the year, leading to excessive harvests. In 1930, the United States and Canada agreed to manage the fishery using an annual quota. The initial management success increased profits, which led to a larger fleet. Managers responded by reducing the season length to 2 months in the 1950s and to less than a week in the 1970s (Homans and Wilen 2005).

12.5 Property Rights–Based Regulation

Objectives and skills: Understand how property rights–based regulation can increase profits and protect stocks.

Regulated open access can enforce an annual catch limit, solving the problem of overfishing but also leading to overcapitalization and low profits. Property rights–based regulation solves some of these problems while allowing fishers, instead of regulators, to choose how many days to fish and the type and number of boats. Both individual quotas (IQs) and individually transferable quotas (ITQs) use a (typically) species-specific annual total allowable catch (TAC); individuals buy or are given shares of that quota. An individual with share s is entitled to harvest s times that year's TAC. Under ITQs, owners can sell or lease ("transfer") their shares.

Property rights–based regulation can decrease costs, increase revenue, and protect fish stocks. Only about 2% of the world's fisheries (25% of volume) currently use this type of regulation (Costello et al. 2010; see also the symposium on rights-based fisheries edited by Costello 2012b).

12.5.1 Reducing Industry Costs

Property rights induce fishers to internalize the externalities that lead to overcapitalization, reducing costs. The Mid-Atlantic surf clam fishery switched from restricted entry regulation to ITQs in 1990. Prior to the switch, there were 128 vessels in the fishery. The estimated optimal number of boats for the industry was 21–25, leading to an estimated 45% cost reduction (Weninger 1999). By 1994, the fleet size had fallen to 50 vessels, and costs had fallen by 30%. This section explains why property rights–based regulation has these effects.

If catch from a fishery with TAC A_t sells for price p_t^{fish}, then revenue from this fishery is $p_t^{\text{fish}} A_t$. We first consider the case where trade in permits is not allowed: IQs are used instead of ITQs. We assume that the price of fish is high enough that all fishers want to catch their full allocation, so fisher i who owns the share s_i obtains revenue $s_i A_t p_t^{\text{fish}}$. With fixed revenue, this fisher maximizes profits by choosing effort and other harvest decisions to minimize the cost of catching $q_{it} = s_i A_t$. Denote this fisher's cost function as $c_i(q)$, the minimum cost of catching q. Because all fishers minimize costs, conditional on their harvest, there is no need for a regulator to interfere with their harvest decisions. The assignment of property rights leads to efficient decisions, conditional on the individual harvest levels.

Full efficiency (conditional on aggregate harvest, A_t) requires that harvest be allocated efficiently across the fishers. Efficient allocation minimizes industry costs:

$$\min_{\{q_i \geq 0\}} \sum_i c_i(q_i), \text{ subject to } \sum_i q_i = A$$

(dropping the time subscript). If it is efficient for fishers i and j to harvest positive levels ($q_i^* > 0$ and $q_j^* > 0$), then at the optimum their marginal costs are equal: $c_i'(q_i^*) = c_j'(q_i^*)$. If the two marginal cost functions are different, then the levels q_i^* and q_j^* are typically different.

Without trade, a fisher's harvest equals their quota; in this case, marginal costs are unlikely to be equalized across fishers: $c_i'(s_i A) \neq c_j'(s_j A)$. If marginal costs happened to be equal without trade, a change in A likely breaks the equality. Because the TAC A changes from year to year, full efficiency is unlikely to be satisfied without trade in quotas. The exception is if all fishers have the same marginal cost functions and equal shares.

If fishers have different marginal cost functions, and transfers in quotas are allowed (ITQs are used instead of IQs), there are potential gains from trade. Efficiency under ITQs requires a market for quotas but not bargaining among individuals. Bargaining becomes unwieldy (transactions costs become large) if it involves many people. Markets, in contrast, tend to work better when many people participate. If there is a market for quotas, and the equilibrium rental price of a license to catch a fish is P^{license}, then fisher i solves

$$\pi_i = \max_{q_i \geq 0} \left(\underbrace{p^{\text{fish}} q_i - c_i(q_i)}_{\text{profits from catching fish}} + \underbrace{P^{\text{license}} \times (s_i A - q_i)}_{\text{profits from buying or selling permits}} \right). \tag{12.4}$$

(Box 12.2 discusses the distinction between buying and renting licenses.) We can imagine the transaction for licenses taking place in two steps. First, the fisher rents out all her permits for the season, earning revenue $P^{\text{license}} \times s_i A$. Then she "rents in" q_i permits, the number needed to enable her to harvest q_i, spending $P^{\text{license}} \times q_i$. The difference equals the net profit or cost from the two transactions.

Box 12.2
Renting Versus Buying

In the static framework used here, there is no distinction between renting and buying. In practice, this distinction is important. P_t^{license} is the price a fisher pays to be allowed to catch a unit of fish in year t. If there are 100 shares, each giving a fisher the right to catch 1% of the annual catch, then the rental rate for one share in year t is $(0.01A_t) \times P_t^{\text{license}}$. One share entitles the renter to catch $0.01A_t$ fish, each of which is worth P_t^{license}. In a riskless world with frictionless markets, the amount a person would pay at $t = 0$ to buy the share equals the present discounted stream of future rents:

$$0.01 \sum_{t=0}^{\infty} \rho^t (P_t^{\text{lisence}} A_t).$$

Buying the share entitles the fisher to the future stream of revenue obtained by renting it out. Buying and renting are equivalent under certainty but not under uncertainty. An unexpectedly high future rental rate benefits an owner but harms a renter. The current price of a share takes into account, or "capitalizes," the (expected) future rental rates.

The first order condition for an active fisher, one who harvests a positive quantity ($q_i > 0$), is

$$\underbrace{p^{\text{fish}} - c_i'(q_i)}_{\text{marginal profit from additional harvest}} = \underbrace{P^{\text{license}}}_{\text{license price}}. \tag{12.5}$$

All fishers face the same price of fish and of licenses, so all active fishers (those who harvest a positive level) have the same level of marginal cost. ITQs lead to the efficient allocation of harvest across fishers, and each fisher minimizes her costs. ITQs (but not IQs) lead to the efficient outcome.

Under ITQs, the rental price and fishers' harvest levels depend on the TAC but not on the shares, s_i.[3] Essentially the same point was made in section 10.5, where we saw that the price of an emissions permit, and the levels of pollution across firms, depend on the total number of emissions permits but not on the allocation of permits. The allocation of permits in the pollution setting corresponds to the quota shares here; the aggregate level of

---

3 If there are n fishers with positive harvests, there are n first order conditions like equation 12.5. An additional equation, $\sum_{i=1}^{n} q_i = A$, states that fishers' aggregate demand for licenses equals the aggregate supply, A. We thus have $n + 1$ equations to determine the n harvest levels and P^{license}. We need to solve these equations simultaneously. Because A enters the "demand for licences = supply of licences" constraint, A affects the equilibrium values of q_i. In contrast, none of the $n + 1$ equations involve the shares (the s_i).

pollution corresponds to A; the emissions permit price corresponds to the fish quota rental price; and the firm emissions levels correspond to the catch levels, q_i.

Example

An example with two fishers (or two groups of fishers) having different harvest cost functions makes these observations concrete. Fishers 1 and 2 have harvest costs $c_1(q_1) = q_1 + q_1^2$ and $c_2(q_2) = 0.5q_2 + 1.5q_2^2$. The TAC is A, and fishers 1 and 2 have shares s and $1 - s$, respectively. Assume that the price of fish is high enough that they both want to catch their limit when trade is not allowed (IQs are used, not ITQs). Then the industry cost is

$$C^{IQ}(A) = c_1(sA) + c_2((1-s)A) = \left[(0.5s + 0.5) + (2.5s^2 - 3.0s + 1.5)A\right]A.$$

If the fishers are allowed to buy and sell permits, we saw above that if they both harvest a positive quantity, then they harvest to the point where their marginal costs are equal. This equality requires $1 + 2q_1 = 0.5 + 3q_2$. The reallocation of harvest never increases (and except for a knife-edge case strictly decreases) total costs. Therefore, the assumption that the fishers want to catch the limit in the absence of quota trade means that they also want to catch the limit under trade; thus, $q_1 + q_2 = A$.

Temporarily ignoring the non-negativity constraint on catch, we solve the last two equations to obtain

$$q_1 = 0.6A - 0.1, \quad \text{and} \quad q_2 = 0.4A + 0.1 \Rightarrow \frac{q_1}{A} = 0.6 - \frac{0.1}{A}. \tag{12.6}$$

The first equation in 12.6 shows that the non-negativity constraint is not binding if and only if $A \geq \frac{1}{6}$. The last equation in 12.6 shows that equality of marginal cost levels requires the share of harvest to vary with the total harvest, A, but not with the allocation, s. For $A > \frac{1}{6}$, both fishers are active, and industry cost equals

$$C^{ITQ}(A) = c_1(0.6A - 0.1) + c_2(0.4A + 0.1) = -0.025 + 0.8A + 0.6A^2.$$

The cost savings obtained by allowing trade in quotas (for $A \geq \frac{1}{6}$) is

$$C^{IQ}(A) - C^{ITQ}(A) = 0.025 + (0.5s - 0.3)A + (2.5s^2 - 3.0s + 0.9)A^2.$$

If $A < \frac{1}{6}$, it is optimal for fisher 2 to catch the entire TAC, because for $A < \frac{1}{6}$, fisher 2's marginal cost when she catches everything is less that 1's marginal cost when he catches nothing: $c_2'(A) < c_1'(0)$. If fisher 2 catches everything, industry costs are $C^{ITQ}(A) = c_2(A)$. The cost savings obtained by allowing trade in quotas (for $A < \frac{1}{6}$) is

$$C^{IQ}(A) - C^{ITQ}(A) = ((2.5s - 3.0)A^2 + 0.5A)s.$$

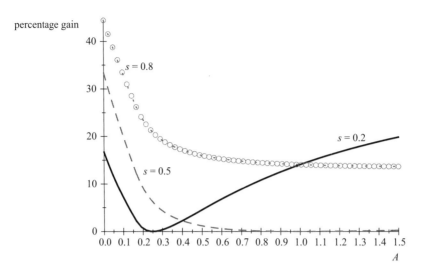

Figure 12.1

The "percentage gain" equals the percentage reduction in total costs, $\dfrac{C^{IQ}(A)-C^{ITQ}(A)}{C^{IQ}(A)}100$ due to allowing trade in quotas, as a function of the TAC A, for different allocations, s.

Figure 12.1 graphs the percentage reduction in aggregate costs due to quota transfers ("percentage gain") as a function of the TAC, A, for different quota shares. The different curves intersect, because the optimal share of harvest depends on A (see equation 12.6). Therefore, the benefit of moving from the allocation sA and $(1-s)A$ to the optimal allocation also depends on s.

12.5.2 Increasing Revenue

For a fixed TAC, IQs and ITQs can increase revenue, in addition to reducing harvest costs. The introduction of ITQs in the Gulf of Mexico reef fish fishery potentially increased revenue by almost 50% and reduced costs by 75%; the efficient fleet size was estimated at 29–70 vessels, compared to the actual level of 387 vessels (Weninger and Waters 2003). Regulated open access leads to too much gear and/or too many boats, requiring regulators to reduce the fishing season. By concentrating the annual harvest in a short period of time, this regulation potentially reduces revenue:

• With inelastic demand for fresh fish, the sudden increase in harvest that occurs during a short fishing season lowers the equilibrium price.

• Transportation constraints may make it hard to bring fresh fish to market, causing fish to be diverted to the lower-priced frozen fish market.

• Fish processors may be able to wield market power if fishers have to unload large catches during short periods of time.

These factors cause a shorter fishing season to reduce the price fishers receive. Moving from regulated open access to IQs or ITQs reduces or eliminates the race to catch fish, causing harvest to be spread out over the season and so increasing the average price of landings (Homans and Wilen 1997).

Before the British Columbia halibut fishery switched to ITQs in 1993, the fishing season lasted about five days, and most of the catch went to the frozen fish market. With the more spread-out and thus steadier supply of fish caused by the move to ITQs, wholesalers found it profitable to develop marketing networks for transporting fresh fish. Prior to the ITQs, the price of fresh fish fell rapidly if more than 100,000 pounds a week became available, but with the development of the new marketing networks, the market could absorb 800,000 pounds before prices dropped (Homans and Wilen 2005).

12.5.3   Protecting Fish Stocks

Regulated open access, like IQs/ITQs, typically relies on an annual catch limit. The mismatch between targets and instruments under regulated open access, and the resulting inefficiencies, lead to high costs, low revenue, and low industry profit. By reducing inefficiencies, an IQ/ITQ with the same annual catch limit can lower costs and increase revenue, thereby increasing profits. Property rights–based regulation can also encourage protection of fish stocks.

Changing Incentives to Protect the Stock
Regardless of the form of regulation, fishers wanting to increase short-term profits might pressure regulators to increase the annual catch limit. Property rights–based regulation may be less susceptible to this type of pressure, making it easier for regulators to follow scientific advice when setting annual limits. First, political pressure to take short-sighted actions may be harder to resist when the fishery is in financial crisis. Because property rights–based regulation can reduce industry costs while increasing revenue (for a given level of annual catch), fisheries under property rights–based regulation are less likely to be in financial crisis. Second, property rights–based regulation potentially changes fishers' incentives, making conservation of stocks more valuable to them. The IQ/ITQ gives fishers a claim on the TAC, not on the stock. Fish move around and cannot be easily identified (unlike cattle, which can be branded), so it may be impractical to assign rights to the fish stock. However, with secure quota rights, individual fishers may have almost the same incentive to protect the stock as would a sole owner, who literally owns the stock.

To explain this claim, suppose first that all fishers have the same marginal cost functions and equal shares, so they have no incentive to trade; in this case, there is no difference between IQs and ITQs. A price-taking fisher obtains a share of fishery profit equal to her quota share. This fisher, with quota share s, has the same incentive to harvest the stock as would a sole owner who faces a constant ad valorem profits tax $1 - s$; they both retain the fraction s of profits in each period. We saw in section 11.2, in the context of a nonrenewable resource, that the constant ad valorem profits tax does not alter the firm's extraction incentives; the same conclusion holds in the renewable resource setting. Thus, if firms have the same marginal cost functions and equal quota shares, every fisher has the same incentives as the sole owner. Moreover, extraction under the price-taking sole owner is efficient, provided there are no externalities (the First Fundamental Welfare Theorem and chapter 15).

In this example, where fishers are identical, any fisher delegated to pick the annual TAC would make the same (efficient) decision. If the fishers vote on the annual harvest, they unanimously vote for the efficient harvest path. Even under these circumstances, property rights to a share of harvest and property rights to a share of the stock are not identical. A person who owns the share of stock can unilaterally decide how to use it. With property rights to harvest shares, there must still be a regulator or some mechanism (e.g., a dictator or voting) for picking the annual harvest. The assignment of a share of harvest aligns individual with group interests, but it still leaves the coordination problem of picking an annual harvest. With unanimity of interests, that coordination problem may be easy to solve. The monitoring problem also differs in the two situations. A fisher who owns the stock is not tempted to "cheat on herself" by harvesting above the socially optimal level, but it is still necessary to keep poachers out of the fishery. Fishers who own shares to the TAC might want to cheat by taking more than the legal amount, because other fishers bear some of the cost of their excessive harvest: there is a dynamic (stock) externality. In this case, it is necessary to deter illegal catch both by outsiders and by quota owners. The monitoring problem is present in both situations, and might be greater in either. The example of the Igbo in section 12.1 illustrates that an apparent strengthening of property rights might make monitoring harder.

Because fishers are unlikely to all have the same marginal cost functions and shares, the analogy of the constant ad valorem profits tax is too optimistic. When marginal costs functions or shares are not the same, we saw that efficiency requires ITQs instead of IQs. Even with ITQs, fishers do not have exactly the same incentive to harvest as a sole owner. When maximizing the present discounted stream of profits, a price-taking sole owner chooses an efficient harvest trajectory, one that also maximizes the discounted stream of social surplus. That trajectory satisfies an Euler equation; neither the sole owner nor the social planner benefits from a perturbation. Now suppose that this fishery has ITQs, and a regulator proposes the efficient trajectory of TACs. Choose an arbitrary fisher, who happens to have the ITQ share s. Would this fisher want to alter the efficient trajectory chosen by the regulator? In general, the answer is "yes." This fisher's share of industry profit in any period depends on both her share of the quota, s, and also on the TAC in the period. But the TAC (in general) changes from year to year, so the fisher's share of industry profit also changes from year to year. In this case, it is as if the fisher faces a time varying ad valorem profits tax; section 11.2 notes that such a tax does alter the firm's (fisher's) extraction (harvest) incentives. In this circumstance, the assignment of property rights to the stock leads to different incentives, compared to the assignment of property rights to ITQs.

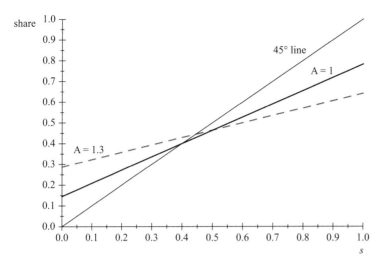

Figure 12.2
Fisher 1's share of profits ("share") as a function of his allocation share, s, under ITQs for two allocations, $A = 1$ and $A = 1.3$. Where share lies above (below) the 45° line, fisher 1's profit share is greater (less) than his allocation share.

Figure 12.2 illustrates this claim, extending the numerical example from section 12.5.1. The figure graphs Fisher 1's equilibrium profit share ("share") as a function of her quota share, s, for two levels of the allocation.[4] Where the share graph lies above (below) the 45° line, the profit share is greater than (less than) the quota share. The figure shows that the profit share is sensitive to the allocation, A, and might be either greater or less than the quota share, s.

A fisher's share of profit exceeds her quota share when s is small, and is less than her quota share when s is large. To understand this relation, consider the extreme cases where $s = 0$ or $s = 1$. For $s = 0$, the fisher without any shares buys quota rights. This fisher obtains profits even though she has no quota shares, so her share of profits necessarily exceeds her share of quotas. If $s = 1$, the fisher with all of the shares sells some shares to other fishers. Those fishers obtain positive profits, so the fisher with $s = 1$ obtains less than 100% of industry profits. (For the parameters used in constructing this figure, the allocation is large enough that both high- and low-cost fishers are active.)

If s is constant but A changes over time, a fisher's share of aggregate profits also changes over time. In this respect, a constant quota share is analogous to a time-varying profits tax.

4 The figure uses the inverse demand $p^{\text{fish}} = 4.1 - A$, so under ITQs, price exceeds the fishers' marginal cost for $A < 1.5$. Using calculations in the example, we know that it is efficient for both fishers to operate for $A > \frac{1}{6}$. Equation 12.5 determines the rental price, p^{license}. Using this value in the expression for a fisher's profit, equation 12.4, we obtain fisher 1's profit as a function of s and A, and industry profit as a function of A. Figure 12.2 graphs the ratio of these functions for $A = 1.3$ and $A = 1$.

Here, assignment of ITQ rights does not give fishers the same incentive to harvest the stock as would assignment of property rights to the stock. Nevertheless, the special case where fishers have the same marginal cost functions and the same quota shares suggests that property rights to ITQs can be a close substitute to the (perhaps impractical) assignment of property rights to stocks.

Empirical Results

Do IQs/ITQs actually lead to healthier fisheries (= larger stocks)? Ideally, we would answer this question by measuring stock size (the outcome of interest) and randomly assigning some fisheries to be regulated by IQs/ITQs (the treatment group) and others (the control group) to alternative regulatory regimes. Additionally, we would ensure that characteristics in the two groups are balanced, as described below. Real world data are not so neat. We do not have accurate stock data, assignment to ITQ status is not random, and the characteristics are not balanced.

Most fisheries lack reliable measures of stock size. Instead, researchers use proxies (as in section 6.4) that are correlated with stock size. One definition calls a fishery "collapsed" in a particular year if the harvest in that year is less than 10% of the maximum historical harvest. To the extent that this measure is strongly correlated with the actual stock size, the relation between IQ/ITQ status and collapse status provides information about the relation between IQ/ITQ status and stocks.

Twenty-seven percent of fisheries were collapsed in 2003, and fisheries with IQ/ITQs were less likely to be collapsed. This negative correlation is consistent with the theory outlined above, which suggests that property rights promote healthy stocks. However, fisheries were not randomly assigned to the treatment and control groups. The resulting selection problem makes it difficult to tell whether the negative correlation between ITQ status and fishery collapse is spurious, or whether the property rights–based mechanism really protects the fishery's health. (Exercise 6.3 illustrates the bias caused by self-selection.) The problem is that the econometrician does not observe the selection process that determines whether a fishery is regulated by IQ/ITQs. Suppose that political considerations make it easy to convert some fisheries to property rights–based management and difficult to convert others; suppose also that the "politically easy" fisheries happen to be less prone to collapse. These two circumstances create a negative correlation between property rights–based management and collapse status, independently of whether there is a causal relation between the two.[5]

---

5 More generally, there is an unobserved "Characteristic Y" that is positively correlated with collapse status and negatively correlated with ITQ status (or vice versa). Characteristic Y creates a negative correlation between collapse status and ITQ status, without any causal connection. If the characteristic were observed, statistical methods (regression analysis) can control for it. The selection problem arises because Characteristic Y is not observed, making it impossible to control for it. Exercise 6.3 illustrates the selection problem and shows that failure to correct it leads to biased estimates.

Statistical methods based on matching can alleviate the selection problem; these methods match pairs of fisheries that are alike except for their ITQ status. By comparing collapse status across these pairs of matches, we can estimate the effect of ITQs. A study based on 50 years of data and more than 11,000 fisheries, taking into account the selection problem, estimates that ITQs reduce the probability of collapse in a year by about 50% (Costello, Gaines, and Lynham 2008). It also estimates that had there been a general movement to ITQs in 1970, the percentage of fisheries collapsed in 2003 would have been about 9% instead of the observed 27%.[6]

A third data problem arises from a particular type of imbalance: all ITQ fisheries have catch limits, but only some of the non-ITQ fisheries have these limits. If none of the non-ITQ fisheries had catch limits, then it would clearly be impossible to determine whether any difference in stock health is due to ITQ status or to the catch limit. The actual data are not so extreme; nevertheless, this imbalance in characteristics across the treatment and control groups decreases the precision of estimates of the effect of ITQ status on stock health.

IQ/ITQs Are Not a Panacea
The property rights created by IQs and ITQs can improve the financial and ecological health of a fishery, but they leave some problems unsolved. If it is cheaper to catch fish earlier in the season, when the stock is larger, there is still an incentive to race for fish, a cause of overcapitalization. In addition, the IQ/ITQ in a specific fishery does not reduce bycatch or otherwise protect other species; that protection requires additional regulations or the creation of additional property rights (Abbott and Wilen 2009, 2011).

Reducing overcapitalization results in fewer boats and (usually) fewer jobs. The loss of employment associated with ITQs can create hardship. The importance of local employment is frequently used as a rationale for supporting shrinking industries, including steel production (e.g., in the United States during the 1980s and 1990s), forestry (e.g., in the United States during the 1990s and 2000s), and agriculture (e.g., the Common Agricultural Policy in the European Union). The Principle of Targeting tells us that even though local unemployment may be a significant social problem, maintaining an inefficiently large industry is unlikely to be the right policy prescription. For natural resource–based industries, this employment argument is particularly problematic if supporting a sector aggravates the decline in resource stocks. Without protecting the stock that the industry relies on, employment in the sector will certainly fall.

The employment effects of IQ/ITQs is harder to document than the reduction in the number of boats. ITQs introduced in the Bering Sea/Aleutian Islands crab fisheries reduced the number of jobs in proportion to the reduction in the number of boats (Abbott, Garber-Yonts, and Wilen 2010). However, total crew hours remained roughly constant: fewer

---

6 A much smaller study based on estimated stock levels (instead of the collapse proxy) found that fish stocks continued to decline in eight of the 20 stocks regulated using ITQs (Chu 2009).

people had longer seasonal fishing employment. Most fishers had higher remuneration after IQs, and there was a reduction in physical risk associated with the easing of the race to catch fish. Fishers had steadier employment during the season and faced less financial risk. Property rights-based regulation led to fewer but better jobs, with similar levels of total hours worked and income.

Other objections to IQ/ITQs involve market power and equity. The ITQ-induced increased concentration conceivably makes it easier for fishers to exercise market power. However, each fishery faces competition from other fisheries and other food products, making monopoly power unlikely. The industry concentration might reduce competition for workers, enabling owners to exercise monopsony power with respect to labor.[7] ITQs are sometimes criticized because they transfer resource rents to individual fishers, instead of to society at large; but this is an argument against the way in which ITQs are distributed (as a gift rather than by auctioning), not against ITQs as a means of rationalizing the industry and protecting a resource stock.

Other approaches protect fisheries on the basis of territory instead of species. Territorial Use Rights Fisheries can alleviate the cross-species problem by giving groups of fishers (e.g., co-ops) exclusive rights to an area, instead of quotas to a species (Deacon, Parker, and Costello 2013). Marine Protected Areas (MPAs) restrict or prohibit fishing, thus protecting nurseries and increasing stocks that migrate outside the MPA, which enhances the profitability of fisheries that rely on those stocks. Only a small fraction of marine habitat is designated as MPAs. A recent widely publicized proposal recommends that all international waters be set aside as an MPA (Wilson 2016). Advocates claim that by improving the oceans' ecology, this MPA would enhance the value of domestic fisheries by enough to offset the economic loss caused by eliminating fishing in international waters.

12.6   Subsidies to Fisheries

Objectives and skills: Recognize that fishing subsidies are large and understand that their distortionary effect depends on the regulatory environment.

Inappropriate regulation can lead to overharvest, reducing stocks, thereby threatening future harvests; it can also lead to overcapitalized and financially stressed fisheries. The policy remedy requires reducing catch to allow stocks to recover, and encouraging rationalization and consolidation of the industry. Reducing catch and encouraging fishers to leave the industry are politically unpopular. Subsidizing the industry is politically easier but ultimately counterproductive. Subsidies disguise the economic costs, enabling fishers to remain in a socially unproductive activity. Subsidies transfer income from one group

---

7 The monopolist exercises market power by reducing quantity produced, raising the output price. The "monopsonist" exercises market power by reducing, for example, the amount of labor it employs, reducing the wage it must pay.

to another, in this case from taxpayers to fishers and indirectly to consumers via lower prices. If subsidies exacerbate the problem of overfishing, the current increase in supply and resulting lower price comes at the cost of reduced future supply and higher future price. In this case, subsidies also transfer welfare from future to current consumers.

Subsidies attract mobile factors of production into a sector. In the static setting with a single distortionary tax (or subsidy), section 10.3 notes that the economic cost of the policy (the deadweight loss) is typically much smaller than the transfer ("triangles are small relative to rectangles"). The example in section 9.4 shows, however, that mutually reinforcing distortions can lead to much higher social losses, exceeding the magnitude of the transfer. That example shows that a subsidized sector might contribute negative value-added to society; in that case, the social value of the mobile inputs used in the sector exceeds the social value of production.

The effect of subsidies depends on the regulatory environment. Under open access, where free entry drives profits toward zero, subsidies exacerbate overharvest (harming future consumers) without increasing sectoral profits. In fisheries where the value of harvest is less than the true cost of harvest, the industry operates at a social loss, disguised by government subsidies.[8] Under regulated open access, catch limits protect stocks. However, just as with open access, subsidies attract more factors to the fishing sector, worsening the problem of overcapitalization. Property rights–based regulation potentially solves both the problems of overfishing and overcapitalization. There, subsidies' main effect is to increase the value of quota rents, transferring income from taxpayers to the quota owners.

Fisheries are not alone in receiving politically motivated but economically unproductive subsidies; section 11.1 discusses fossil fuel subsidies. Agriculture in many developed countries also receives large subsidies, often justified as helping struggling farmers. However, changes induced by the subsidies often undo whatever short-term financial help the subsidies provide. Agricultural subsidies are capitalized into the price of land, in the same way that fishing subsidies are capitalized into the value of quota rights. The expectation that the subsidies will continue into the future makes people willing to pay more for land or the quota right, raising its equilibrium price. In agriculture, current landowners who sell their land, not entering farmers who must buy the land, capture the increased value. Subsidies, and in particular the belief that they will continue into the future, increase young farmers' debt (via the increase in land prices), making them more vulnerable to future financial difficulties and more dependent on the subsidies. The same mechanism operates when subsidies are used in fisheries with property rights–based regulation.

Domestic and international agencies have estimated the magnitude of fishing subsidies and have documented the link between subsidies, overfishing, and overcapitalization. A 2013 European Parliament study estimates annual global subsidies to the fishing sector of

---

8 This situation is reminiscent of many Russian and Eastern European industries after the collapse of the Soviet Union. These industries were not economically viable and had been kept alive by government subsidies; closing them down increased gross national product.

$35 billion (2009 dollars) (Sumaila et al. 2013). A 2009 study commissioned by the World Bank estimates the annual global economic cost of fishery subsidies, including the costs associated with overcapitalization reduced stocks, at $50 billion (Arnason, Kelleher, and Willmann 2009). Developed countries are responsible for the bulk of the subsidies, with more than 40% originating in Asia, chiefly Japan and China. The precise dollar values and subsidy categories are debated. For example, both fishers and farmers are exempt from certain fuel taxes. Should this exemption be counted as a fishing subsidy, or does it merely level the playing field with farmers? There is general agreement that the subsidies are large and that they aggravate problems in the fishing industry.

12.7   Summary

Private property, common property, open access, and state/public property are the leading modes of property rights. Property rights to most resources lie somewhere on the continuum that includes these modes. De facto property rights sometimes differ from de jure rights. Common property can lead to overuse of the resource, a result known as the tragedy of the commons. Many societies developed mechanisms that efficiently manage common property resources; increased trade, migration, and population growth sometimes erode these mechanisms. If transactions costs are small and property rights well defined, agents can (plausibly) reach an efficient outcome through bargaining. The Coase Theorem states that in this case, the efficiency of the outcome does not depend on agents' bargaining power, or more generally, on the distribution of property rights. This result implies that regulation is unnecessary when transactions costs are low and property rights are secure.

Most economically important fisheries fall within nations' exclusive economic zones and are regulated. The impracticality of regulating every facet of fishing leaves regulators in a second-best setting. Many fisheries set annual quotas, enforced using a variety of policies, notably early season closures. The race among fishers to catch fish leads to overcapitalization, which results in high costs and, because much of the harvest is landed during a short period of time, low revenue. Property rights–based regulation, primarily ITQs, can lead to consolidation and rationalization of fisheries, lowering costs; increasing revenue; and via a political dynamic, increasing the prospect for fishery health (adequate stocks). Subsidies provide short-run benefits to fisheries but often exacerbate the causes of low profits and overfishing.

12.8   Terms and Concepts, Study Questions, Exercises, and Sources

Terms and Concepts

Open access, common property, de jure, de facto, congestion, localism, tragedy of the commons, Doctrine of Regulatory Taking, transactions costs, Coase Theorem, fair lottery, outside option, Law of the Sea, exclusive economic zone, Magnuson-Stevens Fishery

Conservation and Management Act, bycatch, Regional Fishery Management Councils, Fishery Management Plans, acceptable biological catch, annual catch limit, biomass, regulatory capture, regulated open access, overcapitalization, Individual Quotas (IQs), individual transferable quotas (ITQs), Territorial Use Rights Fisheries, marine reserves, monopsony power.

Study Questions

1. Recently there have been a spate of disputes on airlines concerning whether a person is entitled to recline their seat. These disputes are essentially about who has the property rights to the several inches of space between a seat and the one in front of it. Some airlines assign property rights: a person is entitled to recline her seat, except during meals (and of course during landing and takeoff). Recently these rules seem to have become more vague, or less well understood. Discuss the increasing occurrence of these disputes among passengers in light of the Coase Theorem.

2. A regulator has a target of a fixed annual allowable catch, A, and can choose the season length. For a given number of boats, explain why the regulator might have to use a short season. Next, explain why increased ability to regulate (e.g., the ability to regulate effort) might lead to a longer season. If there is free entry (so the number of boats is endogenous), explain why the increased ability to regulate effort might induce additional boats to enter.

3. Briefly describe how an IQ and an ITQ work. In what respect are they similar, and how are they different?

4. Suppose that fishers have different cost functions. For a given allowable catch, A, explain why industry costs depend on the distribution of quota rights (the s_i) under IQs but not under ITQs. Explain why the quota price, under ITQs, does not depend on the distribution of quota rights.

5. Explain why the adoption of an ITQ potentially increases industry revenue, decreases industry costs, and protects the stock.

6. Explain the "selection problem" in estimating the effect of ITQs on fishery health.

Exercises

1. A factory that emits e units of pollution obtains the total benefit from emissions, $10e - \frac{1}{2}e^2$. (By polluting more, the factory incurs lower abatement costs, thus increasing its profits.) An old-fashioned downstream laundry dries clothes outside. The pollution makes it more expensive for the laundry to return clean clothes to its customers, increasing the laundry's costs by $2e^2$.

  (a) Find the socially optimal level of pollution, e^*, the level of pollution that maximizes factory profits, e^F, and the level that minimizes laundry costs, e^L.

  (b) The bargaining surplus due to moving from a nonoptimal level of emissions to the optimal level equals the increase in social welfare (factory profits minus laundry costs). Suppose that the factory has property rights to pollute. What is the bargaining surplus in this case? What is the minimum amount that the factory would insist on to reduce emissions to the optimal level? What is the maximum amount that the laundry would pay to reduce emissions to the optimal level?

(c) Without doing any calculations, explain why the laundry and the factory have an incentive to continue bargaining until they agree on the socially optimal emissions level.

(d) What emissions tax supports the socially optimal level of pollution as a competitive equilibrium?

2. Use the cost functions in the example in section 12.5.1 and the inverse demand function $p^{\text{fish}} = 4.1 - q$. The total allocation is A; fisher 1 has share s, and fisher 2 has share $1 - s$. Assume that quotas are traded (ITQs, not IQs), that both fishers operate, and that they want to catch the entire allocation, A. (Using equation 12.6, the assumption that both firms operate implies $A > \frac{1}{6}$.)

(a) Find the expression for the price of a license, p^{license}, as a function of A. [Hint: Begin with equation 12.5, the formula for p^{license}. Substitute in the marginal cost for either fisher, evaluated at the equilibrium level of harvest under ITQs, given by equation 12.6. Because the two types of fishers have equal marginal cost in equilibrium, it does not matter which of the two marginal cost functions you use.]

(b) What is the largest value of A for which the license price is positive? Explain why a license has zero price for larger A.

(c) Give the economic explanation for why the license price does not depend on s.

(d) Figure 12.2 shows that even for $s = 0$, fisher 1 has a large share (15–30%) of industry profits (for $A = 1$ and $A = 1.3$). Explain why fisher 1 obtains a significant share of profits, even if her share of the allocation is zero ($s = 0$).

(e) Use figure 12.2. Suppose that fisher 1 has the share of quotas $s_1 = 0.2$. The regulator announces the efficient trajectory of allowable catch, which increases over time from $A = 1$ to $A = 1.3$. If fisher 1 were able to perturb ($=$ change) this trajectory, would she want to do so? Why?

3. Use the model in section 12.4, where N is fixed, the regulator chooses D, and fishers choose E. Parts (a) and (b) of this exercise require reproducing material in the text, together with filling in a couple of details. Part (c) requires following a series of instructions. Part (d) requires summarizing the interpretation given in the text.

(a) Copy the fisher's optimization problem when she chooses effort, equation 12.1. Write the fisher's first order condition, and solve it to obtain the value of E shown in equation 12.1.

(b) Under the assumption that fishers choose effort, use notation to write the constraint that total harvest equals the allowable catch, A. Solve this equation to find the value of D that satisfies the constraint.

(c) Now consider the case where the regulator is able to choose both D and E. Because harvest is not permitted to exceed A, the total revenue is fixed at pA. Therefore, the regulator's objective is to minimize costs, subject to the constraints that the limit is caught ($NE^{0.5}D = A$) and that D not exceed the maximum number of days, S:

$$\min_{E,D} (wED), \text{ subject to } NE^{0.5}D = A \text{ and } D \leq S.$$

Proceed as follows: (1) Use the constraint involving A to solve for E. (2) Substitute this value of E into the minimand (the quantity being minimized; in this case, costs). (3) Note that the resulting minimand is decreasing in D. Conclude that the value of D that minimizes costs is therefore the maximum feasible value, S. (4) Using $D = S$ from part (3) in the expression you obtained from part (1), write the level of effort as a function of the model parameters.

(d) Explain why the values of E and D are different when the regulator chooses only D, compared to the case when the regulator chooses both D and E.

4. Use the model in section 12.4 when the regulator chooses both E and D to achieve the aggregate harvest, A. Here we treat N as endogenous; ignore the "integer constraint" (i.e., assume that N can be any non-negative number). Set $w = 1$, $p = 1$, $S = 5$, $F = 1$, and $A = 10$.

(a) Find the equilibrium D, N, and E under free entry. [Hint: Use the answer to exercise 3 to determine the value of D, given that the regulator can choose effort. Then use the free entry condition to obtain an equation in N that must be satisfied under free entry In both of the following scenarios. This equation has two roots. The larger root is the correct one.]

(b) Find the equilibrium D, N, and E when the regulator can choose N, in addition to D and E.

(c) Compare aggregate industry costs and the levels of N and E in the two cases. Explain the difference.

Sources

Dietz, Ostrom, and Stern (2003) and Ostrom (1990, 2007) discuss conditions under which societies successfully manage common property without formal regulation.

Hardin (1968) introduced the term "tragedy of the commons."

Gordon (1954) provided the first well-known analysis of fisheries as common property resources.

Kaffine (2009) documents California surfers' efforts to exercise de facto property rights on some beaches. Lovett (2016) describes a court case arising from locals' attempts to exclude outside surfers from a California beach.

The Millennium Ecosystem Assessment (United Nations 2005), Sumaila et al. (2011) and Dyck and Sumaila (2010) provide overviews of the state of fisheries.

Johnson and Libecap (1982) describe the replacement of common property with open access in the Alaska salmon fishery.

Fenske (2012) documents the case of property rights for rubber trees among the Nigerian Igbo.

Strambro et al. (2014) examine the effects on Utah's finances of transferring federal land to the state.

De Janvry et al. (2015) examine the migration effect of formalizing property rights to land in Mexico.

Anderson et al. (2015) introduce Fishery Performance Indicators, a tool to improve management.

NOAA Fisheries (2016) publishes an annual report on the status of U.S. fisheries.

Wittenberg (2014) provides the information for box 12.1.

Smith (2012) surveys the problems of regulating fisheries when there more targets (i.e., margins) than policy variables.

Costello et al. (2010) review the effect of rights-based regulation on economic incentives and fishery sustainability.

The 2012 symposium "Rights-Based Fisheries Management," edited by Costello (2012b) and with papers by Aranson (2012), Deacon (2012), and Wilen, Cancino, and Uchida (2012) reviews the literature on rights-based management.

Homans and Wilen (1997) show how individually rational effort decisions, and the resulting overcapitalization, lead to reductions in the length of a fishing season.

Homans and Wilen (2005) document the effect of ITQs on revenue, and provide the example of the British Columbia halibut fishery.

Weninger and Waters (2003) estimate potential revenue gains, cost reductions, and fleet consolidation due to using ITQs in the Gulf of Mexico reef fish fishery.

Weninger (1999) studies the effect of ITQs on the Mid-Atlantic surf clam.

Abbott and Wilen (2009, 2011) examine fishers' response to quotas on bycatch.

Costello, Gaines, and Lynham (2008) use a proxy for collapse to estimate the effect of ITQs on fishery sustainability.

Chu (2009) examines the effect of ITQs on stock levels.

Deacon, Parker, and Costello (2013) study a situation where fishers had the option of obtaining property rights by joining a co-op.

Abbott, Garber-Yonts, and Wilen (2010) study the employment effect of IQs in the Bering Sea/Aleutian Islands crab fisheries.

Sharp and Sumaila (2009) quantify U.S. fishery subsidies.

Sumaila et al. (2013) quantify global fishery subsidies.

Arnason, Kelleher, and Willmann (2009) estimate the economic cost of global fishery subsidies.

Wilson (2016) presents the argument for setting aside international waters as an MPA.

13 Renewable Resources: Tools

Objective
- Introduce the building blocks of renewable resource models.

Skills
- Understand and be able to work with a growth function and a harvest rule.
- Know the meaning of and be able to calculate steady states.
- Understand the meaning of, and be able to identify, stable steady states.
- Understand the meaning of, and be able to calculate maximum sustainable yield.

A few tools make it possible to analyze a range of renewable resources. Subsequent chapters use these to study the open access fishery, the sole owner fishery, and water economics. Resource models involve one or more "stock variable(s)" that potentially change over time. In the nonrenewable resource setting, the stock variable equals the amount of the resource remaining in the mine or well; extraction decreases the stock. In the renewable resource setting, growth might offset extraction, causing the stock to rise or fall.

For water, we can measure the stock using the volume in an aquifer or a reservoir. Consuming the water reduces the stock, but a natural recharge (e.g., rain) and evaporation also affect the stock. In forestry, the stock can be measured using the biomass of forestry, the number of tons of wood. Cutting down trees reduces the stock, but the forest's natural growth increases it. In the climate context, the stock might be measured using the parts per million of atmospheric CO_2. Carbon emissions increase the stock, some of which is absorbed into other carbon reservoirs (e.g., oceans). In all these cases, the stock might rise or fall over time, depending on the relation between society's actions and natural growth, recharge, and decay.

A Road Map
In the renewable resource setting, the "growth function" describes the change in the stock in the absence of extraction or harvest. Section 13.1 emphasizes the logistic growth function. In many contexts, the amount harvested in a period depends on the stock in that

period. We refer to the relation between harvest and the stock (a function) as a "harvest rule." A "steady state" is a level of the stock that remains constant over time. There might be one or more steady states; the location of these depend on the growth function and the harvest rule (section 13.2).

Most steady states are either "stable" or "unstable." If the stock begins close to a stable steady state, the stock trajectory approaches that steady state over time; if a stock begins close to an unstable steady state, the trajectory moves away from that steady state over time. In a continuous time setting, stability is easy to determine by inspection of a graph; matters are a bit more complicated in a discrete time setting. Therefore, when considering stability, we adopt a continuous time perspective (section 13.3). The "maximum sustainable yield" (MSY) is the largest yield that can be sustained in perpetuity. This yield maximizes consumer surplus and is often adopted as a regulatory target. Section 13.4 identifies the MSY for the logistic growth function.

13.1   Growth Dynamics

Objectives and skills: Understand the meaning of a growth function, and the logistic growth function in particular.

This section introduces renewable resources using fishery economics. The stock of fish equals its biomass, the number of tons of fish. Section 12.3 notes that most regulation targets biomass, even though biomass does not capture age and size distributions. These distributions are hard to measure; their use as regulatory targets potentially increases efficiency but also increases complexity.

The stock of fish in period t is x_t, so the change in the stock is $x_{t+1} - x_t$. The growth function, $F(x)$, determines the evolution of the fish stock with zero harvest. Some fish die and new fish are born, so the stock might increase or decrease over time. Growth depends on the stock:

$$x_{t+1} - x_t = F(x_t).$$

If a period equals 1 year, then $F(x)$ equals the annual growth, $\frac{F(x)}{x}$ equals the annual growth rate and $\frac{F(x)}{x}100\%$ equals the annual percentage growth rate. The Verhulst, or "logistic" model is often used to describe growth:

$$F(x_t) = \gamma x_t \left(1 - \frac{x_t}{K}\right). \tag{13.1}$$

This model uses two parameters, $\gamma > 0$, and $K > 0$. The parameter K is the "carrying capacity," the level of stock that can be sustained with zero harvest. Growth is zero if $x_t = K$ or if $x_t = 0$; the stock grows if $0 < x_t < K$ and it falls if $x_t > K$. As the stock increases, the fish compete for prey, and/or they become more vulnerable to predators.

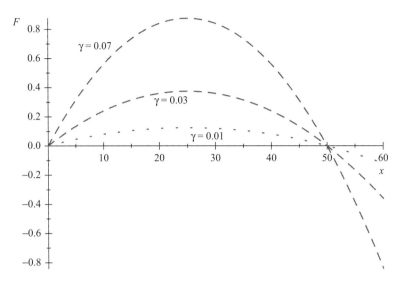

Figure 13.1
The logistic growth function for three values of γ.

This type of "congestion" limits growth of the stock. The more important congestion is, the smaller is the carrying capacity, K.

The growth rate of the stock with the logistic growth function is

$$\frac{x_{t+1} - x_t}{x_t} = \frac{F(x_t)}{x_t} = \frac{\gamma x_t \left(1 - \frac{x_t}{K}\right)}{x_t} = \gamma \left(1 - \frac{x_t}{K}\right). \tag{13.2}$$

The parameter γ is the intrinsic growth rate. In the absence of congestion ($x_t \approx 0$, or $K = \infty$), the growth rate equals γ. A larger value of K implies a higher growth rate (less congestion) for given x. If $K = \infty$, the growth rate is constant at γ. For given γ and finite K, the growth rate falls with x, so the growth rate (*not* growth) reaches the maximum value, γ, at $x = 0$. The value $\gamma = 0.07$, for example, means that in the absence of congestion, the stock grows at 7% per year. For x close to 0, congestion is relatively unimportant, and the growth rate is close to 7%. However, as the stock gets larger, congestion becomes more important, until growth ceases as x approaches the carrying capacity, K. Figure 13.1 shows graphs of the logistic growth function for three different growth rates and $K = 50$. For stocks less than K, a larger γ implies larger growth.

13.2 Harvest and Steady States

Objectives and skills: Understand the meaning of and be able to graph harvest rules and be able to identify steady states.

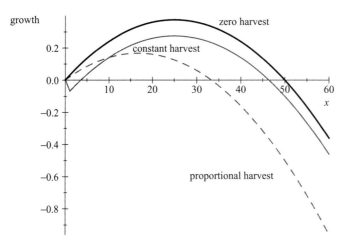

Figure 13.2
Growth with zero harvest (heavy solid curve), with harvest proportional to the stock (dashed curve), and with the stock equal to Y for $x \geq Y$ (light solid curve).

Harvest, $y > 0$, changes the dynamics. The amount harvested at a point in time might depend on the stock of biomass at that point in time. A "harvest rule" gives the harvest level as a function of the stock. With a harvest rule $y(x)$, the change in the stock is

$$x_{t+1} - x_t = F(x_t) - y(x_t).\tag{13.3}$$

Two examples illustrate harvest rules: $y(x) = \min(x, Y)$, where Y is a constant, and $y(x) = \mu x$, with $\mu > 0$ a constant. For the first example, harvest is constant at Y if this level is feasible (i.e., if $x \geq Y$). If the stock is less than Y, all of it is harvested. For the second example, harvest is a constant fraction of the stock. For example, for $\mu = 0.01$, annual harvest equals 1% of the fish stock. It is not possible to take more than the entire stock, so in the discrete time setting, $\mu \leq 1$. Figure 13.2 shows the growth functions with the zero, constant, and the proportional harvest with $K = 50$, $\gamma = 0.03$, $Y = 0.1$, and $\mu = 0.01$. Under these two harvest rules, the change in the stock is

$$\text{constant harvest: } x_{t+1} - x_t = \gamma x_t \left(1 - \frac{x_t}{K}\right) - \min(x_t, Y);$$

$$\text{harvest proportional to stock: } x_{t+1} - x_t = \gamma x_t \left(1 - \frac{x_t}{K}\right) - \mu x_t.\tag{13.4}$$

A "steady state" is any level of the stock at which growth minus harvest equals 0. A stock beginning at a steady state remains there. We have three examples of harvest rules: zero harvest, and the two rules shown in equation 13.4. We obtain the steady states, denoted

x_∞, in these three cases by setting the growth minus harvest equal to 0 and solving for x (using $K = 50$, $\gamma = 0.03$):

$$y = 0: \ \gamma x \left(1 - \frac{x}{K}\right) = 0 \Rightarrow x_\infty, \in \{0, 50\}$$

$$y = \min(x, 0.1): \ \gamma x \left(1 - \frac{x}{K}\right) - \min(x, 0.1) = 0 \Rightarrow x_\infty \in \{0, 3.6, 46.4\} \tag{13.5}$$

$$y = 0.01x: \ \gamma x \left(1 - \frac{x}{K}\right) - 0.01x = 0 \Rightarrow x_\infty \in \{0, 33\}.$$

13.3 Stability

Objectives and skills: Using graphical methods and the continuous time model, identify steady states and determine whether each is stable or unstable.

A steady state is "stable" if the stock trajectory approaches that steady state when the stock begins sufficiently close to it. A steady state is "unstable" if the stock trajectory beginning close to it, moves away from it. The stability or lack of stability of a steady state provides important information about the dynamics of the fish stock, and is therefore important in policy questions. Often there are multiple steady states, including $x = 0$. If $x = 0$ is a stable steady state, a small stock eventually becomes extinct; if $x = 0$ is unstable, a small stock grows.

13.3.1 Discrete versus Continuous Time

Discrete and continuous time models have different advantages. With the discrete time model, we can derive the necessary condition for optimality (the Euler equation) using only elementary calculus. The no-intertemporal-arbitrage interpretation of the Euler equation is also more intuitive in the discrete time setting. The continuous time model has three advantages. First, the graphs of the continuous time equilibrium trajectories are easier on the eye, because they are smooth instead of step functions. Second, some computations are easier in the continuous time setting. Third, the analysis of stability is easier in the continuous time setting. We take advantage of both the discrete and continuous time approaches. We use the discrete time setting to present and interpret the models and the Euler equation, but we use the continuous time analog to construct graphs and to study stability. This section explains the difficulty arising with discrete time stability analysis, and then discusses the relation between the two models (see appendix D).

In the discrete time setting, there is a non-negligible change in the stock of fish from one period to the next, outside of a steady state. The stock might jump from one interval to another, where the behavior is quite different. This possibility can lead to "chaos," where trajectories are very irregular (they do not repeat in a finite amount of time) and are very sensitive to the initial condition. It is possible to rule out chaotic behavior by restricting parameter values, but that still leaves special cases. A steady state might be stable, but the approach path might be "monotonic" (steadily increasing or decreasing over time) or cyclical (first increasing, then decreasing, then increasing, and so on). These possibilities are tangential to our concerns; the continuous time setting avoids them. Finally, in the discrete time setting, we cannot determine the stability or instability of a steady state merely by examining a graph showing growth minus harvest; we require calculation.

For the purpose of considering stability, consider "the continuous time analog" to the discrete time model. For our one-dimensional models, the dynamics in continuous time are simple, and stability can be determined by inspection of a graph without calculation. We develop the continuous time analog using the general growth function and harvest rule, $F(x)$ and $y(x)$, replacing equation 13.3 with the continuous time analog, the ordinary differential equation[1]

$$\frac{dx_t}{dt} = F(x_t) - y(x_t). \tag{13.6}$$

These two equations have the same steady states, where $F(x) - y(x) = 0$.

A Caveat

One subtlety arises in moving from discrete to continuous time. Suppose that we pick a unit of time equal to a year; in the discrete time setting, y equals the amount harvested in a year, and we require $y \leq x$, because it is not possible to harvest more fish than the level of biomass. This constraint does not apply in the continuous time setting.

To explain this claim, consider the situation where we have $1,000 (a stock of money), we cannot borrow, and we receive no interest on savings; our unit of time is a year. In the discrete time setting, y equals the amount spent in a year; because we cannot borrow, we cannot spend more than $1,000: $y \leq x = 1,000$. In the continuous time setting, y equals spending per unit of time, and y can take any non-negative value. For example, it is feasible to spend $1,000 per year for the duration of a year. It is also feasible to spend $5,000 per year for the duration of one-fifth of a year. We can spend at any rate—but possibly not for very long.[2]

13.3.2   Stability in Continuous Time

In the continuous time setting, inspection of a graph enables us to determine whether a steady state is stable. First, we identify the steady state(s) by finding the value(s) of x where

---

1 Equations 13.3 and 13.6 have the same steady states: $x_{t+1} - x_t = 0$ if and only if $\frac{dx_t}{dt} = 0$. Provided that the length of a period in the discrete time setting is sufficiently small, the dynamics of the continuous and discrete systems are similar in the neighborhood of a steady state.

2 For this example, where savings earns no interest, the area under the curve $y(t)$, between $t = 0$ and $t = T$, equals the amount that we spend over $0 \leq t \leq T$. This curve must lie on or above the t-axis to satisfy the constraint $y(t) \geq 0$, and the area under the curve must be no greater than 1,000 to satisfy the constraint $x(t) \geq 0$. The curve can be at any height, but only for a short enough interval that the area beneath it does not exceed 1,000.

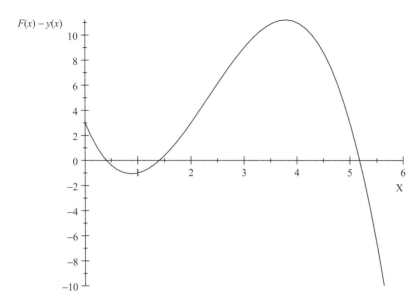

Figure 13.3

The graph of $\frac{dx}{dt} = F(x) - y(x)$. There are three steady states, at $x = 0.4$, $x = 1.4$ and $x = 5.2$. The first and third are stable, and the middle steady state is unstable.

the graph of $F(x) - y(x)$ crosses the x-axis; that is, we find the roots of $F(x) - y(x) = 0$, exactly as in the discrete time setting. For now, we assume that $F(x) - y(x)$ is continuous in x; later we discuss a case where this function is discontinuous at $x = 0$.

Figure 13.3 shows the graph of an arbitrary function $F(x) - y(x)$ (one without a specific resource interpretation). This function has three roots (i.e., three steady states), where the graph crosses the x-axis. For a value of x close to but slightly below the low steady state, $x = 0.4$, $\frac{dx}{dt} = F(x) - y(x) > 0$; this inequality states that x is becoming larger over time. For a value of x close to but slightly above 0.4, $\frac{dx}{dt} = F(x) - y(x) < 0$; this inequality states that x is becoming smaller over time. Therefore, $x = 0.4$ is a stable steady state: a trajectory beginning close to, but not equal to, $x = 0.4$ approaches the level $x = 0.4$. A parallel argument shows that the middle steady state, $x = 1.4$, is an unstable steady state, and the large steady state, $x = 5.2$, is a stable steady state.

Noticing that the slope of $F(x) - y(x)$ is negative at the two stable steady states in figure 13.3, and the slope is positive at the unstable steady state, we obtain the following rule for checking stability of a steady state.[3]

---

[3] If the second derivative of $F(x) - y(x)$ is continuous, and $\frac{d(F(x_\infty) - y(x_\infty))}{dx} = 0$, then points on one side of the steady state approach the steady state, and points on the other side move away from the steady state. We do not discuss this knife-edge case.

Provided that $F(x) - y(x)$ is continuous at a steady state x_∞:

x_∞ is a stable steady state if and only if $\dfrac{d(F(x_\infty) - y(x_\infty))}{dx} < 0$

x_∞ is an unstable steady state if and only if $\dfrac{d(F(x_\infty) - y(x_\infty))}{dx} > 0.$

(13.7)

We can determine the sign of these derivatives by inspection of the graph of $F(x) - y(x)$: under the assumption of continuity, *a steady state is stable if and only if the slope of the graph is negative at the steady state.*

13.3.3   Stability in the Fishing Model

Figure 13.4 shows the graphs of $F(x) - y(x)$ (the growth function minus the harvest function) using the logistic growth function $F(x)$ and three harvest rules: $y(x) = 0$ (solid curve); $y(x) = 0.01x$ (dashed curve); and $y(x) = 0.3$ for $x > 0$ (dotted curve). The intersections of the graphs in figure 13.4 and the x-axis are steady states. With zero harvest, the solid curve shows that the steady states are $x = 0$ and $x = K = 50$. Using the rule in equation 13.7, we see that $x = 0$ (where the slope of the solid curve is positive) is an

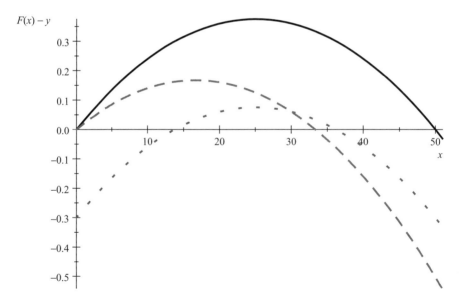

Figure 13.4
Solid curve: the graph of the logistic curve, $F(x)$. Dashed curve: the graph of $F(x) - 0.01x$. Dotted curve: the graph of $F(x) - 0.3$.

unstable steady state, and $x = K$ (where the slope of the solid curve is negative) is a stable steady state. The dashed curve shows that under proportional harvest, $y = 0.01x$, the two steady states are $x = 0$ and $x = 33.33$. Again, the low steady state is unstable and the high steady state is stable.

The dotted curve, corresponding to constant harvest $y(x) = 0.3$ for $x > 0$, has two points of intersection with the x-axis: $x = 13.8$ and $x = 36.2$. Applying the rule in equation 13.7 shows that the low steady state is unstable, and the high steady state is stable. However, $x = 0$ is also a *stable* steady state under the rule $y(x) = 0.3$ for $x > 0$, even though the graph of $F(x) - 0.3$ does not intersect the x-axis. The function $y(x)$ is not continuous at $x = 0$: it equals 0.3 for positive x and it equals 0 for $x = 0$. Therefore, $F(x) - y(x)$ is not continuous at $x = 0$, and the rule in equation 13.7 is inapplicable. For our example, y can remain at 0.3 as long as $x > 0$. If the stock is small (in this case, lower than 13.8), constant harvest $y = 0.3$ exceeds natural growth, and the stock falls. As soon as the stock hits $x = 0$, harvest must stop. The stock heads to extinction, $x = 0$.

Figure 13.4 illustrates an important possibility that we will encounter again. Under zero harvest or harvest proportional to the stock, the stock always approaches the high steady state ($x = 50$ and $x = 33.33$ in the two examples), provided that the initial stock is positive. In contrast, under constant harvest, beginning with a positive stock, the stock might eventually approach either stable steady state, $x = 0$ or $x = 36.2$. The unstable steady state, $x = 13.8$, is a critical stock level. For initial stocks above this critical level, the stock approaches the high steady state, and for initial stocks below this level, the stock approaches the low steady state, 0.

A Different Perspective

Figure 13.4 shows graphs of growth minus harvest, $F(x) - y(x)$. In contrast, Figure 13.5 shows the graph of $F(x)$ and the graphs of $y(x)$ (not their difference). We can use either figure to identify steady states and their stability. You should confirm that, as we move from left to right in Figure 13.5:

(i) If the harvest function cuts the growth function from above, the associated steady state is unstable.

(ii) if the harvest function cuts the growth function from below, the associated steady state is stable.

For example, under constant harvest, $y = 0.3$, harvest exceeds growth for stocks below the low unstable steady state, $x = 13.8$. There, the stock falls over time, moving away from the low steady state. For $x > 13.8$, the stock moves toward the high stable steady state, $x = 36.2$.

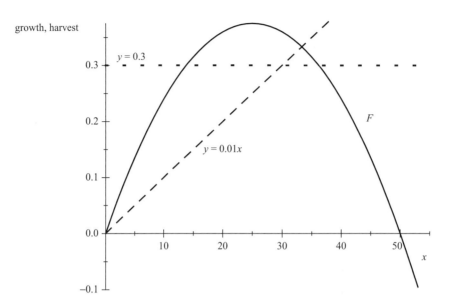

Figure 13.5
The logistic growth function, $F(x)$, and two harvest rules: constant harvest, $y = 0.3$ (dotted line) and harvest proportional to stock, $y = 0.01x$ (dashed line).

13.4   Maximum Sustainable Yield

Objectives and skills: Know the definition of maximum sustainable yield (MSY), be able to calculate it, and understand the economic factors that determine whether optimal steady state harvest should be above or below MSY.

The "maximum sustainable yield" (MSY) is the largest harvest that can be sustained in perpetuity. Any point on the graph of the growth function is a sustainable harvest/stock combination. We can pick any point on this graph and draw a second graph intersecting that point; this second graph is a particular harvest rule for which the chosen point is a steady state, and thus a sustainable harvest. The MSY occurs at the highest point on the graph of the growth function. We identify this highest point by solving $\frac{dF(x)}{dx} = 0$, the first order condition for the problem of maximizing $F(x)$. For the logistic growth function, this condition is

$$\frac{d\left(\gamma x \left(1 - \frac{x}{K}\right)\right)}{dx} = \frac{1}{K}\gamma(K - 2x) \overset{\text{set}}{=} 0 \Rightarrow x = \frac{K}{2}.$$

Substituting this value into the growth function, $\gamma x \left(1 - \frac{x}{K}\right)$, gives the MSY:

$$y = \frac{1}{4}K\gamma.$$

(The MSY is a level of y, not a level of x.) An increase in either the intrinsic growth rate, γ, or the carrying capacity, K, increases the MSY.

13.5 Summary

We measure the stock of fish as biomass, the number of tons of fish. The growth equation determines the stock in the subsequent period as a function of the current stock. The logistic growth function depends on two parameters: the intrinsic growth rate, γ, and the carrying capacity, K. A harvest rule (a function of the stock of fish) determines the harvest in a period. We emphasized two harvest rules, one equal to a constant level, and the other equal to a constant fraction of stock.

At a steady state, the fish stock remains constant over time. The steady state depends on both the growth function and the harvest rule. There may be multiple steady states. A steady state is stable if and only if stocks that begin sufficiently close to the steady state converge to that steady state. If a trajectory beginning at any initial condition close to but not equal to the steady state moves away from that steady state, the steady state is unstable.

The continuous time model makes it easy to determine the stability or instability of a steady state. With a growth function, $F(x)$, and a harvest rule, $y(x)$, any solution to $F(x) - y(x) = 0$ is a steady state. In the continuous time setting, the slope of $F(x) - y(x)$ is negative at a stable steady state and positive at an unstable steady state, provided that $F(x) - y(x)$ is continuous at that point. We also need to consider points of discontinuity, levels of the state at which an inequality constraint binds. In the fishing context, the biomass cannot be negative, so $x \geq 0$; $x = 0$ is a steady state, which might be either stable or unstable, depending on the relation between the growth and harvest functions. The maximum sustainable yield equals the vertical coordinate of the maximum point on the growth function. For the logistic growth model, the maximum sustainable yield equals growth when the stock is half of its carrying capacity.

13.6 Terms and Concepts, Study Questions, Exercises, and Sources

Terms and Concepts
Stock variables, annual growth rate, logistic growth function (or logistic model), carrying capacity, intrinsic growth rate, harvest rule, steady state, chaos, stability, monotonic path, cyclical path, maximum sustainable yield (MSY).

Study Questions
1. Given the graph of a growth function $x_{t+1} - x_t = F(x)$, identify the carrying capacity and the maximum sustainable yield, and describe in a few words what each of these mean.

2. Given the graph of $G(x)$, where $\frac{dx}{dt} = G(x)$, identify the steady state(s) and determine which, if any, stable. Explain your answer in a couple of sentences.

3. Given a single figure that shows both the graph of the growth function, $F(x)$, and the harvest rule, $y(x)$, identify the steady states and explain (in very few words) which is stable and which is unstable. Given a figure showing the graphs of the two functions, sketch a graph of their difference, $\frac{dx}{dt} = F(x) - y(x)$, and use the rule in equation 13.7 to confirm that your answer to part (a) was correct.

Exercises

1. Using an argument that parallels the discussion of the low steady state in figure 13.3, explain why the middle steady state is unstable and why the high steady state is stable.

2. Consider the logistic growth function, $F(x) = \gamma x \left(1 - \frac{x}{K}\right)$.

   (a) Identify the proportional harvest rule (the value of μ in the rule $y = \mu x$) that supports the maximum sustainable yield as a steady state.

   (b) Is this steady state stable? Explain.

3. The "skewed logistic" growth function is

$$F(x_t) = \gamma x_t \left(1 - \frac{x_t}{K}\right)^{\phi},$$

with $\phi > 0$. For $\phi = 1$, we have the logistic growth function in equation 13.1.

   (a) How does the magnitude of ϕ affect the growth rate, for $x < K$? [Hint, you need to use the formula for the derivative of an exponent: $\frac{dx^{\alpha}}{d\alpha} = x^{\alpha} \ln x$.]

   (b) At what stock does the MSY occur? What is the MSY? (These are both functions of ϕ.)

   (c) Sketch the skewed logistic function for $K = 50$, $\gamma = 0.03$, and for both $\phi = 2$ and $\phi = 0.5$.

Sources

Clark (1996) is the classic text on renewable resource economics and on fishery economics in particular.

Hartwick and Olewiler (1986) cover much of the material in this chapter.

Conrad (2010) presents the discrete time material.

Readers interested seeing how the deterministic models discussed in this book can be extended to the stochastic setting should consult Mangel (1985).

14 The Open Access Fishery

Objective
- Analyze policy in an open access fishery.

Information and Skills
- Use the zero-profit condition to obtain the open access harvest rule.
- Determine the evolution of biomass under open access.
- Understand how a tax affects harvest and the evolution of biomass.

The fish stock affects the population growth via the function $F(x)$, thereby affecting the number of fish that can be caught in the future and possibly also affecting the cost of harvest. Absent property rights, fishers have little or no reason to think about the effect of their harvest on stocks, even though those stocks are important to society. The absence of property rights creates "stock externalities" (or "dynamic externalities") in the industry. The fish stocks might also provide ecological services external to the industry (e.g., serving as a food source to other species). A tax or other regulation, or the introduction of property rights, alters the harvest, changing the evolution of the stock. Section 12.4 introduced the regulated limited/open access fishery in a static setting, where everything happens in the same period. Dynamics are central to many resource problems, including fisheries, where the externality unfolds over time: current aggregate harvest decisions affect future stocks, which may affect future harvests and costs.

"Static" externalities can also be important in natural resource settings. Trawling (a method of fishing) disperses schools of fish, making them harder to catch. In this case, boats create congestion in fishing grounds, much as automobiles do on highways.[1] An additional boat owner does not consider the effect of her presence on other boats' profits. Negative static externalities occur at the same time the additional boat is present, reducing industry profits for a given level of the stock; negative dynamic externalities reduce future

---

1 Congestion is a negative externality. Additional boats can also reduce search costs, making it easier to find schools of fish and resulting in a positive static externality.

profits by reducing future stock. Both of these effects can be important, but their combined effect may be less than the sum of their individual effects. By lowering industry profits (for a given level of the stock), the static negative externality reduces the number of boats and/or the amount of gear and labor per boat, lowering the equilibrium level of aggregate catch and reducing the severity of the dynamic externality. For the North Carolina shrimp fishery, Huang and Smith (2014) find that the static externality, on balance, increases industry profits.

This result can be viewed through the lens of the Theory of the Second Best. Suppose that there was a fishing technology, some alternative to trawling, that could eliminate the congestion externality. This technology increases industry profits for a given level of the stock and a given number of boats. The increased profits induce fishers to increase inputs (e.g., work more days, hire more deckhands) and may induce additional boats to enter (see section 12.4). These changes increase current harvest, reducing future stocks and exacerbating the dynamic externality. In this case, the improved technology fixes the static externality but worsens the dynamic externality, possibly reducing the present discounted stream of industry profits. By the same logic, a restriction on gear that increases costs without conferring any direct benefit (e.g., increased safety) might increase industry profits. Requiring boats to carry a ton of sand slows them down and increases their fuel costs; if this requirement leads to a large enough fall in current harvest and subsequent increase in future stock, with attendant reduction in future harvest cost, it might increase industry profits.

We consider an open access fishery in which average costs are independent of harvest, although possibly they depend on the stock. This setting enables us to focus on the dynamic/stock externality; there is no static externality here. Industry profits are always zero; the social surplus associated with the fishery arises from consumer surplus and any ecological services the fishery provides. We consider a "landing fee," a tax levied on harvest, illustrating the effect of a particular means of regulating stock externalities. A landing fee and a restriction on fishing gear that increases harvest costs potentially have the same effect on harvest. However, the tax generates revenue, whereas the gear restriction might only increase costs.

A Road Map
Section 14.1 sets up the machinery for the analysis. We consider two cost functions where open access leads to zero rent. We find the open access harvest rule, the function that relates equilibrium harvest to the stock. Section 14.2 uses this machinery, together with the tools developed in chapter 13, to examine the steady state effect of a constant landing fee. This effect may be sensitive to the "initial condition," the level of stock at the time the landing fee is first imposed.

14.1 Harvest Rules

Objectives and skills: Obtain and graph the open access harvest rule and determine the steady states and their stability.

We consider two cases, the first with constant stock-independent average and marginal harvest costs, $c(x, y) = Cy$, and the second with stock-dependent average and marginal cost, $c(x, y) = C\frac{y}{x}$. Free entry and exit and the assumption that marginal costs do not depend on harvest imply that profits are zero at every point in time: price equals average cost (= marginal cost).[2] If profits were positive, new entrants would increase supply, lowering the price and lowering profits; if profits were negative, current fishers would leave the industry, lowering supply, increasing the price, and increasing profits.

14.1.1 Stock-Independent Costs

With stock-independent constant harvest costs, $c(x, y) = Cy$, "price equals average cost" requires $p_t = C$. For the inverse demand function, $p = a - by$, this condition implies $y = \frac{a-C}{b}$. For $C < a$, open access harvest is positive whenever the stock is positive; the open access harvest rule is[3]

$$y(x) = \min\left(x, \frac{a-C}{b}\right). \tag{14.1}$$

Chapter 13 examines the dynamics under this kind of harvest rule. Figure 14.1 reviews this material, showing the graph of a logistic growth function and the graphs of two harvest rules, corresponding to a low cost and a high cost, C (the dashed and dotted lines, respectively). For both of these costs, there are three steady states; $x = 0$ and the high steady states, at points D and D', which are both stable. The intermediate steady states, at points B and B', are unstable.

14.1.2 Stock-Dependent Costs

We begin by showing that a particular production function leads to a particular harvest cost function, $c(x, y) = C\frac{y}{x}$. Using this cost function, we derive the open access harvest rule.

---

2 If marginal cost increases with harvest, the condition for competitive production, "price equals marginal cost" implies that price exceeds average cost. In that case, producer surplus is positive. To "close the model" (make it internally consistent and complete), we could introduce fixed but not sunk entry costs, so that producer surplus minus the entry cost is zero in every period.

3 Equation 14.1 is the harvest rule in the discrete time setting. In the continuous time setting, where the rate y can be arbitrarily large, the harvest rule is $y = \frac{a-C}{b}$ for $x > 0$ and $y = 0$ for $x = 0$.

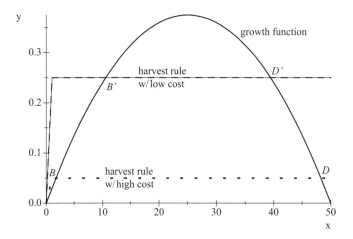

Figure 14.1
The logistic growth function with $\gamma = 0.03$ and $K = 50$. The harvest rules correspond to $C = 1$ and $C = 3$, for inverse demand $p = a = by$, with $a = 3.5$ and $b = 10$.

Production Function and the Cost Function

Aggregate fishing "effort," E_t, is an amalgam of all inputs (including boats) in the fishery sector in period t. Greater effort increases harvest, and fish are easier to catch when the stock is large. The fishery production function shows how effort, E, and the stock, x, determine harvest, y. A simple production function has harvest per unit of effort proportional to the size of the stock, $\frac{y}{E} = \lambda x$, or

$$y = \lambda E x \Rightarrow E = \frac{y}{\lambda x}. \tag{14.2}$$

The parameter $\lambda > 0$ is the "catchability coefficient." A larger λ means that for a given stock size, fishers need to expend less effort to obtain a given level of harvest. The cost per unit of effort is constant, w. If one unit of effort equals one boat and 200 hours of labor and a particular net, then w equals the cost of renting the boat and other gear and paying the crew. The cost, c, of harvesting y, given the stock, x, is

$$c(x, y) = wE = \frac{w}{\lambda x} y = \frac{C}{x} y, \tag{14.3}$$

where $C \equiv \frac{w}{\lambda}$. Harvest costs fall as the stock of fish (x) rises, the cost per unit of effort (w) falls, and the catchability coefficient (λ) increases.

The Harvest Rule

If harvest is positive in the open access equilibrium, then the zero-profit condition implies price equals average costs; with linear inverse demand, $p(y) = a - by$, zero profit requires

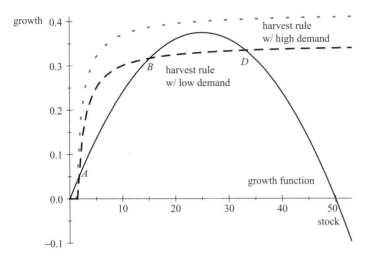

Figure 14.2
The logistic growth function with $\gamma = 0.03$ and $K = 50$ and harvest rules for $p = a - 10y$ with $a = 4.2$ (high demand) and $a = 3.5$ (low demand). Dashed curve: harvest rule for $a = 3.5$. Dotted curve: harvest rule for $a = 4.20$.

$a - by = \frac{C}{x}$. If cost exceeds the choke price, a, then harvest equals zero. These two facts imply the harvest rule[4]

$$
y(x) = \begin{cases} \frac{1}{b}\left(a - \frac{C}{x}\right) & \text{for } \frac{1}{b}\left(a - \frac{C}{x}\right) \geq 0, \\ 0 & \text{for } \frac{1}{b}\left(a - \frac{C}{x}\right) < 0. \end{cases} \tag{14.4}
$$

Figure 14.2 shows the graph of the logistic growth function and the open access harvesting rule in equation 14.4 for low demand, $p = 3.5 - 10y$ (dashed curve) and high demand, $p = 4.2 - 10y$ (dotted curve) with $C = 5$. The figure identifies the three interior steady states (where $x > 0$), points A, B, and D, under low demand. In the high demand scenario, the only interior steady state occurs at a low stock level, close to but slightly lower than point A. Extinction, $x = 0$, is a steady state in both cases.

In the low demand scenario, moving from left to right, the dashed curve cuts the growth function from below at points A and D, and it cuts the growth function from above at point B. Thus, points A and D are stable steady states, and point B is an unstable steady state. (See the final paragraph in section 13.3.3.) The point $x = 0$ is an unstable equilibrium. For

---

4 A necessary and sufficient condition for $y(x) < x$ for all $x \geq 0$ is $a < 2\sqrt{bC}$. When this inequality holds, equation 14.4 is the harvest rule for both the discrete and continuous time settings.

sufficiently small but positive stock, $a - \frac{C}{x} < 0$, so $y = 0$. In this case, the stock is so low, and the harvest costs so high, that the equilibrium harvest is 0. Because growth is positive for small positive x, the fish stock is growing in this region. Therefore, if the initial stock is positive and below point B, the stock in the open access fishery converges to point A. If the initial stock is above point B, the stock converges to point D. The stock corresponding to point B is a "critical" level, because the trajectory is completely different depending on whether the initial stock is above or below that level.

In the high demand scenario (dotted curve), there are two steady states. The stable steady state is slightly below point A; $x = 0$ is an unstable steady state. Here, for any positive initial stock, the stock under open access converges to a level slightly below point A.[5]

The graphs of the two harvest rules in figure 14.2 show that an increase in demand (raising the inverse demand function from $p = 3.5 - 10y$ to $p = 4.2 - 10y$) increases the harvest level and potentially changes the qualitative nature of the steady states. Under low demand, there exist both high and low stable steady states; high demand eliminates the high steady state.

14.2 Policy Application

Objectives and skills: Understand why the long-run effect of a tax may depend on the level of the stock at the time the tax is imposed.

Here we consider the effect of a tax when average harvest costs depend on the stock. Exercise 2 confirms that a particular cost-increasing gear restriction leads to the same harvest rule as the tax. The tax and this gear restriction therefore have the same effect on the trajectory of the stock and harvest, and thus on consumer surplus. However, the tax raises revenue, benefiting taxpayers. The gear restriction (depending on its precise nature) might create no benefit beyond protecting the stock. In this case, the tax and the gear restriction are similar in some but not all dimensions.

Chapter 10 showed that (in a closed economy) a tax has the same effect regardless of whether consumers or producers have statutory responsibility for paying it. If consumers face price, p, and have inverse demand, $p = a - by$, producers facing the unit tax v receive the net-of-tax price, $p - v$. Zero profits requires that this price equals average cost, or $a - by - v = \frac{C}{x}$. Modifying equation 14.4, the open access harvest rule under the tax is

$$y(x) = \begin{cases} \frac{1}{b}\left(a - v - \frac{C}{x}\right) & \text{for } a - v - \frac{C}{x} \geq 0, \\[2mm] 0 & \text{for } a - v - \frac{C}{x} < 0. \end{cases} \tag{14.5}$$

---

5 Appendix E provides a different way of visualizing the equilibrium, using the concept of a "bioeconomic equilibrium."

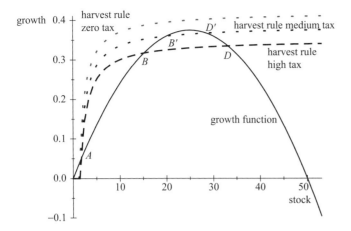

Figure 14.3
The logistic growth function (solid curve) and harvest rules for: zero tax (higher dotted curve), $v = 0.35$ (lower dotted curve), and $v = 0.7$ (dashed curve). Demand is $p = 4.2 - 10y$.

A one unit decrease in a or a one unit increase in v have the same effect on $a - v$, and thus have the same effect on the harvest rule. Figure 14.3 shows harvest rules for $a = 4.2$ and three values of the tax: $v = 0$, $v = 0.35$ (so $a - v = 3.85$), and $v = 0.7$ (so $a - v = 3.5$).

Role of the Initial Condition

The "initial condition" is the level of the stock, x_0, at the time the tax is first imposed. The long-run (steady state) effect of the tax might depend on the initial condition. The low steady states for the three harvest rules (corresponding to the three tax levels) are slightly different, but they all occur so close to point A, where $x_A = 1.7$, as to be indistinguishable in figure 14.3. However, the intermediate and the high steady states are appreciably different under the two positive taxes; these steady states do not exist if $v = 0$. The points B' and D' are steady states under the tax $v = 0.35$, and B and D are steady states under the tax $v = 0.7$. The stocks at these points are

$$x_A = 1.7, \ x_B = 15.4, \ x_{B'} = 20, \ x_{D'} = 28.6, \text{ and } x_D = 33.2.$$

The initial stock—not just the policy level—can have a significant effect on the steady state to which the stock converges. If $x_0 < 15.4$, neither tax has an appreciable effect on the steady state: the stock converges to a point close to $x_A = 1.7$ for $v \in \{0, 0.35, 0.7\}$. If $15.4 < x_0 < 20$, the tax $v = 0.35$ has a negligible effect on the steady state (close to $x_A = 1.7$), but the tax $v = 0.7$ causes the stock to converge to 33.2. If $x_0 > 20$, then the stock converges to $x = 28.6$ for $v = 0.35$ and to $x = 32.2$ for $v = 0.7$. In this example, if the initial stock is moderately small ($15.4 < x_0 < 20$), then $\nu = 0.35$ has a negligible effect on the steady state, whereas the tax $\nu = 0.7$ leads to a large increase in the steady state. If the initial stock is moderately large ($x_0 > 20$), then both taxes lead to qualitatively different steady states compared to $\nu = 0$. Under the zero tax, the stock converges to the low steady state stock for any positive x_0. We discuss the policy implications of these results, after first considering the steady state welfare in greater detail.

Steady State Welfare Effects of the Tax
To avoid the need to consider many cases, here we assume that $x_0 > 20$. The low tax leads to a lower steady state stock, but a higher steady state harvest, compared to the high tax: point D' is to the left and above point D (figure 14.3). A higher harvest corresponds to a lower consumer price and to higher consumer surplus. In the high steady state under the high tax, $x_D = 33.2$, so harvest = consumption:

$$y = \gamma x_D \left(1 - \frac{x_D}{K}\right) = 0.335.$$

Consumers are willing to purchase this amount if they face the tax-inclusive price $4.2 - 10 \times 0.335 = 0.853$. At this price, consumer surplus is

$$\int_{0.853}^{4.2} \left(\frac{4.2 - z}{10}\right) dz = 0.56,$$

and tax revenue is $\nu y = 0.7(0.335) = 0.2345$. Profits are 0 at every point, so social welfare equals the sum of consumer surplus plus tax revenue, 0.794. Table 14.1 collects these numbers at the high stable steady states under the two taxes. For this example, steady state consumer surplus is higher, tax revenue is lower, and their sum, social welfare, is higher under the smaller tax.

Policy Implications
Even if a tax has only a negligible effect on the steady state to which the stock converges, it may nevertheless have a significant effect on welfare by slowing the decline of the fishery. For example, if x_0 is slightly lower than 15.4, the tax $\nu = 0.35$ causes a 9% reduction in the initial harvest (relative to harvest under $\nu = 0$), and the tax $\nu = 0.7$ causes an 18% reduction in the initial harvest. Neither reduction in harvest is large enough to keep the stock from converging to approximately the same low level, but the higher tax slows the fishery's decline.

The effect of the tax on the steady state depends on the initial condition. In view of the uncertain relation between the model and the real world, the regulator might want to build in a margin of safety. The larger tax protects against the possibility that we overestimated the initial biomass or were wrong about some other key parameter.

Table 14.1
High stable steady state stock, harvest, price, consumer surplus, tax revenue, and social surplus for two taxes

Tax (v)	Stock	Harvest	Price	Consumer surplus	Tax revenue	Social welfare
0.7	33.2	0.335	0.853	0.56	0.234	0.794
0.35	28.6	0.367	0.528	0.67	0.129	0.803

Here we considered only a constant tax, a number. That single number can be used to target (i.e., to select) a single endogenous variable. We took the steady state stock, and corresponding payoff, as the target of interest. However, the regulator may care about the payoff along the trajectory en route to the steady state. A richer description of the regulatory problem includes "state-contingent" taxes, defined as taxes that vary with the level of the stock (see section 15.2).

14.3 Summary

In an open access equilibrium with costless entry and exit, profits are 0, implying that price equals average harvest cost. We obtained the open access harvest rule under linear demand and two types of cost function. Using these harvest rules and the logistic growth function, we identified the steady states, determined their (in)stability, and studied the evolution of the stock of fish under open access. For the case of stock-dependent harvest costs, there might be either a single interior (= positive) steady state or three interior steady states. In the former case, the unique interior steady state is stable. In the latter case, the low and the high interior steady states are stable, and the middle steady state is unstable. The stock $x = 0$ is an unstable steady state under stock-dependent harvest cost, and it is a stable steady with constant average harvest costs.

A unit tax on harvest shifts down the open access harvest rule, reducing harvest for any level of the stock. Under a stock-dependent harvest cost, a sufficiently high unit tax moves the fishery from the situation where there is a single interior steady state to the situation where there are three interior steady states. In this case, the tax creates a stable steady state with high stock and harvest. The effect of a tax depends on both the magnitude of the tax and on the level of the stock at the time the tax is first imposed (the initial condition). We also used this example to determine the steady state level of welfare (= consumer surplus plus tax revenue) under different taxes.

A tax and more complex policies, such as cost-increasing gear restrictions, might have the same effect on harvest, and therefore offer the same protection to the stock. In this case, the simple tax is capable of describing one aspect of the complex restrictions. However, the tax generates tax revenue, a benefit to society. The gear restrictions might have no additional benefit beyond protecting the stock.

14.4   Terms and Concepts, Study Questions, Exercises, and Sources

Terms and Concepts
Catchability coefficient, initial condition.

Study Questions
1. (a) For the case of constant average harvest cost, Cy, linear inverse demand, $p = a - by$, and logistic growth, obtain the open access harvest rule and sketch it on the same figure as the growth function. Illustrate how a change in C alters the steady state and the dynamics of the fish stock.

(b) Illustrate and explain the effect of a constant unit tax, v, on the steady states.

(c) Use a graph and short discussion to illustrate the fact that the effect of a tax depends both on its magnitude and on the stock level at the time the tax is imposed.
(i) The production function for harvest is $y = \lambda Ex$, where E is effort and x is biomass. Explain the meaning of E (perhaps by using an example) and the meaning of the parameter λ. What is the name given to λ?

(ii) Suppose that a unit of effort costs w. Derive the cost function for the example in question 2. Explain your derivation.

(iii) Using the cost function derived in question 3 and the inverse demand curve $p = a - by$, derive the open access harvest rule, explaining each step.

(iv) Sketch the logistic growth function and the harvest rule obtained in question 4. Use the sketch to show how an increase in b, the inverse demand slope, alters the harvest rule and thereby alters steady state(s). Explain how this change in b can qualitatively alter the evolution of the stock, depending on the initial condition.

(v) Explain why the effect of a tax depends on both the magnitude of the tax and on the initial condition of the biomass at the time the tax is first implemented.

Exercises
1. Absent restrictions, firms and fishers choose inputs to minimize their costs. A binding restriction (one that alters the agent's choice) increases their costs. "Effort" depends on the size of the boat, B (the "number of boat units"), and the amount of labor, L, in the following manner: $E = B^{\alpha} L^{1-\alpha}$ (a Cobb Douglas production function). The cost of the boat, bB, is proportional to its size, with a price per boat unit of b. The wage is w, so the labor bill is wL. Thus, the cost of providing one unit of effort is C, with

$$C = \min_{B,L}(bB + wL), \text{ subject to } B^{\beta} L^{1-\beta} = 1.$$

Set $\alpha = 0.5$, $w = 1$ and $b = 2$.

(a) With B on the horizontal axis, graph the unit isoquant (the curve showing the combination of B and L that produce one unit of output). Use a tangency condition (from intermediate microeconomics) to identify the cost minimizing level of inputs that produce one unit of effort. Identify this point by F and identify the slope of the tangent line.

(b) Draw a ray from the origin through point F. What is the slope of this line? How do you know?

(c) Suppose that a regulation requires six units of labor per "unit of boat." Identify the input mix needed to produce one unit of effort under this restriction; label it G. Explain, using the graph, how you know that costs are higher at G than at F.

(d) What is the percentage increase in the cost of a unit of effort due to this restriction? (To answer this question use the fact that production of a unit of effort requires $L^{0.5}B^{0.5}=1$, or $L=\frac{1}{B}$. Also use the fact that, with the Cobb Douglas production function, the optimal expenditure shares of each input equals its exponent, so the ratio of optimal expenditures on each input equals the ratio of their exponents: $\frac{wL}{bB}=\frac{1-\alpha}{\alpha}$.)

2. This problem illustrates the claim that different policies can have the same effect on harvest. Under constant marginal harvest costs, a landing fee of v and a gear restriction that increases the cost parameter from C to $C+v$ both increase the harvest rule in the first line of equation 14.1 to

$$y(x)=\min\left(x,\frac{a-C-v}{b}\right).$$

These two policies have the same effect on harvest.

Now consider the case of stock dependent harvest costs. In Scenario A, fishers face a landing fee of v, and in Scenario B, they face gear restrictions that increase the cost parameter from C to $(\mu+\beta x)C$.

(a) Equation 14.5 shows the harvest rule under the landing fee. Use the zero profit condition and the inverse demand function $p=a-by$ to find the harvest rules under the gear restrictions. (Consider only the case where harvest is positive.)

(b) Find the values of μ and β such that the harvest rule is the same in the two scenarios for all levels of x. [Hint: Set the two harvest rules equal, and simplify to obtain a linear function of x that must equal 0 for all x (not merely for a particular x). This requirement can hold only if the intercept and the slope of the linear function you obtained are both zero. Setting the intercept and the slope to zero gives you two equations that identify the values of the parameters μ and β.]

3. Consider an open access fishery with constant harvest costs, $c(x,y)=Cy$, linear inverse demand, $p=a-by$, and the logistic growth function. Producers have the statutory obligation to pay a unit tax, v.

(a) What is the harvest rule? (The text provides the answer.)

(b) What is the tax incidence in this model?

(c) Does your answer to part (b) mean that the tax makes consumers worse off?

(d) Suppose that the resource is never driven to extinction, either without or with the tax. In this case, how does the tax affect consumer welfare? How does the tax affect social welfare? (Is tax revenue valuable to society?)

(e) In this closed economy, does it matter whether producers or consumers have the statutory obligation to pay the tax?

Sources

In the model presented in this chapter, the size of the fishing fleet adjusts instantaneously, so profits equal zero at every moment. Conrad (2010) discusses extensions in which the industry's speed of adjustment depends on current profits; in this setting, profits can be nonzero outside a steady state.

Berck and Perloff (1984) consider a model with costly adjustment and rational expectations: firms' entry and exit decisions depend on their expectations of future profits.

Huang and Smith (2014) show that the congestion externality in the North Carolina shrimp fishery increases the value of the fishery by reducing the stock externality.

15 The Sole-Owner Fishery

Objective
- Analyze equilibrium in a price-taking sole-owner fishery.

Information and Skills
- Know the steps in deriving the Euler equation for the fishery model.
- Understand the role of growth in the Euler equation.
- Describe optimal policy in the presence of market failures.
- Identify the steady states and their comparative statics.

This chapter studies the price-taking sole-owner fishery, extending earlier results on non-renewable resources. Absent other market failures, the sole owner harvests efficiently. By maximizing the present discounted stream of profits, she also maximizes the present discounted sum of producer and consumer surplus. Even though sole owner fisheries are rare, there are two reasons for focusing on them. First, it provides a baseline for determining policy when property rights are imperfect. To determine the socially optimal steady state stock, for example, we need a criterion for optimality. The sole-owner fishery provides that criterion. The tools developed here are useful in many renewable resource settings, where the social planner (or sole-owner) outcome provides information on optimal regulation. Second, we saw that the outcome under property rights–based regulation might be similar to (and in a special case, the same as) that of the sole owner (see section 12.5). Here, the sole-owner model provides a tractable, even if only approximate, description of the actual outcome.

A Road Map
Section 15.1 states the sole owner's optimization problem and provides the intuition for the optimality condition, the Euler equation. This optimality condition differs from the Hotelling rule because of the presence of growth in the renewable resource setting. As in the nonrenewable resource setting, we use the definition of rent to simplify the Euler equation.

Section 15.2 compares the open access and sole-owner equilibrium conditions, showing that a tax equal to the sole owner's rent supports an efficient outcome under open access. We also consider the situation where the fishery provides ecological services, a positive externality.

Manipulation of the growth function and the Euler equation enable us to determine the sole-owner steady state(s) (section 15.3), which we compare to the open access steady states. We then provide empirical examples of regulation, emphasizing the relation between targets that are actually used, and the maximum sustainable yield (MSY), introduced in section 13.4.

15.1   The Euler Equation for the Sole Owner

Objectives and skills: State the sole owner's optimization problem, write and interpret the Euler equation, and then express that equation using rent.

We consider two specializations of the parametric cost function. In the first, average harvest costs are constant in harvest and independent of the stock: $c(x, y) = Cy$. In the second, average harvest costs are constant in the harvest and decreasing in the stock: $c(x, y) = \frac{C}{x} y$, so $\frac{\partial c(x,y)}{\partial x} = -\frac{C}{x^2} y < 0$. The owner of the resource takes the sequence of prices, $p_0, p_1, p_2, \ldots$, as given; these prices are endogenous, via the inverse demand function, $p_t = p(y_t)$, but the resource owner treats them as exogenous. In both cases, the owner chooses the sequence of harvests, $y_0, y_1, y_2, \ldots$, to maximize the present discounted stream of profits:

$$\underbrace{\max \sum_{t=0}^{\infty} \rho^t (p_t - C) y_t}_{\text{PDV of profits w/ constant costs}}, \text{ or } \underbrace{\max \sum_{t=0}^{\infty} \rho^t \left(p_t - \frac{C}{x_t} \right) y_t}_{\text{PDV of profits w/stock dependent costs}}.$$

In both cases, the owner faces the constraint $x_{t+1} = x_t + F(x_t) - y_t$ where $F(x)$ is the growth function.

For the sole owner facing constant harvest costs, C, the Euler equation is

$$\overbrace{p_t - C}^{\substack{\text{increased profit due to} \\ \text{additional unit of harvest}}} = \rho \times \underbrace{(p_{t+1} - C)}_{\substack{\text{reduction in profit per unit} \\ \text{reduction in harvest}}} \times \underbrace{\left(1 + \frac{dF(x_{t+1})}{dx_{t+1}} \right)}_{\substack{\text{reduction in harvest to offset} \\ \text{increase in period-t harvest}}} . \tag{15.1}$$

The Euler equation for the stock-dependent case is (see appendix F).

$$p_t - \frac{C}{x_t} = \rho \left[\left(p_{t+1} - \frac{C}{x_{t+1}} \right) \left(1 + \frac{dF(x_{t+1})}{dx_{t+1}} \right) + \underbrace{\frac{C}{x_{t+1}^2} y_{t+1}}_{\substack{\text{higher cost due to} \\ \text{inceased period-}t \text{ harvest}}} \right] \tag{15.2}$$

The two Euler equations are the same, except for the addition of the underbracketed term on the right side of equation 15.2.

15.1.1 Intuition for the Euler Equation

We emphasize the case of stock-dependent harvest costs, equation 15.2. With one important difference, this necessary condition is identical to the Euler equation 5.2 for the nonrenewable resource. The first term on the right side of equation 15.2 is

$$\left(p_{t+1} - \frac{C}{x_{t+1}} \right) \left(1 + \frac{dF(x_{t+1})}{dx_{t+1}} \right).$$

The corresponding term with nonrenewable resources is

$$\left(p_{t+1} - \frac{C}{x_{t+1}} \right) (1 + 0).$$

These two expressions differ unless $\frac{dF(x_{t+1})}{dx_{t+1}} = 0$. Stock-dependent growth is important in the renewable resource setting.

A trajectory consists of a sequence of harvest and stock levels. Along an optimal trajectory, a small change in harvest in some period, and an "offsetting change" in some other period, leads to a zero first order change in the payoff: a perturbation does not improve the outcome. The left side of equation 15.2 equals the marginal benefit of increasing harvest in period t, and the right side equals the marginal cost of the offsetting change in the subsequent period. Growth affects the change needed in period $t + 1$ to offset the change in period t.

A Savings Example for Intuition

To provide intuition, we consider a savings problem unrelated to resources. An investor earns a per-period return of r: investing a dollar at the beginning of a period produces $1 + r$ dollars at the end of the period. This investor has a "candidate savings plan," a trajectory of savings and wealth. If the individual begins the period with wealth W_t and invests s_t, her wealth in the next period is $W_{t+1} = (1+r)(W_t + s_t)$. The savings decision corresponds to harvest in the fishery setting, and wealth corresponds to biomass.

The investor considers perturbing this candidate in period t by saving one dollar less than the candidate plan prescribes. To return wealth to the candidate trajectory by period $t+2$, she has to invest an additional $1+r$ dollars in period $t+1$, over and above the amount that the candidate calls for. The extra \$1 makes up for the dollar that she did not save in period t, and the extra \$$r$ makes up for the interest that she lost by not saving that dollar. The same consideration applies in the fishery setting.

Using This Intuition

Harvesting an extra unit in period t generates p_t additional units of revenue, and $\frac{C}{x_t}$ additional units of cost, for a net increase in profits of $p_t - \frac{C}{x_t}$, the left side of equation 15.2. This perturbation leads to lower and more expensive harvest in $t+1$. Each unit of stock contributes $\frac{dF(x_{t+1})}{dx_{t+1}}$ units of growth. The owner must reduce harvest in period $t+1$ by one unit to offset the direct effect of the increased harvest in period t, and by $\frac{dF(x_{t+1})}{dx_{t+1}}$ units to make up for the reduced growth. The term $\frac{dF(x_{t+1})}{dx_{t+1}}$ corresponds to the interest payment in the savings example.

Each unit of reduced harvest in period $t+1$ reduces profits by $\left(p_{t+1} - \frac{C}{x_{t+1}} \right)$, so the reduction in $t+1$ harvest reduces profits by

$$\left(p_{t+1} - \frac{C}{x_{t+1}} \right) \left(1 + \frac{dF(x_{t+1})}{dx_{t+1}} \right),$$

which equals the first term on the right side of equation 15.2. The lower $t+1$ stock (caused by the perturbation) increases harvest cost by

$$-\frac{\partial \left(\frac{C}{x_{t+1}} y_{t+1} \right)}{\partial x_{t+1}} = \frac{C}{x_{t+1}^2} y_{t+1},$$

the underbracketed term on the right side. The time t present value cost of the perturbation equals the right side of equation 15.2.

15.1.2 Rent

We use the definition of rent to write the Euler equation more concisely. As in the nonrenewable resource setting, we define rent as the difference between price and marginal cost. For our example (but not in general), marginal cost equals average cost, so rent equals profit per unit of harvest.

For stock-independent average costs, rent is

$$R_t = p_t - C.$$

Using this definition, we rewrite the Euler equation 15.1 as

$$R_t = \rho R_{t+1}\left(1 + \frac{dF(x_{t+1})}{dx_{t+1}}\right). \tag{15.3}$$

For stock-dependent harvest costs, rent is

$$R_t = p_t - \frac{C}{x_t} \tag{15.4}$$

and the Euler equation 15.2 becomes

$$R_t = \rho\left[\underbrace{R_{t+1}\left(1 + \frac{dF(x_{t+1})}{dx_{t+1}}\right)}_{\text{change in profit due to change in harvest}} + \underbrace{\frac{C}{x_{t+1}^2}y_{t+1}}_{\substack{\text{change in cost due to}\\\text{change in stock}}}\right]. \tag{15.5}$$

Using $\rho = \frac{1}{1+r}$, we multiply both sides of equation 15.5 by $1+r$, then subtract R_t from both sides and simplify to obtain

$$rR_t = \underbrace{(R_{t+1} - R_t)}_{\text{capital gain}} + \underbrace{R_{t+1}\frac{dF(x_{t+1})}{dx_{t+1}}}_{\text{value of additional stock}} + \underbrace{\frac{C}{x_{t+1}^2}y_{t+1}}_{\text{stock-related cost change}} . \tag{15.6}$$

Recall that rent can be interpreted as the shadow price of the stock: the amount that the owner would be willing to pay to have one more unit of stock. The modifier "shadow" reminds us that a market for this transaction is unlikely to exist; but by reducing current harvest, it is "as if" the fisher buys an additional unit of stock. Equation 15.6 is similar to equation 5.14, apart from our use of a specific cost function here, and the presence of the middle term that accounts for growth. To interpret equation 15.6, we can think of the fish stock as if it were a share in a company. Suppose that a person can borrow at rate r, and imagine that they could buy an additional unit of fish stock in period t at the shadow price R_t. The cost of borrowing is the left side of equation 15.6. The benefit of the transaction equals the sum of the three terms on the right side: the capital gain, the value of the additional stock, and the reduction in harvest costs. The middle term is positive or negative, depending on whether the stock is growing or shrinking.

The sole owner never sells when price is below marginal cost, so rent is never negative, and often (but not always) is positive. The open access fishery eliminates profits, driving rent to zero. Section 12.5 notes that individual transferable quotas (ITQs) create property rights to a flow, making an open access or common property fishery more like a sole-owner fishery. The equilibrium annual lease price of an ITQ equals the amount of profit a fisher can expect to obtain for the volume of harvest covered by the quota licence. The lease price thus provides an estimate of the rent. Many lease prices range from 50% to 80% of the "ex-vessel" fish price (the price fishers receive); rent is large in these fisheries (Homans and Wilen 2005).

15.2   Policy

Objectives and skills: Understand why the optimal stock-dependent tax under open access equals the rent for the agent who harvests at the first-best level.

Section 9.2 explains how to find an optimal tax in the presence of a market failure (e.g., market power or pollution): we first find the socially optimal level of output, and we then find a tax that supports this level of output. We say a tax "supports outcome X" if the market equilibrium in the presence of the tax is the same as outcome X. The construction of optimal taxes in the dynamic setting follows the same logic. By solving the sole-owner's problem (absent externalities), we obtain an efficient trajectory, one that maximizes the discounted stream of the sum of producer and consumer surplus. Information about that trajectory enables us to find the tax that supports the optimal trajectory under a particular market failure, such as open access. An empirical application to the Gulf of Mexico reef fishery shows that improved (but still suboptimal) management can double the value of a natural resource (Fenichel and Abbott 2014).

We consider two scenarios. In the first, there is a single market failure: lack of property rights to the fishery. To find the tax that supports the socially optimal harvest, we first find rent under the sole owner. If open access fishers are charged a tax, per unit of catch, equal to this level of rent, then open access fishers harvest at the optimal level. In the second scenario, the biomass provides ecological services (e.g., food for another fishery) that fishers ignore. An owner who is not compensated for these services treats them as external to his decision problem, leading to excessive harvest and underprovision of the ecological services and creating a role for regulation even under the sole owner. Under open access, the optimal tax must correct two market failures: the absence of property rights and the ecological externality.

We discuss this policy problem in the fishery context, but the goal is for you to become accustomed to thinking about common features of resource problems. Forests and fisheries give rise to similar market failures. There may be imperfect property rights in both cases and unpriced benefits that are external to harvesters. Forests contribute to biodiversity, and they sequester carbon. Absent policy intervention, foresters do not obtain these benefits. What is the right policy response when these types of externalities are important? How does that policy response depend on the nature of property rights? This section helps you develop the skills needed to think systematically about these kinds of questions.

15.2.1 Optimal Policy under a Single Market Failure

If there are no externalities, the sole owner harvests efficiently. Under open access, there is a single market failure: the absence of property rights to the fish stock. If open access fishers face the tax $v(x)$, they harvest up to the point where their tax-inclusive profits equal 0:

$$p(y_t) - \frac{C}{x_t} - v(x_t) = 0. \tag{15.7}$$

Comparing equations 15.4 and 15.7, we see that the levels of the price and harvest are the same in the two cases if and only if the open-access tax equals the sole owner's rent:

$$v(x_t) = R(x_t). \tag{15.8}$$

To use this tax rule, we need an estimate of rent under the sole-owner. If we can estimate the demand and harvest cost function, the growth function, and the initial stock, we can solve the sole-owner problem and calculate the stock-contingent optimal open access tax, $R(x_t)$.

15.2.2 Optimal Policy under Two Market Failures

If the stock of fish provides ecological services with per-period value $V(x_t)$, external to the sole owner, harvest under the sole owner is not efficient. The efficient level of harvest maximizes the present value of the stream of profits plus the value of the flow of ecological service.

$$\sum_{t=0}^{\infty} \rho^t \left[\left(p_t - \frac{C}{x_t} \right) y_t + V(x_t) \right]. \tag{15.9}$$

Harvest under the sole owner is efficient if this owner receives a state-contingent subsidy $V(x_t)$.

The Euler equation when the sole owner receives the subsidy $V(x_t)$ is

$$R_t = \rho \left[R_{t+1} \left(1 + \frac{dF(x_{t+1})}{dx_{t+1}} \right) + \underbrace{\frac{C}{x_{t+1}^2} y_{t+1}} + \underline{\underline{\frac{dV(x_{t+1})}{dx_{t+1}}}} \right]. \tag{15.10}$$

The right sides of equations 15.5 and 15.10 are identical, except for the double-underlined term in equation 15.10, equal to the reduction in the $t + 1$ subsidy resulting from the additional unit of harvest at t. Given estimates of the inverse demand function, the harvest cost function, growth function, and the external benefit ($V(x)$), we can numerically solve the optimization problem and calculate rent in the presence of the subsidy $V(x)$. The stock-contingent optimal tax for the open access fishery equals the subsidized sole-owner's rent.

Section 9.3 notes that a tax on pollution emissions and a subsidy on pollution abatement can have the same effect on incentives to pollute. This equivalence between taxes and subsidies is quite general and also holds in the fishery setting. Instead of giving the sole owner a stock-dependent per-period subsidy of $V(x_t)$, as in the payoff 15.9, suppose that the owner must pay a per-period licensing fee $L(x_t)$, so her profit in period t is $\left(p_t - \frac{c}{x_t}\right) y_t - L(x_t)$. If the licensing fee is less than per-period profit, the owner still wants to use the resource. Moreover, if the licensing fee satisfies

$$\frac{dL(x_t)}{dx_t} = -\frac{dV(x_t)}{dx_t} \text{ for all } x, \tag{15.11}$$

then the fisher facing this fee has the same incentives, and harvests at the same level, as the fisher who receives the subsidy.[1] The two policies have different fiscal effects, as with the pollution tax and abatement subsidy.

15.2.3 Empirical Challenges

Managers are unable to directly observe the growth function, the cost function, or the biological stock. The management tools described above require estimates of these functions and of the stock. We discuss two approaches to estimating these model components.

The first approach uses data for multiple boats for multiple years ("panel data"); an observation consists of effort and catch for a particular boat in a particular year. Effort data (a vector) include characteristics of the boats and expenditures. In a particular year, all boats confront (approximately) the same level of the stock. Researchers estimate parameters relating harvest to the effort characteristics, and also estimate a stock index; these can be used to estimate optimal harvest (Zhang and Smith 2011).[2] This procedure results in parameter estimates of a harvest cost function and a growth function.

The second approach uses data collected by dragging nets across fishing areas. By counting rings in the bones (e.g., in the ear canal or the jaw), scientists estimate the age of individuals in the sample, in much the same way that counting tree rings identifies the tree's age. These data are used with a dynamic model and a measurement model. The

---

1 If $V(x) = gx - \frac{h}{2}x^2$, with $g, h > 0$, then setting the annual license equal to $L(x) = k - gx + \frac{h}{2}x^2$ satisfies equation 15.11. The fisher has the same incentive to protect the stock under the subsidy $V(x)$ as under the license fee $L(x)$. This license is equivalent to a two-part policy: the fisher pays the fixed fee k to use the resource, and also receives a subsidy, $V(x)$. The fixed fee, k, does not change incentives to harvest (provided that it is not large enough to cause the fisher to cease harvesting). The two-part license leads to the same extraction decisions as the subsidy, but the license extracts rent from the fishery.

2 An "index" is a measurement related to the object of interest (here, the stock), not the object itself. For example, the economy-wide price level is a theoretical construction, not an observable price. We use the consumer price index to measure this price level.

dynamic model consists of a system of equations that describe the evolution of the stock and age classes. Taking as given the equations' functional form, the goal is to estimate the parameters of the functions. In the simplest case, with a single stock variable, scientists might assume the logistic growth function and then estimate the two parameters of that function, the natural growth rate and the carrying capacity. The measurement model relates the underlying but unobservable variables of interest (e.g., stock size for different ages) to the measured variables (e.g., age estimates of the sample).

Estimation of the unknown parameters and unknown stocks uses an iterative procedure (International Scientific Committee for Tuna 2011). Beginning with a guess of the unknown values of the parameters and the stocks, we can calculate what the measurements would have been, had the guess been correct. Because the guess is not correct, the calculated values differ from the observed measurements. We then change our guess, in an effort to make the calculated values closer to the observed measurements. We stop the iteration when it is not possible to get a closer fit between the calculated values and the observed measures. The final iteration yields estimates of the parameters and stock variables.

15.3   The Steady State

Objectives and skills: Obtain and analyze the steady state(s) under the sole owner and compare them with open access steady states.

Comparison of the sole-owner and the open access steady states provides information about the relation between property rights and equilibrium outcomes. Under what circumstances do open access and sole ownership lead to the same (or almost the same) steady state? When are the steady states significantly different?[3]

By definition, at a steady state the harvest, stock, and rent are unchanging over time. We drop the time subscripts to indicate that these variables are constant in a steady state. The equation of motion of the stock is $x_{t+1} - x_t = F(x_t) - y_t$. In a steady state, the left side of this equation is zero; dropping the time subscripts, we write this equation, evaluated at the steady state, as $0 = F(x) - y$. The definition of the steady state rent can be written as $R = p(y) - \frac{\partial c(x,y)}{\partial y}$. We obtain a third equation by evaluating the Euler equation at a steady state. We then have three algebraic equations in three unknowns, the steady state stock, harvest, and rent. We can solve these three equations to determine the steady state values. We consider the cases of constant and stock-dependent average extraction costs separately.

---

3 Chapter 14 obtained the harvest rule under open access by solving the zero-profit condition, price = average cost. There, we could easily determine which of the steady states is stable. In the sole-owner setting, we only have an optimality condition (the Euler equation), not an explicit harvest rule. We can still identify the steady states, but determining their stability requires methods discussed in Chapter 16.

15.3.1   Harvest Costs Are Independent of Stock

Evaluating equation 15.3 at an interior steady state $(x > 0)$, we have the condition[4]

$$0 = R\left(r - \frac{dF(x)}{dx}\right). \tag{15.12}$$

Equation 15.12 implies that at a steady state either $R = 0$ or

$$r = \frac{dF(x)}{dx}. \tag{15.13}$$

Equation 15.13 states that at an interior steady state with $R > 0$, the sole owner is indifferent between two investment opportunities. The owner can increase current harvest, and invest the additional profit in an asset that earns the annual return r, or she can keep the extra unit of stock in the fishery, where it contributes to growth, thus contributing to future harvests and future profits. At an interior $(x > 0)$ optimum, the owner is indifferent between these two investments.

For concave F, there is a unique solution to equation 15.13. This solution, denoted x_∞, depends only on the discount rate and the growth function. If $x_\infty \leq 0$, there is no interior steady state with positive profits. If $x_\infty > 0$, we perform one further test. The harvest that maintains x_∞ as a steady state is $y_\infty = F(x_\infty)$. The price at this level of harvest is $p(y_\infty)$, and the rent is $R(y_\infty) = p(y_\infty) - C$. If $x_\infty > 0$ and $R(y_\infty) \geq 0$, then x_∞ is a steady state. If either of these inequalities fail, x_∞ has no significance, and there are no interior steady states with positive profits. There might still be interior steady states with zero profits.

In summary, the solution to equation 15.13, x_∞, is a steady state if and only if it satisfies both of the inequalities

(i) $x_\infty > 0$,   and   (ii) $R(y_\infty) \geq 0$. \tag{15.14}

We use the logistic growth function, $F(x) = \gamma x(1 - \frac{x}{K})$ and figures 15.1 and 15.2 to explain how to determine interior steady states.

Figure 15.1 shows the graph of $\frac{dF(x)}{dx} = \gamma\left(1 - \frac{2x}{K}\right)$ for $\gamma = 0.04$ and $K = 50$. The intercept of this graph is $\gamma = 0.04$, the intrinsic growth rate. The figure also shows two horizontal lines labeled $r = 0.05$ and $r = 0.03$. The intersection of each of these lines and the graph of $\frac{dF}{dx}$ is the solution to equation 15.13 for the particular value of r. For $r = 0.05$, this solution occurs where $x_\infty < 0$. Because the stock cannot be negative, we conclude that

---

4 We can obtain equation 15.12 using the same steps that led to equation 15.6. Alternatively, we can directly use equation 15.6, eliminating the last term on the right side, because here there is no stock-related cost change. In the steady state, capital gains are zero, so the capital gain term in equation 15.6 also vanishes. We are left with the middle term on the right side. Dropping time subscripts (because variables are constant in the steady state) and rearranging gives the steady state condition 15.12.

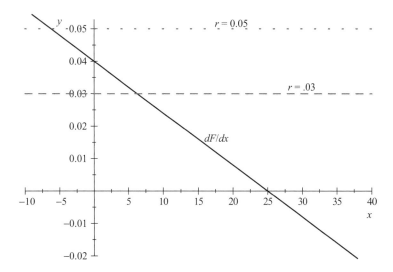

Figure 15.1
The derivative of the logistic growth $F(x) = 0.04x \left(1 - \frac{x}{50}\right)$, $\frac{dF}{dx} = 0.04x \left(1 - \frac{2x}{50}\right)$, and two values of r.

for $r = 0.05$, there is no interior steady state with positive profits. For $r = 0.03$, the solution to equation 15.13 occurs where $x_\infty > 0$. More generally, there is a positive solution ($x_\infty > 0$) to equation 15.13 if and only if $r < \gamma$. This inequality implies that for small stock levels (where the growth rate is close to γ), the value of harvesting an additional fish is less than the value of allowing the fish to remain alive and reproduce.

To find x_∞, we use $\frac{dF(x)}{dx} = \gamma \left(1 - \frac{2x}{K}\right)$ and solve $r = \gamma \left(1 - \frac{2x}{K}\right)$ to obtain

$$x_\infty = \frac{K}{2}\left(1 - \frac{r}{\gamma}\right) < \frac{K}{2}. \tag{15.15}$$

Equation 15.15 confirms that $x_\infty > 0$ if and only if $r < \gamma$. The candidate steady state decreases with $\frac{r}{\gamma}$: a higher discount rate (greater impatience) lowers the candidate, and faster growth increases the candidate. The inequality in equation 15.15 states that the candidate steady state is less than $\frac{K}{2}$, the stock level that maximizes growth (i.e., leads to MSY). At a steady state with positive rent, harvest is less than MSY.

Sensitivity of the Steady State to the Discount Rate
The steady state stock with positive rent tends to be more sensitive to the discount rate, the more slowly the stock grows. Using equation 15.15, the elasticity of the steady state stock, with respect to the discount rate in the logistic model, is $\frac{r}{\gamma - r}$. For fast-growing Pacific halibut, γ is estimated (with an annual time step and a continuous time model) at 0.71; for the slow-growing Antarctic Fin-Whale, the estimate is 0.08 (Clark 1996). As r ranges

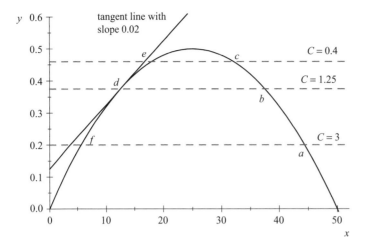

Figure 15.2
For $F = 0.04x \left(1 - \frac{x}{50}\right)$ and $r = 0.02$, one candidate for a steady state under the sole owner is point d, where $x = 12.5$ and $y = .375$. For inverse demand $= 5 - 10y$, open access steady states (where rent and growth are both zero) are points e and c for $C = 0.4$, points d and b for $C = 1.25$, and points f and a for $C = 3$. These points are also steady states under the sole owner for these levels of C.

from 2% to 5%, the elasticity of the steady state for the Fin-Whale is 11–22 times greater than the elasticity for halibut: the steady state of the more slowly growing stock is more sensitive to the discount rate.

Numerical Example

We use the logistic growth function $F(x) = 0.04x \left(1 - \frac{x}{50}\right)$ and $r = 0.02$. Here, $\gamma = 0.04 > r$, so $x_\infty > 0$. We find x_∞ by solving equation 15.15 to obtain $x_\infty = 12.5$ and then obtain

$$y_\infty = F(x_\infty) = 0.04(12.5)\left(1 - \frac{12.5}{50}\right) = 0.375.$$

Figure 15.2 identifies the candidate steady state as point d, $(x_\infty, y_\infty) = (12.5, 0.375)$, the tangency between the graph of the growth function and the line with slope $r = 0.02$. To determine whether the candidate is a steady state, we check whether rent is positive at this value (i.e., whether the candidate satisfies part (ii) of equation 15.14). Here we use the inverse demand function $p(y) = 5 - 10y$. With a choke price of 5, the fish has value if and only if $C < 5$, as we hereafter assume. Rent at the candidate steady state, point d, is $R = 5 - 10(.375) - C$: $R \geq 0$ requires $C \leq 1.25$.

Figure 15.2 shows three horizontal lines, each at the level of harvest where rent is 0 for a particular value of C. Rent is 0 if $R = 5 - 10y - C = 0$, implying $y = \frac{5-C}{10}$. Rent is positive below the $R = 0$ line, and rent is negative above this line. We now have the information needed to determine whether $R(y_\infty) \geq 0$. Point d, our candidate steady state, lies below the $R = 0$ line for $C = 0.4$. Thus, if $C = 0.4$ (harvest costs are low), rent is positive at point d; in this case, point d is a steady state. In contrast, if $C = 3$ (harvest costs are high), rent is negative at point d; for this level of costs, point d has no significance. If $C = 1.25$, point d is an interior steady state with rent 0.

Comparing Open Access and Sole-Owner Steady States

We use the numerical example and Figure 15.2 to discuss the relation between the open access and the sole-owner fisheries. From section 14.1.1 we know that under open access there are three steady states: 0, an intermediate steady state (e, d, f for the three values of C), and a high steady state (c, b, a for the three cases). Under open access, the high steady state and $x = 0$ are stable steady states, and the intermediate steady state is unstable.

Now consider the steady states under the sole owner. The open access high steady states, (c, b, a) also satisfy the sole-owner steady state conditions for the different levels of cost, C. At these points: (i) $y = F(x)$, so the stock is unchanging; (ii) $R = 0$, so the steady state Euler equation 15.12 is satisfied; and (iii) the definition of rent is also satisfied. Exactly the same reasoning holds at the open access intermediate steady states and at $x = 0$. Thus, for this problem, all steady states under open access are also steady states under the sole owner. If $C < 1.25$, then point d is also a steady state under the sole owner (but not under open access).

In summary, every point that is a steady state under open access is also a steady state under the sole owner. (This conclusion holds for constant average harvest costs but not for general harvest costs.) At all of these points, either rent or harvest is zero. For sufficiently low costs ($C < 1.25$ in our example), there is an additional steady state under the sole owner that does not exist under open access. At that steady state, the sole owner has positive rent. The Chapter 16 turns to the question of determining which of the sole-owner steady states is stable.

15.3.2 Harvest Costs Depend on the Stock

When harvest costs depend on the stock:

1. The sole-owner steady state stock might be below or above the stock corresponding to the MSY.

2. Harvest costs have ambiguous effects on both steady state rent and steady state consumer surplus.

In the steady state, rent is constant; there are no capital gains. Using this fact, evaluating equation 15.6 in the steady state (merely dropping the time subscripts), and rearranging, we have the steady state condition:

$$\left(r - \frac{dF(x)}{dx} \right) R = \frac{C}{x^2} y. \tag{15.16}$$

Rearranging this equation gives the steady state value of rent:

$$\underbrace{R}_{\text{steady state value of rent}} = \cfrac{\overbrace{\dfrac{C}{x^2}y}^{\text{cost reduction due to larger stock}}}{\underbrace{r - \dfrac{dF(x)}{dx}}_{\text{modified discount rate}}}. \tag{15.17}$$

The numerator on the right equals the cost reduction due to an extra unit of the stock. The denominator is a modified discount rate, equal to the discount rate r minus $\frac{dF(x)}{dx}$ to account for growth.

Section 5.3 notes that rent can be interpreted as the shadow value of the resource: the amount the owner would be willing to pay for one more unit of the resource in situ. Section 2.6 notes that the present discounted value of a constant flow, received in perpetuity, equals that flow divided by the discount rate (equation 2.13). Thus, equation 15.17 says that the steady state rent equals the value of the cost reduction achieved by an additional unit of the stock (the numerator on the right side), received in perpetuity and discounted using the modified discount rate.

In deciding whether to reduce harvest by one unit, the owner weighs two consideration: the modified discount rate accounts for both. A reduction in harvest at a point in time leads to a fall in profit and a corresponding reduction in funds available for investment. The discount rate, r, determines the opportunity cost of a reduction in investment. However, the one unit reduction in harvest increases the stock at the end of the period by one unit, thereby changing growth by $\frac{dF}{dx}$. The change in growth provides a benefit if positive and a cost if negative. If the stock is below the MSY, then $\frac{dF}{dx} > 0$; if the stock is above the MSY, then $\frac{dF}{dx} < 0$. If, for example, the stock is below MSY, then the modified discount rate is less than r. In this case, the opportunity for increased growth, resulting from a higher stock, lowers the net opportunity cost associated with a reduction in harvest. If the stock is above the MSY, growth increases the opportunity cost of reducing harvest. Here, the modified discount rate exceeds the discount rate.

We collect the steady state conditions:

$$F(x) - y = 0, \quad \left(r - \frac{dF(x)}{dx}\right)R - \frac{C}{x^2}y = 0, \quad \text{and} \quad R = p(y) - \frac{C}{x}. \tag{15.18}$$

The first two equations repeat the steady state conditions for the stock and the rent, and the third equation repeats the definition of rent.

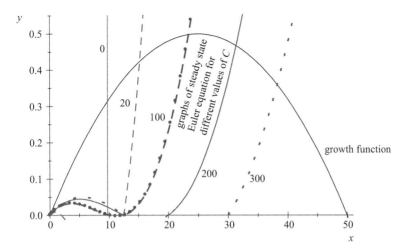

Figure 15.3
The logistic growth function and graphs of the steady state Euler equations (the positively sloping curves) each labeled with the value of the cost parameter, C. The sole-owner steady state occurs at the intersection of the growth function with these curves. An increase in C increases x_∞ and has an ambiguous effect on y_∞.

System 15.18 contains three equations in three unknowns, x, y, and R.[5] Figure 15.3 shows the graph of the growth function and the graphs of the steady state Euler equation (the upward sloping curves) corresponding to different values of C. (The figure uses $p = 10 - y$, $F = 0.04x \left(1 - \frac{x}{50}\right)$, and $r = 0.02$.) At all points on the growth function, harvest equals growth: the first equation in system 15.18 is satisfied. At all points on an upward sloping curve (corresponding to a particular value of C), the second two equations in the system are satisfied. The equilibrium occurs at the intersection of the curves. An increase in C causes the graph of the steady state Euler equation to shift to the right, increasing the value of x_∞. Larger values of the cost parameter increase costs and also make costs more sensitive to the the stock. A larger value of C therefore gives the sole owner an incentive to conserve the stock.

The sole-owner steady state might lie below or above the MSY stock level. As C increases, raising x_∞, the harvest level, y_∞, rises and then falls: the steady state harvest is nonmonotonic in the cost parameter C. Table 15.1 shows sole owner (superscript "so") steady state stock, harvest, and rent, under three values of the cost parameter, C. The last

5 For $C > 0$, rent is positive for the solution to this system. For $C > 0$, the second equation in system 15.18 implies $R = \left(\frac{C}{x^2} y\right) / \left(r - \frac{dF(x)}{dx}\right)$. This equality implies that steady state rent is positive if and only if $\left(r - \frac{dF(x)}{dx}\right) > 0$. For concave $F(x)$, this inequality holds for any x greater than the solution to equation 15.13, which is the candidate steady state under zero costs. Stock-dependent harvest costs ($C > 0$) lead to a higher steady state, compared to zero costs. Therefore for $C > 0$, the second equality in system 15.18 implies that steady state rent is positive.

Table 15.1
Steady state stock, harvest, and rent for the sole owner (so), and stock and harvest under open access (oa)

C	x_∞^{so}	y_∞^{so}	R_∞^{so}	x_∞^{oa}	y_∞^{oa}
0	12.5	0.38	9.6	0	0
50	18.6	0.47	1.7	5.1	0.18
300	38.2	0.36	1.8	31.47	0.47

two columns of the table show the open access (superscript "oa") steady state stock and harvest for those values of C. Open access rent is always 0.

Steady state harvest, and thus consumer surplus, might be either higher or lower under the sole owner, compared to open access. For $C > 0$, the sole owner has an incentive to conserve the stock and so reduce future harvest costs; the open access fisher ignores future harvest costs. Therefore, the sole-owner steady state stock is higher than the open access steady state. If both these steady states are above the level that maximizes yield, steady state harvest (and consumer surplus) is lower under the sole owner than under open access.

The price and harvest combination lies on the demand function. Higher harvests therefore correspond to lower prices and higher consumer welfare. We noted above that the sole owner steady state harvest is non-monotonic in C, first increasing and then decreasing with larger C. Consequently, a higher C might make consumers either better or worse off in the steady state (under the sole owner). In the static competitive setting, in contrast, higher costs shift the equilibrium supply function in and up, leading to a higher equilibrium price and lower consumer surplus. Why do higher costs have different effects in the (steady state) sole-owner fishery, compared to the static market? In the fishery context, a higher C reduces the incentive to harvest, leading to a higher steady state stock. The higher steady state stock might correspond to either a higher or a lower steady state harvest, depending on whether the stock lies below or above the level corresponding to MSY. These considerations are absent in the static setting.

Steady state rent can also be non-monotonic in the cost parameter. The larger C increases costs for a given level of stock, but it also leads to a higher steady state stock. Table 15.1 shows that steady state rent is lower at $C = 50$ compared to either $C = 0$ or $C = 300$. The fact that an increase in costs might increase steady state rent or consumer surplus, does not imply that either consumers or producers are better off with higher costs. To evaluate their welfare, we need to consider the present discounted stream of their payoffs. Suppose that we begin at the steady state corresponding to $C = 50$ and then increase the cost parameter to $C = 300$. The rent is higher at the new steady state, but the stock does not instantly jump from the original to the new steady state. The adjustment process takes time. Rent is lower during much of the trajectory that takes the stock to the new, higher, steady state; the present discounted stream of rent is also likely to be lower.

A decrease in the discount rate makes future profits more valuable, increasing the steady state stock regardless of whether harvest costs depend on the stock. For stock-independent harvest costs, a lower discount rate causes the tangency point d in Figure 15.2 to move up the growth function, resulting in higher steady state harvest and higher consumer surplus. In this case, a more patient manager (one with lower r) benefits consumers. If harvest costs depend on the stock, the steady state might be above the MSY level. Then a lower discount rate can lead to lower steady state harvest and consumer surplus; consumers might not benefit from a more patient manager.

15.3.3   Empirical Evidence

The optimal steady state stock depends on harvest costs, the growth function, and the demand function; these vary across fisheries, so the optimal steady state stock might be above or below the MSY level. A study of four fisheries (including slow-growing orange roughy) finds that in all cases, the socially optimal stock level exceeds the MSY stock level, implying that the optimal steady state harvest is below the MSY (Grafton, Kompas, and Hilborn 2007). Section 15.3.1 notes that a low growth rate tends to reduce the optimal steady state stock and possibly leads to extinction. Thus, it might be optimal to drive down stocks of the slow-growing orange roughy. However, other considerations, such as strongly stock-dependent harvest costs, promote a higher steady state. A study for North Pacific albacore concludes that the optimal steady state lies below the MSY level (Squires and Vestergaard 2013). This study emphasizes the role of cost-reducing technology improvements. As figure 15.3 illustrates, lower harvest costs (smaller C) reduce the sole-owner steady state.

Many actual management practices try to keep stock at the level of MSY. There is a plausible argument and a dubious one in favor of this practice. The plausible argument is that, lacking a strong a priori basis for thinking that the stock should be to the right or the left of this level, and in view of the measurement difficulties, the MSY level is neutral. The dubious argument is that a positive discount rate is unfair to future generations, because it gives them less weight in the social welfare function. Whatever the merits of this ethical position, it does not imply that the steady state occurs at MSY. MSY maximizes consumer surplus, but when harvest cost depends on the stock, it does not maximize social welfare, the sum of consumer and producer surplus. With stock-dependent costs, low discount rates require a higher steady state stock to take advantage of cost reductions. Because these stocks occur to the right of the MSY level, they correspond to lower harvests and lower consumer surplus but higher producer surplus, and a higher social surplus.

15.4   Summary

We derived and interpreted the Euler equation for the price-taking sole-owner fishery, emphasizing the difference between the renewable and nonrenewable resources. For a renewable resource, we have to take growth into account. The sole owner internalizes the effect of her current harvest decisions on future stocks. Absent externalities, the First

Fundamental Welfare Theorem implies that the outcome under the sole owner is efficient. In that case, there is no efficiency rationale for regulation. Moving from open access to the sole owner solves the only market failure.

If it is not practical to establish property rights to the fishery, the open access fishery can be induced to harvest efficiently by charging a tax per unit of harvest equal to rent under the sole owner. We also considered the case where the stock of fish provides ecological services that are external to the sole owner. A subsidy or a tax can induce the sole owner to internalize that externality, causing the sole owner to harvest efficiently. A tax equal to the sole owner's rent, when that owner harvests efficiently, induces the open access fishery to harvest efficiently. This efficiency-inducing tax varies with the stock of fish, so a constant tax is not first best.

For the nonrenewable resource, extraction eventually ceases as the resource is exhausted or as extraction becomes too costly. For the renewable resource, the sole owner might drive the stock to a positive steady state, where harvest and the stock remain constant; or the owner might drive the fishery to extinction. A model with constant (stock-independent) average harvest costs illustrates these possibilities. Here, if the intrinsic growth rate is less than the rate of interest ($\gamma < r$), there is no interior steady state with positive rent: either the owner drives the stock to extinction, or he maintains the stock at a positive level with zero rent. If the intrinsic growth rate exceeds the rate of interest ($\gamma > r$), there is a candidate interior steady state at which the actual growth rate equals the rate of interest. This candidate is a steady state for the sole owner if and only if rent is greater than or equal to zero there.

Stock-dependent harvest costs give the sole owner an incentive to restrict harvest to let the stock grow, reducing future harvest costs. Thus, stock dependence tends to increase the sole-owner steady state, while discounting tends to decrease it. The sole-owner steady state might lie above or below the MSY stock level. Lower discount rates increase the sole-owner steady state but have an ambiguous effect on steady state harvest and consumer surplus. With zero discounting and stock-independent harvest costs, the sole owner steady state stock equals the MSY. With zero discounting and stock-dependent harvest costs, the sole owner steady state stock exceeds the MSY level; steady state harvest is less than the MSY.

15.5   Terms and Concepts, Study Questions, Exercises, and Sources

Terms and Concepts
Stock-dependent efficiency-inducing tax, ecological services.

Study Questions
1. Given a growth function $F(x)$, a cost function $c(x, y)$, and discount factor ρ, write down the sole owner's objective function and constraints. Without doing calculations, describe the steps needed to obtain the Euler equation in this model.

2. Provide an economic interpretation for the Euler equation in the fishing model both with and without stock-dependent harvest costs.

3. Consider the case where marginal = average harvest costs depend on the stock. Identify the stock-dependent tax that induces the open access industry to harvest at the same rate as the untaxed sole owner.

4. (a) For the model with constant (stock-independent) average harvest costs, C, and logistic growth $F(x) = \gamma x \left(1 - \frac{x}{K}\right)$, write down the Euler equation evaluated at the steady state. (b) Under what conditions is there an interior steady state with positive rent? Explain. (c) If the conditions in part (b) are not satisfied, are there other interior steady states? If so, describe these.

5. Consider the following two claims "(i) An open access fishery leads to excessive harvest. (ii) It is never socially optimal to exhaust the stock." Discuss these two claims in light of the model described in question 4.

6. Discuss the claim "Consumers are better off under a more patient manager (one with lower discount rate r)."

Exercises

1. Write down and interpret the Euler equation for the monopoly owner of a renewable resource facing inverse demand $p(y)$ and constant average harvest costs, Cy. [Hint: Use the same methods that we applied to the nonrenewable resource problem.]

2. Suppose that $F = 0.8x \left(1 - \frac{x}{100}\right)$, $r = 0.4$, inverse demand is $p = 60 - y$, and the constant extraction cost is C.

   (a) Find the candidate interior steady state with positive profits. Does this candidate satisfies part (i) of equation 15.14?

   (b) Find a condition on C such that the candidate satisfies part (ii) of equation 15.14.

3. Derive the formula for the elasticity of the steady state with respect to the discount rate presented in section 15.3.

4. Show that, provided that $F(x)$ is concave, an interior steady state with positive profits, in the case where costs do not depend on the stock, always lies below the maximum sustainable yield.

5. Consider the model with constant harvest costs C and logistic growth $F(x) = \gamma x \left(1 - \frac{x}{K}\right)$. Suppose that $\gamma < r$. Are there circumstances where the sole owner drives the stock to a positive steady state? Explain and justify your answer. [Hint: Is there any reason to suppose that rent is positive in this model?]

6. Using equation 15.15 for the case of stock-independent harvest costs with logistic growth, verify (by taking derivatives) that if $\gamma > r$, then a larger value of K or γ increases

the candidate interior steady state with positive profits. Provide an economic (not mathematical) explanation for these results. You need to explain how changes in these parameters changes the owner's incentive to conserve the fish.

Sources

Clark (1996) provides the estimates of growth rates used in section 15.3.

Homans and Wilen (2005) provide the estimate of the annual lease prices for fishing quotas, as a percentage of ex vessel price of catch.

Fenichel and Abbott (2014) show how estimates of stock dynamics and the production function can be used to estimate the gain from better management of fish stocks.

Zhang and Smith (2011) describe and implement, for Gulf Coast reef fish, the first estimation approach discussed in section 15.2.3.

The NOAA Fisheries website (http://www.nmfs.noaa.gov) explains the second estimation approach in section 15.2.3.

International Scientific Committee for Tuna (2011) illustrates the second estimation approach, for the case of tuna stocks.

Grafton, Kompas, and Hilborn (2007) provide evidence that the socially optimal stock exceeds the MSY stock.

Squires and Vestergaard (2013) provide evidence that increases in technical efficiency cause socially optimal steady state stocks to be below the MSY stock.

16 Dynamic Analysis

Objective

• Use descriptions of sole-owner harvest rules to evaluate resource policy.

Information and Skills

• Use "careful reasoning" to describe the sole-owner harvest rule under constant marginal costs.

• Use phase portrait analysis to describe this harvest rule under stock-dependent harvest cost.

• Compare harvest rules under the sole owner and under open access to characterize optimal policy.

When is it important to intervene in an open access fishery, and what level of intervention is needed? This chapter takes a step toward answering these questions by comparing the efficient outcome with the open access outcome. To this end, we have to move beyond steady state analysis and study the efficient evolution of the fish stock. We assume that there are no market failures under the price-taking sole owner, who harvests efficiently. We could achieve efficient resource use by establishing property rights where they are absent. However, only about a quarter of fish stocks (by volume) are currently managed using property rights–based regulation. Other regulation, including taxes, can increase efficiency under open access. The tools developed here are applicable to a wide range of renewable resources.

To find the optimal tax for the open access fishery, we need to know the optimal outcome. We then look for the policy that supports this outcome in the open access setting. The discussion of the Pigouvian tax (see chapter 9) illustrates this procedure. We apply the same logic here, where we want to support a particular "harvest rule" (= a relation that determines harvest as a function of the stock) instead of a particular harvest level. By approximating that rule and comparing it with the open access harvest rule, we can begin to answer the questions that introduce this chapter.

A Road Map

Section 13.3.1 notes that a continuous time model may be easier to analyze than a discrete time model. Section 16.1 presents the continuous time analog of the discrete time Euler equation, introduced in section 15.1. Section 16.2 uses careful reasoning to describe the sole-owner harvest rule with constant marginal costs. By comparing the sole-owner and the open access harvest rules, we identify circumstances where policy intervention is important. Section 16.3 considers the more interesting case where marginal harvest costs depend on the stock. We discuss the type of policy information obtained by inspection of a graph and then work out the construction of this graph.

16.1 The Continuous Time Limit

Objectives and skills: Have an intuitive understanding of the continuous time analog of the discrete time Euler equation.

We need one intermediate result: the continuous time version of the discrete time Euler equation. In deriving the discrete time Euler equation, we did not specify whether the length of a period is 1 year or 1 second. Here we assume that the length of period in the discrete time setting is sufficiently small that the continuous time limit provides a reasonable approximation.

As in section 13.3, the continuous limit of the discrete time equation of motion for the stock is $\frac{dx}{dt} = F(x) - y$. The missing piece is the continuous time Euler equation. We begin with the discrete time equation 15.3 for constant average harvest cost and equation 15.5 for stock-dependent cost, and take limits, letting the length of each period become small. The continuous time limits are, respectively (appendix G),

$$\frac{dR_t}{dt} = R_t \left(r - \frac{dF(x_t)}{dx_t} \right), \tag{16.1}$$

$$\frac{dR_t}{dt} = R_t \left(r - \frac{dF(x_t)}{dx_t} \right) - \frac{C}{x_t^2} y_t. \tag{16.2}$$

If harvest costs do not depend on the stock $\left(\frac{C}{x_t^2} y_t = 0 \right)$, equation 16.1 shows that in a steady state (where $\frac{dR_t}{dt} = 0$), either $R = 0$ or $r = \frac{dF(x)}{dx}$; section 15.3.1 shows this result in the discrete time setting.

Interpreting the Euler Equation

For $r \neq \frac{dF(x)}{dx}$, we can rearrange equation 16.2 and divide by $r - \frac{dF(x)}{dx}$ to write rent as

$$R_t = \frac{\overbrace{\frac{C}{x_t^2}y_t}^{\text{cost reduction due to larger stock}} + \overbrace{\frac{dR_t}{dt}}^{\text{capital gains or losses}}}{\underbrace{\left(r - \frac{dF(x_t)}{dx_t}\right)}_{\text{modified discount rate}}}. \tag{16.3}$$

Equation 15.17 gives the formula for rent evaluated at the steady state. Equation 16.3 is more general, giving rent at any time, even outside the steady state. The right sides of the two equations equal the present discounted value of a constant flow, received in perpetuity and discounted using the modified discount rate. The two equations differ because equations 16.3 takes into account capital gains or losses; these are 0 at the steady but can be positive or negative outside the steady state.

Outside the steady state, both the numerator and the denominator of equation 16.3 are changing over time. However, the equation states that rent equals the value of a hypothetical investment that generates a constant flow benefit, in perpetuity, discounted at a constant rate. The constant flow in this hypothetical investment equals the sum of the cost reduction due to a larger stock $\left(\frac{C}{x_t^2}y_t\right)$ and the capital gains $\left(\frac{dR_t}{dt}\right)$; we discount this flow using the modified discount rate.

16.2   Harvest Rules for Stock-Independent Costs

Objectives and skills: Compare the sole owner and open access harvest rules and then describe the optimal open access tax.

This section uses the example introduced in section 15.3.1, with growth function $F(x) = 0.04x\left(1 - \frac{x}{50}\right)$, inverse demand $p(y) = 5 - 10y$, discount rate $r = 0.02$, and constant average costs C. By varying C, we determine the relation between harvest costs and the sole-owner equilibrium. The Euler equation 16.1 holds on the sole-owner's harvest path.

Figure 16.1 reproduces Figure 15.2. We first review the open access equilibrium. The horizontal dashed lines in Figure 16.1 are the open access harvest rules corresponding to three values of C. (These dashed lines show the open access harvest rules for $x > 0$; at $x = 0$, harvest is always 0: you cannot get blood out of a turnip.) These constant values of y satisfy the zero-profit open access condition, $5 - 10y = C$, or $y = \frac{5-C}{10}$. Using the analysis of chapter 14, the points a, b, and c are stable steady states, and f, d, and e are unstable steady states, for the three values of C. The origin, $x = 0$, is a stable steady state in all three cases. At $C = 0.4$, the open access stock approaches point c if the initial stock is greater than the horizontal coordinate of point e; if the initial stock lies below this level, the

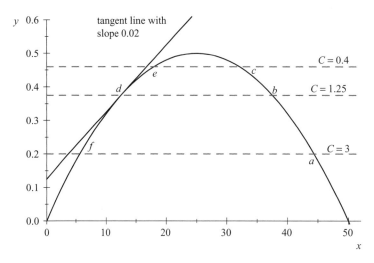

Figure 16.1
For $F = 0.04x \left(1 - \frac{x}{50}\right)$ and $r = 0.02$, one candidate for a steady state under the sole owner is point d, where $x = 12.5$ and $y = .375$. For inverse demand $= 5 - 10y$, open access steady states (where rent and growth are both zero) are points e and c for $C = 0.4$, points d and b for $C = 1.25$, and points f and a for $C = 3$. These points are also steady states under the sole owner for these levels of C.

Table 16.1
Open access steady state, x_∞, for different initial conditions, x_0

	x_0 above unstable steady state (e, d, or f)	x_0 below unstable steady state (e, d, or f)
$C = 0.4$	$x_\infty = c$	$x_\infty = 0$
$C = 1.25$	$x_\infty = b$	$x_\infty = 0$
$C = 3$	$x_\infty = a$	$x_\infty = 0$

open access stock approaches $x = 0$. The entries in table 16.1 show the open access steady state, x_∞, corresponding to different values of C and different initial conditions, x_0. In writing $x_\infty = a$, for example, we mean that x_∞ equals the horizontal coordinate of point a.

For the sole owner, we are not able to find an explicit function for the harvest rule for all values of x; however, we know that rent is non-negative whenever extraction is positive: $y > 0 \Rightarrow R \geq 0$. This fact, and some reasoning discussed below, enable us to identify the steady state that the stock approaches as a function of the parameter C and of the initial condition, x_0. Table 16.2 summarizes this information, and section 16.2.2 explains how we obtain it. First, we consider the policy implications of tables 16.1 and 16.2.[1]

---

1 For $C = 1.25$ and $C = 3$, the sole-owner middle steady states (d and f, respectively) are "semi-stable": for initial conditions to the left of these points, the trajectory converges to the point (d or f, depending on the value of C), and for initial conditions to the right, the trajectory moves away from that point.

Table 16.2
Sole-owner steady state, x_∞, for different initial conditions, x_0

	x_0 above middle steady state $(e, d,$ or $f)$	positive x_0 below middle steady state $(e, d,$ or $f)$
$C = 0.4$	$x_\infty = c$	$x_\infty = d$
$C = 1.25$	$x_\infty = b$	$x_\infty = d$
$C = 3$	$x_\infty = a$	$x_\infty = f$

16.2.1 Tax Policy Implications of Tables 16.1 and 16.2

Tables 16.1 and 16.2 imply a simple and intuitive policy recommendation:

It is important to regulate an open access fishery when the stock is small; regulation may be unnecessary when the stock is large.

We say that the initial stock is "large" if it exceeds the middle steady state, points e, d, or f (depending on the value of C); the initial stock is "small" if it is below these levels. The meaning of "large" and "small" depends on C. For all three values, if the initial stock is large, the equilibrium is the same under open access and under the sole owner. In these cases, the stock is large enough that the sole owner's rent, along the equilibrium trajectory, is 0, exactly as under open access. Here, the resource is not scarce; there is no reason to tax open access harvest, because there is no market failure.

In contrast, if the initial stock is small (but positive), open access drives to the stock to extinction, whereas the sole owner drives the stock to the socially optimal positive level. In this case, the resource is scarce; there is a market failure, and regulation is needed under open access. For $C < 1.25$ and small x_0, the sole owner drives the stock to point d. Rent is positive en route to and at the steady state.[2] Open access drives the stock to extinction: preserving the stock requires regulating open access harvest. The first-best tax policy for small stocks varies with the level of the stock. We previously noted (section 15.2) that in a resource setting, the optimal tax is typically stock dependent. Optimality might be too much to ask for, but the analysis suggests second-best alternatives. The manager can close down the open access fishery until the stock recovers to point d and then maintain a constant tax that supports open access harvest at point d. A less extreme alternative uses a high tax to permit recovery of low stocks, reducing the tax as the stock increases.

In summary, there is no need to regulate an open access fishery with large stocks, but regulation is important when the stock is small. Taxes can alter the open access steady state and also the speed at which the stock changes. At low stocks, the optimal open access

---

2 If $5 > C > 1.25$, rent is negative at point d. If x_0 is small, the sole owner drives the stock to a steady state to the left of and below d (point f for $C = 3$). In this case, rent is positive en route to the steady state, but is 0 at the steady state. The open access fishery drives the stock to extinction.

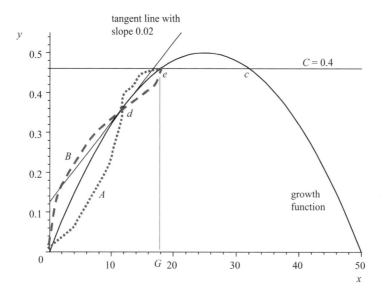

Figure 16.2
The growth function $F(x)$ and two hypothetical harvest rules (dashed and dotted curves) for $x < G$.

tax depends on the stock. If it is impractical to use the optimal tax, second-best taxes can ensure that the stock approaches the first-best steady state, even if not at the optimal speed.

16.2.2 Confirming Table 16.2*

We use figure 16.2 to examine the case $C = 0.4$. This figure contains a vertical line at $x = G$, through the unstable steady state; the initial stock is large if $x_0 > G$ and small if $x_0 < G$. Beginning with $x > G$, if the owner harvests at a rate that drives profits to 0, the stock approaches the higher steady state, point c. Along that trajectory, $R = 0$, so the Euler equation 16.1 is satisfied. A trajectory that satisfies the necessary conditions for optimality and converges to a steady state is (in our setting) optimal, so for $x > G$, the sole owner harvests (efficiently) at the open access level.

The interesting situation arises for $x < G$. We established (section 15.3.1) that there is a unique candidate steady state with positive rent: point d. For $C = 0.4$, this point lies below the zero-profit (horizontal) line, so d satisfies both conditions in equation 15.14; it is the unique steady state with positive profit. Because point d is a steady state, the harvest rule must intersect the growth function at d. The harvest rule cannot intersect the growth function at any other positive stock level below G. Any other point of intersection would be a steady state with positive rent, but we know that d is the only such point.

Therefore, to the left of point d, the harvest rule is either above the growth function (e.g., the dashed curve through B), or it is below the growth function (e.g., the dotted curve through A). There is a similar choice for initial conditions between d and G. In fact, the harvest rule is below the growth function to the left of d and above the growth function to the right of d. We confirm this claim for $0 < x < d$; the proof for $d < x < G$ mirrors the argument provided here. We begin by collecting six facts that hold regardless of whether the harvest rule lies above or below the growth function for $x < d$.

Fact 1: The harvest rule intersects the origin, because harvest must be 0 if there are 0 fish.

Fact 2: The harvest rule is continuous in x. A discontinuous harvest rule implies a jump in harvest at a point of discontinuity, and an associated jump in price and rent, violating equation 16.1.

Fact 3: There is an interval of stocks where $x < d$, the harvest rule is increasing in x, and rent is positive.[3] Call such an interval J (merely to give it a name).

Fact 4: The logistic growth function is concave, so $F'(x)$ falls with x; therefore, for $x < d$, we have $r < F'(x)$.

Fact 5: Rent is falling ($\frac{dR_t}{dt} < 0$) for all $x < d$ where rent is positive. This fact follows from equation 16.1 and fact 4.

Fact 6: Because J is a subset of $[0, d]$, fact 5 implies that rent is falling for $x \in J$.

Now consider the two possibilities: the harvest rule lies above the growth function or it lies below the growth function for $0 < x < d$. The first possibility implies that the stock is decreasing over time. For $x \in J$, the harvest is therefore decreasing over time, because for $x \in J$, the harvest changes in the same direction as the stock, which is decreasing over time. Consequently, for $x \in J$, price, and therefore rent ($=$ price $- C$), increases over time. But this conclusion contradicts fact 6. Therefore, we conclude that the harvest rule cannot lie above the growth function for $0 < x < d$.

The only remaining possibility is that the harvest rule lies below the growth function, as shown by the dotted curve through point A in figure 16.2. In this situation, the stock grows over time (because the harvest rule lies below the growth function), so for $x \in J$, harvest increases over time (because the harvest is positively related to the stock), so the rent falls over time (because the rent is negatively related to the harvest, due to the downward-sloping inverse demand). Thus, a harvest rule that lies below the growth function (for $0 < x < d$) is consistent with the above mentioned six facts and with the Euler equation, whereas a harvest rule above the growth function is not.

3 To confirm fact 3, begin with figure 16.2, and draw a continuous curve intersecting the origin and point d. It is apparent that any such curve must have an interval where the curve increases with x and lies below the horizontal line $C = 0.4$. In the interest of simplicity, figure 16.2 shows the dashed curve through point B as increasing for all x.

16.3   Harvest Rules for Stock-Dependent Costs

Objectives and skills: Use graphs of the open access and the sole-owner harvest rules to estimate the optimal tax under open access, and introduce the phase portrait.

This section uses the following parametric example:

$$c(x, y) = \frac{C}{x}y, \text{ with } C = 5;$$

$$F(x) = \gamma x \left(1 - \frac{x}{K}\right), \text{ with } K = 50 \text{ and } \gamma = 0.04; \text{ and} \qquad (16.4)$$

$$p = a - by, \text{ with } a = 3.5 \text{ and } b = 10, \text{ and } r = 0.03.$$

We summarize the policy implications of this example and then develop the methods used to obtain those results. The "phase portrait" is the important new tool introduced in this chapter. The example illustrates both the construction and the usefulness of phase portraits.

16.3.1   Tax Policy

Here we discuss the meaning and implications of figure 16.3. For the model in equation 16.4, there is a unique positive steady state under the sole owner, $x_\infty = 39.35$, $y_\infty = 0.335$. We obtain this steady state by setting stock and harvest constant in the growth equation and the Euler equation, just as in section 15.3.2. In the interest of brevity, we emphasize the behavior of the fishery for x below the steady state. Figure 16.3 shows the growth function, the heavy solid curve, for $x \leq 39.35$. The dotted curve shows the harvest rule under the sole owner for x below the steady state. Most of the work involved with this analysis lies in identifying this harvest rule (i.e., in constructing the dotted graph). For the time being, we put those difficulties aside and discuss the meaning of this graph.

The dashed curve (the "zero rent locus") shows the harvest rule under open access, obtained (as always) by setting rent $= 0$ and solving for harvest as a function of the stock. There are three positive steady states under open access, the intersections between the dashed and the heavy solid curve. The middle point ($x = 8$) is unstable, and the higher ($x = 39.3$) and the lower ($x = 2$) points of intersection are stable.

The harvest rule under the sole owner (dotted curve) lies everywhere below the harvest rule under open access (dashed curve): the sole owner harvests less than the open access fishery. For stock levels close to $x = 39.35$, the sole owner harvests only slightly less than under open access; at the level of resolution in figure 16.3, the difference is not appreciable. For x close to 39.35, it is relatively unimportant to regulate the open access fishery. For stocks above but close to the open access unstable steady state ($x = 8$), harvest under open access is low enough to allow the fish stock to reach almost the optimal steady state; regulation allows the fish stock to recover more quickly, but it has no significant long-term

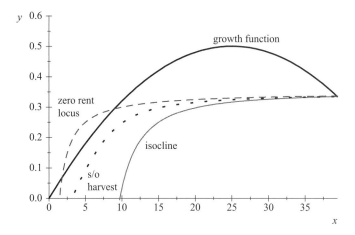

Figure 16.3
A part of the phase portrait for stocks below the steady state level. The solid curve shows the growth function; the dashed curve shows the combination of stock and harvest leading to zero rent; the dotted curve shows the sole owner (s/o) harvest rule. The next section discusses the isocline.

effect: the unregulated open access and the sole-owner steady states are almost the same. For stocks $x < 8$, the stock approaches $x = 2$ under open access, whereas under the sole owner, it eventually recovers to 39.35. Regulation is important for $x \leq 8$.

We can use the two harvest rules to estimate the optimal tax for any level of the stock. An example, with the arbitrary value $x = 7$, illustrates the procedure. Reading from the harvest rules, we see that at $x = 7$, the open access harvest is approximately $y = 0.29$, and the sole owner harvest is approximately $y = 0.2$; the corresponding open access price is $3.5 - 10(0.29) = 0.6$, and the sole owner price is $3.5 - 10(0.2) = 1.5$. The tax $1.5 - 0.6 = 0.9$ induces the open access fishery to reduce harvest to $y = 0.2$; at that level, the market price minus the tax equals the average harvest cost, and industry rent is 0. The tax $\tau = 0.9$ thus supports the efficient level of harvest at $x = 7$. Here we use the same logic as in chapter 9, which introduces the Pigouvian tax for a pollution externality: we first find the optimal outcome (here, harvesting $y = 0.2$ when the stock is $x = 7$) and then we find the tax that supports this outcome.

Because the vertical distance between the open access and the sole-owner harvest functions changes with the level of the stock, the optimal tax also changes with the stock. The optimal tax is negligible for large stocks, but it is large for small stocks. For our example, the optimal tax comprises 60% of the equilibrium consumer price at $x = 7$. Recalling section 15.2.1, the optimal tax under open access equals the rent under the sole owner. For this example, rent under the sole owner comprises about 60% of the market price when $x = 7$. Section 15.1.2 notes that estimates of rent, based on lease prices, are of this order of magnitude in fisheries with individual transferable quotas (ITQs).

Box 16.1
Back to Huxley and Gould

Box 1.2 contains quotes from two nineteenth-century figures, one explaining why regulation is
not needed, and the other explaining why it is needed. The analysis here illustrates the circumstances where one or the other is correct. If stocks are above the unstable open access steady
state, the open access outcome might be approximately socially optimal. Stock-dependent
costs reinforce this tendency by inducing fishers to reduce harvest as the stock falls. These
forces provide a kind of automatic protection, as Huxley suggested, and there is little need for
regulation. However, at low stocks, neither the market (which limits demand) nor technology
(which limits supply by increasing costs) is adequate to protect the stock: regulation is needed,
as Gould stated.

The tax implications of the models with constant and stock-dependent costs are similar.
In both, it is unimportant to tax the open access fishery at high stock levels. At high stock
levels, the optimal tax is 0 under constant harvest costs, and the optimal tax is close to 0 in
our example of stock-dependent harvest costs. At low stocks, the tax is important in both
models; it avoids physical extinction in one case and economic irrelevance in the other. At
intermediate stock levels, an open access tax enables to fishery to recover more quickly but
possibly has little or no long-run effect.

16.3.2   The Phase Portrait*

Equations 13.6 and 16.2 give the differential equations for the stock and for the rent under
the sole owner. We can use these two equations, together with the definition of rent,
$R = p(y) - \frac{C}{x}$, to obtain a third differential equation, for the harvest, dy/dt. For ease
of reference, we give this differential equation a name, denoting it as $dy/dt = H(x, y)$.
(Appendix G.2 explains how we find this function H.) The solution to these three differential equations (for x, R, and y) gives the optimal paths of the stock, rent, and harvest. Apart
from the simplest problems, we cannot solve these equations analytically. Our first goal is
to learn as much as possible about the solution without actually solving the equations: we
use the phase portrait to obtain qualitative information about the solution.

The phase portrait contains two "isoclines." An isocline is a curve along which the time
derivative of a variable is constant, here equal to 0. Consider the logistic growth func-
tion, $dx/dt = \gamma x \left(1 - \frac{x}{K}\right) - y$. Setting this derivative equal to 0 gives $y = \gamma x \left(1 - \frac{x}{K}\right)$;
the graph of this function is the x isocline (the curve where $dx/dt = 0$). The x isocline
is simply the growth function. Figure 16.4 labels the graph of the growth function "stock
constant" to indicate that this graph shows the combinations of stock and harvest that cause
the stock to remain constant.

We can also obtain the y isocline using $dy/dt = H(x, y)$ and setting $H(x, y) = 0$. The
dashed graph in figure 16.4, labeled "harvest constant," shows the combinations of harvest

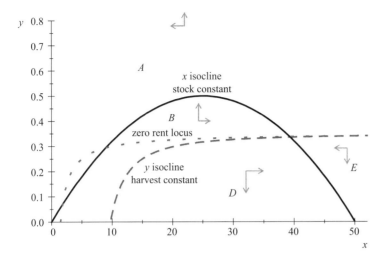

Figure 16.4
The solid curve is the growth function, which is also the x isocline, where $\frac{dx}{dt}=0$. The dashed curve is the y isocline, where $\frac{dy}{dt}=0$. The two isoclines divide the plane into four regions, A, B, D, and E, known as isosectors. The arrows show the direction of motion in each isosector. The dotted curve is the locus of combinations of stock and harvest where rent is 0.

and stock at which the harvest is constant: the y isocline. The steady state occurs at the intersection of the x and the y isoclines, where $dx/dt=0=dy/dt$. For our example, the steady state is $x=39.35$, $y=0.335$.

Outside the steady state, the stock and the harvest are changing over time. Imagine that there is a third axis, labeled time, t, perpendicular to the page. A point on the page represents a particular value of x and y at $t=0$. A point above the page represents a particular value of x and y at a time $t>0$. Suppose that we start at $t=0$, with some initial condition, x_0, and we pick some initial harvest, y_0. Starting from this point, there is a path (a curve in three-dimensional space) call it (x_t, y_t, t), along which the differential equations $dx/dt=F(x)-y$ and $dy/dt=H(x,y)$ are satisfied. Now imagine shining a light perpendicular to the page; if curves could cast shadows, the curve (x_t, y_t, t) would project a shadow onto the page. We refer to this shadow (projection) as a trajectory. The phase portrait provides information about such a trajectory; we use that information to infer facts about the behavior of the stock and the harvest over time. To this end, we note that the two isoclines divide the x, y plane into different regions, called "isosectors." In this case, there are four isosectors, whose boundaries consist of the two isoclines. Figure 16.4 identifies these four isosectors as A, B, D, and E.

Consider isosectors B and D, the region below the x isocline. For any point in either of those two isosectors, $y < F(x)$. Consequently, at such a point, $dx/dt = F(x) - y > 0$

Table 16.3
Direction of change of x and y and overall direction of motion of trajectory in the four isosectors

Isosector	A	B	D	E
Motion of x	Decreasing (west)	Increasing (east)	Increasing (east)	Decreasing (west)
Motion of y	Increasing (north)	Increasing (north)	Decreasing (south)	Decreasing (south)
Overall motion of trajectory	Northwest	Northeast	Southeast	Southwest

(i.e., x is increasing over time). For short, we say that the trajectory is "moving east" (x is getting larger). Similarly, above the x isocline, in isosectors A and E, $y > F(x)$, so $dx/dt = F(x) - y < 0$. In these two isosectors, x is getting smaller, so we say that the trajectory is "moving west." The second row of table 16.3 summarizes this information.

We can identify the direction of movement in the north-south direction by using information about the differential equation for y, $dy/dt = H(x, y)$ (details in appendix G.2). Below the y isocline (in isosectors D and E), $dy/dt = H(x, y) < 0$ (i.e., y is decreasing, so the trajectory is moving south). Above the y isocline (in isosectors A and B), $dy/dt = H(x, y) > 0$ (i.e., y is increasing, so the trajectory is moving north). The third row of table 16.3 summarizes this information. The fourth row identifies the overall direction of motion of a trajectory in each isosector. The arrows in each isosector in figure 16.4 convey this information graphically. For example, any trajectory in isosector A moves northwest, in the direction between the perpendicular arrows in that isosector: y increases and x falls.

This qualitative information tells us that a trajectory that obeys the Euler equation and approaches the steady state x_∞ from a smaller value of x (to the west of x_∞) lies in isosector B. Similarly, a trajectory that approaches the steady state from a larger value of x (to the east of x_∞) lies in isosector E. To explain and confirm these statements, we consider the case where the optimal trajectory approaches the steady state from below (from the west).

A trajectory approaching the steady state from below cannot lie in isosector E, because that isosector contains no stock levels less than the steady state. The path cannot lie in isosector A, because trajectories there involve westward movements (i.e., reductions in the stock). It cannot lie in D, because from any point in D, y must increase en route to the steady state; but trajectories in D move south (i.e., y falls there). Consequently, trajectories that approach the steady state from stocks below the steady state do so in isosector B.

Recall that the dotted curve in figure 16.4 is the set of points where rent is 0. Rent is positive below the dotted curve and negative above it. If the stock begins below the steady state, it approaches the steady state in isosector B. The sole owner never harvests where rent is negative, so the trajectory must be on or below the dotted curve. Therefore, we conclude that if the initial stock is below the steady state, the trajectory must be sandwiched between the dashed and the dotted curves. We obtain this information *without actually solving the optimization problem*, using only the necessary conditions for optimality and graphical analysis. This procedure illustrates the power of the phase portrait.

The Full Solution

Figure 16.3 contains the graph of the sole owner's optimal harvest rule (the dotted curve in that figure). To construct that graph, we need the solution to the pair of differential equations, $dx/dt = F(x) - y$ and $dy/dt = H(x, y)$, that includes the point (x_∞, y_∞), the steady state. The steady state is a "boundary condition" for this mathematical problem. As noted above, except for a very few functional forms (not including our parametric example), there is no analytic solution to this problem. However, there are numerical routines that are straightforward to implement. The harvest rule shown in figure 16.3 is obtained using Mupad, imbedded in ScientificWorkplace.

16.4   Summary

Two examples, one with constant harvest costs, and the other with stock-dependent-harvest costs, show how to analyze the dynamics under the sole owner. The chapter explains how to determine the sole owner steady state(s), and to determine which steady state the sole owner fishery approaches, as a function of the initial condition. With constant harvest costs, this determination requires careful economic reasoning but no new mathematical tools. To study the model with stock-dependent harvest costs, we discussed the phase portrait, which has many uses in dynamic problems.

By comparing the harvest rules under open access and the sole owner's harvest rule, we can estimate the optimal tax for the open access fishery. In particular, we learned that regulating this fishery is important if the stock is low; for sufficiently high stocks, regulation of the open access fishery is unimportant. In dynamic resource problems, the optimal tax is stock dependent. A second-best alternative is to close down the open access fishery at low stock and leave the fishery untaxed at high stocks. A more nuanced policy imposes low or 0 taxes at high stocks, and high taxes at low stocks.

Examples of this sort are useful for developing intuition. The pedagogic danger of these examples is that they may make the problem of regulation appear too simple. It might appear that all we need is a few parameter estimates and a modest knowledge of mathematics to propose optimal policy measures. That conclusion is too optimistic. The models studied here offer insight but are too simple to be directly useful in policy environments. There, it may be important to consider multiple species or multiple cohorts of a single species, or different kinds of uncertainty. Nevertheless, simple models provide a good place to begin.

16.5   Terms and Concepts, Study Questions, Exercises, and Sources

Terms and Concepts
Continuous time Euler equation, isocline, isosector, phase portrait.

Study Questions
1. Using figure 16.1, for each of the three values of C, sketch the sole owner's harvest rule that is consistent with the claims in table 16.2. (You can assume that the owner's harvest rule is a monotonic function of the stock. The answer to part (c) of exercise 3 will verify that feature.)

2. (a) Using your sketch from question 1 and $C = 3$, pick two values of x to the left of point f. Explain how you would use this graph to obtain the optimal tax under the sole owner at these two values of x.

   (b) What qualitative statement can you make about the magnitude of the optimal taxes for the two values of x?

Exercises
1. By adapting the arguments used in section 16.2.2, confirm the claims in the first row of table 16.2 for x_0 between the point G and the horizontal coordinate to point d (figure 16.2).

2. By adapting the arguments used in section 16.2.2, confirm the claims in the last row of table 16.2.

3. Suppose that $F(x) = 0.04x \left(1 - \frac{x}{50}\right)$, inverse demand is $p(y) = 5 - 10y$, the discount rate is $r = 0.02$, and harvest costs are constant at $C = 0.4$. Suppose also that the initial condition, x_0, is below the horizontal coordinate of point e in figure 16.1.

   (a) What tax (a number) supports an open access steady state at point d?

   (b) If the policymaker uses this constant tax, does it drive the stock to point d for all initial conditions below e? Explain.

   (c) For initial conditions below e, does the optimal tax rise or fall with higher x?

4. For the model in equation 16.4, use figure 16.3 to estimate the optimal tax for the open access fishery at $x = 5$. Explain your reasoning.

Sources
Kamien and Schwartz (1991) provide many economic applications demonstrating the use of phase portrait analysis.

   Clark (1996) uses phase portrait analysis for the fishery model.

   Readers interested in extending the deterministic methods to a stochastic setting should consult Mangel (1985).

17 Water Economics

Objective
• Use the tools developed in previous chapters to study water economics.

Information and Skills
• Be familiar with market failures associated with water.

• Use both static and dynamic methods to study water problems and to analyze policy remedies.

We used the examples of oil and fish to develop analytic tools for studying nonrenewable and renewable resources, respectively, and to illustrate market failures and appropriate policies. This chapter introduces water economics, emphasizing the generality of both the policy problems and the tools discussed in previous chapters. Nonrenewable resources, like oil, do not regenerate on a time scale relevant for human planning. Renewable resources, like fish, potentially regenerate quickly, over a period of years or decades. Water, forests, and many other resources are intermediate cases. Groundwater in a slowly recharging aquifer (a geological formation that stores water) and the stock of old-growth redwood trees are similar to nonrenewable resources. Water in a lake with inflows and new-growth forests are renewable resources.

Water is an essential, and in many parts of the world, poorly managed natural resource. During the next decade, many countries will likely experience water shortages, poor water quality, and floods, increasing political instability and regional tensions. Absent policy changes, growing water demand will outstrip supply, jeopardizing food and energy production and so threatening economic growth. Only about 2.5% of the earth's water is freshwater. Glaciers contain about 69% of the freshwater, and groundwater contains about 30%. The surface (rivers, lakes) and atmosphere contain about 0.4% of freshwater (Intelligence Community Assessment 2012).

"Consumptive" water use removes water from available supply; "nonconsumptive" use returns the water, making it available for subsequent uses. Most water use has both consumptive and nonconsumptive features. Water used to generate hydroelectric power is nonconsumptive to the extent that it is available for downstream uses. However, the dams built to generate this power reduce the availability of water for fish runs and other environmental or recreational purposes; they also reduce water quality due to the buildup of silt and increased salinity, and they increase evaporation. Downstream users and hydroelectric power generators have conflicting objectives if they want water to be released from the dam at different points in time; people may disagree about water management, even if they all eventually use the same water molecule. Much of the water used for agricultural irrigation is absorbed by plants and the atmosphere, a consumptive use, but some of it returns to rivers and aquifers, a nonconsumptive use. Even if the returned water is pristine, people have to use the same molecule at different times and therefore may disagree about water management. When agricultural runoff is polluted, the return flows create costs, not benefits. Agriculture accounts for about 68% of total (consumptive plus nonconsumptive) use, with household and industrial (19%) and power generation (10%) making up most of the remainder. Agriculture accounts for more than 90% of consumptive water use.

A larger, more prosperous population increases water demand, as more people eat a more water-intensive diet. Drought-resistant crops and more efficient irrigation reduce the amount of water needed to grow a given amount of food, but they potentially increase water usage. Infrastructure investments can reduce leaks. Technical remedies are important in solving water shortages, but without policy changes, they are unlikely to be adequate.

A Road Map

Section 17.1 provides an overview of water-pricing structures. It explains the importance of including the full social cost in a water price, and provides examples of political constraints that impede obvious solutions and create perverse incentives. Static market failures result in the inefficient use of a given flow of water. Dynamic market failure results in inefficient (usually too-rapid) use of water stocks. Efficiency requires a mechanism for allocating water over different uses at a point in time, and also over time. With strong property rights, markets provide that mechanism. When property rights are weak, markets can exacerbate inefficiencies.

Section 17.2 illustrates a static inefficiency when agents have water rights but are not permitted to trade among themselves or to sell their water to third parties. The problem here is similar to the situation discussed in section 12.5, where fishers have individual nontransferable quotas.

The "rebound effect," important in many environment and resource contexts, is usually invoked to explain why an improvement in technology might have an unexpected effect on resource use. Section 17.3 explains the idea and applies it to a political economy setting, showing that a market reform that increases efficiency can also increase competition for the resource.

Section 17.4 discusses dynamic market failures, beginning with an overview of an important U.S. aquifer. We then compare extraction from an aquifer under a sole owner (or social planner) and under common property. In a particular setting, weaker property rights have the same effect on extraction as does less concern for the future. Inefficiencies found in fisheries and many other resources are similar to those related to water. The lessons of property rights–based fishery management are relevant here.

Section 17.5 discusses the relation between trade and the environment. Trade liberalization increases efficiency in a first-best setting, but it can reduce efficiency when property rights are weak: another example of the Theory of the Second Best.

17.1 The Policy Context

Objectives and skills: Have an overview of water-pricing structures, and understand the role of resource rent for efficient pricing.

Current water laws and policies result from the accretion of decades or centuries of social interactions and in many cases are inefficient. This section discusses water pricing and then considers two types of inefficiency: (i) water is priced inefficiently, or not at all; (ii) policies not directly targeted to water use make water problems worse. Water provision requires large infrastructure costs for storage and transportation. It would be inefficient to duplicate this infrastructure, so it is efficient to have a single provider: water provision is a "natural monopoly." In many places, it is organized as a public utility; in some places, it is a publicly regulated private enterprise.

Types of Pricing Structures

Pricing (or "tariff") structures seek, to varying extent, to recover the cost of water provision and to achieve efficient allocation. Some tariffs have equity goals. A fixed connection charge and a fixed price per unit (a "volumetric charge") are the two simplest tariff structures. Each has a single policy parameter (the connection charge or the price per unit), so they can address a single target. A fixed connection charge can recover costs, but it provides no incentive for conservation and it requires everyone to pay the same amount. A price (= volumetric charge) that recovers infrastructure and delivery costs typically does not equal the full social marginal cost of provision, leading to inefficient consumption levels. A price equal to the full social marginal cost of provision achieves efficiency but may not cover infrastructure costs.

A "two-part tariff," consisting of a connection charge and fixed price per unit, contains two policy levers and can achieve two targets. Setting the price equal to full social marginal provision costs achieves efficiency; the connection charge can recover infrastructure costs. By varying the connection charge over households (e.g., according to average income in the area), the tariff can also address the goal of fairness. The French water sector requires the use of two-part tariffs, but there the volumetric charge is often above the marginal cost of provision, leading to the underuse of water (Porcher 2014).

Table 17.1
Types of tariffs across water utilities

Country	Fixed charge	Fixed price	Increasing tiers	Decreasing tiers
Australia	—	68%	27%	5%
Canada	56%	27%	4%	13%
Japan	—	42%	57%	1%
Norway	87%	—	13%	—
Spain	—	10%	90%	—
United Kingdom	90%	10%	—	—
United States	2%	33%	31%	34%

Source: Whittington, Boland, and Foster (2002).

Many parts of the world use tiered (or "block") pricing (table 17.1). This tariff structure changes the price of a marginal unit when usage crosses a threshold. The price might either increase or decrease with usage, resulting in increasing and decreasing tiered pricing. Increasing tiered pricing confronts high-use consumers with higher marginal, and also average, price.[1] By raising more money per unit of sales from these consumers, the utility can reduce the average price for low-use consumers: high-use consumers subsidize low-use consumers. If the former are richer, this scheme transfers money from the rich to the poor. In some countries however, many poor people share a single water connection. Their aggregate use may be high, even though their individual use is low; in this circumstance, under increasing tiered pricing, the poor may subsidize the rich. With decreasing tiered pricing, low-use consumers have higher average price than high-use consumers. This pricing structure makes sense if economies of scale make it cheaper to provide water to high-use consumers.[2]

Figure 17.1 illustrates increasing tiered pricing where a representative low-demand consumer has inverse demand $p = 15 - q$ and the representative high-demand consumer has inverse demand $p = 15 - 0.5q$. The aggregate demand, the horizontal sum of individual demands, is $p = 15 - \frac{1}{3}q$. The solid step function shows the low-tier price, 2, for quantities below 10.8, and the high-tier price, 6, for higher quantities. (Ignore, for now, the labels "marginal cost" and "marginal cost + rent.") The low-demand consumer purchases at the threshold, 10.8, with marginal utility of consumption $p = 15 - 10.8 = 4.2$; the high-demand consumer purchases at point B', with marginal utility equal to price, 6. These consumers have different marginal valuations of water, so the allocation is inefficient.

---

1 If the price is p^L for $q \leq x$ and p^H for $q > x$, a person consuming less than x has marginal = average price p^L. A person consuming $q > x$ has marginal price p^H and average price $\frac{p^L x + (q-x)p^H}{q} = p^H - \frac{(p^H - p^L)x}{q}$, which increases with q.

2 A literature known as "mechanism design" provides methods for designing incentives that make it possible to reach complex policy objectives under uncertainty. All tariff structures described here are mechanisms.

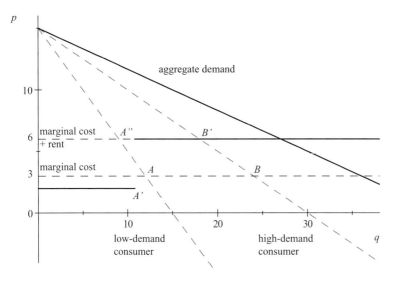

Figure 17.1
Dashed curves show inverse demand functions for low-demand and high-demand consumers. The solid sloping curve shows aggregate demand, the horizontal sum of individual demand. The step function (solid horizontal lines) shows the tiered pricing when the price equals 2 for $q \leq 10.8$, and 6 for $q > 10.8$.

Including Rent in the Water Price

The efficient use of water creates water rents, just as the efficient extraction of oil creates oil rents. These rents equal the opportunity cost of water use, arising from water's scarcity and from higher future pumping costs. When water is allocated using the price mechanism, efficient management requires the price to equal the full social marginal cost: the sum of the marginal cost of providing water and the rent. A price excluding rent is too low and leads to excessive water use. We consume water as a "bundle," consisting of the liquid and its location at a point in time. Apart from contamination arising during transportation, the physical object is the same in our kitchen tap or in a reservoir hundreds of miles away. If we pay only the cost of storing and transporting the water, without paying rent, then we pay only part of the real cost of consuming it.

Efficient water pricing requires that all consumers face the same price "at the margin" (i.e., for the last unit they consume); that price must include rent. If all consumers face that price, the utility's revenue exceeds its variable costs. A California law forbids municipalities from charging more for utilities (e.g., water) than the cost of provision.[3]

---

3 A 2015 California State Supreme Court ruling upheld an appellate court's decision that struck down a municipality's use of tiered pricing. The appellate court did not ban tiered pricing, but it required that its structure be tied to the cost of providing service (Kassler 2015). By 2015, over half of California's water districts used some form of tiered pricing, but in many communities, water was not even metered. In Riverside, California,

More generally, utilities face political pressure not to raise rates. Figure 17.1 shows the lines labeled "marginal cost" (at $p = 3$) and "marginal cost + rent" (at $p = 6$). The tiers and threshold are set so that the utility's revenue equals its variable cost (in this case, marginal cost times quantity). Under this tariff, high-demand consumers face the price of 6 and consume at the optimal level, but low-demand users consume too much water (10.8) instead of the efficient level (9).[4] Aggregate consumption exceeds the efficient level; the allocation across users is also inefficient. By reducing the threshold from 10.8 to the efficient level for low-demand consumers (9, where their marginal valuation equals 6) and also reducing the low price (from 2 to 1.5), the utility obtains revenue equal to variable cost and achieves both efficient aggregate use and efficient allocation.

With many types of consumers, a tiered pricing structure that achieves efficiency and also equates revenue to variable costs (exclusive of rent) typically requires many different tiers. The price for each tier has to be set to ensure that consumers purchase at the right threshold; otherwise, a consumer might decide to purchase at an inefficient level in order to obtain a low price. (This requirement is known as an "incentive compatibility constraint.") This kind of plan often involves an impractical level of complexity. It may also be ineffective because of buyers' limited attention and the cost of information. Firms and farms that pay careful attention to their costs are likely to respond to tiered pricing, but many households are unclear about the difference between their average and marginal cost of water. It is easier to understand and base our decisions on a single price, compared to a price schedule; simplicity has real value. The two-part tariff is simple, efficient, and it can balance revenue with costs while also achieving some equity goals. A price equal to the full social marginal cost of provision achieves efficiency; the average connection fee can be adjusted to balance revenue and variable + fixed costs; and the differential in the connection fee, across households, can achieve equity goals.

Policies That Encourage Waste

Many policies ostensibly unrelated to water have major implications for water use. U.S. sugar lobbies have propped up domestic sugar prices by maintaining restrictions on U.S. imports of lower-cost foreign sugar. This method of supporting U.S. producers is politically attractive, because, unlike direct subsidies (which have been widely used for export crops, e.g., corn) the trade restrictions have no direct budgetary costs; consumers, not taxpayers, pay for the trade-induced implicit subsidy to producers. The high domestic

---

tiered pricing reduced water consumption by 10–15% (Baerenklau, Schwabe, and Dinar 2015). Santa Fe, New Mexico, used tiered pricing with high marginal prices and had a per capita consumption of about 100 gallons per day; Fresno, California, with a low uniform water price, had a per capita consumption of more than 220 gallons per day (Schwartzmay 2015).

4 Under the tiered structure, low-demand consumers purchase at the threshold, point A' in figure 17.1. At price $p = 3$, they would consume at point A. Under the efficient price $p = 6$, they would consume at point A''. Under the tiered pricing structure, high-demand consumers purchase at the efficient level, point B'. At price $p = 3$, they would purchase at B.

prices encourage domestic production, which has led to wasteful use of water and associated pollution in the Florida Everglades. Section 9.4 provides an example where output and input subsidies reinforce each other, magnifying the welfare loss arising from underpriced natural resource inputs. Elsewhere, U.S. subsidies have promoted the production of water-intensive crops in drought-prone areas (e.g., rice production in California). U.S. ethanol policy (section 9.6), an indirect subsidy to corn producers, has encouraged irrigated corn production, adding pressure to the Ogallala aquifer (see section 17.4).

Similar problems arise in many parts of the developing world. The Zayanderud River, running through the Iranian city of Isfahan, went dry in the early 2010s; groundwater levels fell, and wells dried up. A drought that began in 1999 and worsened in 2008 precipitated the crisis, and mismanagement exacerbated it. To increase local support, the central government transferred control of the watershed from a unified authority to local leaders, who then allocated water without regard to the resource constraint. Crop subsidies that increased the demand for water and local leaders' support for water-intensive industries worsened the problem (Nair 2014).

In India, tube wells increased irrigation in the Ganges watershed. In the 1980s, the Indian state Uttar Pradesh subsidized well construction, and banks extended credit for pumps. Users' low electricity price encouraged pumping, and landowners were not charged for groundwater extraction. Overextraction caused water tables to fall, increasing pumping costs and endangering public hand pumps used primarily by the landless poor. India's Ground Water Authority banned private extraction and sale of groundwater in some areas, but illegal pumping continued. The aquifer that serves the capital, New Delhi, might dry up in a few years (Acciavatti 2015).

Examples of this nature can be found in many countries. Increases in water demand due to higher population and higher living standards put pressure on limited resources. In some cases, these supplies are further stressed by droughts and pollution. New infrastructure that reduces leaks in transporting water and more efficient irrigation and desalinization plants potentially help solve or at least postpone crises. Rationalizing water pricing and reforming policies that worsen water shortages can make the problem more tractable. Economists have spent decades explaining why current policies are irrational and suggesting improvements (Griffin 2012, 2016).

17.2 A Static Market Failure

Objectives and skills: Understand the source and the measurement of a static distortion, and understand some reasons for its continued existence.

In many parts of the world, including Eastern U.S. states and British Commonwealth countries, water rights are based on "riparian" (i.e., pertaining to riverbanks or wetlands) law; landowners have the right to use water on their land, provided that their use does

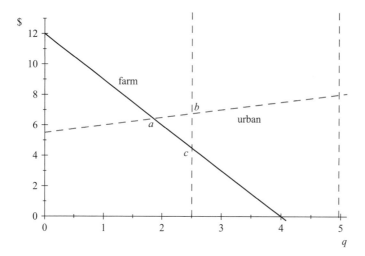

Figure 17.2
Water inverse demand functions for "urban" (sloping dashed line), $p = 8 - 0.5(y - q)$, and "farm" (solid line), $p = 12 - 3q$, when the aggregate supply is $y = 5$. Farm consumption is q, and urban consumption is $y - q$. The efficient allocation occurs at point a, where both groups have the same marginal valuation. If the two groups have equal shares of total supply, $q = \frac{y}{2}$, then they have different marginal valuations, at points b and c.

not conflict with other riparian users. In the Western U.S. states, water rights arise from "prior appropriation," having been the first to make "beneficial use" (e.g., irrigation) of unclaimed water. This basis for water rights sometimes led to fraudulent water claims and inefficient use, partly to forestall others from making their claims. In the first half of the twentieth century, Western U.S. states rushed to build dams and irrigation projects, acquiring property rights. The resulting property rights are incomplete if, for example, farmers with water rights are unable to sell their water allocation to users outside their area. We discuss the welfare cost of this restriction, and some of the reasons (apart from inertia) for its continued existence. The restriction is a "static" market failure, creating an inefficient allocation across users of a given quantity of water.

Figure 17.2 shows the inverse aggregate demand functions for urban and farm groups when the aggregate supply is $y = 5$. Figure 17.2 looks like figure 2.1; the urban inverse demand is read "right to left." Moving to the right along the horizontal axis corresponds to increased farm consumption, and an equal decrease in urban consumption, because the sum of quantities is fixed at 5. For a household, the inverse demand function equals the marginal willingness to pay for an additional unit. For a farm, the inverse demand is the value of marginal productivity of water: the additional value arising from the use of an additional unit of water. An efficient outcome occurs where each group has the same marginal willingness to pay, at point a; there, farmers consume $q = 1.9$ units, and households consume 3.1 units.

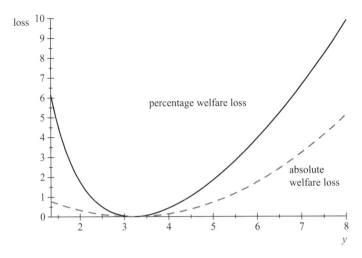

Figure 17.3
The solid curve shows the welfare loss (as a percentage of welfare), under the constraint $q = \frac{1}{2}y$, as a function of aggregate supply, y. The dashed curve shows the absolute welfare loss.

Measuring the Cost of the Restriction

If both groups have property rights to half of the total allocation and cannot trade, they each consume 2.5 units and have the willingness to pay shown by points b and c in figure 17.2. The trade prohibition causes a welfare loss equal to the area of the triangle abc. Households would be willing to pay $p = 6.75$ for an extra unit of water, and farmers would be willing to sell a unit for $p = 4.5$. At the constrained outcome there are potential, but unrealized, gains from trade.

Figure 17.3 graphs, as a function of y, the welfare loss (the area of the triangle abc) arising from the constraint that each group uses half the available quantity, $\frac{y}{2}$. At a particular value of y (equal to 3.2 for this example), it is optimal for each group to consume the same amount. At that point, the welfare cost of the constraint is 0. For levels of y close to 3.2, the welfare loss due to the constraint is small. However, it begins to rise quickly as y moves away from 3.2: the welfare cost is convex in the aggregate supply of water.[5] Incomplete property rights, and the resulting prohibition against water trades, creates a "missing market"; people are prevented from making mutually beneficial transactions. In this setting, allowing trade would achieve an efficient outcome.

---

5 The graph shows welfare cost for $1.34 \leq y \leq 8$. Outside these levels, non-negativity constraints bind. For $y < 1.34$, the urban group consumes nothing under efficient allocation, and for $y > 8$ farmers' consumption remains at 4, where their value of marginal product is 0.

Reasons for the Prohibition on Trade

The analysis above ignores third parties, who may have a legitimate basis for objecting to transferring water out of their area. Some water used in irrigation returns to rivers and aquifers, where it subsequently benefits other users, the third parties. Irrigation creates a positive externality for them; removing water from the hydrologic system eliminates this positive externality and harms the third parties. If these people had formal property rights to the return flows from irrigation, they could block the trade or demand a portion of the surplus it generates. The prohibition against out-of-area or off-farm trades provides an imperfect substitute for the third parties' lack of explicit property rights. There are also externalities associated with the infrastructure to transport water. In some places, farmers jointly maintain the irrigation ditches that transport water for all of them. When Los Angeles bought water rights from some farmers along irrigation ditches in the Owens Valley in the early 1920s, those farmers no longer contributed to maintenance. The added costs fell on the farmers who had not sold their water rights, decreasing the value of their land and water rights and placing them in a weaker bargaining position vis-à-vis the city of Los Angeles (Reisner 1987).

Aggregate welfare equals the sum of all agent's welfare (or surplus), measured in a monetary unit. If the third parties' loss, arising from the water transfer, exceeds the direct welfare gain (the triangle abc in figure 17.2), the transfer lowers aggregate welfare. A change constitutes a "Pareto improvement" if and only if it benefits some agent without harming anyone. The transfer might increase aggregate welfare, but if the third parties are not compensated, it is not a Pareto improvement.

The third-party effects associated with the return flows are genuine externalities: consequences that are not reflected in market prices. The discussion of water transfers often involves other kinds of third-party effects. Agricultural-to-urban transfers potentially lower the demand for farm labor and locally provided farm services, such as machine sales and maintenance. The people harmed by these changes might oppose the water transfers. These kinds of effects, arising through the normal operation of the market (not as a consequence of market failure) are "pecuniary externalities." They are externalities, because they are unintended consequences, but they do not result from market failures; the modifier "pecuniary" (meaning related to money) distinguishes these from genuine externalities.

Most significant transactions create these kinds of pecuniary effects; foreign imports might reduce employment in a sector, but international trade is not a market failure. However, these pecuniary externalities are salient where they interact with market failures. Unemployment may be a consequence of poorly functioning labor markets; if opening a new market (e.g., liberalizing international trade or allowing farm-urban water transfers) leads to higher unemployment, the new market can reduce welfare. The Principle of Targeting reminds us that the efficient remedy corrects the labor market distortion responsible for unemployment. However, labor market distortions exist for complicated reasons; if they were easy to fix, they would not persist. Prohibitions against trade or water transfers are often defended as second-best remedies for the underlying intractable problems.[6]

These kinds of third-party arguments have to be examined critically, because they can be constructed to oppose almost any reform. Even if they do not provide an efficiency rationale for prohibiting water transfers, they help explain the resistance to those transfers. The examples given above involve harm to third parties, but transfers can also create third-party benefits. The actual third-party losses tend to be more visible than the potential third-party gains; there is already a constituency to oppose the former, but there may not be one to support the latter.

Many of these issues are present in fisheries and in other resource settings. In the fishery context, we noted the importance of creating individual transferable quotas (ITQs, not just IQs) in chapter 12. The transferability enables the market to reallocate quotas to the most efficient fishers. This reallocation creates a welfare gain, just as does the water reallocation in the example in figure 17.2. There are also third-party pecuniary externalities in the fishing context (e.g., employment and other community-related issues; section 12.5). Each natural resource gives rise to specific problems, but the different resources share many of the same features. The skills and intuition acquired in studying one type of resource often help in studying a different resource.

Other arguments, based on sentiment, are sometimes invoked to oppose water transfers. One such argument is that water is a gift of nature: people should be allowed to use but not to own it, and they should not profit from its sale. This view is inconsistent with the fact that people own land and mineral rights, which are equally gifts of nature. A related fairness argument recognizes that often the value of water arises partly from previous social policy, not just nature's largess. In many parts of the world, publicly funded water projects created dams to store water and aqueducts to transfer it, principally to farmers.[7] Current farmers bought or inherited land, and with it, the attached water rights. The increase in the value of water, resulting from allowing transfers, would provide a windfall to current owners and would also benefit buyers. Taxing the surplus created by water transfers can finance public projects or compensate third parties.

---

6 The political discourse seldom uses this terminology. Liberalized international trade is frequently challenged as being the cause of unemployment, instead of something that exacerbates a labor market failure. Many people would consider this to be a distinction without a difference; it is certainly too subtle for a television sound bite. The distinction might not change a person's opinion about trade liberalization, but it is still important to distinguish underlying causes from contributing factors. Labor market distortions are hard to fix under the best circumstances; they cannot be fixed unless they are recognized.

7 Projects in Western U.S. states were designed to be funded by the water users, but low- and no-interest loans resulted in substantial taxpayer subsidies to users (section 2.6).

17.3   The Rebound Effect

Objectives and skills: Understand technology and political economy applications of the rebound effect.

Increased efficiency, whether arising from a technological innovation or a market reform (e.g., water trade), increases the value of a given quantity of water. This increase makes it possible to obtain the same economic value from a smaller quantity of the resource. The technological innovation or market reform therefore potentially contributes to resource conservation; changes in behavior occurring in the market place or the political arena might not actually lead to conservation. If the number of miles driven were constant, then an increase in fuel efficiency lowers fuel consumption. However, by lowering the cost of driving a mile, the greater fuel efficiency increase the number of miles driven, a result known as "the rebound effect." If the rebound (e.g., the increase in miles driven) is sufficiently large, greater fuel efficiency can lead to increased fuel consumption. The rebound effect is usually discussed in the context of technological improvement, but it also arises in a political economy setting associated with market reform.

Rebound and Technology

In the 1800s, the economist William Stanley Jevons noted that increased efficiency in coal, made possible by the Watt steam engine, increased the use of coal in many industries, an observation known as the "Jevons paradox." The increased efficiency resulted in greater usable energy per unit of coal, thereby decreasing the price of a unit of energy (for a fixed price of coal). The demand for energy was sufficiently elastic that coal consumption increased. The Jevons paradox arises when the rebound effect is sufficiently large. If the rebound effect exists but is not large enough to create this paradox, the technological change reduces resource use, but by less than one might expect.

Suppose that for each unit of water the farmer uses, $\beta < 1$ units reach the plant; the rest is lost to leakage or evaporation. An increase in β represents an increase in efficiency (e.g., due to improved irrigation). Let p denote the price of water, and $\eta(p; \beta)$ denote the (absolute value) price elasticity of demand for water. A change in efficiency potentially alters the demand elasticity.[8] The elasticity of demand for water, w, with respect to β is

$$\frac{dw}{d\beta}\frac{\beta}{w} = -1 + \eta(p; \beta). \tag{17.1}$$

(See exercises 2 and 3) If the total amount of water reaching the plant were fixed, the elasticity of demand for water with respect to β would equal -1: a 10% increase in efficiency would lead to a 10% reduction in water demand. The elasticity $\eta(p; \beta)$ accounts for the

---

8 We write the price elasticity of demand for water as $\eta(p; \beta)$ instead of using the more familiar form $\eta(p)$ as a means of emphasizing that the elasticity depends not only on the price of water but also on the efficiency parameter, β.

increased demand due to the lower cost of each unit of water reaching the plant (because fewer units of water must be bought). For $0 < \eta < 1$, the rebound effect occurs, but is not great enough to offset the direct effect: the percentage reduction in water demand is less than the percentage increase in water efficiency. If $\eta > 1$, improved technology increases water demand: the Jevons paradox occurs.

The rebound effect has been discussed extensively in water economics and in other fields of resource economics. A recent review (Berbel et al. 2015) of 17 model-based (simulation) studies and nine empirical studies finds a number of cases where better technology potentially (for the simulation studies) or actually (for the empirical studies) leads to increased water use. A more efficient sprinkler system was associated with a 1–2.5% increase in groundwater use in Kansas (Pfeiffer and Lin 2014).

Rebound and Political Economy

The rebound effect can also arise with efficiencies obtained from market reforms. The basic logic is the same in both cases: a change that we might expect to shift in the demand function (lower demand for a given price), actually causes the demand function to shift out. The mechanism is less transparent in the case of market reforms, so we merely illustrate it using the example in figure 17.2. Suppose (for reasons exogenous to our model) that the urban and farm groups each obtain an equal share of water allocation. In one world, they are allowed to trade water; in the other world, trade is prohibited. A given quantity of water is more valuable in the world with trade. An additional (marginal) unit of allocation is valuable in both worlds. We can imagine these two groups lobbying jointly to increase their total water allocation. (In our story, they are unable to change the sharing rule.) To obtain an additional unit of allocation, it is rational for the two groups (acting jointly) to be willing to spend the marginal value, to them, of that additional unit. The groups' aggregate demand function for water equals their marginal value of water.

Denote by $V(y)$ the farm + urban joint value of allocation y in the presence of the trade prohibition. Their demand function, the marginal value of their allocation, is $D(y) = V'(y)$. Denote by $V^{\mathrm{opt}}(y)$ ("opt" for "optimal") their combined payoff when a water market permits trade between them. The loss in surplus arising from the constraint prohibiting water transfers (the area of the triangle abc in figure 17.2) is $\Delta(y) \equiv V^{\mathrm{opt}}(y) - V(y) \geq 0$. This loss is positive, except for the knife-edge value of y where the equal-sharing constraint is not binding (3.2 in the example in figure 17.2). The constraint unambiguously lowers the value of water. But how does the constraint affect the demand for water? The model provides a simple answer. The inverse demand (= marginal value) under water transfers equals

$$\overbrace{D^{\mathrm{opt}}(y)}^{\text{demand w/trade}} = \frac{dV^{\mathrm{opt}}(y)}{dy} = \frac{d(V(y) + \Delta(y))}{dy} = \underbrace{D(y)}_{\substack{\text{demand w/o trade}}} + \underbrace{\Delta'(y)}_{\substack{\text{marginal loss} \\ \text{due to no trade}}} . \tag{17.2}$$

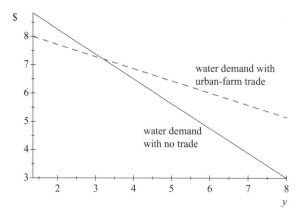

Figure 17.4

The solid line shows the aggregate (urban + farm) demand for water $\left(\frac{dV}{dy}\right)$ under the constraint $q = \frac{y}{2}$. The dashed line shows the aggregate demand for water $\left(\frac{d(V+\Delta)}{dy}\right)$ when users can trade their allocations. Water markets increase the demand for water if and only if $y > 3.2$.

The dashed curve in figure 17.3 graphs $\Delta(y)$; this curve shows that $\Delta'(y)$ is positive or negative, depending on the magnitude of y.

Figure 17.4 shows the farmer + urban aggregate demand functions with and without water markets, $D^{\text{opt}}(y)$ and $D(y)$, respectively. In this case, allowing water markets increases urban + farm water demand if and only if $y > 3.2$.[9] In general, a reform that moves us closer to efficiency increases the value of water but may or may not increase the marginal value = demand for water. The actual urban + farm allocation, y, emerges from a political economy equilibrium. Water users, including environmental representatives, compete in the political arena to allocate water across different uses. By increasing potential surplus, water markets in principle make it easier to strike a political bargain; by making the economic pie larger, it is possible to satisfy more people. However, water markets potentially increases a group's willingness to devote resources to obtaining a larger slice of the larger pie. For our example, if $y > 3.2$, allowing farm-urban transfers increases the joint demand from these two groups for additional water allocation, possibly reducing the equilibrium allocation reaching environmental uses.

---

9 If $V(y)$ and $V^{\text{opt}}(y)$ are both concave and increasing in y, then the two marginal utility (= inverse demand) functions have negative slopes. If, in addition, $V^{\text{opt}}(y) \geq V(y)$, with equality holding at the point of tangency, y_0, then the two demand functions intersect at y_0. Finally, if the loss function, $\Delta(y)$, is convex, then y_0 is the only point of intersection, and the demand function under the constraint lies above (respectively, below) the demand function without the constraint, for $y < y_0$ (respectively, $y > y_0$), as shown in figure 17.4.

17.4   A Dynamic Market Failure

Objectives and skills: Understand the dynamic inefficiencies (stock externalities) in a common property aquifer, and examine possible policy remedies.

The static question is: "How should we use a given amount of water (a flow) in a period?" The dynamic question is "How should we manage a given stock of water (i.e., choose the flow trajectory)?" Static efficiency requires that competing users have the same marginal valuation for water in a period; dynamic efficiency requires that water be allocated over time to satisfy an intertemporal optimality condition (the Euler equation). If all of our water came from free-flowing rivers or from annual rainfall, then the policy problem is static: nature determines the availability of water in each year, and policy, property rights, and trading rules determine the allocation across uses. Dynamics are important, because much of our water supply is stored in reservoirs, lakes, and aquifers. The Ogallala Aquifer illustrates dynamic water problems; we then build on resource models from previous chapters.

17.4.1   The Ogallala Aquifer

The Ogallala Aquifer, located beneath eight U.S. states from Texas to South Dakota, exemplifies the problem of managing a common-property resource. This million-year-old aquifer, ranging over 174,000 square miles, provides water for almost a fifth of U.S. wheat, corn, cotton, and cattle production. Agriculture accounts for about 95% of water use from the aquifer, which contains enough water to cover all 50 states with 1.5 feet of water. If it went dry, it would take natural processes 6,000 years to refill. Extraction during the first decade of the twenty-first century was a third of total extraction during the previous century. The stock of water in the aquifer declined 10% from the early twentieth to the early twenty-first century. Water levels in 25% of the land above the aquifer fell by more than 10 feet. There may be enough water in northern regions to last hundreds of years, while in the southern High Plains, a third of farmland may lose irrigation over the next several decades (McGuire 2007; Braxton 2009; Steward et al. 2013).

Withdrawals from the Ogallala accelerated in the 1940s and 1950s, spurred by the center-pivot irrigator which increased irrigation efficiency. Technological advances, including more efficient irrigation or drought resistant crop varieties, might reduce water demand; recall the rebound effect. Switching to less water-intensive crops (e.g., sunflowers instead of corn), changing cultivation practices (e.g., adopting no-till methods), or retiring land from cultivation potentially reduce water use. Those changes require short-run sacrifices, which are hard to enforce when decisions are made by thousands of farmers in a common-property setting.

The Ogallala is nominally a regulated resource, with rules varying across states. Nebraska passed laws in the 1970s limiting water allocations and using rotating water permits, and the state has maintained groundwater supplies. Elsewhere, regulation has not prevented rapid declines in the aquifer. Regulators have known for decades that the Ogallala is a finite resource; in the mid-1980s, heads of water conservation boards in Colorado and New Mexico stated that their goal was to make this resource last for 25–50 years (Reisner 1987). With this objective, it is not surprising that the aquifer is being depleted rapidly. Texas regulation uses minimum distance restrictions between wells and from wells to property lines. The Texas High Plains groundwater conservation district attempted to limit the amount of water pumped, hoping to conserve half of the stock available in 2010 until 2060. A Texas Supreme Court 2012 opinion delayed this ruling, questioning its legality on the basis that landowners have the same property rights to the water beneath their land as to the oil and gas (Galbraith 2012).

Kansas law enables farmers to create groups that, with a two-thirds vote, can restrict water withdrawals for all farmers in the area. This procedure is similar to compulsory unitization in the oil and gas industry, where a majority of producers can require that all companies pumping from a reservoir manage the reservoir jointly (section 9.6). These laws reduce transactions costs, making it possible to implement a management plan without unanimity, and so easing the common action problem. Two years after Kansas legalized these associations, only one, consisting of a group of 110 farmers, was formed (Dillon 2014). A successful farmer group must include a large enough area to ensure that most of the water saved by the group stays below land owned by members. Otherwise, the group's conservation largely benefits nonmembers.

17.4.2   Stock Externalities for Groundwater

Stock externalities occur with groundwater, just as with the open access/common-property fishery; in both cases, the externalities may have effects outside the sector that is the focus of analysis. In the fishing context, the stock affects growth and thereby affects the number of fish that can be caught in the future; the stock also likely affects the cost of catching fish. If the stock provides environmental services (e.g., as food for a different fishery), there are stock effects external to the fishery, not just to the individual fisher. With groundwater, a lower water table, resulting from a smaller stock in the aquifer, requires deeper wells and higher pumping costs. Drawing down the stock can cause land subsidence and reduce springflow, affecting streams and wildlife habitat, which creates stock externalities outside the farming sector.

Only landholders (or those with water rights) can pump water; this barrier to entry results in common property instead of open access. An owner's incentives to conserve groundwater, and thus generate rent, depends on the aquifer's lateral permeability ("transmissivity"), which determines how rapidly water moves in response to pressure differentials. If landowner A makes rapid water extractions, reducing the stock beneath her property, and the neighboring landowner B extracts slowly, the pressure differential eventually causes some of the water beneath B's land to flow beneath A's land. With no lateral movement across property boundaries, there is no common-property problem. If there is a market for the extracted water, extraction and use is then efficient. The common-property problem arises because water in the aquifer flows underground across property lines in response to pressure differentials. If this flow happens quickly, the aquifer is like a large tub.

Absent stock externalities, it is possible to achieve efficiency by separating property rights to the stock and the inflow, even if the aquifer resembles a large tub (Smith 1977). This system requires an estimate of the initial stock and an assignment of shares to it. People can sell their allocation of the stock and extract it at any rate they wish. The system of property rights must also allocate the inflow, perhaps by using a combination of shares and seniority. For example, suppose that the inflow of water to the hydrologic system in year t is α_t, and there are three water users, "the environment" (environmental services), farmer 1, and farmer 2. If the environment has senior rights to a flow f, with the two farmers having shares s and $1 - s$ to any residual, then farmer 1 receives the flow $s \times \max\{0, \alpha_t - f\}$. If the inflow α_t is variable, it might be efficient to save some of it in high-flow years. If owners can "bank" all or part of their flow allocation by sending it to the aquifer instead of using it, they increase their stock account. The assumption that there are no stock externalities means that this system is efficient; owners internalize all of the benefit of conservation and use water efficiently. This scheme has not been used, perhaps because stock externalities are important and because the scheme is perceived as complicated.

Some water districts use "correlative shares," the water analog of ITQs in fisheries. A rule or a regulator determines the annual allowable aggregate withdrawal of water, and the owner of a correlative share is entitled to the fraction corresponding to her share. Much of the discussion of IQs and ITQs (section 12.5) is relevant here. In the fishery context, all fishers send their catch to approximately the same market; there, trade in shares (ITQs instead of IQs) is important to minimize the industry cost of catching a particular harvest. In the water context, trade might be important for reducing aggregate extraction costs, but it is especially important for achieving an efficient allocation across users (section 17.2). We noted that if fishers are identical and have equal quota shares, then each fisher's incentive to allocate catch over time is the same as that of a sole owner. In that case, if there is a regulatory structure that solves the coordination problem (e.g., voting on aggregate harvest), the industry with ITQs can achieve the efficient harvest trajectory; here, property rights to a flow are a good substitute for property rights to a stock. This unanimity of interests vanishes if fishers have different harvest cost functions or unequal shares. These comments also apply to water. ITQs and tradable correlative shares both increase efficiency for a given level of harvest/withdrawal, and both are likely to help align the individual fisher's/farmer's incentives with the group objectives, but they do so imperfectly. Neither helps correct stock externalities that occur outside the fishing/farm sectors, such as reduced springflow arising from a lower water table.

17.4.3   A Dynamic Model of Water Economics

The stock of water in the aquifer at the beginning or period t is x_t, and y_t is the aggregate withdrawal in period t. The recharge is $F(x_t)$, and the change in the stock is

$$x_{t+1} - x_t = F(x_t) - y_t. \tag{17.3}$$

Abstracting from static efficiencies, we assume that all users have the same value of water; the aggregate value of a given flow y is $V(y)$. The recharge might (but need not) depend on the stock. The cost of extracting and transporting y units of water when the stock is x equals $(c_0 - cx)y$. For $c > 0$, a larger stock reduces these costs. Increased pumping reduces the stock of water, making less available in the future and increasing future pumping costs. Scarcity and extraction costs were important in our discussion of rent for both the nonrenewable resource (chapter 5) and the renewable resource (chapter 15). Agents' incentives to extract water depend on the relation between the marginal utility and marginal cost of water extraction, $V'(y)$ and $(c_0 - cx)$, respectively.

The Sole Owner or Social Planner

The discount factor is ρ, and the present discounted value of the stream of water use, $\{y_0, y_1, y_2, \dots, y_T\}$ is

$$\sum_{t=0}^{T} \rho^t [V(y_t) - (c_0 - cx_t)y_t], \tag{17.4}$$

where T is the last period during which extraction is positive. Depending on the parameters of the model, extraction might continue indefinitely $(T = \infty)$ or end in finite time. The Euler equation under a social planner (first-best regulation) is

$$\underbrace{V'(y_t) - (c_0 - cx_t)}_{\text{gain from extracting an extra unit at } t}$$

$$= \rho \left[\underbrace{(V'(y_{t+t}) - (c_0 - cx_{t+t}))}_{\text{loss per unit reduction in extraction}} \times \underbrace{\left(1 + \frac{dF(x_{t+1})}{dx_{t+1}}\right)}_{\text{reduction in extraction}} + \underbrace{cy_{t+1}}_{\text{higher costs}} \right]. \tag{17.5}$$

We can perturb a candidate trajectory by extracting one more unit of water in the current period, obtaining the gain on the left side of equation 17.5; the underlined term on the right equals the $t + 1$ period loss per unit reduction in extraction, and the underbracketed term equals the reduction needed to offset the change at period t; the final term equals the higher extraction costs due to lower stock. If the candidate is optimal, the marginal gain from this perturbation equals the present value of its marginal loss.

In previous chapters, where the single-period payoff equals revenue minus costs, we defined rent as marginal revenue (= price for the competitive firm) minus marginal cost. Here, the single-period payoff equals $V(y_t) - (c_0 - cx_t)y_t$, the current benefit minus the cost of extracting y; we accordingly define water rent as marginal benefit minus marginal cost:

$$R_t = V'(y_t) - (c_0 - cx_t).\tag{17.6}$$

Using equation 17.6, we can simplify equation 17.5 to obtain

$$R_t = \rho\left(R_{t+1}\left(1 + \frac{dF(x_{t+1})}{dx_{t+1}}\right) + cy_{t+1}\right).\tag{17.7}$$

Regulation potentially leads to a high steady state stock if the sole owner or social planner cares enough about the future (has a high discount factor). A social planner with a low discount factor might drive the stock to a low level or exhaust the aquifer. Figure 17.5 uses the example

$$V = 10y - \frac{1}{2}y^2, \quad (c_0 - cx)y = (10 - 0.1x)y, \quad F(x) = 1 + 0.1x\left(1 - \frac{x}{100}\right).$$

Here, there is a stock-independent inflow, 1, available even when the stock falls to 0, and a stock-dependent component. The figure shows the steady state extraction, and 0.05 times the steady state stock (in order to make the two magnitudes comparable). The steady state

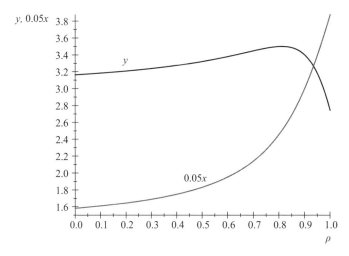

Figure 17.5
The steady state extraction, y, and the fraction 0.05 of the stock, x, as functions of ρ.

stock increases monotonically with the discount factor, but the steady state extraction is non-monotonic. A larger stock reduces extraction costs. For stocks below the level corresponding to MSY (here equal to $x = 50$, with MSY $1 + 0.1(50)\left(1 - \frac{50}{100}\right) = 3.5$), a larger stock increases the steady state withdrawal; for stocks above 50, an increase in the stock leads to lower withdrawals (section 15.3).

The Steady State Focus
The steady state is easy to compute, but it might be insensitive to the discount factor, even if the extraction path and welfare are very sensitive to it. In this case, emphasis on the steady state (ignoring the extraction path) can be misleading. With a nonrenewable resource, extraction eventually approaches 0 (chapter 5). In the nonrenewable resource model from section 7.4.2, the steady state stock is independent of the discount factor, but the extraction trajectory is sensitive to it. It might be optimal to eventually exhaust an aquifer with a low recharge rate, just as it might be optimal to drive a slowly growing fish stock to extinction.

If we consider only the steady state, we might mistakenly conclude that the discount rate in not important to the planning problem. For the same reason, we might mistakenly conclude that the common property and sole owner (= social planner) outcomes are similar, simply because their steady states are similar. In many contexts, the steady state is less interesting than the path that takes us to the steady state. (As Keynes remarked, "In the long run, we are all dead.") Exhaustion might occur in 50 years under one scenario and in 200 years under a different scenario; the steady states are the same, but the welfare trajectories might be very different.

Uncertainty   We consider only the deterministic setting because of its comparative simplicity, but one insight about the stochastic (nondeterministic) setting is readily available. Efficiency requires an allocation across users both at a point in time and across time. We can describe the optimal allocation as "arbitraged" over users and time periods. Arbitrage might arise from market forces, but we use the term here without associating it with a particular institution; the efficient allocation might be due to a social planner's decision. The optimal allocation in a stochastic setting must be arbitraged over states of nature. For example, if random inflows are high or low, $\alpha \in \{\alpha_H, \alpha_L\}$, we refer to the two realizations, α_H and α_L, as "states of nature." "Arbitrage over states of nature" means that we adjust the extraction decision depending on α; for example, we might use more water if inflows are high.

A Common Property Game
We examine how the outcome changes as we move from the sole owner/social planner with $n = 1$ to common property with $n \geq 1$ self-interested farmers. A two-period example illustrates the consequence of increasing n; we then return to the dynamic water model. An increase in n (resulting in a more serious common-property problem) and a smaller

discount factor (indicating that people care less about the future) both increase period-0 extraction.

A Two-Period Game For the two-period model, suppose that farmer i obtains the benefit (net of extraction cost) $B(y^i)$ from extracting y^i in period 0. In the next period, the remaining water, $x_1 = x_0 - \sum_{j=1}^{n} y^j$, is split equally among the n farmers, and each obtains the present-value benefit, $\rho W\left(\frac{x_1}{n}\right)$. ($B$ and W are arbitrary concave functions.) The social planner wants to maximize the aggregate welfare of all farmers. This planner's objective and first order conditions are

$$\max_{\{y^1, y^2, \ldots, y^n\}} \left(\sum_{j=1}^{n} B\left(y^j\right)\right) + \rho n W\left(\frac{x_1}{n}\right) \Rightarrow B'(y^i) = \rho W'\left(\frac{x_1}{n}\right), \quad i = 1, 2 \ldots n.$$

(17.8)

Farmer i chooses first period extraction, taking as given the decisions of all other farmers (the "Nash assumption"). The farmer's objective and the first order condition in a Nash equilibrium are

$$\max_{y^i} B(y^i) + \rho W\left(\frac{x_1}{n}\right) \Rightarrow B'(y^i) = \frac{\rho}{n} W'\left(\frac{x_1}{n}\right).$$

(17.9)

The first order conditions for the individual farmer and the planner differ, because the farmer weighs the next period marginal benefit, W', by $\frac{\rho}{n}$, whereas the planner weighs the next period marginal benefit by ρ. The farmer knows that if she consumes one more unit of water in the first period, her subsequent allocation will fall by $\frac{1}{n}$. She does not take into account the fact that her additional first-period consumption reduces the subsequent allocation of the remaining $n - 1$ farmers. The planner, in contrast, takes into account that by giving farmer i an additional unit of water in the first period, all farmers' subsequent allocation falls by $\frac{1}{n}$ The marginal loss to all of these farmers is $nW'\left(\frac{x_1}{n}\right)\frac{1}{n} = W'\left(\frac{x_1}{n}\right)$.

In moving from the sole owner/social planner to common property with n farmers, it is as if the discount factor falls from ρ to $\frac{\rho}{n}$. The discount factor does not literally change: it is constant at ρ. However, an agent attaches less value to conserving a resource stock when he knows that other people will obtain some of the benefit of his conservation. As a consequence, the first-period equilibrium level of extraction is higher in the Nash equilibrium to the common-property game compared to the social optimum.

The Dynamic Game We obtained intuition in the two-period setting by comparing the optimality conditions for a social planner with those of an individual farmer in a game. In the multiperiod setting, we compare the two Euler equations, identifying the two externalities that lead to excessive extraction in the dynamic common-property game: the cost externality and the strategic externality. Both lead to higher extraction and lower welfare under common property. In a Nash equilibrium, the actions of individual farmers are individually rational but collectively inefficient (see appendix H).

The cost externality arises because in making her current extraction decision, the individual farmer does not take into account that the lower future stock caused by her marginal unit of extraction at t, raises neighbors' future extraction costs. She considers only the effect of her current extraction on her own current and future costs.

The strategic externality is a bit more subtle. To decide how much to extract in the current period, the farmer has to take a view concerning (i.e., form expectations about) the future evolution of the stock. A rational farmer understands that other farmers' future aggregate extraction decisions depend on the future stock. A lower future stock increases neighbors' extraction costs and also makes the resource scarcer. Both these features lower the neighbors' incentive to extract. Therefore, an individual farmer understands that by extracting an extra unit today, the lower stock will (likely) reduce his neighbors' future extraction. The farmer has a strategic incentive to increase extraction today, partly as a means of decreasing his neighbors' future extraction. No such incentive exists under the sole owner (or social planner), who understands that an additional unit of extraction today takes that unit away from the owner/planner in the future.

17.5   Trade under Weak Property Rights

Objectives and skills: Understand why trade liberalization might reduce efficiency when property rights are weak.

The assumption that farmers using the aquifer are identical means they have no incentive to trade among themselves, but it leaves open the possibility that they might want to trade outside their aquifer. Trade, if permitted, occurs when price (or marginal valuation) differs across the two regions by more than transportation costs. A water market that allows northern states to ship water to the south increases the exporting regions' incentive to extract water, possibly reducing pumping in the south. In the absence of other market failures, this interstate market increases social surplus, because it transfers water from a region where the value of marginal product of water is low to one where it is high. The common-property problem, leading to excessive pumping, creates a complication. Suppose that regulators have solved the common-property problem in the north but not in the south, and that water imports from northern states decrease pumping in the south. The assumption that the north has solved the common-property problem means that the additional pumping there is efficient. The assumption about the south means that the water imports reduce the distortion associated with excessive pumping there. In this case, trade creates two types of welfare gain: it improves the allocation of a given flow of water, and it reduces excessive pumping. If there are market failures in both regions, the welfare effect of trade is ambiguous; recall the Theory of the Second Best.

The trade and natural resource nexus is even more important in the international context. Neoclassical trade theory explains why trade increases aggregate national income in trading partners, and thus increases the potential welfare of everyone.[10] This theory assumes a first-best setting (e.g., the absence of common-property distortions). Many resource-rich countries, particularly developing countries, have weak property rights for natural resources. Both their resource abundance and weak property rights contribute to low domestic resource prices (e.g., cheap water or forest products). When they open up to international trade, their low domestic prices make them an attractive source for foreign buyers, resulting in exports of natural resources or of commodities that use natural resources for production.

To the extent that these countries' low domestic resource prices derive from resource abundance, they have a "real" comparative advantage in the resource sector, and international trade tends to increase their welfare. However, to the extent that their low domestic price derives from weak property rights (leading to excessive extraction) they have an "apparent" but not a real comparative advantage. In that situation, trade exacerbates a market failure and possibly reduces their welfare (Chichilnisky 1994). The market does not care about, and cannot distinguish between, real and apparent comparative advantage (Copeland and Taylor 2009; Bulte and Barbier 2005).

Trade in mammals, for which there are weak or nonexistent property rights, has often reduced resource stocks. Examples include seals, beaver, the Arctic Bowhead whale, buffalo, elephants, and rhinos. The trade-resource nexus is also important for forests, fish stocks, and water supplies. In such cases, it is difficult to distinguish the impact of trade liberalization from the impact of concurrent changes, such as increased migration or population growth. Consequently, much of the empirical literature on natural resources and trade relies on case studies. Researchers tend to select "interesting" cases, those likely to exhibit an important trade-resource connection. Because the case studies are not randomly chosen, we have to be cautious in using them to reach general conclusions.

Despite this limitation of case studies, it is worth noting that they find mixed effects; sometimes trade aggravates resource degradation. In Argentina and Senegal, trade and investment liberalization contributed directly to the overharvesting of fish stocks. Here, an additional distortion, EU subsidies to EU fleets, compounded the problem of weak domestic property rights. Other examples show why there is not a simple relation between trade and resource use. An EU policy to stimulate livestock production in Ile de la Réunion led to a temporary surge in maize exports from Madagascar, accelerating deforestation; however, previous import restrictions in Madagascar, aimed at increasing domestic production of food, led to even greater deforestation. In regions of China and Vietnam, shrimp

---

10 The Stolper Samuelson Theorem shows that trade reduces welfare to owners of some factors of production in both trading partners. The increase in aggregate national income makes it possible to compensate these people, making them better off. If the compensation does not actually occur, trade makes them worse off.

farming for the export market contributed to the decline of mangroves. EU biofuel policy contributed to deforestation to develop palm oil plantations in Southeast Asia. Those environmental damages elicited EU measures to prohibit imports from these plantations. Palm oil producers complained to the WTO that these restrictions violated WTO trade rules. Trade has complicated effects on natural resources, sometimes benefiting and sometimes harming them. All these examples involve developing countries. Rich countries face similar but less pronounced problems. Canada restricted water exports to the United States out of concern that the trade would harm Canadian water stocks.

Institutions typically adjust more slowly than markets. Society may have developed common-property management practices well suited to specific and stable conditions. Economic development, migration, or trade liberalization might overwhelm these institutions. These changes alter incentives both to extract and to protect natural resources. Trade increases landowners' incentives to pump water, and it also increases their incentives to protect the aquifer, to maintain future sales. Either of those forces may dominate. The potential to obtain short-run profits from trade might overwhelm previously successful common-property management, leading to resource degradation. Alternatively, the opportunity to trade might make the resource so valuable that society develops better ways to protect it. Both these possibilities are responses to changing incentives, but they have an important difference. Resource degradation tends to obey the logic of the market, without requiring an organized response from society. Protection, in contrast, typically arises from political activity, not the self-governing market. Without intentional societal intervention, institutions may be unable to change quickly enough to protect resources.

17.6   Summary

Water, like many resources, is often inefficiently priced, often leading to overuse. Efficient pricing includes water rents. A two-price tariff makes it possible to price water efficiently, recover fixed costs, and also achieve equity goals. Many areas use tiered prices.

Incomplete property rights can create inefficient allocations across users at a point in time or across periods. People might have the right to a particular flow of a resource but might not be allowed to trade it, preventing the resource from being used where its marginal value is highest. Third parties, who lack explicit property rights, often benefit from return flows; these groups have an incentive to block water transfers to outside their area. In many places, land ownership gives people the right to pump from a common-property aquifer, or use some other stock of water, leading to excessively fast extraction. The common-property problem arises because property rights to land give people access to the water but not ownership of it. Scarcity and stock-dependent pumping costs, the two sources of rent under perfect property rights, are also sources of stock externalities when property rights are incomplete. A farmer's increased pumping raises neighbors' future pumping costs and also leaves less in the aquifer for them to use.

The Theory of Second Best is important in water economics, as in other fields of resource economics. Market failures that appear incidental to the problem at hand might make reform more urgent. Crop subsidies create inefficiencies, attracting factors of production (e.g., land, labor, water) to the subsidized crop and away from more efficient uses. A water price below the efficient level also attracts inputs to the subsidized sector, compounding the distortion created by the output subsidy.

The rebound effect explains why the magnitude and possibly even the direction of the effect of improved technology might be unexpected. There can also be "political rebound": an increase in efficiency might increase political competition for a scarce resource. In a first-best setting, trade liberalization encourages the movement of inputs or commodities to places where their marginal valuation is higher. However, if property rights for natural resources are weak, liberalized trade can exacerbate the market failure and reduce efficiency.

17.7 Terms and Concepts, Study Questions, Exercises, and Sources

Terms and Concepts
Aquifer, consumptive and nonconsumptive uses, tiered pricing, block rates, two-part tariff, mechanism design, water as a "bundle," riparian rights, prior appropriation, rebound effect, stochastic, real versus apparent comparative advantage.

Study Questions
1. Explain the difference between consumptive and nonconsumptive use, and give examples where uses have both consumptive and nonconsumptive features.

2. What are some of the reasons that a water price that reflects only the cost of transporting water leads to inefficient allocation of water?

3. Define a two-part tariff. Explain how it can lead to efficient consumption of water and also result in revenue covering fixed + variable costs. Explain how a variant of the two-part tariff can also achieve equity goals.

4. Consider the case where there are two types of consumers. Explain how tiered pricing can lead to efficient consumption of water and also result in income transfers from high-demand to low-demand consumers.

5. Discuss the meaning of static and dynamic market failures (as used in this chapter) in the water context.

6. Explain why agents' incentives to lobby for higher resource allocations likely depend on the marginal, not the total, value of their allocation. Discuss some possible political economy implications of this observation.

7. Use a two-period common-property game to show that the Nash equilibrium with $n > 1$ owners leads to higher extraction in the first period compared to the socially optimal level.

8. Discuss the effect of allowing international (or interregional) trade in a natural resource for which there are imperfect property rights. Explain the difference between real and apparent comparative advantage.

Exercises

1. Aggregate consumer benefit from consuming y^c units of water is $(10 - y^c)y^c$, and farm benefit of consuming y^f units of water is $(7 - 0.5y^f)y^f$.

(a) What is the total (consumer + farm) benefit (a function of y) of consuming y units of water, under the sharing rule $y^c = 0.5y$ and $y^f = 0.5y$?

(b) If these two groups could overcome the collective action problem (section 9.6) and lobby for increased water, how much would they be willing to pay (a function of y) to obtain an additional unit of water (under the fixed sharing rule)?

(c) Now suppose that consumers and farmers receive a joint allocation y and are allowed to trade. After trading, consumers use the fraction s and farmers use the fraction $1 - s$ of the allocation. What is the equilibrium value of s? (Assume that y is such that there is an interior solution, where $0 < s < 1$.)

(d) Denote the total benefit to the two groups, under trade, as $B(y)$. Find the expression for $B(y)$. How much would the two groups (combined) be willing to pay for an additional unit of water (if they solve the collective action problem)?

(e) There is a particular allocation of y at which the consumer + farm groups would be willing to pay the same amount for an additional unit of water. What is this value? What is the interpretation of this value?

2. Let one unit of water provide β units of "effective water," defined as the amount of water that actually reaches the plant. Letting w denote the quantity of water and w^e the quantity of effective water, $w^e = \beta w$. Let p equal the price of a unit of water; the price of a unit of effective water is $\tilde{p} = \frac{p}{\beta}$. (For example, if $\beta = 0.5$, the farmer must buy two units of water to obtain a unit of effective water.) The price elasticity of demand for water equals the (effective) price elasticity for effective water:

$$-\frac{dw}{dp}\frac{p}{w} = -\frac{dw^e}{d\tilde{p}}\frac{\tilde{p}}{w^e}. \tag{17.10}$$

Without performing any calculations, explain why this equality is true. [Hint: review section 2.3.]

3. This exercise takes you through the derivation of equation 17.1, the elasticity of demand for water with respect to the efficiency parameter β. This expression treats the price of water, p, as constant. However, a change in β alters the price of effective water, $\tilde{p} = \frac{p}{\beta}$. Denote the demand for effective water as $w^e(\beta) = D^e\left(\frac{p}{\beta}\right)$ and the demand for water as

$w(\beta)$. Proceed as follows. (i) Begin with $w^e(\beta) = \beta w(\beta) = D^e\left(\frac{p}{\beta}\right)$. The first equality uses the relation between effective water and water, and the second merely defines the demand function for effective water written as a function of the price of effective water. The demand for effective water, $w^e(\beta)$, and the demand for water, $w(\beta)$, are shown as functions of only β, because for this experiment we hold the price, p, fixed. (ii) Divide through by β to write the last relation as $w(\beta) = \frac{1}{\beta}D^e\left(\frac{p}{\beta}\right)$. (iii) Take the derivative with respect to β of both sides of the previous equation. In taking this derivative, use the product rule, the chain rule, and the quotient rule. (iv) Multiply by $\frac{\beta}{w}$ to convert to an elasticity. You will get a somewhat complicated looking expression, which simplifies to equation 17.1. In performing this simplification, you need to use two pieces of information: the starting relation, $\beta w(\beta) = D^e\left(\frac{p}{\beta}\right)$, and the answer to exercise 2.

4. This exercise shows how the tools that we developed to study nonrenewable resources, fisheries, and water can also be applied to climate economics. Define S_t as the difference between the stock of atmospheric carbon at t and the pre-industrial level. Suppose that S_t evolves according to

$$S_{t+1} - S_t = (\delta - 1)S_t + E - A_t; \tag{17.11}$$

δ is the "persistence factor," so $1 - \delta$ is the decay rate. (If $\delta = 0$, the emissions dissipate in a single period; in this case, we have a "flow pollutant"; if $\delta = 1$, the stock never dissipates. In general, $0 \le \delta \le 1$.) E equals "business as usual" anthropogenic emissions (the level that would occur without any policy intervention), assumed here to be constant, and A_t is the amount of abatement (the decision variable). Abatement reduces anthropogenic emissions from E to $E - A_t$. Society has decided to keep the stock at or below the ceiling $\bar{S}$. Assume that $\frac{E}{1-\delta} > \bar{S}$. The cost of abatement in period t is $C(A_t)$, an increasing convex function. Society's goal is to minimize the present discounted stream of abatement costs,

$$\sum_{t=0}^{\infty} \rho^t C(A_t),$$

subject to equation 17.11 and the constraint $S_t \le \bar{S}$.

(a) This model is designed to shed light on a specific question (see below), but it does not provide an accurate model of the climate or the policy problem. Very briefly, describe some of the limitations/inaccuracies of this model.

(b) What is the business as usual (zero abatement) steady state? What is the role of the assumption $\frac{E}{1-\delta} > \bar{S}$?

(c) This model is essentially the same as the water model studied in section 17.4.3, except that we call things by different names, and functions have different appearances.

The remaining components of the model consist of the single-period payoff, the equation of motion for the stock, and the decision variable. Identify these components for the water model and for the climate model.

(d) Use your answer to part (c) and equation 17.5 to write the Euler equation for the climate model. (Replace the water component with the climate component, being careful about the derivatives.) Interpret the Euler equation.

(e) If firms pay a tax v_t on emissions at time t, their costs equal

$$(E - A_t)v_t + C(A_t).$$

What tax must society use to support a specific level of abatement, A_t^*?

(f) Use your answer to parts (d) and (e) to determine the rate of change over time of the socially optimal tax. (The socially optimal tax trajectory supports the socially optimal level of abatement.) Does the optimal tax increase or decrease over time? Does a more persistent stock (larger δ) cause the optimal tax to rise more or less quickly? Provide an economic explanation for your answers.

Sources

The U.S. government's Intelligence Community Assessment (2012) provides the quoted statistics on water availability and use; it describes likely consequences of future water problems.

Griffin (2016) is an authoritative textbook on water economics.

Whittington, Boland, and Foster (2002) provide the information in table 17.1 and discusses water policy in South Asia.

Pottinger (2009) describes some of the problems created by large dams.

Schoengold and Zilberman (2007) provide a recent survey of water economics.

Howitt (1994) provides an empirical analysis of water market institutions.

Griffin and Hsu (1993) describe efficient water markets where there are both diversionary and instream water uses.

Griffin (2012) discusses the U.S. history of water marketing and pricing, and cost-benefit analysis for water projects.

Porcher (2014) discusses the use of two-part tariffs in French water pricing.

Baerenklau, Schwabe, and Dinar (2015) provide empirical results on the effect of water block pricing in Riverside, California.

Schwartzmay (2015) compares water use in Santa Fe, New Mexico, and Fresno, California.

Chong and Sunding (2006) review water markets.

Kassler (2015) reports the California Supreme Court ruling involving tiered water rates.

Nair (2014) describes the causes of the drought in Isfahan, Iran.

Acciavatti (2015) describes the water crisis in Uttar Pradesh, India.

Dinar and Zilberman (1991) is an early paper studying the rebound effect in water use.

Berbel et al. (2015) review the literature on the rebound effect associated with water savings measures.

Pfeiffer and Lin (2014) find empirical evidence of increased water in Kansas resulting from improved technology.

Krause et al. (2014) provide an overview of a collection of papers that study the dynamics of the aquifer-surface water interface.

The USDA Natural Resources Conservation Service website (http://www.nrcs.usda.gov/) describes the Ogallala Aquifer and the problems it faces.

Braxton (2009) provides an overview of the Ogallala Aquifer.

McGuire (2007) summarizes changes in water levels in the Ogallala Aquifer.

Steward et al. (2013) project water availability over the Ogallala Aquifer for the next 100 years.

Galbraith (2012) reports on the dispute over the Texas High Plains Underground Water Conservation District rule to restrict groundwater pumping.

Reisner (1987) gives an engaging history of the water in Western states of the United States and describes the water extraction plans promoted by commissioners of state water conservation boards in the early 1980s.

Dillon (2014) describes the attempt to form farmer-directed conservation groups in Kansas.

Chichilnisky (1994) is among the first to discuss the role of trade when resource-rich countries have weak property rights; this paper introduces the distinction between real and apparent comparative advantage.

Copeland and Taylor (2009) provide a model of endogenous property rights under trade; these authors (jointly with Brander) have made many contributions to this literature.

The summary in section 17.5 is adapted from Karp and Rezai (2015), who discuss endogenous property rights in an overlapping generations framework.

Bulte and Barbier (2005) review applications of the Theory of the Second Best in the trade and resources setting.

Exercise 4 is adapted from Nordhaus (1982). Lemoine and Rudik (2015) note that accounting for temperature inertia leads to qualitative and significant quantitative changes in policy recommendations.

18 Sustainability

Objective

• Understand definitions of, and attempts to measure, sustainability.

Information and Skills

• Have an overview of how economists estimate prices of resources where markets are imperfect or missing.

• Know the meaning of strong and weak sustainability and understand the meaning and the application of the Hartwick rule.

• Become familiar with the relation between income and wealth, green national accounts, and other sustainability measures.

Sustainable development "meets the needs of the present without compromising the ability of future generations to meet their own needs" (World Commission on Environment and Development 1987, 16). People born in the future are not responsible for, and cannot insure themselves against, our actions. The view that self-interested actions are unethical if they harm people who are blameless, and who cannot protect themselves against those actions, provides a moral foundation for the sustainability criterion.[1] The idea of sustainability is straightforward, but its measurement is not. A path is sustainable if the stocks of productive assets that we leave our successors are, in their totality, at least as great as the stocks that we inherited. These stocks include produced capital, human capital, and natural resources. Markets exist for some resources (e.g., oil, copper, fish, timber) but not for others (e.g., biodiversity and a resilient climate).

It is hard to determine whether we are on a sustainable path, because for many stocks, we can measure neither the price nor the change in level. Without both these measures, we cannot estimate the value of the change (the price times the change); therefore, we do not

---

1 "Brute luck" is the outcome of an involuntary and uninsurable lottery; "luck egalitarians" consider it morally wrong to disadvantage others as a consequence of brute luck. One's date of birth is a matter of brute luck, so luck egalitarians consider actions that harm people born in the future unethical (Roemer 2009).

know whether we are leaving our successors a larger or smaller totality of wealth than we inherited. The rising living standards during the past two centuries do not imply sustainability; society may be living off its capital. The stocks of produced capital, knowledge capital, and human capital have risen, but many stocks of natural capital have fallen (chapter 1).

The measurement of resource stocks and their prices present different types of difficulties. Some resource stocks are abstract; the "stock of biodiversity" is clearly important but is hard to measure. We can use proxies for biodiversity, such as the number of species in a given area, but we do not know how to price these stocks or their proxies. For other resources, measurement of the stock is conceptually straightforward but practically difficult. The biomass of fish has a precise meaning, but measuring biomass is challenging (section 15.2.3).

Under a sole owner and absent market failures, the resource rent equals the shadow price of the resource, the amount that an owner or a social planner (acting on the behalf of society) would pay for an additional unit of the stock (section 5.3). Private and social prices diverge under market failures. Rent in the open access fishery is 0, because entry occurs until the price of fish equals the cost of catching them. A resource owner would pay nothing for an extra unit of fish in the water. The zero resource rent does not mean that the extra fish create no additional value for society, because consumers obtain surplus in purchasing fish.

A Road Map

Section 18.1 explains how economists estimate the value of resources where market prices are missing or do not reflect societal values. Section 18.2 then explains the concepts of weak and strong sustainability. Here we discuss the Hartwick rule, which prescribes the amount of savings needed to maintain a sustainable path.

Income is a flow variable, and social wealth is a stock variable. These variables are easy to understand and to measure at the level of an individual, but not at a societal level. Of the two, social wealth is harder to measure, but it also provides a better indication of future consumption possibilities and is more useful for determining sustainability. Section 18.3 explains the relation between a nation's income and its wealth in the simplest setting, without natural resources, and then describes a modification when natural resources are important. The lack of data on natural resource stocks and prices makes it difficult to implement this modification. One strand of literature "greens" national accounts by including a small number of natural resource stocks omitted in standard accounts. A second strand produces indices that aggregate disparate categories.

18.1   Measuring Resource Value or Price

Objectives and skills: Be aware of several methods for valuing natural resources.

Oscar Wilde claimed that an economist is someone who knows the price of everything but the value of nothing. It is worse than that: for many resources, we do not know the value, the price, or the stock level. But at least we can be clear about the distinction between value and price (= marginal value). If markets work well, the market price reflects the marginal value to individuals and to society of a marginal change in consumption. However, we are interested in situations where markets do not work well—where the resource price, if it exists, does not reflect the societal value of the resource. Public policy requires striking a balance among competing demands on resources; assessing whether our actions are sustainable requires estimating changes in the value of natural capital. For these purposes, we need estimates of a resource's value or its marginal value (= shadow price).

When do we care about the value, and when is it sufficient to have an estimate of the marginal value? Suppose that the true value of a resource stock, x, is a function $W(x)$. If we knew that function, then we could calculate the change in value due to the reduction, Δ, in the resource stock, as $W(x) - W(x - \Delta x)$. If the change in stock is small, we can approximate the change in value using $W(x) - W(x - \Delta x) \approx -W'(x)\Delta x$: marginal value times the change in stock (appendix A.9). If $W(x)$ is a concave function (decreasing marginal value), this approximation understates the true change in value; the approximation error is small for small stock changes, but the approximation may be misleading for large changes. Suppose that we are considering a policy that diverts water from a river, reducing a fish stock by Δx. If this reduction is small, the approximation using marginal value, $-W'(x)\Delta x$, provides a reasonable estimate of the change in value. If the policy leads to a large reduction in the stock, the approximation is less useful; we need an estimate of the value at two stock levels to obtain an estimate of $W(x) - W(x - \Delta x)$. In the first case, it is enough to estimate marginal value; in the second, we need to estimate the value at two levels.

Travel cost models and contingent value surveys provide two ways of estimating values or marginal values. Travel cost models use data on the amount of time and money people spend in reaching places where they can (for example) fish or hike, to estimate the implicit price they pay for those activities. Those implicit prices, together with data on how often people go fishing or hiking, can be used to construct the value to them (and thus to society) of a marginal change in recreational opportunities. This approach confronts difficult estimation problems and at best measures one component of the value of natural capital; natural capital typically has value beyond the recreational services it provides. Contingent valuation surveys ask people how much they would be willing to spend to achieve a particular environmental outcome. These methods provide information about people's hypothetical willingness to substitute income for changes in natural resources. The survey questions can involve nonmarginal changes, so they provide estimates of the difference in value across two outcomes.

A third approach uses estimates of the flow benefit arising from resource services, the growth function for the stock (inclusive of human use), and the relation between resource use and the resource stock. Fenichel and Abbott (2014) apply this method to estimate the value and the shadow price of Gulf of Mexico reef fish stock, and also to estimate the effect (on value and the price of the stock) of reforms that alter harvest rules. In the fishery context, the flow benefit equals the consumer surplus minus harvest cost; growth equals the natural growth rate minus the harvest, and the harvest rule gives the relation between resource use and the stock. The method requires estimates of the flow benefit, the growth function, and the harvest rule:

$$\text{flow benefit: } B(x) = \overbrace{CS(y(x))}^{\text{consumer surplus}} - \overbrace{\frac{c}{x}y(x)}^{\text{harvest cost}},$$

$$\text{growth: } \frac{dx}{dt} = \overbrace{F(x)}^{\text{natural growth}} - \overbrace{y(x)}^{\text{harvest}}, \text{ and}$$

$$(18.1)$$

harvest rule: $y(x)$.

If the resource provides nonmarket environmental services (as in section 15.2), we need to include an additional term in the function $B(x)$ to capture the benefit of those services. Previously we considered ad hoc harvest rules (chapter 13), and harvest rules under open access (chapter 14) and under the sole owner (chapters 15 and 16). Here we want an estimate of the actual (not theoretical) relation between harvest and the stock. Regulation can affect the value of the stock by changing the harvest rule. We would like to know the value to society of the stock, x, under current regulation (the current harvest rule), and also be able to assess how a change in regulation affects the value of the stock via the change in the harvest rule.

Denote the value to society of the stock under the existing harvest rule as $W(x)$, and denote the marginal value (= shadow price) as $\lambda(x) \equiv W'(x)$. With a constant discount rate, r, and a current stock, x, the value of the resource is defined as the present discounted stream of the flow benefit,

$$W(x) = \int_0^\infty e^{-rt} B(x_t)dt,$$

and the shadow price satisfies (appendix I.1)

$$W'(x) = \lambda(x) = \frac{\overbrace{B'(x)}^{\text{marginal value of stock}} + \overbrace{\dfrac{d\lambda}{dt}}^{\text{capital gains}}}{\underbrace{r - \left(F'(x) - y'(x)\right)}_{\text{modified discount rate}}}.$$

$$(18.2)$$

Outside the steady state, all these variables are changing. However, equation 18.2 states that the shadow price equals the price of a hypothetical asset that returns a constant flow, received in perpetuity (the numerator on the right), whose present value is calculated using the "modified" discount rate (the denominator).[2] The numerator is the sum of the marginal flow benefit due to an additional unit of the stock and the capital gains. Given estimates of the functions in equation 18.1, it is possible to calculate both the value function, $W(x)$, and the shadow price, $\lambda(x)$, and to estimate the effect of a policy that changes the harvest rule.

18.2 Weak and Strong Sustainability

Objectives and skills: Know the meaning, strengths, and limitations of the concepts of strong and weak sustainability; understand the meaning of the Hartwick rule.

"Weak sustainability" requires that future utility levels do not fall below the current level; it accommodates substitution in production and consumption, using a utility function to aggregate all goods and services into utility. "Strong sustainability" requires that capital stocks, including stocks of natural capital, not fall below current levels. It is conceptually simple, but it neglects the possibility of substitution both in production and consumption, and in the case of nonrenewable resources, it sets an impossible standard. We cannot consume oil while also keeping the stock of oil from falling. Why should we want to do so? Higher stocks of produced capital, technology, and human capital, which require current oil consumption, might eventually eliminate our dependence on oil. In the case of renewable resources, strong sustainability might be feasible, but because of opportunities for substitution, not be a sensible objective. Farmland is a renewable resource; we can use it without depleting its stock. If our concern is with agricultural production, not farmland per se, then technological improvements that increase yield make it possible to increase production and also convert some farmland to other uses. That conversion violates the strong sustainability criterion but might be in society's interest.

Some sustainability measures use a hybrid of the weak and strong concepts. The "ecological footprint" (EF) measures the number of hectares of average productivity that it takes to sustain a population of a given size at current levels of consumption. In aggregating all natural capital into a hectare equivalent, the measure assumes perfect substitutability across the different types of natural capital, which builds on weak sustainability. However, the measure does not include produced capital or technology, assuming zero substitutability between natural and produced capital, which builds on strong sustainability.

Weak Sustainability

Weak sustainability takes into account possibilities of substitution in production and consumption, and it can also be applied where stocks necessarily fall while extraction is

2 Equations 16.3 and 18.2 are similar. They both show the shadow price of the resource equal to the present discounted value of a constant flow, discounted using a modified discount rate. The two equations differ because the former emerges in a context where an agent maximizes the value of the stock, whereas the latter uses a (typically) nonoptimal harvest rule.

positive. We address two questions about weak sustainability: (i) What investment policy leads to a sustainable path? (ii) When is a sustainable path feasible? Our model assumes constant population and a single "composite commodity" (i.e., a good that can be used either for consumption or investment). Production uses the stock of human-made capital, $K(t)$, and a resource flow (e.g., oil), $E(t)$. These inputs produce the composite commodity, $Y(t) = F(K(t), E(t))$ under the following assumptions:

1. $F(\cdot)$ is constant returns to scale in K and E: doubling both inputs doubles output.

2. Both inputs are necessary to production: output equals 0 if either input is 0.

3. Human-made capital, K, does not depreciate.

4. The constant average cost of extracting the resource is c.

By choice of units, we can set the price of the composite commodity equal to 1, so Y is both the physical amount of the commodity and the value of the commodity (= income). Therefore, $\frac{\partial F}{\partial K}$ represents both the marginal product of capital and the value of marginal product of capital. Let $p(t)$ be the price of a unit of energy, and $r(t)$ be the rental rate for capital. The competitive equilibrium conditions require that the price of an input equals its value of marginal product:

$$\frac{\partial F(K(t), E(t))}{\partial K} = r(t), \quad \text{and} \quad \frac{\partial F(K(t), E(t))}{\partial E} = p(t). \tag{18.3}$$

The assumption of constant extraction costs implies that the resource rent at time t equals $p(t) - c$. The Hotelling rule for competitive extraction of a nonrenewable resource with constant extraction costs states that rent rises at the rate of interest, $r(t)$:[3]

$$r(t) = \frac{\frac{d(p(t)-c)}{dt}}{p(t) - c}. \tag{18.4}$$

By definition, stock of capital (K) and the resource stock (x) evolve according to

$$\frac{dK}{dt} = I, \quad \text{and} \quad \frac{dx}{dt} = -E.$$

The first equation states that one unit of investment, $I(t)$, adds one unit to human-made capital; the second states that one unit of energy, E, reduces the resource stock by one unit.

The Hartwick Rule

A sustainable consumption path requires that utility remain constant; because utility depends only on consumption, a sustainable consumption path requires a constant level

---

3 Equation 18.4 is the continuous time analog of the discrete time version of the Hotelling rule in equation 5.9.

of consumption. The "Hartwick rule" requires that society invest (rather than consume) the resource rents (appendix I.2):

$$I(t) = (p(t) - c)E(t). \tag{18.5}$$

If there were a single factor of production (e.g., a single capital stock) then it would be obvious that maintaining a constant level of consumption (and thus utility) requires maintaining a constant capital stock. This model, however, has two factors of production: capital and the resource input. Moreover, it is not feasible to maintain a constant positive level of resource extraction, because doing so would eventually exhaust the resource stock. After exhaustion occurs, extraction drops to 0, at which time output and consumption also equal 0. However, by building up the stock of human-made capital, K, society may be able to decrease resource use over time, approaching (but never reaching) zero resource use. The resource stock falls, but it is not exhausted in finite time. Assuming that it is possible to achieve this delicate balancing act, the Hartwick rule explains how it is done: by investing resource rents in human-made capital (Solow 1974b; Hartwick 1977; Asheim et al. 2003; Mitra et al. 2013).

Existence of a Sustainable Path*

When is it possible to maintain a constant consumption trajectory? The answer can be illustrated geometrically for the special case where the production function is Cobb Douglas, $F(K, E) = K^{1-\alpha}E^{\alpha}$, with $0 < \alpha < 1$. The parameter α equals the revenue of the resource sector, pE, as a share of the value of output, $F(K, E) : \alpha = \frac{pE}{F}$. A smaller value of α means that the resource sector contributes a smaller fraction of value-added to the economy. A sustainable trajectory is feasible if and only if $\alpha < 0.5$ (i.e., if the resource is not "too important" in production; appendix I.3).

With Cobb Douglas production and the Hartwick rule, consumption equals the fraction $1 - \alpha$ of output; remaining income pays for investment and extraction. With a constant savings rate, constant consumption requires constant income, so we can recast the question that introduces this section as "When is it feasible to maintain constant income?" We rewrite the production function, $Y = K^{1-\alpha}E^{\alpha}$, to obtain an isoquant, expressing the level of E required to produce Y as a function of $K : E = (YK^{\alpha-1})^{\frac{1}{\alpha}}$. Figure 18.1 shows two isoquants, corresponding to $\alpha = 0.4$ and $\alpha = 0.6$, for $Y = 1$.[4] The $\alpha = 0.4$ isoquant lies above the $\alpha = 0.6$ isoquant for small levels of K, but crosses it and falls more steeply toward 0 as K increases. For large capital stocks, the technology corresponding to $\alpha = 0.4$ requires less of the resource input (compared to the technology with $\alpha = 0.6$).

We can check whether it is feasible to maintain a constant stream of income. With constant income, savings remain positive, so the capital stock continues to grow, compensating

---

4 Setting $Y = 1$ is not an important limitation. With constant returns to scale, the isoquant for any positive value of Y merely scales up or down the isoquant corresponding to $Y = 1$.

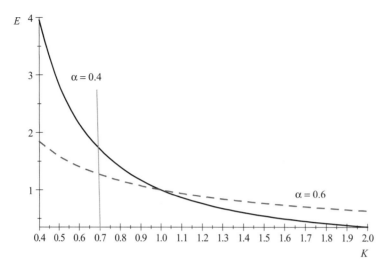

Figure 18.1
Isoquants for two values of α, with $Y = 1$. Given initial stock $K = 0.7$, the area under each isoquant from $k = 0.7$ to $k = \infty$, equals the size of the initial resource stock needed to maintain constant output Y when society follows the Hartwick rule. The area $= 2.4$ for $\alpha = 0.4$, and the area is infinite for $\alpha \geq 0.5$.

for the dwindling use of energy. Given an initial capital stock, constant output requires that the production point slide down the isoquant. Over time, with increasing capital stock, resource use falls, but figure 18.1 shows that it falls much faster the smaller is α.

Suppose that the initial capital stock is $K = 0.7$ (an arbitrary level, located at the vertical line in figure 18.1). The area under the isoquant, from $K = 0.7$ to $K = \infty$, equals the initial resource stock needed to maintain a constant output level $Y = 1$ when society follows the Hartwick rule. For $\alpha = 0.4$ and $K = 0.7$, this area equals 2.4; society needs to begin with 2.4 units of the resource to sustain a constant $Y = 1$. For any $\alpha \geq 0.5$, society would need an infinitely large initial resource stock to maintain the constant level of output. Therefore, the constant output trajectory $Y = 1$ (and indeed, any constant trajectory with $Y > 0$) is not feasible when $\alpha \geq 0.5$. Figure 18.1 suggests that the area under the isoquant is much smaller for $\alpha = 0.4$ compared to $\alpha = 0.6$, simply because the curve falls so much more quickly if $\alpha = 0.4$. If $\alpha \geq 0.5$, it is not feasible to maintain in perpetuity any positive constant level of output (or consumption). In this case, there is no sustainable plan. If $\alpha < 0.5$ and the initial capital stock is positive, it is possible to support a positive sustainable consumption path, one that depends on the initial stocks of capital and the resource, and on α.

18.2.1 Generalizations and Empirics

We have discussed the Hartwick rule in the simplest setting, with a single human-made stock of capital and a single stock of nonrenewable natural capital, along with restrictive

Table 18.1
Total primary energy supply per unit GDP, in tons of oil equivalent per thousand 2000 U.S. dollars using PPP[5]

Country	1971	1990	2000	2005	2010
United States	0.41	0.27	0.23	0.21	0.19
Germany	0.29	0.20	0.16	0.15	0.14
Japan	0.22	0.15	0.16	0.15	0.14
Korea	0.21	0.22	0.23	0.21	0.20
Brazil	0.17	0.14	0.15	0.15	0.15
China	0.88	0.47	0.22	0.21	0.19
World	0.32	0.26	0.22	0.21	0.19

Source: OECD (2012).

assumptions about technology. In some circumstances, by investing natural resource rent into human-made capital, society can sustain a constant level of consumption. In this case, a society that follows the Hartwick rule can gradually use up the resource without harming future generations. In other circumstances, it is not possible to maintain forever any positive consumption level; resource constraints cause consumption to eventually fall to 0.

This model can include depreciation of human-made capital, renewable resources (e.g., fish, not just oil), and multiple stocks of human-made and natural capital, including knowledge and human capital (e.g., education, research and development). By investing in knowledge and human capital, society changes the technology, likely relaxing the resource constraint. A higher stage of economic development is associated with a decrease in required energy per unit of output (table 18.1). Even if sustainability is feasible, there is no presumption that society actually follows a sustainable path. Current generations might want to consume some of the resource rent, violating the Hartwick rule and leading to decreased consumption. Even if consumption remains constant for a period of time, this level of consumption may be unsustainable if it includes a portion of the resource rents.

The model describes a closed economy (one without international trade). It is appropriate for describing the aggregate world economy, because our world currently cannot trade with any other world; the model needs to be modified for individual countries that trade. To see how trade changes the results consider a country that has no resource stock and therefore must import E. This importer earns zero rent, so the Hartwick rule prescribes "invest nothing." If the import price of the resource were constant, this rule would indeed lead to a sustainable consumption path. The importer buys a constant amount of oil at a constant price, exports the fraction α of its income (= output) to pay for resource imports, and consumes the remaining fraction.

If the import price increases over time, the importer must increase its capital stock to maintain a constant level of consumption. The increase in capital stock requires investment,

---

5 PPP is purchasing power parity, a method of converting foreign currency to U.S. dollars based on prices of a reference bundle of commodities instead of on the official exchange rate.

lowering consumption. Because the importer with no resource stock has zero rent, regardless of whether it faces increasing import prices, the Hartwick rule instructs it to invest nothing. But if it invests nothing, its consumption path falls over time, as the import price increases.

The case of an oil exporter is symmetric. Nigeria obtains most of its foreign revenue from oil exports. An increase in oil prices increases the value of its resource stock, thereby increasing Nigeria's wealth, making it possible to maintain a sustainable consumption path while also consuming some of its current rent. In this case, the Hartwick rule instructs the economy to consume too little (for the purpose of maintaining constant consumption). A fall in oil prices reverses this conclusion.

18.3   Welfare Measures

Objectives and skills: Understand the relation between national income and wealth, and be informed about attempts to "green" national accounts and to develop alternative measures of sustainability.

Is society getting richer or poorer? An answer to this question requires a measure of society's wealth. We first consider the relation between measures of income and measures of wealth. We then discuss modifications to national accounts that account for resource depletion and other changes that affect sustainability. Changes in wealth per capita depend on population growth and on estimates of adjusted net savings. The World Bank (2014b) estimates that almost half of the world's countries have falling per capita wealth. Of 24 low-income countries, and 32 sub-Saharan African countries, almost 90% having falling estimated per capita wealth.

National Income Accounts and Welfare

A person's lifetime welfare (as a function of their future stream of consumption) depends on their wealth, not on their income in a particular year. Similarly, a society's future consumption possibilities, and thus social welfare, depends on its wealth, not on national income in a given year. As hard as it is to measure national income, it is vastly harder to measure national wealth. Wealth includes tangibles (e.g., stocks of infrastructure, capital), and also intangibles (e.g., human capital). It is difficult to measure changes in some stocks and to assess their prices; we need prices to add up the different categories to obtain an estimate of wealth. Economists and statisticians have made progress in measuring income but much less progress in providing direct measures of wealth. Theory provides guidance on the relation between income and wealth. We consider this relation, first ignoring and then including natural resources.

Measures of national income, including gross domestic product (GDP), gross national product (GNP), and gross national income (GNI), differ due to their treatment of international trade and remittances (box 18.1). In the interest of simplicity, we consider a closed

Box 18.1
Measures of Income

> GDP and GNI measure economic activity within a country's borders, and GNP measures economic activity of the country's residents.
>
> GDP = consumption + investment + government spending + exports − imports.
>
> GNP = GDP + net income receipts from assets abroad minus income of foreign nationals in the country.
>
> GNI = GDP + payments into the country of foreign nationals' interest and dividend receipts, minus similar payments out of the country.
>
> Example 1: The output of a U.S.-owned factory in China contributes to China's GDP. Profits from this factory that are repatriated to the U.S. reduce China's GNP and increase U.S. GNP.
>
> Example 2: Profits that a foreign national living in the U.S. earns outside the U.S. and brings into the U.S. contributes to U.S. GNI but not to U.S. GDP.

economy (no trade, foreign investment, or overseas workers) with no government sector, where all these measures are the same. We also assume that there is no technological or population change. In this economy, national income depends on an aggregate stock of capital, K, via a production function, $F(K)$. Output can be used either for consumption, C, or net investment, I, so $GDP = F(K) = C + I$.

Under what circumstances, if any, does GDP provide a good measure for wealth? Suppose that the interest rate in the economy is constant at r, and that a competitive equilibrium maximizes the present discounted stream (discounted at rate r) of future consumption. Define wealth at t, $W(t)$, as the present discounted stream of consumption from t to infinity. With these assumptions, we have

$$rW(t) = C(t) + I(t)(= GDP(t)) \tag{18.6}$$

(Weitzman 1976b; appendix I.4). Society derives income from production, $F(K)$. Equation 18.6 states that it is as if society, with wealth, W, can invest in an asset that pays the return, r; this fictional society uses the return on the asset, rW, for the purpose of consumption and savings. In this economy, GDP is proportional to wealth, with r the factor of proportionality. The equation is important because it provides the relation between wealth, the object that we care about, and income (GDP), the object that we have some hope of measuring.

Greening the National Accounts

Introducing natural resources does not change the basic idea, provided that these resources are priced efficiently. Efficient pricing requires secure property rights and well-functioning markets for the resource. To incorporate natural resources and maintain a simple model, suppose that production depends on capital and on a single nonrenewable resource (e.g., oil); suppose also that oil can be extracted costlessly. When extraction (= consumption) of

Table 18.2
Incorporating human capital and resource changes into national accounts

	World	EAP	LAC	MENA	SSA
Gross savings	24.5	47.6	19	25.9	26.3
(−) Consumption of fixed capital	13.6	12.0	12.2	9.9	13.0
(+) Educ. expenditure	4.3	2.1	5.1	4.5	3.4
(−) Energy depletion	2.4	2.7	4.7	12.9	10.3
(−) Mineral depletion	0.6	1.4	1.2	0.5	1.8
(−) Net forest depletion	0.1	0.1	0.4	0.2	1.8
(−) CO_2 damage	0.5	1.0	0.3	0.7	0.6
(−) Particulate emissions damage	0.6	1.6	0.8	0.9	1.2
Adjusted net savings	11.1	30.0	4.5	5.3	0.9

Note: All numbers are percentages of gross national income. EAR, East Asia and Pacific; LAC, Latin America and Caribbean; MENA, Middle East and North Africa; SSA, sub-Saharan Africa.
Source: World Bank (2014b).

the resource is E (energy), output is $F(K, E) = C + I$. In a competitive equilibrium, we know from chapter 5 that the price of this resource, denoted $p(t)$, rises at the rate of interest. Moreover, because of the assumption of costless extraction, the price equals the resource rent, which equals the shadow price of the resource. In this setting, with secure property rights and efficient markets, the resource price is an accurate measure of the value, both to the resource owner and to society, of an additional unit of the resource stock. The reduction in society's stock of capital due to the extraction of a unit of the resource is $p(t)E(t)$. The proper measure of "adjusted" GDP is therefore $C(t) + I(t) - p(t)E(t)$, and the measure of wealth becomes (Weitzman 1999)

$$rW^*(t) = C(t) + I(t) - p(t)E(t). \tag{18.7}$$

Research during the past quarter century has attempted to "green the national accounts" by including the value of changes in productive assets that are not already incorporated into GDP (Hamilton 2003; Hartwick 2011). Estimating GDP requires estimating the value of production of society's goods and services, a daunting measurement problem, but one that has been studied and refined over many decades. Measuring the correction required by changing resource stocks is a harder problem. Researchers have to decide which stocks to include in the correction, then attempt to estimate the reduction in the stock, and finally attribute a price to this stock. For resources with well-functioning markets, such as oil and forestry products, the market price can be used to value the change in stock. However, the correction is also important where property rights and markets are weak or nonexistent, requiring researchers to estimate (often with little data) the prices used in the correction.

Table 18.2 shows World Bank estimates of savings, and adjusted savings, for the world and for different regions. The measure of adjusted net savings includes the externality cost of GHGs and particulate emissions, and also changes in human capital resulting from education. After accounting for depreciation ("consumption of fixed capital"), the World

Bank estimates that the world saves about 11.1% of GNI. Educational investments, which increase the stock of human capital, almost exactly offset the reductions due to resource depletion and pollution, so adjusted net savings are also close to 11% for the world. Gross savings rates and consumption of capital in sub-Saharan Africa are close to world levels. Investment in education there is slightly lower than world levels, but the correction for resource depletion and pollution damages is much higher, resulting in an estimated adjusted net savings for sub-Saharan Africa of 0.9%. Increases in population imply that per capita wealth is falling in these regions.

Alternatives to Adjusted National Accounts
GDP or GNI include some components that do not belong in a measure of welfare, and they exclude some that do belong. Increased construction of prisons and employment of prison guards might stimulate the economy, increasing overall employment and GDP. If this increased activity is the result of stricter laws for minor infractions, and if those laws increase social dysfunction, the additional prisons and the guards do not represent an increase in social welfare. GDP measures only market-based transactions. If a couple divorces, and one person begins paying for services that were previously unpaid, those payments (if recorded) show up as an increase in GDP. However, the change might not represent a real increase in welfare. GDP statistics do not reflect inequality, which may reduce social cohesion and individual happiness, lowering welfare. Higher levels of pollution or congestion likely decrease welfare, but because these are typically unpriced, GDP does not capture them. Green national accounts attempt to remedy this omission but not the others.

A literal interpretation of strong sustainability is impractical, because it would require a long list of stocks, many of which we have no hope of measuring. Even if it were possible to measure the components of this list, it would be too complex to understand, and therefore useless for policy guidance. A useful welfare measure must present information in an intelligible manner. The simplicity of national accounts (e.g., GDP) is an important part of their appeal. Politicians routinely use changes in GDP as evidence of their own or their rivals' economic (in)competence. An index combines different pieces of information into a single number. GDP adds up the value of goods and services in an economy. Green national accounts include the estimated value of some unpriced (or mis-priced) goods and services. Because all these components are in the same units (e.g., dollars) it is sensible to add them together. For indices that involve noncommensurable components, merely summing the components is arbitrary.

The United Nations (UN) produces the Human Development Index (HDI), a widely used measure of welfare that includes estimates of health, education, and material well-being. The HDI aggregates these three components using their "geometric mean" (the cube root of the product of the components). A 1% change in any of the components has the same effect on the geometric (but not the arithmetic) mean. The geometric mean also implies less substitutability among the different components, compared to the arithmetic mean. Both the geometric mean and the arithmetic mean are ad hoc ways of aggregating noncommensurable components. The UN also produces broader indices of well-being that include inequality, human security, and gender disparity.

Other indices include the Measure of Economic Welfare (MEW), Sustainable Measure of Economic Welfare (SMEW), Index of Sustainable Economic Welfare (ISEW), the Genuine Progress Indicator (GPI), and Ecological Footprint (EF) (Stiglitz et al. 2009). MEW adjusts standard national accounts by adding the value of activities that contribute to welfare (e.g., leisure) and subtracting activities that do not (e.g., commuting). SMEW modifies MEW by accounting for changes in wealth. ISEW and GPI deducts other costs, including those related to the loss of wetlands and CO_2 damage. Over the past quarter century, GDP has continued to grow, whereas such alternatives as the GPI and the HDI have been flat (Kubiszewski et al. 2013). Different measures of welfare lead to different conclusions about sustainability.

The EF calculates the amount of "average quality" productive land needed to support a population at current consumption levels. Humans' estimated EF exceeded the earth's carrying capacity by 25% in 2003. There are an estimated 1.8 hectares of average quality land per person available globally; Europeans use about 5 hectares per person, and North Americans use twice that amount. Changes in consumption levels or in production methods could alter our EF. The EF takes into account the forest area needed to absorb carbon emissions. Cross-country differences in CO_2 emissions explain a large part of the cross-country differences in EF. A country's carbon footprint, an alternative to the EF, is easier to calculate and to communicate.

18.4   Summary

It is easy enough to define sustainability. However, even under a host of assumptions, it is not easy to determine whether our development path is likely to be sustainable (i.e., whether future generations are likely to be richer or poorer than the current generation). Economic development is sustainable if it meets current needs without sacrificing future generations' ability to meet their needs. Attempts to rigorously define and to measure sustainability rely on concepts of weak or strong sustainability. The former recognizes substitutability in production and consumption, and it focuses on future utility levels. The latter assumes limited substitutability and focuses on maintaining constant or increasing stocks. In a simple model, weak sustainability requires that resource rents be invested in human-made capital. This investment program transforms natural capital into human-made capital, achieving weak sustainability if and only if natural capital is not too important in production. A constant or increasing stream of future utility is feasible only if human-made capital provides an adequate substitute for a dwindling supply of natural resources. Even if weak sustainability is feasible, there is no reason to assume that society is on a sustainable trajectory.

Attempts to measure sustainability have followed two principle avenues, closely related to the concepts of weak and strong sustainability. The first begins with the positive relation between wealth (a stock) and GDP (a flow). Standard national accounts (e.g., GDP) measure the value of market-based economic activity. These statistics ignore the value of changes in many natural resources and in other stocks. During the past quarter century, economists have attempted to include the value of these kinds of changes, resulting in green national accounts. Recent estimates show that many poor countries are not increasing their stock of human-made plus natural capital fast enough to accommodate population growth. By this measure, these countries are not on a (weakly) sustainable development path.

The second approach to measuring sustainability focuses on resource stocks. There are many of these measures; some rely on a single number (e.g., the amount of average quality productive land needed to support a population in perpetuity at current levels of income). This measure concludes that our development trajectory is not sustainable, because the actual population exceeds the level that can be supported by available land. Other measures create indices that aggregate measures of health, education, material wellbeing, and sometimes other components. These indices attempt to provide welfare measures without necessarily enquiring whether this level of welfare is sustainable. The large number of different sustainability and welfare measures provide alternatives that focus on different aspects of the same general question.

18.5 Terms and Concepts, Study Questions, Exercises, and Sources

Terms and Concepts
Weak and strong sustainability, travel cost models, contingent valuation, composite commodity, constant returns to scale, Cobb Douglas production function, purchasing power parity (PPP), national income accounting identity, Hartwick rule, isoquant, gross domestic product (GDP), gross national product (GNP), gross national income (GNI), Human Development Index (HDI), ecological footprint (EF), geometric mean.

Study Questions
1. Explain the meaning of weak and strong sustainability; discuss some of the advantages and disadvantages of both concepts.

2. State the Hartwick rule, and describe the question to which it provides an answer.

3. Given the Cobb Douglas production function, $F(K, K) = K^{1-\alpha} E^{\alpha}$, state the condition under which a sustainable consumption path is feasible, and provide an intuitive justification for this condition.

4. Consider the closed economy model with no government sector, where GDP = consumption + investment. When all inputs are correctly priced, what is the relation between

GDP and wealth (defined as the present value of the stream of future consumption)? Explain the adjustments to GDP that must be made (to use GDP as a measure of wealth) when production uses unpriced (or incorrectly priced) natural resources.

5. Green national accounts and the EF are two attempts to shed light on the issue of sustainability. Briefly explain both measures; your explanation should describe the relation between both measures and the concepts of weak and strong sustainability.

6. Discuss the context in which equation 18.1 arises, and explain the meaning of the equation.

Exercises

1. Using the Cobb Douglas production function given in section 18.2, write down the equilibrium conditions for competitive firms "value of marginal product equals input price."

(a) Show that α equals expenditures on natural resources as a share of the value of output (= national income), and $1 - \alpha$ equals the rental cost of capital as a share of the value of output.

(b) Use part (a) to show that expenditures on factors of production equals the value of output; therefore, profits are 0.

Sources

World Commission on Environment and Development (1987) sets out a framework for sustainability, relating economic development and environmental protection.

Roemer (2009) discusses the idea of brute luck and the school of luck egalitarians.

Fenichel and Abbott (2014) measure the shadow price and value of the Gulf of Mexico reef fishery.

Solow (1974b) and Hartwick (1977) introduce the Hartwick rule.

Asheim et al. (2003) discuss some of the misconceptions that have arisen related to this rule. Mitra et al. (2013) summarize and extend results on the issue of sustainability in resource markets.

Table 18.1 is taken from the OECD Factbook (2011–2012).

Table 18.2 is based on the World Bank (2014b).

Weitzman (1976b) demonstrates the relation between GDP and welfare.

Weitzman (1999) shows the effects of mineral depletion on welfare.

Hamilton (2002) provides estimates of changes in total and per capita wealth.

Hartwick (2011) explains the relation between green national income and green national product.

Stiglitz et al. (2009) discuss the theory and the practicalities of measuring economic performance and social progress. They describe the various indices used to measure sustainability.

Kubiszewski et al. (2013) compare measures of sustainability.

19 Valuing the Future: Discounting

Objective
• Understand the role of discounting in evaluating a policy that has consequences over long spans of time.

Information and Skills
• Know the difference between discounting utility versus consumption, and understand the "tyranny" of discounting.

• Understand how beliefs about future policy, technology, and wealth affect consumption discount rates, thereby affecting evaluations of policy proposals.

• Understand the relation between impatience and discounting, and the difference between intra- and intergenerational transfers.

Many environmental and resource issues—climate change in particular—involve welfare trade-offs over long spans of time. How much should society be willing to spend today to reduce the risk of future climate damage? Climate scientists' consensus views provide the proper foundation for evaluating climate policy. However, policy-based models require economic assumptions and ethical judgements, along with climate science. Most of these models use discounted utilitarianism. We explore this framework and discuss how it affects policy recommendations.

Carbon taxes have been enacted or seriously considered in only a few places (including Sweden, and for a time, Australia). Despite its lack of political traction, most climate policy models express their policy recommendation as a social cost of carbon (SCC) or a carbon tax. The SCC equals the present discounted cost to society of an additional unit of carbon emissions; it is the social price of the marginal unit of emissions. If people were charged this price, they would internalize the effect of their emissions. The magnitude of estimates of the SCC reflects assumptions about the severity of the environmental problem and the valuation of future welfare. The U.S. Environmental Protection Agency (EPA) uses estimates of the SCC in conducting cost-benefit analysis for policies with significant effects on carbon emissions.[1] The World Bank uses these estimates in calculating the effect of increased atmospheric carbon on net savings (section 18.3).

Economic models produce a wide range of estimates of the SCC, from less than $10 to well over $100 per ton of carbon. We do not know the true SCC, but we can understand and evaluate the assumptions that lead to current estimates. Many climate policies that are actually used, including cap and trade, green subsidies, and renewable fuel portfolio standards, can be expressed as a "tax equivalent," a tax that would yield approximately the same level of emissions reductions, although usually at greater economic cost. A higher tax leads to lower carbon emissions and thus corresponds to a stricter policy.

Previous chapters use a partial equilibrium setting where the sum of consumer and producer surplus (sometimes augmented to include tax revenue and environmental costs) is the measure of welfare in a period. In the climate context, we use utility as the measure of well-being in a single period, and we again take the discounted stream as the overall measure of welfare. Uncertainty about the future requires discounting expected utility.

A Road Map
We begin with a discussion of the SCC and its relation to the optimal carbon tax (section 19.1). Today's optimal climate policy depends on beliefs about features of the economy in the future, such as growth, technology, and policies. We saw that the resource owner's optimal extraction depends on her beliefs about future prices (chapter 5), the future availability of the backstop (chapter 7), or future resource taxes (section 11.4). In the climate context, optimal policy today depends on what we think will happen in the future.

The use of discounted utilitarianism is one reason that many economic models support only modest climate policy. Section 19.2 explains the difference between discounting utility and discounting consumption, and it illustrates the "tyranny" of discounting. Due to the power of compounding, the use of a non-negligible discount rate encourages us to place little weight on severe and long-lasting damages that begin in a century or two. We examine the role of uncertainty, describing a situation where we are willing to spend much more to avoid an event that occurs at a random instead of a known time.

Discounting depends on beliefs about future growth. Growth optimism includes the belief that technological change and increased accumulation of (human-made) capital will make people in the future richer than those currently alive. Optimists recommend only modest climate policy, to avoid requiring the relatively poor current generations to make sacrifices that benefit relatively rich future generations. In addition, if future inventions lower the cost of reducing carbon emissions, it makes sense to delay emissions reductions until they become cheaper. Events of the past two centuries support growth optimism, but

---

1 Most estimates of the SCC consider the cost to the world as a whole, not specifically to the United States, of an additional unit of atmospheric carbon. The EPA, a U.S. agency, uses a global cost of carbon in assessing the cost/benefit ratio of a U.S. policy. To date, U.S. courts have accepted this procedure.

they provide a questionable basis for policy that might have major effects on our species (section 19.3).

People dislike delaying gratification, even apart from uncertainty about whether they will live to enjoy the future. If individuals are impatient about their future utility, perhaps the social planner who acts on their behalf should exhibit the same kind of impatience. This view does not distinguish between transfers a young person makes to her older self (e.g., by saving for retirement), and transfers the current generation makes to future generations (e.g., by protecting the environment). The distinction between these two types of transfers can lead to a planning problem with "time-inconsistent preferences," where a planner's willingness to make trade-offs between people living at different points in the future changes over time (section 19.4).

19.1   The Social Cost of Carbon

Objectives and skills: Understand why the SSC and the optimal carbon tax typically depend on current beliefs about the future.

The SCC today equals the present discounted stream of future marginal damages arising from an additional unit of carbon emitted today. If the marginal damage associated with carbon is constant, as for the example in section 2.6, then the future stream of marginal damage is also a constant. In that case, the SCC does not depend on anything that happens in the future. If, however, marginal damage depends on the carbon stock, then (apart from special cases) future marginal damages depend on the future stock, which depends on future emissions, which depend on future policy.[2] In this case, the SCC depends on future policies.

A review of figure 8.2 helps explain this claim. This figure shows the stock trajectories corresponding to two extraction trajectories. If damages equal $\frac{1}{2}S^2$, then marginal damages equal $S(t)$, so here figure 8.2 also shows the trajectories of marginal damages in the two scenarios. The present discounted values of these two streams are different. When marginal damages depend on the stock, the SCC today (typically) depends on future emissions.

This observation means that the optimal policy today generally depends on beliefs about what will happen in the future, including beliefs about future policies. The optimal tax today equals the marginal cost to society of an additional unit of emissions today: the SCC. Because the SCC depends on what happens in the future, we cannot sensibly speak of an optimal policy today without making assumptions about what policies will be carried

---

2 Nonlinearities in a model might offset one another in such a way that the SCC does not depend on future emissions (or anything that happens in the future), even though marginal damages are not constant (Golosov et al. 2014). A slight change in model assumptions destroys this independence between current policy and things that happen in the future. Despite this fragility, this model is powerful, because it leads to a relatively transparent and easily interpreted expression for the optimal carbon tax.

out in the future. The EPA and World Bank applications use projections of nonoptimal emissions trajectories. Some models calculate the SCC under the assumption that future carbon emissions are optimally regulated.

19.2   Discounting Utility or Consumption

Objectives and skills: Understand the difference between discounting utility and discounting consumption, the sense in which discounting is "tyrannical," and the interaction between uncertainty and discounting.

Discounting utility is different than discounting consumption, but in either case it can be "tyrannical," inducing people today to (almost) ignore the future. This section shows how a particular type of uncertainty interacts with discounting. Throughout this discussion, we use a continuous time setting. If the discount rate under annual compounding is 5%, the discount rate under continuous compounding is about 4.9% (section 2.6).

The discount factor makes objects at different points in time comparable. The logic of discounting is the same regardless of whether we apply it to dollars or utility (or anything else), but the interpretation and the numerical value of the discount rate may vary with the context. To keep this distinction in mind, we use different symbols to represent discount rates applied to different objects. In this chapter only, ρ denotes the (continuously compounded) discount rate for utility, and r denotes the discount rate for consumption (measured in dollars).[3] A higher discount rate corresponds to a lower discount factor, which means that we value future utility or consumption less and therefore are willing to sacrifice less today to benefit the future. *A higher discount rate leads to a lower recommended carbon tax.* For constant values of ρ and r, the utility and the consumption discount factors are

$$
e^{-\rho t} = \left\{ \begin{array}{c} \text{utility discount} \\ \text{factor} \end{array} \right\} = \left\{ \begin{array}{c} \text{number of units of utility a} \\ \text{person will sacrifice} \\ \text{today to obtain one additional} \\ \text{unit of utility at time } t \end{array} \right\}
$$

$$
e^{-rt} = \left\{ \begin{array}{c} \text{consumption} \\ \text{discount factor} \end{array} \right\} = \left\{ \begin{array}{c} \text{number of units of consumption (\$)} \\ \text{a person will sacrifice today to} \\ \text{obtain one additional unit of} \\ \text{consumption at time } t \end{array} \right\}.
$$

3 In previous chapters, ρ denotes the discount factor associated with the discount rate r. Our usage here is different. Here, ρ and r are both discount rates, but they are used to discount different object: utility and consumption.

19.2.1   The Tyranny of Discounting

Even for near-term events, discount rates can have a significant effect on our decisions. The example in table 2.2, involving the levelized cost of electricity, shows that for an investment with a maximum lifetime of 45 years, the relation between the present value of two alternatives changes significantly when the annual discount rate changes from 2% to 4%. Discounting can be even more important when considering distant events.

The "tyranny" of discounting refers to the fact that, at non-negligible discount rates, events in the distant future have almost no effect on current decisions: the present discounted value of a cost, measured in either utility or dollars, in the distant future can be very small, even if the absolute cost in the future is very large. As a consequence, people today may not want to incur even a small current cost to avoid a large future cost. The logic of discounting compels us to essentially ignore the consequences of our actions on people in the distant future. Here we emphasize utility discounting, so the relevant discount rate is ρ, but the same logic applies to consumption discounting. A larger value of ρ implies that the planner is more impatient with regard to future utility: he is willing to give up less current utility to obtain an extra unit of future utility.

Environmental policy provides a kind of insurance. A person who buys standard insurance makes a fixed payment (the premium) that entitles her to a payout under particular contingencies. People can buy insurance against some natural events, such as floods or earthquakes, but society as whole cannot obtain insurance against a world-wide occurrence of climate change: there is no cosmic insurer standing outside our world, able to make a contract exchanging premiums for a payout in the event of a bad outcome. However, society can decide to incur near-term costs to reduce the likelihood or the severity of future climate-related damages (e.g., by replacing fossil fuels with a more expensive alternative). These policies are analogous to insurance, because they involve current costs (the "premium") to mitigate the consequences of random future events.

Climate-related damages associated with current emissions might not arise for many decades, or even centuries, but if they do occur, they are likely to persist a long time. Our model incorporates both delay and persistence. Suppose that in the absence of costly changes (e.g., moving toward low-carbon energy) an event, such as the melting of the Western Antarctic Ice Sheet (WAIS) will occur in 200 years and will result in a loss of 100 units of utility in each subsequent period. (Such an "event" would actually unfold over long periods of time, possibly centuries.) Society can avoid this event by paying, in perpetuity, a "premium" of z. The payment z is the flow cost of taking actions that eliminate the event, such as using expensive alternatives to carbon-based energy.

Figure 19.1 illustrates this scenario. The step function (solid line) shows the trajectory of utility if society does not pay the premium: utility falls by 100 units, from 150 to 50, at the event time $t = 200$. The dashed and dotted lines represent two scenarios. If society can avoid the loss by paying a premium $z = 13.5$ and chooses to do so, the dashed line (constant

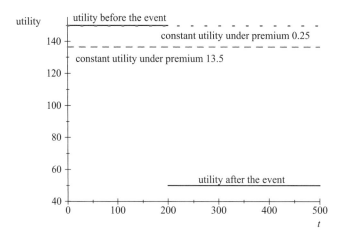

Figure 19.1
Step function (solid line): Utility trajectory if society does not pay the premium. Dashed line: Utility trajectory if society avoids the event by paying a premium of 13.5. Dotted line: Utility trajectory if society avoids the event by paying premium of 0.25.

at $150 - 13.5$) shows its utility trajectory. If society can eliminate this loss by paying a premium of only $z = 0.25$ and chooses to do so, the dotted line (constant at $150 - 0.25$) shows its utility trajectory.

The largest premium society would be willing to pay, denoted Z, makes society indifferent between the trajectory shown by the step function and the trajectory with constant utility $150 - Z$. We can compare these two trajectories by comparing the present discounted value of costs along each of them. If society pays the premium, z, in every period, then the present discounted value of the premium cost is $\frac{z}{\rho}$. If society does not pay the premium, it incurs no cost until $t = 200$, and thereafter occurs the cost 100 in every period, leading to a present discounted cost of $\frac{100}{\rho} e^{-200\rho}$.[4] The maximum premium that society would pay equates these two costs: $Z(\rho)$ is the solution to $e^{-200\rho} \frac{100}{\rho} = \frac{z}{\rho}$, so $Z(\rho) = e^{-200\rho} 100$. Society is willing to pay any premium less than or equal to $Z(\rho)$ to avoid the loss beginning at $t = 200$.

The solid graph in figure 19.2 shows this premium as a function of ρ, for an event time $T = 200$, illustrating the tyranny of discounting. At a discount rate of 1%, the maximum premium is about 13.5% of the loss, but at a discount rate of 3%, the premium falls to less

---

4 The discussion below equation 2.13 notes that in the continuous time setting, the present discounted value of a constant flow, received in perpetuity, equals that flow divided by the discount rate. In the setting here, the flow is z and the (utility) discount rate in ρ, so the present discounted value of the perpetual flow is $\frac{z}{\rho}$. Similarly, the present discounted value of the constant flow, 100, paid in perpetuity, is $\frac{100}{\rho}$. In our example, this cost does not begin until 200 years. The present value, at time 0, of the perpetual flow that begins in 200 years in $\frac{100}{\rho} e^{-\rho 200}$.

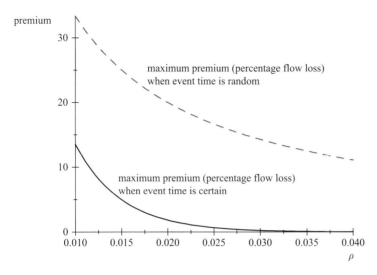

Figure 19.2
Maximum premium as a percentage of the flow loss when the certain event time is $T = 200$ (solid curve) and when event time is exponentially distributed with $E(T) = 200$ (dashed curve).

than 0.25%. With discounting at a non-negligible level, decisionmakers value the (finitely long) near future vastly more than they value the (infinitely long) distant future. In this case, society has little incentive to incur even modest current costs associated with climate change policy, to avoid large future costs. Box 19.1 provides a different perspective on discounting.

19.2.2 Uncertain Timing

The example above assumes that the event time is certain; random timing likely increases the willingness to pay. If there is a 50% chance that, absent climate policy, the event will occur in 150 years, and a 50% chance that it will occur in 250 years, then the expected occurrence time, 200 years, equals the certain time in the example above. The present-value cost of the event is much greater if it occurs in 150 years, and only slightly less if it occurs in 250 years, compared to if it occurs in 200 years. Therefore, the expected cost (the probability-weighted average of the two costs) is closer to the higher, earlier cost: the expected costs in the stochastic scenario are greater than the known costs in the deterministic scenario.[5]

---

5 This result is a special case of "Jensen's inequality": if T is a random variable, and $Z(T)$ is a convex function of T, then $E(Z(T)) > Z(E(T))$, where $E(\cdot)$ denotes expectation. The present value, $\exp(-\rho T)$, is a convex function of T. In other contexts, introducing uncertainty lowers (expected) costs. The comparison depends on whether a function is convex (as in the present context) or concave in the random variable.

Box 19.1
A Different Perspective on the Tyranny of Discounting

The present discounted value of a perpetual annual loss of x equals the sum of the loss for the next 200 years $\left(\frac{1-e^{-\rho 200}}{\rho}x\right)$ and the loss for the infinitely many years beginning 200 years from now $\left(\frac{e^{-\rho 200}}{\rho}x\right)$. The ratio of these two losses, $\frac{e^{-\rho 200}}{1-e^{-\rho 200}}$, equals the value, to the decision maker today, of the infinitely many years starting 200 years from now relative to the value of the next 200 years. At a 1% discount rate this ratio is 0.157; at a 3% discount rate, the ratio is 0.0025. At 3% discounting, the planner values utility during the next 200 years (about 10 generations) 400 times as much as she values utility for the infinitely many years (and generations) beginning in 200 years.

The dashed graph in figure 19.2 shows the willingness to pay if the time of the event is random (and exponentially distributed), with expected event time $T = 200$ (so that the two graphs are comparable).[6] Moving from the deterministic to the stochastic setting increases the maximum willingness to pay by a factor of 2.5 at $\rho = 0.01$, and by a factor of 57 at $\rho = 0.03$. Mistakenly treating the event time as deterministic, when in fact it is stochastic, can lead to a moderately large underestimate of the amount society should be willing to spend to avoid the event at small discount rates ($\rho = 0.01$), and a very large underestimate at higher discount rates ($\rho = 0.03$).

In the real world, stochasticity is important. We do not know whether an event such as the melting of the WAIS will happen sooner or later, or perhaps never (in a span relevant to human existence). If we ignore our uncertainty about the time of the event, and instead merely replace the random time by its expectation, we may vastly understate the amount that we should be willing to spend to prevent the event from happening. Our example assumes that the cost of the event is known and that payment of the premium eliminates the possibility of the event. In fact, both the costs and the timing are uncertain, and costly actions (e.g., the reduction of emissions) might decrease but not eliminate the possibility of future climate events. The general point is that using a deterministic model (one that ignores uncertainty) to approximate a stochastic world might lead to large errors in formulating policy prescriptions. Most climate policies are deterministic (Nordhaus 2008; Anthoff and Tol 2010). Stochastic models have only recently become widely used in climate economics (Lemoine and Traeger 2014; Lontzek et al. 2015).

---

6 If the probability that the event will occur over the next small unit of time, dt, given that it has not yet occurred, is approximately $h \times dt$ (with $h > 0$ a constant), then the event time is exponentially distributed; h is known as the "hazard rate," and the expected time of the event is $\frac{1}{h}$. For figure 19.2, $h = \frac{1}{200} = 0.005$.

19.3 The Consumption Discount Rate

Objectives and skills: Understand the consumption discount rate (CDR) and its sensitivity to assumptions about growth.

For policy applications, the consumption discount factor, and the associated CDR, is more useful than the utility discount factor and rate. The SCC is computed using the CDR. Most people, including policymakers, care about consumption, income, jobs and the other things that produce utility, not utility itself. Asking a policymaker how many units of utility society should sacrifice today to obtain an extra unit of utility at some time in the future will elicit a blank stare. (You know that the answer is "the utility discount factor.")

"How many dollars of consumption should society be willing to give up today to obtain one extra dollar of consumption at a future time?" is an intelligible question for policy makers, one that captures the trade-off arising in policy that has costs and benefits at different points in time, such as climate policy. That policy may reduce consumption today by requiring greater expenditures on pollution abatement or the switch to more expensive types of energy. By protecting the climate, the policy may make people in the future better off.

19.3.1 The Ramsey Formula

The Ramsey formula shows the relation between the CDR, r, and the utility discount rate, ρ (appendix J.1):

$$r(t) = \rho + \eta_t g_t,$$

$$\text{with } \eta_t \equiv -\frac{u''(c_t)}{u'(c_t)} c_t, \quad \text{and} \quad g_t \equiv \frac{1}{c_t}\frac{dc}{dt}, \tag{19.1}$$

where g_t is the consumption growth rate. Equation 19.1 shows that the CDR may change over time, but we first discuss the case where it is constant. To achieve this simplicity, we assume: (i) utility equals $u(c) = \frac{c^{1-\eta}}{1-\eta}$, so that $-\frac{u''(c_t)}{u'(c_t)}c_t = \eta$, a constant, and (ii) the growth rate for consumption is a constant, g. With these assumptions, the CDR is a constant: $r = \rho + \eta g$. The parameters have the following interpretations:[7]

ρ: a measure of impatience. A larger ρ implies a less patient planner, one who places less weight on future utility; the less patient planner is less willing to sacrifice utility today to increase future utility.

---

7 The parameter η has a second interpretation: the elasticity of marginal utility of consumption (i.e., the percentage reduction in marginal utility for a 1% increase in consumption). In symbols, $\eta = -\frac{\Delta MU}{MU}\frac{c}{\Delta c}$, where Δ denotes "change in" and MU denotes marginal utility; the growth rate is $g = \frac{\Delta c}{c}$. Thus, $\eta g = \frac{\Delta MU}{MU}\frac{c}{\Delta c}\frac{\Delta c}{c} = -\frac{\Delta MU}{MU}$, the rate of decrease in marginal utility. The larger is ηg, the greater is the fall in marginal utility due to a shift in consumption from today to the future. Therefore, larger ηg makes the planner less willing to reduce today's consumption to increase future consumption.

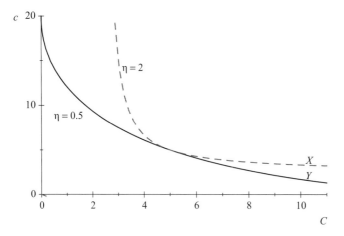

Figure 19.3
Combinations of consumption in two periods, C and c, that lead to a constant sum of utility, $U(c) + U(C)$, for $\eta = 0.5$ (solid curve) and $\eta = 2$ (dashed curve).

η: a measure of inequality aversion. A larger η implies a more inequality-averse planner; this planner is more reluctant to distribute wealth from a poorer to a richer generation.
g: the growth rate. Faster growth makes people in the future richer relative to people today.

Figure 19.3 helps visualize the role of η in determining the willingness to move consumption from one period to a different period (or from one person to a different person). Each curve shows the combination of consumption levels in two periods (or for two people), denoted C and c, that lead to a constant sum of utility, $u(c) + u(C)$. The dashed curve corresponds to $\eta = 2$, and the solid curve corresponds to $\eta = 0.5$. The two curves are tangent, and represent the same sum of utility, at $c = C = 5$.[8] This figure abstracts from impatience, setting $\rho = 0$. The less inequality-averse planner ($\eta = 0.5$) is willing reduce c by more to increase C from 5 to 10, compared to the more inequality-averse planner ($\eta = 2$): compare points X and Y. *The larger is η, the less consumption the planner is willing to take away from a poorer person to increase the consumption of a richer person.*

With decreasing marginal utility (a concave utility function) each additional unit of consumption provides a smaller increase in utility: a rich person values an extra \$100 less than a poor person does. A positive value of g (= consumption growth) means that people in the future are getting richer, decreasing their marginal valuation of still-higher consumption.

---

8 Each of the curves is analogous to an isoquant; instead of showing combinations of factors of production leading to a constant level of output, the figures show the combination of consumption levels, in the two periods, leading to a constant level of total utility. A normalization causes the two curves in figure 19.3 to be tangent at $C = c = 5$.

Faster growth (larger g) makes the planner less willing to sacrifice consumption today to increase consumption for the richer future. Larger growth increases the consumption discount rate (decreases the consumption discount factor). An increase in g has a greater effect on the CDR, the more averse the planner is to income inequality (the larger is η).

In summary, a planner has a higher CDR (lower consumption discount factor) the more impatient she is with regard to future utility (the larger is ρ), or the more rapidly people in the future are getting richer (the larger is g), or (for $g > 0$) the more averse she is to income inequality (the larger is η).

19.3.2   The Importance of the Growth Trajectory

If ρ, g, and η are constant, then the CDR is also constant, and the insights from section 19.2 apply, replacing "utility" with "consumption." The parameters ρ and η measure preference characteristics: the planner's impatience (ρ) and aversion to (intertemporal) inequality (η). Those parameters might change over time or with levels of consumption, but they are often treated as constants. The growth parameter, g, in contrast, describes the economy, not preferences; there is no reason to think that it is constant. Growth rates over long spans of human history have been close to 0, but growth rates over the past two centuries have been around 1.5–2%. Given the consensus view that η is not close to 0, a positive value of g has a significant effect on the CDR, and thus on society's willingness to sacrifice consumption today to protect future generations from climate damages.

If we expect high growth to continue over future centuries, then our successors will be much richer than we are; if we are somewhat averse to intergenerational income inequality (η is not close to 0), then we should be reluctant to incur costs to protect our much richer successors from (noncatastrophic) climate-related damages. This view relies on the assumption that growth over the next several centuries will resemble that of the past two centuries, not growth over the previous millennia. It is not reasonable to assume that growth will abruptly stop, but it may be presumptuous to make long-lasting decisions based on optimism about growth. Growth experts were asked for their assessment of likely growth over the next two centuries. Most anticipate growth in the 1–3% range, but some expect negative growth, and one expects growth above 6%. There is little consensus among growth experts (Gillingham et al. 2015; Gordon 2015).

Appendix J.2 presents a model in which growth starts out at 2% and falls to 0 gradually over time. We compare society's willingness to pay to avoid damages that begin in T years when it correctly anticipates this growth trajectory, versus when it is either "falsely pessimistic" (believing incorrectly that future growth will always be 0) or "falsely optimistic" (believing incorrectly that future growth will always be at 2%). False optimism makes society willing to spend too little, and false pessimism makes society willing to spend too much to avoid the future damages. Which of these errors is greater in magnitude? If the damages begin soon (T is small), then near-term growth is important. Our assumption that actual growth falls slowly means that the falsely optimistic view is closer to being correct in the near term, compared to the falsely pessimistic view. In this circumstance (T small), the error under pessimism is greater than that under optimism. The reverse holds if damages begin in a century (T large), when the pessimistic view about growth is closer to being correct. For large T, the error under false optimism is much greater than that under false pessimism.

The main effects of climate change are likely to occur a century or more in the future: T is large. The model suggests that the error we make in being too optimistic about growth (spending too little to avoid climate damages) is likely to be much greater than the error we make in being too pessimistic about growth (spending too much to avoid damages). This conclusion favors the use of caution (erring on the side of safety) in setting climate policy.

19.3.3   Growth Uncertainty

Economists incorporate uncertainty, including uncertainty about growth, using two principal strategies. The first, most straightforward, and widely used approach, changes the planner's welfare criterion to discounted expected utility (DEU). This criterion also adds up the discounted utility in different periods, but it now takes expectations of the sum with respect to future consumption (or whatever variable is random). The second approach replaces DEU with a more general alterative.

Both approaches produce a "certainty equivalent" CDR, which can be used to evaluate how much society should be willing to invest today to increase consumption (reduce damages) in an uncertain future world. In both cases, the certainty equivalent CDR generalizes the Ramsey formula 19.1; it involves the parameters of the distributions of the random variables and also parameters that describe attitudes toward impatience, risk, and intertemporal consumption transfers. The name "certainty equivalent" means that the discount rate can be used to assess a public investment as if the world were nonrandom; the randomness is already built in to the certainty equivalent discount rate.

Discounted Expected Utility
The simplest modification replaces deterministic constant growth, g, with a random process, $\tilde{g}(t) = \bar{g} + \tilde{\varepsilon}_t$, where $\bar{g}$ equals expected growth, and $\tilde{\varepsilon}_t$ is a mean-zero "serially uncorrelated" random variable: here, growth in one period does not affect growth in subsequent periods. This model of uncertainty increases the amount we are willing to spend to avoid future damages, but not by much.

Positive correlation between growth in different periods increases this correction (lowers the CDR by more), because positive correlation makes the future riskier. An example, in which a person might get $0 or $1 in each of two periods, makes this relation intuitive. In one scenario, the probability of receiving either amount is the same, and the amount received in the first period has no effect on the likelihood of receiving a dollar in the second: the gifts are uncorrelated. In this case, the person receives a total of $0 or $2, each with 25% chance, and $1 with 50% chance. In the other scenario, the person has an equal chance of receiving $0 or $1 (as in the first scenario) but the gifts are perfectly positively correlated: she receives the same amount in both periods. In this scenario, she has a 50% chance of obtaining either $0 or $2. In expectation, she obtains the same amount in both scenarios ($1), but the variance of total receipts is higher in the second scenario; that scenario is riskier. Therefore, positively correlated random growth increases the amount society is willing to spend today to avoid future damages by substantially more, compared to uncorrelated random growth.

A richer model of stochastic growth uses

$$\tilde{g}(t+1) = \bar{g} - \alpha(\bar{g} - \tilde{g}(t)) + \tilde{\varepsilon}_t, \tag{19.2}$$

where $\tilde{\varepsilon}_t$ are serially uncorrelated shocks, and $\bar{g}$ and α are parameters. If $\alpha = 1$, then $\tilde{g}(t+1) = \tilde{g}(t) + \tilde{\varepsilon}_t$. In this case, growth is a random walk: growth in the next period equals current growth plus a random variable. If $0 < \alpha < 1$, then growth is mean reverting, approaching its long-run level $\bar{g}$: when the current growth is above $\bar{g}$, growth in the next period is expected to be less than current growth. Other models involve longer lags or different assumptions about the distribution of the shock.

An alternative incorporates the risk of "catastrophic" shocks. The shock $\tilde{\varepsilon}_t$ might be the sum of two random variables. The first has a familiar (perhaps bell-shaped) distribution, and a second equals 0 in most years but occasionally equals a large negative number, reflecting the possibility of a catastrophe, such as a world war (Barro 2006). Using stochastic growth models requires estimating parameters of an equation similar to 19.2. Researchers might then calculate the certainty equivalent CDR as if the growth process really had the hypothesized form, with actual parameters equal to the estimated parameters. An alternative approach treats the function describing growth as known, but recognizes that the parameters are estimates. This alternative provides a model both of changes in growth and changes in our beliefs about growth (i.e., learning; Weitzman 2009).

These alternatives (positively correlated growth, the possibility of catastrophes, models that update parameter estimates) lead (almost always) to further reductions in the certainty equivalent CDR, increasing estimates of the amount that society should spend today to reduce damages in an uncertain future world. The alternatives improve on naive models that assume deterministic growth, but they are still based on the premise that the distant future will look like the recent past; without that premise, growth data would be useless for estimating future growth rates.

These methods of estimating the certainty equivalent CDR consider a single type of uncertainty—often, uncertainty about growth. An extension focuses on the correlation between growth and climate-related damages. Climate policy is an investment, requiring higher costs and reduced consumption due to the use of more expensive energy sources; the payoff of this investment is a reduction in future damages, and a corresponding increase in future consumption. The policy transfers consumption from today to future periods. Because growth is uncertain, we do not know the level of future consumption, absent this transfer. We therefore do not know the marginal value, to people in the future, of an additional unit of consumption. Because of all the uncertainties of climate science, we do not know how current policy would change the magnitude of future climate damages. Therefore, the "return on investment" of current climate policy is a random variable.

An investor deciding how to allocate funds between a "market portfolio" (e.g., an index fund) and a particular stock faces a similar problem. The outline of the CAPM model (section 6.4) notes that a stock negatively correlated with the market return provides a hedge against market risk, and therefore might be worth buying even if its expected return is below the expected market return. If climate policy is likely to yield a large return (reduce future damages by a large amount) in circumstances where the future is relatively poor, then climate policy provides a hedge against future growth uncertainty. In this case, investing in climate policy may be economical even if its expected return is below that of other social investments. In contrast, if climate policy is likely to provide a high return in circumstances where the future is rich, then climate policy should be required to pass a more stringent cost-benefit test compared to other social investments. Currently, there is no consensus about which of these two possibilities is more likely (Traeger 2014; Gollier 2014; Lemoine 2015).

A Different Paradigm

The stochastic extensions of the Ramsey formula described above use discounted expected utility (DEU), adding up the discounted utility in different periods and taking expectations with respect to the random variables. For decades, economists have been aware that important implications of DEU are inconsistent with stock market data. The risk premium equals the difference between the expected return on a risky asset (e.g., a portfolio of stocks) and the return on a riskless asset (e.g., U.S. government bonds). For long periods, this risk premium has exceeded 6% in the United States and has also been high in other countries. Explaining this difference using DEU requires a value of η much larger than consensus estimates. This inconsistency is known as the "equity premium puzzle" (Mehra 2006).[9]

Attempts to resolve this puzzle within the framework of DEU use some of the extensions discussed above. An alternative replaces the DEU model with "recursive utility," which has enough free parameters to be reconciled with market data (Epstein and Zinn 1991). DEU uses a single parameter, η, to represent two characteristics of preferences. In the deterministic framework, η describes intertemporal inequality aversion. In the stochastic framework, η also describes risk aversion. That is, η describes both the decision maker's attitude to transferring consumption across time periods (or people), and also his attitude

---

9 Resolving this puzzle by simply assuming that the actual value of η is much larger than consensus estimates, leads to the "risk-free rate puzzle": the conclusion that the riskless rate is much higher than observed rates.

about transferring consumption over different "states of nature," corresponding to different realizations of a random variable. There is no reason risk aversion and aversion to intertemporal transfers should be governed by the same parameter. The DEU model uses one parameter to represent two different characteristics. Recursive utility disentangles these preference characteristics.

A related objection to DEU can be explained using an example. Consider a trajectory consisting of only two periods, with no impatience regarding utility (a utility discount factor equal to 1). Consumption might be low or high, yielding low or high utility, u^L or u^H, respectively. In one deterministic scenario, an agent obtains first high and then low utility, $\{u^H, u^L\}$, and in a second deterministic scenario, she receives $\{u^L, u^H\}$. Because she is not impatient and faces no uncertainty, the discounted utilitarian assigns the same payoff, $u^H + u^L$, to both scenarios; she is indifferent between them. Consider a third scenario in which the agent faces a lottery. With probability 0.5, she obtains $\{u^H, u^H\}$ and with probability 0.5, she obtains $\{u^L, u^L\}$. This agent faces intertemporal risk: she might have two good periods or two bad periods. Discounted expected utilitarianism evaluates this payoff by taking expectations over the random payoffs, assigning the value $0.5(u^H + u^H + u^L + u^L) = u^H + u^L$ to this lottery.

This example shows that the DEU model implies that the social planner, or the people she represents, are indifferent about intertemporal fluctuations in utility. Models of recursive utility include an additional parameter that measures intertemporal risk aversion. A planner who is intertemporally risk averse prefers the trajectory $\{u^H, u^L\}$ (equivalently, $\{u^L, u^H\}$) to the lottery where she either receives high utility in both periods or low utility in both periods. With empirically plausible levels of intertemporal risk aversion, stochastic growth might have little effect on the CDR even though deterministic growth would lead to a substantially higher (certainty equivalent) social discount rate (Traeger 2014). Taking into account intertemporal risk aversion, and also recognizing that future growth is stochastic, can lead to a certainty equivalent CDR close to the (deterministic) CDR under zero growth. An intertemporally risk-averse planner facing stochastic growth might be willing to spend more today to avoid future damages compared to the same planner facing zero growth (Jensen and Traeger 2014).

19.4 Hyperbolic Discounting

Objectives and skills: Understand the meaning of and rationale for hyperbolic discounting, its relation to time inconsistency, and the relevance to climate policy.

With a constant level of impatience, ρ, we are willing to make the same utility transfer between any two successive generations, regardless of how far in the future. To understand this assumption, consider an analogy unrelated to time. Suppose we have a large family, with many cousins; forget about the other relatives. We care more about nearer relatives, so we can rank our cousins by kinship: first, second, third, and so on. Distance in cousinage here corresponds to temporal distance in the climate setting. Using the constant ρ to measure our preference for near relatives, we are willing to take $e^{-\rho}$ units of utility from our nth cousin to give one unit of utility to our $(n+1)$th cousin, regardless of the value of n.

The objection to this conclusion is that we are likely to know our first and second cousins, and therefore have a genuine preference for the former over the latter. In contrast, our 33rd and 34th cousins are strangers to us. For both comparisons, we prefer the nearer relations, but the distinction between our first and second cousins may be appreciable, whereas the distinction between the 33rd and 34th cousins is negligible. In the temporal setting, we may have an appreciable preference for our own versus the next generation's utility, whereas we can scarcely distinguish between the 33rd and 34th future generations. The assumption of a constant discount rate (for time or for cousins) does not accommodate this difference, but a decreasing discount rate does. "Hyperbolic discounting" replaces the constant ρ with a decreasing function $\rho(t)$.[10] Hyperbolic discounting can be applied to transfers across time for a single individual or generation, and also transfers across different generations. Climate policy involves both kinds of transfers; current actions may be costly to a young person today but benefit him when he is old, and may also benefit future generations. In this section, we abstract from growth, setting $g = 0$.

19.4.1   Transfers Affecting a Single Person or Generation

Hyperbolic discounting provides a model of excessive procrastination: deferring unpleasant tasks longer than we would like. Suppose we are told that a project due on December 11 will take 5 hours to accomplish if done on December 10, and only 4 hours if done on December 9. Because the project requires work (disutility), we prefer to put if off as long as possible; but we also prefer to spend as little time as possible on it, so we face a trade-off. On September 1, we can make a provisional plan to do the project on either December 9 or 10. By delaying for an extra day we increase by 1% the amount of time we can put off the work (101 instead of 100 days), but we increase the amount of time the work will take by 25%. The 25% extra work may seem more important (salient) than the 1% additional delay, leading us to prefer, on September 1, to do the project on December 9.

On December 9, a minute before we are scheduled to begin, we reconsider our earlier plan. By postponing for a day, we have a 1,441 minute delay, instead of the 1 minute delay if we carry out our original plan; the delay still requires a 25% increase in the amount of time needed to work. From the standpoint of December 8, the 144,100% increase in delay might be more salient than the 25% increase in working time, possibly causing us to

---

10   The argument t is the *distance* from the current time. Thus, $t = 40$ at calendar time 2020 for an event at 2060, and also at calendar time 2050 for an event at 2090.

reverse our earlier decision. Hyperbolic discounting can explain why a person changes an earlier plan and procrastinates "excessively."

A particularly simple form of (quasi) hyperbolic discounting represents this situation using two time preference parameters, $0 < \beta \leq 1$ and $0 < \delta < 1$. The utility discount factor for $t \geq 1$ periods in the future is $\beta \delta^t$. A constant utility discount rate corresponds to $\beta = 1$, and hyperbolic discounting corresponds to $\beta < 1$. Suppose that the disutility of working 4 hours is $D(4)$ and the disutility of working 5 hours is $D(5) > D(4)$. On September 1, the present value disutility of doing the project on December 9 is $\beta \delta^{100} D(4)$, and the present value disutility of doing the project on December 10 is $\beta \delta^{101} D(5)$. On September 1, the person prefers to do the project on December 9 if and only if $\beta \delta^{100} D(4) < \beta \delta^{101} D(5)$, that is, if and only if $D(4) < \delta D(5)$. Once December 9 arrives, the choice is between doing the project on that day, having disutility $D(4)$, or procrastinating, and having present value disutility $\beta \delta D(5)$. On December 9, the person procrastinates if and only if $\beta \delta D(5) < D(4)$.

A preference reversal occurs, causing plans to be "time-inconsistent" if a person wants to change an earlier plan, despite having received no additional information since the original plan was made. Combining the two previous inequalities shows that the plan made on September 1 is time inconsistent (there is a preference reversal) if and only if[11]

$$\beta \delta D(5) < D(4) < \delta D(5). \tag{19.3}$$

If there is time inconsistency, the modeler must decide what outcome is reasonable. If the agent has a "commitment device" on September 1 that somehow binds them to completing the project on December 9, the optimal plan (from the September 1 perspective) will be carried out. The person may commit to getting married on December 10, making it prohibitively expensive to procrastinate when December 9 arrives. Commitment devices can be costly. Absent such a device, there is nothing to keep the person from procrastinating, and the reasonable outcome is for the project to be completed December 10. A sophisticated person, one with self-awareness, understands that she will procrastinate, and so does not bother to plan on doing the project on December 9; she knows that she will procrastinate. A naive person, without that self-awareness, may confidently plan on doing the project on December 9, and be surprised when she later decides to procrastinate.

19.4.2 Transfers across Generations

Time inconsistency arises with intergenerational transfers for the same reason as in the single-agent example. We discuss an example and then examine its relevance to climate policy. People currently alive constitute generation 0, their successors are generation 1, and the next group is generation 2. There are two investments opportunities, A and B,

---

11 Sections 10.3 and 11.3 note that time inconsistency can arise for reasons unrelated to discounting, as when a government is tempted to behave opportunistically and confiscate quasi-rent.

Table 19.1
Benefits for different generations

Utility change	$t=0$	$t=1$	$t=2$	Present discount value for generation 0	Present discount value for generation 1
Investment A	**0**	**−0.64**	**1**	0.1638	−0.01
Investment B	**−0.17**	**−0.625**	**1**	0.00325	0.005

Note: Columns 2–4 show flow benefits for different generations; columns 5–6 show the present discount value for generations 0 and 1. $\beta = 0.7, \delta = 0.9$.

having different cost structures, but the same payout, a one unit utility gain to generation 2. Columns 2–4 of table 19.1 show the utility loss or gain to the different generations. Investment *A* requires a technological development and becomes available only in period 1. It has no direct cost to generation 0, and costs 0.64 to generation 1. Investment *B* must be started in period 0 and finished in period 1; generation 0 pays 0.17 to begin the project, and generation 1 pays 0.625 to complete it. If both generations 0 and 1 do nothing, all three generations obtain a zero change in utility.

People have quasi-hyperbolic discounting with $\beta = 0.7$ and $\delta = 0.9$, so $\beta\delta = 0.63$. Columns 5 and 6 show the net PDV of the two investments, from the perspectives of generations 0 and 1. Generation 1 ignores sunk costs incurred by generation 0. Generation 0 prefers investment *A* to *B* but would accept either (0.1638 > 0.00325 > 0). Generation 1 would complete investment *B* but would not undertake investment *A* (0.005 > 0 > −0.01).

If generation 0 can costlessly compel generation 1 to carry out investment *A*, it chooses that option. It is not easy for a generation to tie its successors' hands.[12] (Ask your parents.) Absent a commitment device, the sophisticated generation 0 knows that generation 1 would not undertake investment *A*, but would complete investment *B*. ("Sophisticated" means "understands successors' incentives.") Generation 0 has the choice of doing nothing, obtaining a zero payoff, or beginning investment *B*, obtaining 0.005. In equilibrium, generation 0 begins investment *B*, and generation 1 completes it

This example illustrates the considerations that determine the equilibrium under hyperbolic versus constant discounting. In both cases, there are three possible actions: (i) do not invest, (ii) begin investment *B* in period 0 and complete it in period 1, and (iii) undertake investment *A* in period 1. With a constant discount factor $\hat{\delta}$, the solution is to undertake investment *A* in period 1 if $\hat{\delta} \geq 0.64$ and to do nothing if the inequality is reversed. To determine the equilibrium under hyperbolic discounting, we have to imagine generation 0 putting itself in generation 1's shoes, anticipating how generation 1 would respond to

12 Generation 0 would be willing to spend up to $0.1638 - 0.00325 = 0.16055$ units of utility be able to commit its successor to undertaking investment *A*. If generation 0 could somehow pay generation 1 slightly more than 0.01 units of utility, conditional on generation 1 undertaking investment *A*, that would induce generation 1 follow generation 0's wishes. Making a transfer from the current to a future generation contingent on something that the future generation does, presents the same difficulty as do other types of commitment devices.

generation 0's decision. The situation under hyperbolic discounting is an "intergenerational game," not a standard optimization problem.

Lessons for Climate Change Policy

Protecting the future from climate damage requires investment in low-carbon alternative energy supplies. From the standpoint of the current generation, the best policy might be to do nothing, waiting for improved technology that makes future investment cheaper, and trusting the next generation to undertake the entire cost of creating the low-carbon alternative. If the subsequent generation prefers to do nothing, when it has to bear the full investment cost, the current generation might be better off making an expensive down payment on the low-carbon technologies, knowing that the future generation would complete the investment needed to protect against climate damage.

19.4.3   Individual versus Generational Discounting

Climate policy creates transfers both within and across generations. A switch to low-carbon fuels that decreases the (current) utility of those currently alive may benefit some of these people late in their lives, and may also benefit people who have not yet been born. The first is a transfer from a person at one point to another point in his life. The second is an intergenerational transfer. People might discount their own future utility at a constant rate and also discount the utility of future generations at a constant rate. However, there is no reason to think that they would use the same constant rate to discount their own and future generations' utility. Agents might discount these distinct types of transfers at different rates.

  The distinction between individual and intergenerational transfers requires an "overlapping generations model," one that recognizes that at any point in time, some people are old and some are young; over time, the old die, the young become old, and new youngsters are born. If people use a lower discount rate to evaluate intergenerational transfers compared to individual transfers, their preferences exhibit hyperbolic discounting (Ekeland and Lazrak 2010).[13] A person might be impatient for her own future utility but egalitarian toward future generations.

19.4.4   The Policy Relevance of Hyperbolic Discounting

Economists disagree about the policy relevance of hyperbolic discounting. One view is that for such intergenerational problems as climate change, no utility discounting is ethical. If we require $\rho = 0$, there is no reason to be interested in the possibility that ρ decreases over time.[14] Our discussion of transfers both within and across generations identifies a problem

---

13 In the simplest overlapping generations model, the population is constant and people live for two periods. This model gives rise to the β, δ quasi-hyperbolic discounting discussed above.

14 Alternatively, instead of insisting that $\rho = 0$, we might set it at a very small value to account for the possibility that our species will suddenly become extinct (e.g., by a comet striking the earth).

with this view. One might agree that intergenerational transfers be discounted at rate 0, but recognize that people appear to be impatient for, and therefore discount, their own future utility. Why should social policy not take those preferences into account? Allowing the intergenerational discount rate to be lower than the individual rate results in hyperbolic discounting.

Setting ρ to a constant close to 0 overcomes the tyranny of discounting, but it also implies (in DEU models) that current generations should be willing to save human-made capital at rates far in excess of those actually observed. Hyperbolic discounting makes it possible to construct models that avoid the tyranny of discounting while still matching observed investment rates. Climate applications of hyperbolic discounting include Karp (2005), Gerlagh and Liski (2012), and Iverson (2015).

19.5   Summary

Climate policy (like natural resource policy in general) is a type of public investment, incurring costs with the expectation of future benefits. Economists base climate policy models on consensus views from climate science. Recognizing that resource policy involves trade-offs, most of these models involve discounting. Discounting renders costs and benefits in different periods and for different projects comparable, making it possible to evaluate policies and to recommend tax or other policy levels.

Economic models produce a range of estimates of the SCC. Some environmental activists view the lower estimates as inconsistent with the severity of the problem of climate change. Discounting is an important component of economic climate models, affecting the level of policy prescriptions. A higher discount rate (= lower discount factor) places less weight on the future, leading to lower tax recommendations. Consumption discount rates (CDRs) depend on levels of impatience and growth optimism.

If the economy grows during the next several centuries at rates seen during the past two centuries, people in the future will be much richer than we are and will be able to tolerate the reduced consumption caused by noncatastrophic climate change. If we accept that the poor should not sacrifice to benefit the rich, and if indeed future generations will be richer than current generations, and furthermore we are confident that climate damage will be noncatastrophic, then society today should make no more than modest investments to protect the climate.

However, we do not know whether growth will continue to be high during the next centuries, or if climate change will be noncatastrophic. The effect of growth uncertainty on the certainty equivalent CDR is sensitive to model specification. If we think of future growth as a sequence of serially uncorrelated random shocks (so that growth in one period does not affect growth in another), recognition of uncertainty leads to a small decrease in the certainty equivalent CDR and a correspondingly small increase in the optimal level of environmental policy. Positive serial correlation of future growth increases the variance of future income. Variable income is "less valuable" than certain income, so positively correlated growth leads to a larger reduction in the CDR and a larger increase in recommended policy.

The recognition that not only economic growth but also climate change are uncertain further complicates matters. If a lower carbon stock is particularly valuable to future generations when growth has been relatively low, then growth and the return on the investment in climate policy are negatively correlated. In that case, climate policy provides a hedge against stochastic growth, making it easier to justify strict climate policy. If, however, a lower carbon stock is particularly valuable when future generations are rich, the case for climate policy is weaker.

The standard paradigm uses a single parameter to measure a person's attitude to random income and to changes in income over time. A generalization disentangles these two characteristics, leading to a different calibration and, in some cases, to significant differences in policy prescriptions. This generalization also incorporates a particular type of intertemporal risk aversion, which the standard paradigm of discounted expected utility assumes is 0.

The standard paradigm also treats the parameter that measures impatience with respect to future utility as a constant. A declining rate of impatience can explain excessive procrastination. More important for environmental policy, a declining rate also can distinguish between transfers that a person makes to herself in the future and to future generations. Climate policy involves both types of transfers. If people discount the second type of transfer at a lower rate than the first type, they have hyperbolic discounting. This situation often creates time inconsistency, and requires solving a game instead of an optimization problem to assess environmental policy. A declining rate of impatience can reconcile observed savings rates with strong protection for the climate.

19.6 Terms and Concepts, Study Questions, Exercises, and Sources

Terms and Concepts
Positive and normative statements; social cost of carbon (SCC), Discounted expected utilitarianism, utility discount rate and factor, consumption discount rate (CDR) and consumption discount factor, tyranny of discounting, hazard rate, Ramsey formula, elasticity of intertemporal substitution, inequality aversion, consumption growth rate, certainty equivalent discount rate, recursive utility, intertemporal risk aversion, equity premium puzzle, (quasi) hyperbolic discounting, intra- and intergenerational transfers, time inconsistency, overlapping generations.

Study Questions
1. Explain the difference between discounting utility and discounting consumption.
2. Explain what it means to say that discounting is "tyrannical."

3. Explain the sense in which climate policy provides a kind of insurance.

4. Given the Ramsey formula for the consumption discount rate, explain the meaning of each term.

5. Explain why near-term growth is particularly important in evaluating a public investment project that has a payoff in the near term, whereas growth over long periods of time are important in evaluating a public investment project that has a payoff in the distant future.

6. Give an example in which an individual may have time-inconsistent preferences.

7. Discuss hyperbolic discounting in the context of climate policy.

Exercises

1. For the example at the beginning of section 19.3.3 (where income in two periods is either 0 or 1), calculate the variance of the payoff in the two cases, first where the two income levels are uncorrelated, and second where they are perfectly correlated.

2. Using the utility flows shown in table 19.1 and the values $\beta = 0.7$ and $\delta = 0.9$, confirm the values shown in the last two columns of the table. (Calculate the net present values of the two investments, from the perspectives of generations 0 and 1.)

Sources

Llavador, Roemer, and Silvestre (2015) criticize the discounted utilitarianism model, particularly as applied to climate change policy; they suggest a sustainability-based alternative.

The examples in section 19.2 are taken from Karp (2016).

Nordhaus (2008) (and in many other publications) has developed the field of integrated assessment models for climate change.

Anthoff and Tol (2010) use an integrated assessment model to examine the effect of international equity weights in climate policy.

Lemoine and Traeger (2014) and Lontzek et al. (2015) use stochastic integrated assessment models to study abrupt and irreversible changes.

Arrow et al. (2012) examine discounting in an intergenerational context.

Traeger (2014), Gollier (2014), and Lemoine (2015) analyze models that incorporate correlation between the market return and the return to protecting the climate.

Gillingham et al. (2015) provide a survey of growth experts' assessment of future growth.

Gordon (2015) provides a comprehensive history of U.S. growth and explains why he expects that high growth rates during the past century will not continue into the future.

Mehra (2003) discusses the equity premium puzzle and reviews some of the explanations offered for it.

Epstein and Zinn (1991) provide an early empirical application of recursive utility.

Traeger (2014) explains the theory of intertemporal risk aversion and shows how it alters the relation between stochastic growth and the consumption discount rate.

Barro (2006) models the effect of rare catastrophic events on discount rates.

Weitzman (2009) uses Bayesian learning about growth to construct a parable about catastrophic changes.

Laibson (1997) discusses the role of quasi-hyperbolic discounting in a model of savings.

Angelotos et al. (2001) explain hyperbolic discounting and survey the literature.

Karp (2005) applies hyperbolic discounting to climate policy in partial equilibrium settings.

Ekeland and Lazrak (2010) note the relation between overlapping generations and hyperbolic discounting.

Gerlagh and Liski (2012) and Iverson (2015) apply hyperbolic discounting to climate policy in a general equilibrium setting.

Appendix A: Math Review

This appendix reviews concepts from calculus. It serves as a reference, and also gives prospective readers an idea of the level of mathematics used in the book. The text assumes that readers have seen much this material before.

A.1 Derivatives and Graphs

The derivative of a function, $f(x)$ at a point x_0, written $\frac{df(x_0)}{dx}$, is the tangent ("slope") of a function, evaluated at a particular point, here x_0. If $f(x) = a + bx$, where a and b are independent of x (and therefore constants for our purposes here), then $\frac{df}{dx} = b$, a constant.

More generally, however, the value of the derivative depends on x. Figure A.1 shows the graph of $f(x) = 2 + 3x - 4x^2 - 5x^3$ (the solid curve), the graph of $g(x) = \frac{df(x)}{dx}$ (the dashed curve), and the graph of $h(x) = \frac{dg(x)}{dx} = \frac{d^2 f(x)}{dx^2}$ (the dotted curve). This figure illustrates: (i) A derivative is a function, not (in general) a constant. (ii) Where a differentiable function reaches an extreme point (a maximum or a minimum), the derivative of that function equals 0. (iii) At an inflexion point, where the graph switches from being concave to convex, the second derivative of the function equals 0.

Subscripts indicate that a function is evaluated at a particular point, say, $x = 2$. In the next equations, the subscript "$|x = 2$" indicates that we evaluate the function f and its derivative at $x = 2$:

$$f(x)_{|x=2} = 2 + 3(2) - 4(2)^2 - 5(2)^3,$$

$$\frac{df(x)}{dx}_{\;|x=2} = 3 - 8(2) - 15(2)^2.$$

An extreme point is a local maximum if the function is concave at the extreme point (the second derivative is negative at that point). The extreme point is a local minimum

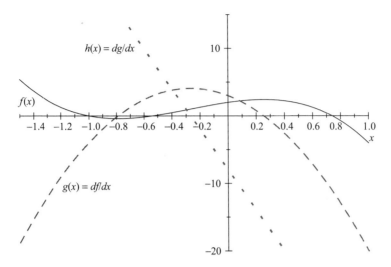

Figure A.1
The solid curve shows the graph of $f(x)$, the dashed curve shows the graph of $g(x) = \frac{df}{dx}$, and the dotted curve shows the graph of $h(x) = \frac{dg}{dx} = \frac{d^2f}{dx^2}$.

if the function is convex at the extreme point (the second derivative is positive at that point).

x_0 is a local maximum: $\quad \overbrace{V'(x_0) = 0}^{x_0 \text{ is an extreme point}}$, and $\quad \overbrace{V''(x_0) < 0}^{V \text{ is concave at } x_0}$;

x_0 is a local minimum: $\quad \overbrace{V'(x_0) = 0}^{x_0 \text{ is an extreme point}}$ and $\quad \overbrace{V''(x_0) > 0}^{V \text{ is convex at } x_0}$.

It is worth repeating that (in general), $\frac{df(x)}{dx}$ is itself a function of x; above we called this function $g(x)$. Similarly, $\frac{d^2 f(x)}{dx^2}$ is a function of x; above we call it $h(x)$. The "prime sign," $'$ provides another way to denote a derivative:

$$\frac{df(x)}{dx} \equiv f'(x).$$

A.2 Derivatives of Exponents

The following rule is important: if a is a constant (with respect to x), then

$$\frac{d(x^a)}{dx} = ax^{a-1}.$$

We write that "a is a constant with respect to x," instead of merely writing "a is a constant," because the formula above is correct even if a is a function of variables other than x. In taking this derivative, it does not matter whether a is a literally a constant or merely a constant with respect to x. What matters is that a change in x does not change a.

A.3 The Sum, Product, and Quotient Rules

We frequently use several other rules for derivatives. Suppose we have two functions of x, $a(x)$ and $b(x)$. (Previously, we treated a as a constant. Here we treat it as a function. In general, we should be careful *not* to use the same symbol to mean two different things. Here, I intentionally use the same symbol, a, to mean two different things, first a constant and then a function. I want to encourage you to pay attention to definitions!) We can form other functions using these two functions.

If c is the *sum of these two functions*, then

$$c(x) = a(x) + b(x), \quad \text{and} \quad \frac{dc}{dx} = \frac{da}{dx} + \frac{db}{dx}.$$

The derivative of a sum equals the sum of a derivative. For brevity we write, for example, $\frac{da}{dx}$ instead of $\frac{da(x)}{dx}$.

If c is the *product of the two functions*, then

$$c(x) = a(x) \times b(x), \quad \text{and} \quad \frac{dc}{dx} = \frac{da}{dx}b + \frac{db}{dx}a.$$

If c is the *quotient of two functions*, then

$$c(x) = \frac{a(x)}{b(x)}, \quad \text{and} \quad \frac{dc}{dx} = \frac{b\frac{da}{dx} - a\frac{db}{dx}}{b^2}.$$

A.4 The Chain Rule

The chain rule enables us to take the derivative of a function of a function. Suppose that y is a function of x, and x is a function of z. Then y is a function of z, via the effect of z on x. The chain rule states

$$\frac{dy}{dz} = \frac{dy(x(z))}{dx}\frac{dx(z)}{dz}.$$

For example, if $y = x^{0.3}$, and $x = 7z$, then $\frac{dy(x)}{dx} = 0.3x^{0.3-1}$, and $\frac{dx}{dz} = 7$, so

$$\frac{dy}{dz} = \frac{dy(x(z))}{dx}\frac{dx(z)}{dz} = 0.3x^{0.3-1} \times 7 = 2.1(7z)^{-0.7}.$$

A.5   Partial Derivatives

Some of our functions involve two arguments instead of one. Throughout the book, we use a cost function that depends on the stock of the resource, x, and the amount that is extracted in a period, y. We write this cost function as $c(x, y)$. A partial derivative tells us how the value of the function (here, costs) changes if we change just one of the variables, either x or y. We use the symbol ∂ instead of d to indicate that we are interested in the partial derivative.

We frequently illustrate concepts using the following cost function:

Parametric example: $c(x, y) = C (\sigma + x)^{-\alpha} y^{1+\beta}$,

where C, α, σ, and β are non-negative parameters. (Note that lower case c is a function, and upper case C is a parameter. It is important to pay attention to definitions.) The partial derivatives of this function with respect to x and y are

$$\frac{\partial C(x+\sigma)^{-\alpha}y^{1+\beta}}{\partial x} = -\alpha C(x+\sigma)^{-\alpha-1}y^{1+\beta}, \quad \text{and}$$

$$\frac{\partial C(x+\sigma)^{-\alpha}y^{1+\beta}}{\partial y} = (1+\beta)C(x+\sigma)^{-\alpha}y^{\beta}.$$

The first partial derivative shows the change in costs due to a change in stock. The second shows "marginal cost," defined as the change in cost due to a change in extraction. In taking the partial of c with respect to x, for example, we recognize that $Cy^{1+\beta}$ does not depend on x; thus in evaluating this partial derivative, we treat $Cy^{1+\beta}$ as a constant. Although not literally a constant, this term is constant with respect to x. In English: $Cy^{1+\beta}$ does not depend on x, so changes in x do not affect this term.

The two partial derivatives of c with respect to x and y are themselves functions of x and y. Thus, we can differentiate either of these functions, with respect to either x or y, to obtain a higher order partial derivative. For example, the "second partial derivative,"

$$\frac{\partial^2 C(x+\sigma)^{-\alpha}y^{1+\beta}}{\partial y^2} = \frac{\partial\left[\frac{\partial C(x+\sigma)^{-\alpha}y^{1+\beta}}{\partial y}\right]}{\partial y} = \frac{\partial\left[(1+\beta)C(x+\sigma)^{-\alpha}y^{\beta}\right]}{\partial y}$$

$$= (1+\beta)\beta C(x+\sigma)^{-\alpha}y^{\beta-1},$$

equals the slope of the marginal cost. The "cross partial derivative,"

$$\frac{\partial^2 C(x+\sigma)^{-\alpha}y^{1+\beta}}{\partial y \partial x} = \frac{\partial\left[\frac{\partial C(x+\sigma)^{-\alpha}y^{1+\beta}}{\partial y}\right]}{\partial x} = \frac{\partial\left[(1+\beta)C(x+\sigma)^{-\alpha}y^{\beta}\right]}{\partial x}$$

$$= (1+\beta)(-\alpha)C(x+\sigma)^{-\alpha-1}y^{\beta},$$

equals the change in the marginal cost due to a change in the stock.

A.6   Total Derivatives

A function may depend on two variables, and each of those variables might depend on a third variable. The "total derivative" tells us how much the function changes for a change in this third argument. For example, suppose that costs depend on x and y, as above, and x and y both depend on ε. We show this dependence by writing $x(\varepsilon)$ and $y(\varepsilon)$. With this notation, we write costs as $c(x(\varepsilon), y(\varepsilon))$. The total derivative of c with respect to ε is

$$\frac{dc\,(x\,(\varepsilon)\,,\,y\,(\varepsilon))}{d\varepsilon} = \frac{\partial c}{\partial x}\frac{dx}{d\varepsilon} + \frac{\partial c}{\partial y}\frac{dy}{d\varepsilon}. \tag{A.1}$$

In writing this equation, we merely apply the chain rule twice: the first term accounts for the fact that a change in ε alters c via the change in x, and the second term accounts for the fact that a change in ε alters c via the change in y. The total change in c due a change in ε is the sum of these two terms.

This expression might seem complicated, but most of the applications in this book are extremely simple. We will be interested in the case where $x = x_1 - \varepsilon$ and $y = y_1 - \varepsilon$, where x_1 and y_1 are treated as constants for the purpose here. For these two functions, we have

$$\frac{dx}{d\varepsilon} = -1, \quad \text{and} \quad \frac{dy}{d\varepsilon} = -1. \tag{A.2}$$

Substituting equation A.2 into equation A.1 gives the total derivative:

$$\frac{dc\,(x\,(\varepsilon)\,,\,y\,(\varepsilon))}{d\varepsilon} = -\frac{\partial c\,(x_1 - \varepsilon,\, y_1 - \varepsilon)}{\partial x} - \frac{\partial c\,(x_1 - \varepsilon,\, y_1 - \varepsilon)}{\partial y}.$$

We often want to evaluate this derivative at $\varepsilon = 0$. In this case, we write

$$\frac{dc\,(x\,(\varepsilon)\,,\,y\,(\varepsilon))}{d\varepsilon}\bigg|_{\varepsilon=0} = -\frac{\partial c\,(x_1,\, y_1)}{\partial x} - \frac{\partial c\,(x_1,\, y_1)}{\partial y}.$$

Remember that the subscript "$|\varepsilon = 0$" on the left side of this equation means that we evaluate the derivative of c with respect to ε where $\varepsilon = 0$.

A.7   Constrained Optimization

Suppose that the problem is to maximize $V(z)$ ("value") subject to $0 \leq z \leq 4$. Assume that V is concave ($V''(z) < 0$), so that an interior extreme point is a maximum. We might have either an interior equilibrium (a solution where $0 < z < 4$) or a boundary equilibrium (where $z = 0$ or $z = 4$). The function V represented by curve B in figure A.2 has an "interior" optimum (the optimal z is between the two boundaries, 0 and 4). At this interior

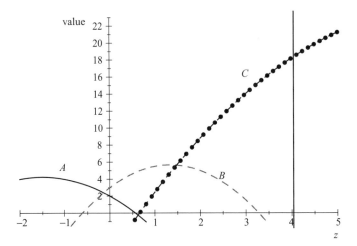

Figure A.2
The curve *B* has an interior maximum. The curves *A* and *C* have boundary maxima.

optimum, $\frac{dV}{dz} = 0$: a marginal increase or decrease in z does not change $V(z)$. The function V represented by both curves A and C have "boundary" optima: $z = 0$ for A, where $\frac{dV}{dz} < 0$, and $z = 4$ for C, where $\frac{dV}{dz} > 0$. For A, a decrease in z at $z = 0$ increases V and for C, an increase in z at $z = 4$ increases V, but either of these changes violates a constraint and thus is not feasible.

A.8 First and Second Order Effects

Figure A.3 illustrates the meaning of "first order" and "second order" effects. The figure shows a graph (the solid curve), and tangents (dashed lines) at two points, the maximum point *A* and an arbitrary point *B*. The first derivative of the function at $x = 2.5$ (the horizontal coordinate of *A*) is zero, and the second derivative is nonzero (negative). A "very small" (or infinitesimal) movement away from $x = 2.5$ results in negligible change in the value of y: the first order effect, on y, of the change in x is zero, and the second order effect is negative. In contrast, a very small movement away from $x = 5$ (the horizontal coordinate of point *B*) results in a non-negligible ("first order") change in y, because the derivative of the function at $x = 5$ is nonzero.

A.9 First Order Approximations

We can use the value of a function and its derivative at a point to approximate the value of the function at a neighboring point. For example, if the value of a stock is

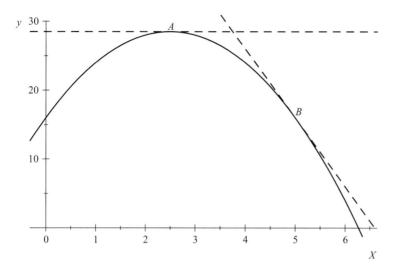

Figure A.3
A change in x away from point A has only a second order effect on y. A change in x away from point B has a first order effect on y.

$W(x) = ax - \frac{b}{2}x^2$, the amount a person who owns x_0 units would pay for an extra unit is approximately $W'(x_0) = a - bx_0$. The increase in value in moving from x to $x + \Delta$ units is $W(x + \Delta) - W(x)$, which can be approximated as $W'(x)\Delta$. The difference between the actual change and the approximation of this change is the approximation error. For this example, the approximation error is

$$\overbrace{a(x+\Delta) - \frac{b}{2}(x+\Delta)^2 - \left(ax - \frac{b}{2}x^2\right)}^{\text{exact change in value}} - \overbrace{(a-bx)\Delta}^{\text{approximate change in value}} = -\frac{1}{2}b\Delta^2.$$

The absolute value of the approximation error increases and is convex in Δ. The approximate is good for small values of Δ but not for large values.

Exercises

1. For the function $f(x) = -2x + x^{0.4}$, graph $f(x)$, $f'(x)$, and $f''(x)$. (A sketch is adequate—it does not have to be precise.)

2. Find the condition (an equation) for an extreme point of f defined in exercise 1. Is this extreme point a maximum or a minimum? (How do you know?)

3. Consider the function $g(x, y) = x^2 y^{0.2} - 3y$,

   (a) Write the partial derivatives of g with respect to x and y.

(b) Evaluate these derivatives at $x = 3$, $y = 1$.

4. Suppose that you are told $x = t^2$ and $y = 7t$.

   (a) Write the total derivative with respect to t of $h(t) = g(x(t), y(t))$, where $g(x, y) = x^2 y^{0.2} - 3y$.

   (b) Evaluate this derivative at $t = 1$.

5. Evaluate

$$\frac{d\left(\frac{4z^2 + 3z}{7z^{0.5}}\right)}{dz}\bigg|_{z=1}.$$

6. Evaluate

$$\frac{d\left((4z^2 + 3z)(7z^{0.5})\right)}{dz}\bigg|_{z=1}.$$

7. For $c(x, y) = C(\sigma + x)^{-\alpha} y^{1+\beta}$ with $\beta = 1$, $\alpha = 2$, and $\sigma = 0$, write the expressions for the marginal cost, the derivative of marginal cost with respect to y, and the derivative of marginal cost with respect to x.

8. Suppose that demand is $D = 10 - 2P$, where P is price.

   (a) Evaluate the elasticity of demand at $P = 2$.

   (b) Evaluate the elasticity of demand at $P = 3$.

   (c) Write the marginal revenue, evaluated at these two prices.

9. Suppose that demand is $D = 10P^{-1.2}$.

   (a) Evaluate the elasticity of demand at $P = 2$.

   (b) Evaluate the elasticity of demand at $P = 3$.

   (c) Write marginal revenue, evaluated at these two prices.

10. For the constrained maximization problem,

$$\max_{x,y} \quad 4xy - 3x^2 - y^2,$$

$$\text{subject to} \quad x + 4y = 17,$$

Use the constraint to solve for x as a function of y. Substituting this result into the maximand (the object you are maximizing) write the first order condition for the optimal y.

Appendix B: The Hotelling Model

This appendix provides details on the derivation of the Hotelling rule (Euler equation). An example shows how to use that equation, together with the transversality condition, to complete the solution.

B.1   Derivation of the Hotelling Equation

By definition, T is the last period during which extraction is positive, so extraction at $T+1$ is 0. In the class of problems we consider, extraction is also positive at earlier times: $y_t > 0$ for all $t < T$. This fact means that we can make small changes (perturbations) in any of the y_ts, and offsetting changes in other y_ts, without violating the non-negativity constraints on extraction or on the stocks. A perturbation is "admissible" if it does not violate these constraints.

A "candidate" is a series of extraction and stock levels that satisfy the non-negativity constraints. At the optimum, any admissible perturbation of the candidate yields zero first order change in the payoff. In the two-period setting, only "one-step" perturbations, in which we make a small change in period-0 extraction and an offsetting change in period-1 extraction, are possible. In a multiperiod setting, in contrast, many types of perturbations are possible. For example, we can reduce extraction by ε in period t, make no change in period $t+1$, and increase extraction by $\varepsilon/3$ in each of the subsequent three periods. To test the optimality of a particular candidate, we have to be sure that no admissible perturbation, however complicated, creates a first order change in the payoff. With many possible perturbations, that sounds like a difficult job. However, the task turns out to be simple, because any admissible perturbation, no matter how complicated, can be broken down to a series of "one-step" perturbations.

Therefore, we can check whether a candidate is optimal by considering only the one-step perturbations affecting pairs of adjacent periods. Let t be any period less than T, so that extraction is positive in periods t and $t+1$. Because we are considering one-step perturbations that affect only these two periods, we only have to check that the perturbation has zero first order effect on the combined payoffs during these two periods. Under the perturbation, the combined payoff in these two periods is

$$g\left(\varepsilon; y_t, x_t, y_{t+1}\right) = \rho^t[(p_t\left(y_t + \varepsilon\right) - c\left(x_t, y_t + \varepsilon\right))$$
$$+ \rho\left(p_{t+1}\left(y_{t+1} - \varepsilon\right) - c\left(x_{t+1} - \varepsilon, y_{t+1} - \varepsilon\right)\right)]. \tag{B.1}$$

This gain function and the gain function from the two-period problem (equation 4.7) are the same, except for the time subscripts (and the fact that ρ^t multiplies the right side of equation B.1). In the two-period setting, we noted that an optimal candidate has to satisfy the first order condition 4.8. The necessary condition in the T-period setting is exactly the same, except for the time subscripts:

$$\frac{dg(\varepsilon; y_t, x_{t+1}, y_{t+1})}{d\varepsilon}\bigg|_{\varepsilon=0} = 0.$$

Evaluating this derivative (repeating the steps used to evaluate equation 4.8) produces the Euler equation 5.2.

B.2   Completing the Solution

If the owner is allowed to decide when to stop extracting, T is unconstrained. In this case, we have to solve for the optimal T along with the optimal trajectory of sales. An owner who is not able to extract beyond $\overline{T}$ (e.g., because a lease expires), where $\overline{T}$ is an exogenous parameter, faces the constraint $T \leq \overline{T}$. To explain the ideas as simply as possible, we restrict attention to the case of competitive sellers with constant marginal extraction costs, C, facing the linear inverse demand function, $p = a - by$, with $a > C$.

T Is Unconstrained
Because sales are positive at T, the price does not exceed the choke price:

$$p_T \leq a. \tag{B.2}$$

We use the weak inequality here to accommodate the limiting case where extraction in period T approaches 0, so the final price approaches the choke price. In the discrete time setting, extraction in T is strictly positive, so the inequality is strict.

For times $t < T$, where extraction is positive at both time t and at $t + 1$, it is possible to increase or decrease time t extraction and make an offsetting change in the subsequent period $(t + 1)$. In contrast, at time T, current extraction is positive, and extraction in the next period is 0: $y_T > 0 = y_{T+1}$. It is possible to decrease y_T and make an offsetting increase in y_{T+1}, but (because negative extraction and a negative stock are infeasible) it is not possible to increase in y_T. Therefore, to test optimality of the candidate at time T, we consider only perturbations that decrease y_T.

Under the candidate trajectory, sales in period $T+1$ are 0, and the price in that period is $p_{T+1} = a - b \times 0 = a$. A feasible perturbation reduces period T extraction, reducing profits in period T by $p_T - C$. By selling the marginal unit in period $T+1$, the present value of profits increases by $\rho(p_{T+1} - C) = \rho(a - C)$. If the candidate is optimal, the loss from this perturbation exceeds the gain, so optimality requires:

$$[p_T - C] \geq \rho[a - C] \quad \Rightarrow \quad p_T \geq \rho[a - C] + C. \tag{B.3}$$

The second inequality in B.3 merely rearranges the first. Inequality B.3, known as a "transversality condition," is a necessary condition for T to be the optimal date to exhaust the mine.

Using equation 5.6 and the definition of rent, we also have

$$p_0 - C = \rho^t(p_t - C) \quad \Rightarrow \quad p_t = (1+r)^t(p_0 - C) + C. \tag{B.4}$$

We obtain the second equality by multiplying the first through by $\rho^{-t} = (1+r)^t$ and simplifying. Our goal is to determine p_0. Once we know the value of p_0, the second part of equation B.4 gives us the value of p_t. With this price, the demand function, $y_t = \frac{a - p_t}{b}$, gives us period-t extraction.

Setting $t = T$ in the second part of equation B.4 gives

$$p_T = (1+r)^T(p_0 - C) + C. \tag{B.5}$$

Substituting this expression in the second equality in equation B.3 gives

$$(1+r)^T(p_0 - C) + C \geq \rho[a - C] + C \quad \Rightarrow \quad T \geq -\frac{\ln\left(\rho\frac{a-C}{p_0-C}\right)}{\ln\rho}. \tag{B.6}$$

We obtain the second inequality by canceling C from both sides of the first inequality, taking logs of both sides of the resulting equation, and then simplifying, using the definition of ρ and the properties of logs. In the discrete time setting, sales are strictly positive in period T, so $a > p_T$, or $a - C > p_T - C$. This inequality and equation B.5 imply that

$$a - C > (1+r)^T(p_0 - C) + C - C \quad \Rightarrow \quad -\frac{\ln\left(\frac{a-C}{p_0-C}\right)}{\ln\rho} > T. \tag{B.7}$$

The second inequality uses the same manipulations used to obtain the final inequality in B.6.

Combining the two final inequalities in B.6 and B.7, we have

$$-\frac{\ln\left(\frac{a-C}{p_0-C}\right)}{\ln\rho} > T \geq -\frac{\ln\left(\rho\frac{a-C}{p_0-C}\right)}{\ln\rho}. \tag{B.8}$$

The difference between the left and the right sides of inequality B.8 is

$$
-\frac{\ln\left(\frac{a-C}{p_0-C}\right)}{\ln\rho} + \frac{\ln\left(\rho\,\frac{a-C}{p_0-C}\right)}{\ln\rho}
$$

$$
= \frac{-\ln(a-C) + \ln(p_0-C) + \ln\rho + \ln(a-C) - \ln(p_0-C)}{\ln\rho} = 1.
$$

Therefore, apart from a knife-edge case, there is a unique integer that satisfies inequalities B.8; that integer is a function of p_0, denoted by $T(p_0)$.

The demand function, $y_t = \frac{a-p_t}{b}$, and the last part of equation B.4 imply that

$$
y_t = \frac{a - \left((1+r)^t(p_0-C)+C\right)}{b}.
$$

Inserting this equation into the stock constraint, which states that the sum of extraction equals the initial stock, gives

$$
\sum_{t=0}^{T(p_0)} y_t = \sum_{t=0}^{T(p_0)} \frac{a - \left((1+r)^t\,(p_0-C)+C\right)}{b} = x_0. \tag{B.9}
$$

Equation B.9 gives p_0 as an implicit function of model parameters, which we can solve using numerical methods. One algorithm uses an initial guess of p_0 to find the integer $T(p_0)$ that satisfies inequalities B.8; using that integer, we evaluate the left side of equation B.9. If this calculation returns a value greater than x_0, we increase our guess of p_0, thereby reducing extraction and lowering the left side of equation B.9; if our guess leads to a value of the left side of equation B.9 less than x_0, we reduce the guess. Proceeding in this way, we improve the guess until the left side is sufficiently close to x_0, giving an approximate solution. We use the approximation of p_0 to calculate p and y in every period.

T **Is Constrained**

Here we consider the case where the owner is not able to extract beyond an exogenous upper limit, $\overline{T}$: we have the constraint $T \leq \overline{T}$. Denote the unconstrained value of T obtained in the previous subsection as T^{endog} (endogenous T). If $T^{\text{endog}} \leq \overline{T}$, then the constraint is not binding, and the solution is as above. If, however, $T^{\text{endog}} > \overline{T}$, then the constraint is binding; in this case, the owner continues extracting until $\overline{T}$.

Now we need to consider two possibilities: the stock constraint is binding or it is not binding. In the first possibility, the firm exhausts the stock and in the second, some of the stock is left in the ground. We begin by assuming that the stock constraint is binding and then check whether that assumption is correct.

To carry out this plan, we find p_0 by solving equation B.9, except that now instead of having the function $T(p_0)$ as the upper limit of the sum, we have the exogenous $\overline{T}$. If the solution to this equation is a value p_0 greater than or equal to the extraction cost, C, we have the correct equilibrium: the assumption that the firm exhausts the stock is correct. If, however, the solution is an initial price less than C, we conclude that exhaustion of the resource is not an equilibrium: $\overline{T}$ is so small relative to the initial stock that exhaustion does not occur. In this case, the equilibrium price is C in every period, and rent is 0 in every period. (Here, exhausting the stock would require the firm to earn negative profits in some periods.)

Relation between Continuous and Discrete Time Models

Suppose that a unit of time equals 1 year, and that the discount rate under annual compounding is r, so the present value of a dollar 1 year from now is $\rho = \frac{1}{1+r}$. The starred subsection of section 2.6 notes that we can write this present value as $e^{-\tilde{r}}$, where $\tilde{r}$ equals the discount rate under continuous compounding. This definition implies that $e^{-\tilde{r}} = \frac{1}{1+r}$, or $\tilde{r} = \ln(1+r)$.

In considering the relation between a discrete and a continuous time model, we hold the annual discount rate, r, fixed, and merely change the length of a period (e.g., from a year to a month to a day). Because r is fixed, so is $\tilde{r} = \ln(1+r)$. The present value of a dollar 1 year from now is $e^{-\tilde{r}}$, so the present value of a dollar 1 month from now is $\exp\left(-\tilde{r}\frac{1}{12}\right)$, and the present value of a dollar 1 day from now is $\exp\left(-\tilde{r}\frac{1}{365}\right)$; the present value of a dollar ε years from now is $\rho(\varepsilon) = \exp\left(-\tilde{r}\varepsilon\right)$. With this notation, we can use the second part of inequality B.3 to write the transversality condition for the model in which each period lasts for ε years as

$$p_T \geq \rho(\varepsilon)[a - C] + C. \tag{B.10}$$

For $\varepsilon = 1$, inequality B.10 reproduces inequality B.3. As ε gets smaller, the length of a period shrinks from a year to a month to a second; as $\varepsilon \to 0$, the model approaches a continuous time model. Using $\lim_{\varepsilon \to 0} \rho(\varepsilon) = 1$, the limiting form of inequality B.10 is $p_T \geq a - C + C = a$. This relation and inequality B.2 imply that $a \geq p_T \geq a$, or $p_T = a$, the transversality condition used in section 5.6.

Writing the second part of equation B.4 for a period of length ε, using $((1+r)^t = e^{\tilde{r}t})$ gives

$$p_t = e^{\tilde{r}t}(p_0 - C) + C.$$

This equation reproduces equation 5.16, except that there we used r instead of $\tilde{r}$ to simplify the notation.

B.3   Inductive Proofs

Exercise 3 in chapter 5 requires understanding the mechanics of an inductive proof. In such a proof, we show that something that depends on an index (an integer) j is true for any positive integer j. In our context, the "something" is an equation. Inductive proofs use two steps. The first step shows that the "something" is true for $j = 1$. The second step shows that *if* the "something" is true for $j - 1$, *then* it is also true for j. These two steps taken together mean that the "something" is true for $j = 1$, therefore it is true for $j = 2$, therefore it is true for $j = 3$, and so on.

As an example, let us use an inductive proof to confirm equation 5.6 for $j = 1, 2, 3 \ldots$.[1] The first step shows that equation 5.6 holds for $j = 1$. This claim follows by setting $j = 1$ in equation 5.6 and noting that the result reproduces the (previously confirmed) Euler equation (the first of the two equations in 5.5). The second step requires showing that if equation 5.6 holds for $j - 1$, then it also holds for j. The hypothesis that equation 5.6 holds for $j - 1$ means that $R_t = \rho^{j-1} R_{t+j-1}$. The Euler equation must hold for all time periods; thus it must hold for period $t + j - 1$, implying $R_{t+j-1} = \rho R_{t+j}$. Combining these two equations implies $R_t = \rho^{j-1} R_{t+j-1} = \rho^{j-1} \rho R_{t+j} = \rho^j R_{t+j}$. We have thus shown that if equation 5.6 holds for $j - 1$, then it also holds for j, completing the inductive proof.

---

1 With finite T, the largest meaningful integer is $j = T - t$. Therefore, a more exact, but also more confusing, statement is that equation 5.6 holds for $j \leq T - t$. We ignore this technical detail in the interest of clarity.

Appendix C: Algebra of Taxes

This appendix collects technical details for chapter 10.

C.1 The Open Economy

For a closed economy, domestic supply equals domestic demand: there is no trade. For an open economy, the difference between domestic demand and supply equals the amount imported or exported. Tax equivalence holds in a closed economy, where all sources of supply or demand are subject to the tax, but not in an open economy. In section 10.1 we noted that in a closed economy, the "Polluter Pays Principle" may be vacuous, because (under some conditions) the tax equivalence result implies that it does not matter whether the polluter or the pollutee pays the environmental tax. Because tax incidence does not hold in the open economy, there it *does* matter whether a consumer or producer tax is used.

We use an example to compare tax incidence in a closed and an open economy. Suppose that domestic demand is $q^d = 10 - p$, domestic supply equals $q^s = bp$, and foreign supply is $q^{s, \text{for}} = cp$. When trade is allowed, the aggregate supply function is the sum of domestic plus foreign supply, equal to $(b + c)p$. Column 2 of table C.1 shows that, for the closed economy, the consumer and producer tax incidence does not depend on which agent, consumers or producers, directly pays the tax. The incidences in this column are calculated using the following steps:

1. Calculate the equilibrium price in the absence of tax by setting the untaxed supply equal to the untaxed demand.

2. Calculate the equilibrium consumer price and producer price when one of these agents directly pays the tax, v, by setting the (taxed) demand equal to the (taxed) supply.

3. Use the tax-inclusive consumer and producer price for the two cases (where one agent or the other directly pays the tax) and the zero-tax price to calculate the incidences.

The third column of the table shows that in the open economy, the incidences do depend on which (domestic) agent directly pays the tax. To calculate the incidences in the open

Table C.1
Consumer and producer tax incidence in a closed and an open economy

	Closed economy	Open economy
Zero tax	$q^d = 10 - p$	$q^d = 10 - p$
	$q^s = bp$	$q^s = bp$ and $q^{s, for} = cp$
	market clearing	market clearing
	$10 - p = bp$	$10 - p = (b + c)p$
Consumers pay tax	consumer incidence $\frac{b}{1+b} 100\%$	consumer incidence $\frac{b+c}{1+b+c} 100\%$
	producer incidence $\frac{1}{1+b} 100\%$	producer incidence $\frac{1}{1+b+c} 100\%$
Domestic producers pay tax	consumer incidence $\frac{b}{1+b} 100\%$	consumer incidence $\frac{b}{1+b+c} 100\%$
	producer incidence $\frac{1}{1+b} 100\%$	producer incidence $\frac{1+c}{1+b+c} 100\%$

economy when consumers directly pay the tax (regardless of the source of supply), we begin with the market clearing condition in the absence of a tax, $10 - p = (b + c)p$. We solve this to find the zero-tax price. If consumers pay the tax, the market clearing condition is $10 - (p + v) = bp + cp$, where now we understand that p is the price received by both domestic and foreign firms, and $p + v$ is the consumer tax-inclusive price. We solve this equation to find the equilibrium producer and consumer prices. Using the formula for tax incidence, we obtain the expressions in the second row and third column of table C.1. If domestic producers pay the tax, the market clearing condition is $10 - p = b(p - v) + cp$. Solving this equation for the equilibrium price and comparing with the no-tax price produces the consumer incidence when domestic producers pay the tax, shown in the third row and third column of the table.

In an open economy, domestic supply does not equal domestic demand. Taxing consumers causes the market demand function to shift in, lowering the price that both domestic and foreign producers face and increasing the consumer's tax-inclusive price. Taxing only domestic supply causes the domestic supply function to shift in, increasing the consumer price, decreasing the domestic tax-inclusive price, and shifting supply from domestic to foreign producers. Under the consumer tax, both the domestic and foreign producers receive the same price. Under the (domestic) producer tax, consumers and foreign producers face the same price, and domestic producers receive a lower after-tax price.

In a closed economy, producer and consumer taxes are equivalent; the two taxes are not equivalent in an open economy. The rest of this appendix considers only the closed economy.

C.2   Algebraic Verification of Tax Equivalence

Denote the producer price as p^s (for supply) and the consumer price as p^c (for consumption) and write the "market price" as p. If consumers pay the tax, the prices are $p^s = p$ and $p^c = p^s + v$ (producers receive the market price, and consumers pay this price plus the tax). If producers pay the tax, $p^s = p - v$ and $p^c = p$ (consumers pay the market price, and producers receive this price minus the tax). We want to confirm that tax-inclusive prices are the same regardless of who directly pays the tax.

If consumers pay the tax, the supply equal demand condition is

$$S(p) = D(p + v). \tag{C.1}$$

Let $p^*(v)$ be the (unique) price that solves this equation; this is the equilibrium producer price (a function of v) when consumers pay the tax: $p^*(0)$ is the equilibrium price when $v = 0$. Because consumers (directly) pay the tax, the price producers receive (the "supply price") equals $p^*(v)$, and the price consumers pay equals $p^*(v) + v$.

If, instead, producers directly pay the tax, the equilibrium condition is

$$S(p - v) = D(p). \tag{C.2}$$

Substitute $p = p^* + v$ into this equation to write equation (C.2) as

$$S(p^*) = D(p^* + v).$$

The last equation reproduces equation (C.1) evaluated at $p = p^*(v)$, the unique solution to that equation. Thus, the two equations (C.1) and (C.2) lead to the same producer and consumer prices.

C.3   Approximating Tax Incidence

We begin by deriving equation 10.2. In a closed economy, it does not matter whether consumers or producers are charged the tax. Suppose that consumers are charged the tax, so that the equilibrium condition is equation C.1. This equation expresses the equilibrium price as an implicit function of the tax: as the tax increases, the equilibrium producer price p falls. The consumer incidence (expressed as a fraction instead of a percentage) equals

$$\frac{p^*(v) + v - p^*(0)}{v} = \frac{p^*(v) - p^*(0)}{v - 0} + 1 = \frac{\Delta p}{\Delta v} + 1. \tag{C.3}$$

The numerator on the left side equals the change in price that consumers pay. We obtain the first equality using the fact that $\frac{v}{v} = 1$ and subtracting 0 from the denominator. We subtract 0 to emphasize that both the numerator and the denominator are changes: the numerator is the change in price, in moving from a zero tax to a nonzero tax, and the denominator is the change in the tax, $v - 0$. We obtain the second equality by using the "delta notation": Δ means "change in." The next step requires a formula for an approximation of $\frac{\Delta p}{\Delta v}$, which we obtain using the fact that the derivative $\frac{dp}{dv}$ is approximately equal to $\frac{\Delta p}{\Delta v}$.

Treating $p = p(v)$ (i.e., price as a function of the tax), we can differentiate both sides of the equilibrium condition C.1 to write

$$\frac{dS(p)}{dp}\frac{dp}{dv} = \frac{dD(p+v)}{dp^c}\left(\frac{dp}{dv}+1\right).$$

Divide both sides by the equilibrium quantity, using $S = D$, and multiply by the equilibrium price p to write

$$\frac{dS(p)}{dp}\frac{p}{S}\frac{dp}{dv} = \frac{dD(p+v)}{dp^c}\frac{p}{D}\left(\frac{dp}{dv}+1\right). \tag{C.4}$$

Because we are considering an approximation for small v, we evaluate equation C.4 at $v = 0$. Using the definitions in equation 10.1 and evaluating equation C.4 at $v = 0$, we rewrite that equation as

$$\theta\frac{dp}{dv} = -\eta\left(\frac{dp}{dv}+1\right).$$

We can solve this equation for $\frac{dp}{dv}$ to obtain

$$\frac{dp}{dv} = -\frac{\eta}{\theta+\eta} = -\frac{1}{\frac{\theta}{\eta}+1}, \tag{C.5}$$

reproducing equation 10.2. The second equality follows from dividing the numerator and the denominator of the middle expression by η. This equation shows the derivative of the equilibrium producer price with respect to the tax, evaluated at a zero tax. Notice that $\frac{dp}{dv} < 0$: the tax, although paid by consumers, reduces the equilibrium price that producers receive.

We use the fact that

$$\frac{\Delta p}{\Delta v} \approx \frac{dp}{dv}$$

and equations C.3 and C.5 to write the expression for the consumer incidence as

$$\frac{\Delta p}{\Delta v}+1 \approx \frac{dp}{dv}+1 = 1-\frac{\eta}{\theta+\eta} = \frac{\theta}{\theta+\eta}.$$

The tax incidence for producers equals

$$\frac{\text{reduction in producer price}}{\text{level of (unit) tax}}.$$

Initially the tax is 0, so the level of the tax (once it is imposed) is $v - 0 = \Delta v$. The producer tax incidence is

$$\frac{-\Delta p}{\Delta v} \approx \frac{\eta}{\theta + \eta}.$$

This expression involves $-\Delta p$ rather than Δp, because the definition of the producer incidence involves the price reduction, not the price change. If the price change is, for example, -3, then the reduction is 3.

C.4   Approximating Deadweight Loss

The graphical representation of the deadweight loss (DWL) of the tax is the area of the triangle bcd in figure 10.1. To verify equation 10.5 for the case of linear supply and demand, we use the formula for the area of a triangle: one half base times height. Turn the triangle bcd in figure 10.1 on its side, so that the base of the rotated triangle is bd, and split the triangle into two triangles, bcg and dcg. The area of bcd equals the sum of the area of the two smaller triangles. Denote the consumer tax incidence (as a fraction, not a percentage) as $1 - \phi$, so the producer incidence is ϕ. The length of bd is v, the tax, so the length of the base of gb is ϕv. Denote the slope of bc as S_1, and denote the absolute value of the slope of dc as S_2. Using the formula slope = rise/run, $S_1 = \frac{\phi v}{\Delta q}$, or $\Delta q = \frac{\phi v}{S_1}$; Δq is the tax-induced reduction in sales. Therefore, the area of triangle bcg is $\frac{1}{2}\phi v \frac{\phi v}{S_1} = \frac{1}{2}\frac{\phi^2}{S_1}v^2$. Using the same reasoning, the area of the triangle dcg is $\frac{1}{2}\frac{(1-\phi)^2}{1-S_2}v^2$. The sum of the areas is $\frac{1}{2}\left(\frac{\phi^2}{S_1} + \frac{(1-\phi)^2}{1-S_2}\right)v^2$, that is, it is proportional to the square of v.

To approximate the DWL when the supply and demand functions are not linear, we again begin with the formula for the area of a triangle, turned on its side. The base of the triangle is the tax, v. As above, denote the height of this triangle as Δq, the change in sales. We have (by multiplying and dividing)

$$\Delta q = \frac{\Delta q}{\Delta p}\Delta p = \frac{\Delta q}{\Delta p}\left(\frac{\Delta p}{\Delta v}\right)\Delta v = \left(\frac{\Delta q}{\Delta p}\frac{p}{q}\right)\frac{q}{p}\left(\frac{\Delta p}{\Delta v}\right)\Delta v. \tag{C.6}$$

Equation 10.2 and the definition of the supply elasticity imply, respectively, the following two equations:

$$\frac{\Delta p}{\Delta v} \approx \frac{dp}{dv} = -\frac{\eta}{\theta + \eta}, \quad \text{and} \quad \left(\frac{\Delta q}{\Delta p}\frac{p}{q}\right) \approx \theta.$$

Inserting these formulae into equation C.6 gives the approximation

$$\Delta q \approx \frac{\theta\eta}{\theta+\eta}\frac{q}{p}v. \tag{C.7}$$

Here we used the fact that $\Delta v = v - 0 = v$, because we are taking the approximation in the neighborhood of a zero tax. This result and the formula for the area of a triangle produces equation 10.5.

C.5   Cap and Trade

This section provides more detail on the comparison of taxes and cap and trade. We discuss how a cap and trade system works, and why the equilibrium level of each firm's emissions does not depend on whether firms are given permits or have to buy them. We then discuss the sense in which a cap and trade policy is equivalent to an emissions tax.

Basic Ingredients of Cap and Trade

The regulator chooses the cap on emissions, denoted by Z. The many competitive firms are able to buy and sell permits. Each of these firms takes the price of an emissions permit as given. Denote the equilibrium price of permits as $p^e(Z)$. This relation recognizes that the equilibrium price of permits depends on the supply of permits. In this case, the supply is a number, Z. Due to the (assumed) fixed relation between output and emissions, by choice of units we can set one unit of output to equal one unit of emissions.

Claims

Claim 1: Permit Price and Firm-Level Emissions Are Independent of the Allocation of Permits   The equilibrium permit price depends on the aggregate number of permits, Z. However, if firms are price taking and profit maximizing, and if the permit market works well, then firm-level pollution levels are independent of the distribution of allowances, (e.g., whether firms are given or sold the permits). To verify this claim, we show that each firm's demand for permits is independent of its own allocation. Consider an arbitrary firm that is given an allowance A (possibly equal to zero). This price-taking firm faces the output price, p, and the permit price, p^e, and wants to maximize profits:

$$pq - c(q) + p^e(A - q).$$

The first two terms equal the firm's revenue from selling the good minus its cost of production; the last term equals the firm's profits from selling (if $A > q$) or its costs of buying (if $A < q$) permits.

The first order condition for the firm's problem states that price equals marginal cost. Marginal cost here equals the sum of the "usual" marginal cost ($\frac{dc}{dq}$), and the cost of buying an emissions permit, p^e. The first order condition,

$$p = \frac{dc}{dq} + p^e, \qquad (C.8)$$

does not depend on its permit allocation, A. A firm's decision about how much to produce, and thus about how many permits to use, does not depend on the allocation of permits.

A firm that buys permits has to pay p^e for the additional permit needed to produce an additional unit. A firm that sells permits incurs an opportunity cost p^e in using an additional permit: by using that permit, the firm cannot sell it. Thus, regardless of whether the firm is a net buyer or seller of permits, it incurs the cost p^e of using an additional unit.

Claim 2: There Exists a Quota-Equivalent Emissions Tax   To simplify the exposition, assume that all firms have the same cost function, so that we can use the representative firm model. As in section 2.4, we denote the cost function for the representative firm as $c(Q)$. Using the fact that $Q = Z$ (because one unit of output produces one unit of emissions), equation C.8 implies that

$$p(Q)_{|Q=Z} = \frac{dC(Q)}{dQ}\Big|_{Q=Z} + p^e(Z), \quad \text{or}$$

$$\left(p(Q) - \frac{dC(Q)}{dQ}\right)_{|Q=Z} = p^e(Z). \qquad (C.9)$$

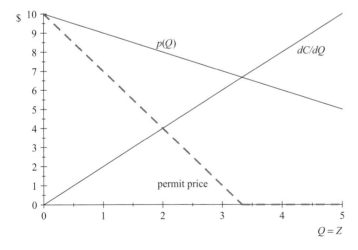

Figure C.1
Solid lines: Inverse demand and marginal cost. Dashed curve: The equilibrium permit price, p^e, is the vertical difference between inverse demand and marginal cost.

The second equation shows that the equilibrium permit price equals the difference between price and marginal cost.

Figure C.1 shows linear (product) demand and marginal cost curves. The dashed line shows the vertical difference between the two solid lines equal to the left side of equation C.9. This dashed line is the inverse demand function for pollution permits. For this example, the equilibrium quantity (= emissions) absent regulation is 3.33. If the regulator chooses $Z \geq 3.33$, then the regulation is vacuous, and the permit price is 0. But for $Z < 3.33$, the emissions constraint is binding, and the permit price is positive. For example, if $Z = 3$, the permit price equals the vertical coordinate of the dashed line at $Z = 3$. Every value of Z below the unregulated "business as usual" level (3.33) corresponds to a different equilibrium permit price.

If the representative firm faces a tax, v, the equilibrium condition (price equals "usual" marginal cost plus the tax) is

$$p(Z) = \frac{dC(Q)}{dQ} + v. \tag{C.10}$$

Comparing equation C.10 to the first line of equation C.9 shows that the tax $v = p^e(Z)$ induces the competitive industry to produce at the same level as under the cap and trade policy with cap Z. The quota-equivalent emissions tax equals the equilibrium quota price under cap and trade.

Exercises

Suppose that consumers are charged the tax, as above. Let the demand function be $D(p) = p^{-\eta}$ with $\eta > 1$, and suppose that firms have constant marginal cost, c. Evaluate the consumer and producer tax incidence under the monopoly, as a function of η. Compare with the consumer and producer tax incidence under competition, with the same demand and cost functions. [Hint: Follow the derivation above, replacing marginal revenue with price.]

Appendix D: Continuous Time

We begin with equation 13.3, multiplying the right side by 1:

$$x_{t+1} - x_t = F(x_t) - y(x_t) = \left[F(x_t) - y(x_t) \right] 1. \tag{D.1}$$

We have to measure time in specific units. It is meaningful to say "That was 3 years ago," but we would never say "That was 3 ago." We choose the unit of time to equal 1 year; this choice is arbitrary.

We use the symbol Δ to represent the length of a period. Given that our unit of time is a year, the symbol $\Delta = 10$ means that a period lasts for a decade. If a period lasts for a day, then $\Delta = \frac{1}{365}$. For our model to show explicitly the length of a period, we can replace the number 1 wherever it appears in equation D.1 (including in the subscripts) with Δ, obtaining

$$x_{t+\Delta} - x_t = \left[F(x_t; \Delta) - y(x_t; \Delta) \right] \Delta \quad \Rightarrow$$

$$\frac{x_{t+\Delta} - x_t}{\Delta} = F(x_t; \Delta) - y(x_t; \Delta). \tag{D.2}$$

By introducing the parameter Δ, we have changed in the definition of $F(x_t)$ and $y(x_t)$; these are now rates (i.e., they give growth and harvest per unit of time (1 year)). To take into account this change, we replace $F(x_t)$ and $y(x_t)$ with $F(x_t; \Delta)$ and $y(x_t; \Delta)$. If a period lasts for a day, then $\Delta = \frac{1}{365}$; if the growth per year is 0.8, and harvest per year is 0.2, then the amount of growth and harvest over one period (= 1 day) equals $\frac{0.8}{365}$ and $\frac{0.2}{365}$, respectively. The change in stock over 1 day is $(0.8 - 0.2)\frac{1}{365}$.

Now that we explicitly recognize that growth and harvest are rates, we no longer need to require that $y \leq x$. It is not possible to extract 60 units of biomass if the stock of biomass equals only 40. However, it is possible to harvest at an annual rate of 60 for a short period of time. If $\Delta = \frac{1}{365}$ and $y = 60$, then after 10 periods (= 10 days) we have extracted $\frac{60}{365} \times 10 = 1.64$ units of biomass. If Δ is sufficiently small, then the annual harvest rate y can be arbitrarily large (for a portion of the year) without violating the non-negativity constraint on the stock of fish.

The last equation in D.2 has the ratio $\frac{x_{t+\Delta}-x_t}{\Delta}$, equal to the change in stock per change in time. With $\Delta = \frac{1}{365}$, this ratio is the change in the stock per day. As $\Delta \to 0$, the ratio $\frac{x_{t+\Delta}-x_t}{\Delta}$ converges to a time derivative. We define

$$F(x) = \lim_{\Delta \to 0} F(x; \Delta), \quad \text{and} \quad y(x) = \lim_{\Delta \to 0} y(x; \Delta).$$

With this definition, the limit (as $\Delta \to 0$) of the last equation in D.2 is

$$\frac{dx_t}{dt} = F(x_t) - y(x_t). \tag{D.3}$$

Equation D.2 is a difference equation, and equation D.3 is a differential equation. They both describe how x changes over time. *When studying stability, we use the continuous time model.*

By construction, equations D.2 and D.3 have the same steady states. In other respects, however, they may contain different information. If one fish stock grows according to equation D.2 and the second grows according to equation D.3, and they begin at the same stock level, they might evolve quite differently; the time-graphs of their trajectories might not be similar. If we want to change the length of a period (e.g., from $\Delta = 1$ to $\Delta = \frac{1}{10,000,000,000}$), while keeping the trajectory qualitatively unchanged, we have to recalibrate the functions $F(x_t)$ and $y(x_t)$. However, if Δ is sufficiently small, then trajectories arising from the continuous and discrete time models are qualitatively similar in the neighborhood of a steady state.

Appendix E: Bioeconomic Equilibrium

Here we offer a slightly different perspective on the open access steady state. The zero profit condition and the production function in equation 14.2, imply that

$$0 = (p\lambda x - w)E \quad \Rightarrow \quad x = \frac{w}{p\lambda} = \frac{C}{p}, \tag{E.1}$$

where the last equality uses the definition $\frac{w}{\lambda} \equiv C$. The steady state condition under logistic growth (harvest equals growth) is

$$y = \gamma x \left(1 - \frac{x}{K}\right). \tag{E.2}$$

Substituting equation E.1 into equation E.2 (eliminating x) gives the steady state supply function:

$$y = \gamma \frac{C}{p} \left(1 - \frac{C}{Kp}\right). \tag{E.3}$$

The steady state supply function for harvest gives the harvest level, as a function of the price, that is consistent with a steady state stock of the fish and zero profits in the fishery. Figure E.1 shows the supply function for parameter values $K = 50$, $\gamma = 0.03$, and $C = 5$. The notable feature is that this supply function bends backward. For prices $p < \frac{1}{Kq} = 0.2$, supply increases with price and is very price-elastic (flat). At higher prices, equilibrium supply decreases with the higher price. At a given stock, the higher price induces greater harvest, but the higher harvest reduces the steady state stock. The net effect in the steady state is that a higher price reduces equilibrium supply over the backward-bending part of the curve.

The dashed line in the figure shows the linear demand curve, $p = 3.5 - 10y$. There are three "bioeconomic equilibria," combinations of output and price where supply equals demand and the stock is in a steady state. The equilibria A and D, corresponding to high price–low harvest and low price–high harvest, respectively, are stable; the intermediate equilibrium B is unstable, just as we saw in section 14.1.2.

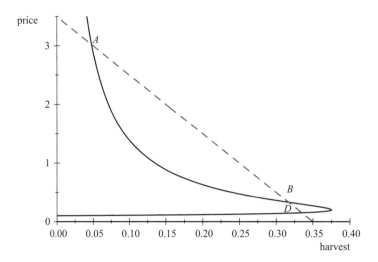

Figure E.1
The backward-bending steady state supply function (solid curve) and a linear demand curve (dashed line).

   To help explain this conclusion, we introduce a fictitious "Walrasian auctioneer." This auctioneer calls out an arbitrary price. If, at that price, supply equals demand, the auctioneer has found an equilibrium. However, if at the price the auctioneer has called out, demand exceeds supply, then the auctioneer raises the price in an effort to bring supply and demand into equilibrium.

   Suppose that this auctioneer calls out a price slightly above the p coordinate of point B; there, demand exceeds supply. In an effort to balance supply and demand, the auctioneer increases the price. The higher price initially elicits greater harvest, which reduces future stock, creating an even larger divergence between steady state supply and demand. The auctioneer continues to raise the price, toward the p coordinate of point A, where steady state supply equals demand. Thus, a price that begins slightly above the p coordinate of point B moves away from that point, so this price is unstable. Parallel arguments show that the prices corresponding to points A and D are stable steady states.

   The story of the Walrasian auctioneer aids intuition, but it is ad hoc. We now explain stability using the excess demand function without invoking this auctioneer. Steady state excess demand is the difference between demand and steady state supply (the horizontal difference between the dashed line and the solid curve in Figure E.1) as a function of the price. By definition, excess demand is zero at an equilibrium price: the prices corresponding to A, B, and D in our setting. In general, the graph of excess demand (as a function of price) has a negative slope at a stable steady state and a positive slope at an unstable steady state. Using Figure E.1 to construct the graph of excess demand, you can confirm that the slope is negative at points A and D and positive at B.

We want to establish that beginning close to but not equal to the price corresponding to A (or D), the price converges to A (respectively, to D). Similarly, beginning close to but not equal to the price corresponding to B, the price moves away from that level. Demand adjusts instantaneously to price, so consumers are always on their demand function. Supply, in contrast, depends on both the price and the resource stock. The resource stock changes smoothly over time (it does not "jump"), so the quantity supplied also changes smoothly. Consequently, the price-quantity pair is off the steady state supply function except at a steady state.

Consider, for example, the situation where the fishery begins with a stock, x_0, that results in an equilibrium price, $p_0 = \frac{C}{x_0}$ (the solution to equation E.1) slightly lower than the price corresponding to point A. At this price, demand exceeds the harvest needed to keep the stock at a constant level. Because the actual harvest equals demand, the stock is initially falling over time. As the stock falls, the equilibrium price rises (using the 0-profit condition $p = \frac{C}{x}$). Thus, if the initial price is below the level corresponding to point A, the price rises continuously over time, approaching the stable price corresponding to point A. A similar argument shows that beginning with a price slightly above point A, the price falls over time. Therefore, point A is stable. The same kind of arguments show that B is unstable and D is stable.

Appendix F: The Euler Equation for the Sole-Owner Fishery

We find the optimality condition where both the stock and the harvest are strictly positive (i.e., along an interior optimum). As in chapter 5, we determine the optimality condition using the perturbation method. Natural growth, the function $F(x_t)$, complicates the problem, but the logic is the same. We begin with a feasible "candidate trajectory" of harvest, $y_0, y_1, y_2, \ldots$, and the corresponding stock sequence, $x_0, x_1, x_2, \ldots$. We obtain the condition that must be satisfied if no perturbation increases the present discounted value of the payoff. As before, we consider a particular one-step perturbation: one that changes harvest in an arbitrary period (t) by ε, and makes an offsetting change in harvest in the next period $(t + 1)$ to keep unchanged the stock in the subsequent period $(t + 2)$. We can build a more complicated perturbation from a series of these one-step perturbations, but for the purpose of obtaining the necessary conditions, it suffices to consider the one-step perturbation. (To simplify the exposition, we refer to the change in harvest at t as an "increase", but the change could be positive or negative.)

We begin by finding the offsetting change needed in period $t + 1$ to keep unchanged (relative to the unperturbed candidate) the stock in period $t + 2$. If we increase harvest in period t by ε, the stock in period $t + 1$ is

$$x_{t+1} = x_t + F(x_t) - (y_t + \varepsilon).$$

This relation implies

$$\frac{dx_{t+1}}{d\varepsilon} = -1. \tag{F.1}$$

The increased harvest in period t reduces the stock in period $t + 1$ from x_{t+1} (the level under the candidate trajectory) to $x_{t+1} - \varepsilon$. Under the candidate trajectory, we plan to harvest y_{t+1} in period $t + 1$. The offsetting change in y_{t+1}, required by the fact that we increased y_t by ε, and by our insistence that x_{t+2} be unchanged, is $\delta(\varepsilon)$. The notation $\delta(\varepsilon)$ emphasizes that δ, the change in y_{t+1}, depends on, ε, the change in y_t. Using the growth function, we have

$$x_{t+2} = (x_{t+1} - \varepsilon) + F(x_{t+1} - \varepsilon) - (y_{t+1} + \delta(\varepsilon)). \tag{F.2}$$

We require that the change in x_{t+2} resulting from the changes in periods t and $t + 1$ equal 0:

$$\frac{dx_{t+2}}{d\varepsilon} = 0.$$

Using this condition and differentiating both sides of equation F.2 implies that

$$\frac{dx_{t+2}}{d\varepsilon} = 0 = -1 + \frac{dF(x_{t+1})}{dx_{t+1}} \frac{dx_{t+1}}{d\varepsilon} - \frac{d\delta}{d\varepsilon} \quad \Rightarrow \quad -1 - \frac{dF(x_{t+1})}{dx_{t+1}} - \frac{d\delta}{d\varepsilon} = 0 \Rightarrow$$

$$\frac{d\delta}{d\varepsilon} = -\left(1 + \frac{dF(x_{t+1})}{dx_{t+1}}\right). \tag{F.3}$$

The first line differentiates both sides of equation F.2 with respect to ε, using the chain rule. We use equation F.1 to eliminate $\frac{dx_{t+1}}{d\varepsilon}$ to obtain the equation after the first "$\Rightarrow$," and rearrange that equation to obtain the final equation.

The derivative $\frac{d\delta}{d\varepsilon}$ in the final equation in F.3 equals the required reduction in y_{t+1}, given that we increase y_t by ε, and given that we want to keep x_{t+2} unchanged. A one-unit increase in y_t leads to a one-unit direct reduction in x_{t+1} and $\frac{dF(x_{t+1})}{dx_{t+1}}$ units loss in growth; the loss in growth affects x_{t+2}. Therefore, if we increase y_t by ε units, we must decrease y_{t+1} by $\left(1 + \frac{dF(x_{t+1})}{dx_{t+1}}\right) \varepsilon$ units, to offset both the direct effect on x_{t+2} and the indirect effect that occurs via the reduced growth.

Under the perturbation, periods' t and $t + 1$ contribution to the total payoff is ρ^t times

$$g(\varepsilon) = \left(p_t - \frac{C}{x_t}\right)(y_t + \varepsilon) + \rho\left(p_{t+1} - \frac{C}{x_{t+1} - \varepsilon}\right)(y_{t+1} + \delta).$$

If the candidate is optimal, then a perturbation must lead to a first order change of 0 in the gain function. Using the product and the quotient rules, we have

$$\frac{dg(\varepsilon)}{d\varepsilon}\bigg|_{\varepsilon=0} = p_t - \frac{C}{x_t} + \rho\left[-\frac{C}{x_{t+1}^2}y_{t+1} + \left(p_{t+1} - \frac{C}{x_{t+1}}\right)\frac{d\delta}{d\varepsilon}\right]$$

$$= p_t - \frac{C}{x_t} + \rho\left[-\frac{C}{x_{t+1}^2}y_{t+1} - \left(p_{t+1} - \frac{C}{x_{t+1}}\right)\left(1 + \frac{dF(x_{t+1})}{dx_{t+1}}\right)\right] = 0$$

$$\Rightarrow p_t - \frac{C}{x_t} = \rho\left[\left(p_{t+1} - \frac{C}{x_{t+1}}\right)\left(1 + \frac{dF(x_{t+1})}{dx_{t+1}}\right) + \frac{C}{x_{t+1}^2}y_{t+1}\right].$$

The last line is the Euler equation 15.2.

Appendix G: Dynamics of the Sole-Owner Fishery

This appendix derives the continuous time analog of the Euler equation and then derives the differential equation for harvest.

G.1 Derivation of Equation 16.2

The continuous time Euler equations can be obtained using the calculus of variations, the Maximum Principle (employing Hamiltonians), or continuous time dynamic programming. These methods require additional mathematics. The approach here is heuristic, using only the discrete time perturbation method, and then taking a "formal limit," but without proving that this limit is mathematically valid. It does, however, give the correct optimality condition. We take equation 15.5 as our starting point and manipulate it to produce the continuous time analog, equation 16.2.

We need to have in mind a unit of time. Because we want the discrete time and the continuous time models to be close to each other, the unit of time should be small. As in section 13.3, we begin with the model in which one period equals one unit of time and then divide that period into smaller subperiods. Mechanically, we do this by replacing the number 1, the length of a period, with Δ. We also need to rewrite the discount factor as $\rho = \frac{1}{1+\Delta r}$ instead of $\rho = \frac{1}{1+r}$. Using the growth equation,[1]

$$x_{t+\Delta} - x_t = [F(x_t) - y(x_t)]\Delta,$$

we replace $F(x_t)$ and $y(x_t)$ with $F(x_t)\Delta$ and $y(x_t)\Delta$. Thus, the terms

$$\frac{dF(x_{t+1})}{dx_{t+1}} \quad \text{and} \quad -\frac{C}{x_{t+1}^2}y_{t+1}$$

---

1 More precise but more cumbersome notation uses $F(x; \Delta)$ and $\frac{dF(x;\Delta)}{dx}$, and reserves $F(x)$ and $\frac{dF(x)}{dx}$ for the limiting values (as $\Delta \to 0$) of the function and its derivative, as in appendix D. We use the simpler but less precise notation.

in equation 15.5 become, respectively,

$$\frac{dF(x_{t+\Delta})}{dx_{t+\Delta}}\Delta \quad \text{and} \quad -\frac{C}{x_{t+\Delta}^2}y_{t+\Delta}\Delta.$$

These substitutions mean that instead of having the length of a period be one unit of time (e.g., 1 minute), we now have the length of a period be Δ units of time. With these substitutions, we rewrite equation 15.5 as

$$R_t = \frac{1}{1+\Delta r}\left[R_{t+\Delta}\left(1 + \frac{dF(x_{t+\Delta})}{dx_{t+\Delta}}\Delta\right) + \frac{C}{x_{t+\Delta}^2}y_{t+\Delta}\Delta\right]. \tag{G.1}$$

Subtract $R_{t+\Delta}$ from both sides of equation G.1 and collect terms on the right side to rewrite the result as

$$R_t - R_{t+\Delta} = \left(\frac{1}{1+\Delta r} - 1\right)R_{t+\Delta} + \frac{1}{1+\Delta r}\left[R_{t+\Delta}\left(\frac{dF(x_{t+\Delta})}{dx_{t+\Delta}}\right) + \frac{C}{x_{t+\Delta}^2}y_{t+\Delta}\right]\Delta.$$

Divide both sides of this equation by Δ to write

$$-\frac{(R_{t+\Delta} - R_t)}{\Delta} = \frac{\left(\frac{1}{1+\Delta r} - 1\right)}{\Delta}R_{t+\Delta} + \frac{1}{1+\Delta r}\left[R_{t+\Delta}\left(\frac{dF(x_{t+\Delta})}{dx_{t+\Delta}}\right) + \frac{C}{x_{t+\Delta}^2}y_{t+\Delta}\right].$$

Now take the limit of both sides of this equation as $\Delta \to 0$, using

$$\lim_{\Delta\to 0}\frac{(R_{t+\Delta} - R_t)}{\Delta} = \frac{dR_t}{dt}, \quad \text{and} \quad \lim_{\Delta\to 0}\frac{\left(\frac{1}{1+\Delta r} - 1\right)}{\Delta} = \lim_{\Delta\to 0}\frac{\left(\frac{1-1-\Delta r}{1+\Delta r}\right)}{\Delta} = -r,$$

to write

$$-\frac{dR_t}{dt} = -R_t\left(r - \frac{dF(x_t)}{dx_t}\right) + \frac{C}{x_t^2}y_t.$$

Multiplying through by -1 gives equation 16.2.

G.2   Differential Equation for Harvest

Section 16.3.2 uses the differential equation for the sole-owner harvest, $\frac{dy}{dt} = H(x, y)$. This appendix explains how we obtain the function $H(x, y)$. The procedure uses the equations of motion for the stock, the rent, and the definition of rent. We repeat these three equations:

$$\frac{dx}{dt} = F(x) - y,$$

$$\frac{dR_t}{dt} = R_t \left(r - \frac{dF(x_t)}{dx_t} \right) - \frac{C}{x_t^2} y_t, \quad \text{and}$$

$$R_t = p(y_t) - \frac{C}{x_t}.$$

(G.2)

The first equation is merely the constraint of the problem (i.e., it is "data," given to us). The second equation is the Euler equation, expressed in terms of rent. Both these equations are the continuous time versions of the discrete time model. The third equation is the definition of rent.

Because the third equation holds identically with respect to time (i.e., it holds at every instant of time), we can differentiate it with respect to time to write

$$\frac{dR_t}{dt} = \frac{d\left[p(y_t) - \frac{C}{x_t} \right]}{dt} = p'(y_t)\frac{dy_t}{dt} + \frac{C}{x_t^2} y_t \frac{dx_t}{dt}.$$

We can use the first two equations in G.2 to eliminate $\frac{dR_t}{dt}$ and $\frac{dx_t}{dt}$:

$$R_t \left(r - \frac{dF(x_t)}{dx_t} \right) - \frac{C}{x_t^2} y_t = p'(y_t)\frac{dy_t}{dt} + \frac{C}{x_t^2} y_t (F(x) - y).$$

We can now use the third equation in G.2 to eliminate R_t:

$$\left(p(y_t) - \frac{C}{x_t} \right) \left(r - \frac{dF(x_t)}{dx_t} \right) - \frac{C}{x_t^2} y_t = p'(y_t)\frac{dy_t}{dt} + \frac{C}{x_t^2} y_t (F(x) - y).$$

Solving this equation for $\frac{dy_t}{dt}$ gives

$$\frac{dy}{dt} = \frac{\left(p(y_t) - \frac{C}{x_t} \right) \left(r - \frac{dF(x_t)}{dx_t} \right) - \frac{C}{x_t^2} y_t - \frac{C}{x_t^2} y_t (F(x) - y)}{p'(y_t)} \equiv H(x_t, y_t).$$

The middle expression is a function of only x, y, and the model parameters. We define this expression as the function $H(x_t, y_t)$.

This function looks complicated, but for the functional forms and the parameter values in our example, it simplifies to

$$\frac{dy}{dt} = 0.000\,02 \frac{-500.0yx + 80.0yx^2 - 28.0x^2 + 195.0x + 750.0}{x} = H(x_t, y_t).$$

Section 16.3.2 uses this function to construct the y isocline, the set of points where $\frac{dy}{dt} = 0$. This isocline is given by

$$\frac{dy}{dt} = 0 \Rightarrow y = -\frac{1}{10x\,(0.08x - 0.5)}\left(-0.28x^2 + 1.95x + 7.5\right).$$

G.3 Finding the Full Solution

To find the solution to the optimization problem—needed to construct the dotted curve in figure 16.3—we take the ratio of the differential equation for y and the differential equation for x to obtain a new differential equation, showing how y changes with changes in x:

$$\frac{\frac{dy}{dt}}{\frac{dx}{dt}} = \frac{dy}{dx} = \frac{H\,(x_t\,y_t)}{F(x) - y}.$$

The solution to this equation is a function giving the optimal harvest as a function of the stock, the optimal harvest rule. Denote this function as $y = Y(x)$. Figure 16.3 shows the graph of $Y(x)$, the dotted curve. Solving the differential equation to obtain the optimal harvest rule, $Y(x)$, requires a boundary condition, giving the value of y at some value of x. Our boundary condition is given by the steady state, denoted by (x_∞, y_∞). We calculate the steady state by finding the intersection of the x and the y isoclines. Our boundary condition is $y\,(x_\infty) = y_\infty$.

Some numerical algorithms encounter a problem when solving the differential equation, because both the numerator and denominator of $\frac{dy}{dx}$ vanish at the steady state, making the ratio an indeterminate form. This problem is easily resolved; we merely sketch the procedure. We can linearize our original nonlinear system and use the eigenvector associated with the stable eigenvalue to replace the boundary condition (the steady state) with a point on the stable eigenvector. We have to (numerically) solve the resulting initial value problem twice, once beginning with a point slightly below the steady state and then beginning with a point slightly above the steady state. Figure 16.3 shows the first of these two parts of the solution.

The dotted curve in figure 16.3 shows the graph of the optimal harvest level as a function of the stock, x. Harvest is positive only when the stock is above 3. As the stock increases over time, the harvest rises. The harvest is nearly constant, once the stock reaches about 20 or 25. The stock continues to grow to its steady state, and the harvest changes very little.

Appendix H: The Common-Property Water Game

We define an individual farmer's benefit of consuming $\frac{y}{n}$ units of water as $v\left(\frac{y}{n}\right)$; when each of n farmers consumes $\frac{y}{n}$ units, the total benefit of consumption is $nv\left(\frac{y}{n}\right) \equiv V(y)$. With this definition, the net benefit to farmer i is $v(y_t^i) - (c_0 - cx_t)y_t^i$, and the aggregate benefit, when each farmer consumes an equal share $(y^i = \frac{y}{n})$ equals $V(y_t) - (c_0 - cx_t)y_t$. Replacing $V(y)$ with $nv\left(\frac{y}{n}\right)$ does not alter the social planner's problem or the Euler equation for that problem, but it provides the notation needed to think about the game when each farmer individually chooses her own extraction. In a symmetric equilibrium, each farmer has the same level of consumption in a period: $y_t^i = \frac{y_t}{n}$. Using the chain rule and $V(y) \equiv nv\left(\frac{y}{n}\right)$, we have $V'(y) = nv'\left(\frac{y}{n}\right)\frac{1}{n} = v'\left(\frac{y}{n}\right)$. When farmer i's benefit of extraction is $v(y_t^i) - (c_0 - cx_t)y_t^i$, her rent in a symmetric equilibrium is

$$R_t^i\left(\frac{y_t}{n}, x_t\right) = v'\left(\frac{y_t}{n}\right) - (c_0 - cx_t) = V'(y) - (c_0 - cx_t) = R(y_t, x_t). \tag{H.1}$$

These equalities state that for a given level of extraction, y_t, and a given stock, x_t, the individual farmer's rent and the social planner's rent are the same. Of course, the equilibrium level of extraction differs in a common-property game and under the social planner.

Consider a noncooperative Nash equilibrium in which farmer i extracts y_t^i units of water at t and takes as given the aggregate extraction policy (a function of the stock, x) of all other farmers.[1] We denote that aggregate extraction policy of the other $n - 1$ farmers by $y^*(x_t)$. Farmer i faces the equation of motion

$$x_{t+t} - x_t = F^*(x_t) - y_t^i, \quad \text{with } F^*(x_t) \equiv F(x_t) - y^*(x_t). \tag{H.2}$$

and her Euler equation is (cf. equation 17.7)

$$R_t^i = \rho\left(R_{t+1}^i\left(1 + \frac{dF^*(x_{t+1})}{dx_{t+1}}\right) + cy_{t+1}^i\right). \tag{H.3}$$

---

1 There are a number of different types of Nash equilibria in dynamic games of this sort. We consider a "feedback" (also known as Markov perfect) equilibrium, in which each agent thinks that all other agents will base their decisions on the payoff-relevant state variable. Here, the payoff-relevant state variable is the stock of water.

As in our two-period example, we want to compare the optimality conditions under the planner (equation 17.7) and in the game (equation H.3), without actually solving for the two equilibria. The left sides of these two equations are the same (by virtue of equation H.1), but their right sides differ (just as is the case with the two first order conditions in our two-period example). The right side of equation 17.7 contains cy_{t+1}, accounting for the higher aggregate costs in period $t+1$ due to the lower stock. In contrast, the right side of equation H.3 contains cy_{t+1}^i, accounting for the higher cost only to farmer i due to the lower stock. When the planner decides whether to extract an extra unit, he takes into account the higher aggregate future cost; the individual farmer only takes into account her own future higher cost. The higher cost that other farmers face is the cost externality discussed in the text.

The strategic externality arises from the fact that the right side of the equation 17.7 contains the term $\frac{dF(x_{t+1})}{dx_{t+1}}$, whereas the right side of equation H.3 contains $\frac{dF^*(x_{t+1})}{dx_{t+1}}$. If farmer i (irrationally) believes that the other farmers would not condition their future extraction decisions on the future water stock, then $y^{*\prime}(x) = 0$, and these two terms are identical. In that case, the strategic externality vanishes. However, a reasonable conjecture for equilibrium is that[2]

$$\frac{dy^*(x_t)}{dx} > 0. \tag{H.4}$$

This inequality states that a higher stock of water leads to higher extraction by the other agents. The assumption is reasonable (and is satisfied in many equilibria), because the higher is the stock of water, the lower are extraction costs, and the less scarce is the water. Both these considerations tend to encourage higher extraction.

Inequality H.4 means that actions are "dynamic strategic substitutes," in the following sense. If agent i extracts an extra unit of water at time t, the stock in the next period will be lower than it otherwise would have been, causing other farmers' extraction decisions to be lower than they otherwise would have been. That is, higher extraction by farmer i at a point in time causes other farmers to reduce their future extraction.

If inequality H.4 holds, then

$$\frac{dF^*(x_{t+1})}{dx_{t+1}} < \frac{dF(x_{t+1})}{dx_{t+1}}.$$

This inequality lowers the reduction in extraction that farmer i needs to make at time $t+1$, following an increase in her extraction at t (to return to the candidate trajectory). By leaving her neighbors with a lower stock, farmer i induces them to lower their future extraction, benefiting farmer i. The neighbors' future response to lower stocks encourages farmer i to increase her current extraction.

---

2 The infinite horizon version of this model has a continuum of stable steady states satisfying the Euler equation. In contrast, a finite horizon model may have a unique equilibrium.

Appendix I: Sustainability

We derive equation 18.2, confirm the Hartwick rule, and then examine the feasibility of sustainability when society follows the Hartwick rule.

I.1 Derivation of Equation 18.2

The value of the program is

$$W(t) = W(x(t)) = \int_t^\infty e^{-r(\tau - t)} B(x(\tau)) d\tau$$

Differentiating this expression with respect to time, using Leibniz's rule and the definition $\lambda(x) \equiv W'(x)$, gives

$$\frac{dW}{dt} = r \int_t^\infty e^{-r(\tau - t)} B(x(\tau)) d\tau - B(t) = \frac{dW(x(t))}{dx} \frac{dx}{dt} = \frac{dW(x(t))}{dx} (F(x) - y(x))$$

$$\Rightarrow r W(x(t)) - B(x(t)) = \lambda(x)(F(x) - y(x)).$$

Differentiating with respect to time once again implies that

$$r W'(x) \frac{dx}{dt} = \left[B'(x) + \frac{d\lambda(x)}{dt} + \lambda(x) \left(F'(x) - y'(x) \right) \right] \frac{dx}{dt}.$$

Canceling $\frac{dx}{dt}$ and using the definition of $\lambda(x)$ gives

$$r\lambda(x) = \left[B'(x) + \frac{d\lambda(x)}{dt} + \lambda(x) \left(F'(x) - y'(x) \right) \right].$$

Rearranging this equation gives equation 18.2.

I.2   Confirming the Hartwick Rule

Here we show that the Hotelling rule + Hartwick rule implies constant consumption ($\frac{dC}{dt} = 0$). Reordering the argument shows that constant consumption + the Hotelling rule implies the Hartwick rule.

The national income accounting identity states that total income, Y must equal total expenditures. Expenditure is the sum of investment, $I = \frac{dK}{dt}$, extraction costs, cE, and consumption, C:

$$\text{Income accounting identity: } Y = \frac{dK}{dt} + cE + C. \tag{I.1}$$

We rearrange this identity to write

$$Y - (I + cE) = C.$$

Using the Hartwick rule, $I = (p - c)E$, we have

$$Y - ((p - c)E + cE) = Y - pE = C. \tag{I.2}$$

Differentiating both sides with respect to time gives

$$\frac{dY}{dt} - \frac{d(pE)}{dt} = \frac{dC}{dt}.$$

We use the differential for $Y(K, E) = F(k, E)$ to write the left side of this equation as

$$F_K I + F_E \frac{dE}{dt} - \frac{d(pE)}{dt} = r(p - c)E + p\frac{dE}{dt} - \frac{d(pE)}{dt}.$$

The equality uses the Hartwick rule and equation 18.3 (which states that the value of marginal product equals factor price). Using the Hotelling rule, we write the right side of the last expression as

$$\frac{dp}{dt}E + p\frac{dE}{dt} - \frac{d(pE)}{dt} = 0.$$

The equality follows from the product rule for differentiation. Thus, we have shown that the Hotelling rule plus the Hartwick rule implies that consumption is constant over time.

I.3   Feasibility of Constant Consumption

Here we assume that technology is Cobb Douglas, $F(K, E) = K^{1-\alpha}E^{\alpha}$, a stronger assumption than constant returns to scale. We show that sustainable consumption is feasible if and only if $\alpha < 0.5$. As a preliminary step, we establish that under the Hartwick rule, consumption is constant if and only if output, Y, is also constant. To demonstrate this claim, use the equilibrium condition that the value of marginal product of E equals the price of E:

$$\frac{\partial K^{1-\alpha}E^{\alpha}}{\partial E} = p \Rightarrow \alpha K^{1-\alpha}E^{\alpha-1} = p \Rightarrow pE = \alpha K^{1-\alpha}E^{\alpha} \Rightarrow \frac{pE}{Y} = \alpha. \tag{I.3}$$

The last equality states that payments to the resource sector, pE, as a share of the value of output, $Y = K^{1-\alpha}E^{\alpha}$, equals the constant α. Using the last parts of equations I.2 and I.3, we have

$$Y = C + pE = C + \frac{pE}{Y}Y = C + \alpha Y \Rightarrow (1 - \alpha)Y = C.$$

The last equality implies that output (= income) is constant if and only if consumption is constant.

To determine whether a constant consumption path (i.e., a constant output path) is feasible, we solve $Y = K^{1-\alpha}E^{\alpha}$ for E to obtain $E = Y^{\frac{1}{\alpha}}K^{\frac{\alpha-1}{\alpha}}$. For $\alpha \neq 0.5$, the integral of this function from an initial capital stock k to a larger stock z gives

$$V(z, k) \equiv Y^{\frac{1}{\alpha}} \int_{k}^{z} \left(K^{1-\frac{1}{\alpha}} \right) dK = \frac{\alpha}{2\alpha - 1} Y^{\frac{1}{\alpha}} \left(z^{2-\frac{1}{\alpha}} - k^{2-\frac{1}{\alpha}} \right).$$

For $\alpha = 0.5$, this integral is $V(z, k) = Y^2 \int_{k}^{z} \left(K^{-1} \right) dK = Y^2 (\ln z - \ln k)$. The function $V(z, k)$ equals the cumulative extraction needed to produce a constant output Y as K varies from the initial level k to some larger level z. As noted in the text, capital becomes infinitely large along the sustainable trajectory, so (for $\alpha \neq 0.5$) a sustainable trajectory requires an initial resource stock of

$$\lim_{z \to \infty} V(z, k) = \lim_{z \to \infty} \frac{\alpha}{2\alpha - 1} Y^{\frac{1}{\alpha}} \left(z^{2-\frac{1}{\alpha}} - k^{2-\frac{1}{\alpha}} \right) = \begin{cases} \infty, & \text{if } \alpha > 0.5, \\ \frac{\alpha}{1-2\alpha} Y^{\frac{1}{\alpha}} k^{2-\frac{1}{\alpha}}, & \text{if } \alpha < 0.5. \end{cases}$$

For $\alpha = 0.5$, the initial resource stock needed to maintain constant output is $\lim_{z \to \infty} Y^2 (\ln z - \ln k) = \infty$. Thus, if $\alpha \geq 0.5$, it is not feasible to maintain *any* positive constant level of output, simply because such a path would require an infinite resource stock. If $\alpha < 0.5$, the initial resource stock is x, and the initial capital stock is k, then it is feasible to maintain the constant level of output y that solves

$$x = \frac{\alpha}{1-2\alpha} Y^{\frac{1}{\alpha}} k^{2-\frac{1}{\alpha}} \Rightarrow Y = \left(\frac{(1-2\alpha)x}{\alpha} \right)^{\alpha} k^{1-2\alpha}.$$

For $Y = 1$, $k = 0.7$, and $\alpha = 0.4$ (as in figure 18.1), $x = 2.4$. If $\alpha = 0.4$, the initial resource stock is 2.4, and the initial capital stock is 0.7, then the constant output path, $Y = 1$, and the corresponding consumption path, $(1 - 0.4)1 = 0.6$, are sustainable.

I.4 Derivation of Equation 18.6

Society's wealth, or welfare, is defined as the present discounted value of the stream of future consumption, $W(t) = \int_t^\infty e^{-r(\tau-t)} C(\tau) d\tau$, discounted using the constant rate r back to the current time, t. Using Leibniz's rule, the derivative of this function is

$$\frac{dW(t)}{dt} = -C(t) + rW(t).$$

In a stationary world (e.g., one without technical progress), the future consumption and investment depend on future levels of capital, which depend on the current (at time t) stock of capital, $K(t)$. We therefore write wealth as

$$W(K(t)) = \int_t^\infty e^{-r(\tau-t)} C(\tau) d\tau.$$

Using the chain rule,

$$\frac{dW(t)}{dt} = \frac{dW(K(t))}{dK} I(t),$$

where $\frac{dW(K(t))}{dK}$ equals the shadow price of capital, defined as the increase in the present discounted value of the stream of future consumption due to an additional unit of capital. Equating the two time derivatives and rearranging gives

$$rW(t) = C(t) + \frac{dW(K(t))}{dK} I(t). \tag{I.4}$$

Consumption is the numeraire good (i.e., its price is 1). Output produces a composite commodity that can be allocated to consumption or investment. An agent can purchase a unit of investment by sacrificing a unit of consumption, so the price of a unit of capital is also 1. In this competitive model without market failures, private and social values are equal, so $\frac{dW(K(t))}{dK} = 1$. Substituting this value into equation I.4 produces equation 18.6.

Appendix J: Discounting

We derive the Ramsey formula for the consumption discount rate and then discuss a numerical example that shows the effects, on willingness to pay to avoid future damages, of excessive optimism or pessimism.

J.1   The Ramsey Formula

We want to know how many units of consumption people today (time 0) are willing to sacrifice to increase time t consumption by 1 unit ($\$1$ or $\$1$ billion, depending on choice of units). Suppose, absent the policy, that society has c_0 units of consumption today for the present value utility $e^{-\rho \times 0} u(c_0) = u(c_0)$, and society has c_t units of consumption at time $t > 0$, with present value utility $e^{-\rho t} u(c_t)$. The utility discount factor, $e^{-\rho t}$, converts the time t utility into its present value (at time 0, today) equivalent. If society gives up $\$x$ today, the utility cost is $u'(c_0) x$, the marginal value of a unit of consumption, times the number of units that society gives up today. The present value of the increased utility due to the extra dollar at time t is $e^{-\rho t} u'(c_t)$. Equating the marginal cost to the marginal gain and dividing by $u'(c_0)$ gives

$$x(t) = \frac{e^{-\rho t} u'(c_t)}{u'(c_0)};$$

$x(t)$ equals the number of units of consumption society is willing to give up today, in exchange for one more unit of consumption at time t; $x(t)$ therefore is the "consumption discount factor," giving the present value today of a future unit of consumption.

A rate of change (with respect to time) of a variable equals the derivative of the variable with respect to time, divided by the variable. Because $x(t)$ is the consumption discount factor, the absolute value of its rate of change is the consumption discount rate, which we denote as $r(t)$. Taking the derivative gives

$$r(t) = -\frac{\frac{dx(t)}{dt}}{x(t)} = -\frac{\frac{d(e^{-\rho t}u'(c_t))}{dt}}{e^{-\rho t}u'(c_t)} = \frac{\rho e^{-\rho t}u'(c_t) - e^{-\rho t}u''(c_t)\frac{dc}{dt}}{e^{-\rho t}u'(c_t)}$$

$$= \frac{\rho e^{-\rho t}u'(c_t) - e^{-\rho t}u''(c_t)c\frac{\frac{dc}{dt}}{c}}{e^{-\rho t}u'(c_t)} = \rho - \frac{u''(c_t)c}{u'(c_t)}\frac{\frac{dc}{dt}}{c} = \rho + \eta_t g_t.$$

The last equality uses the definitions in the second line of equation 19.1

J.2   Optimism versus Pessimism about Growth

We illustrate the relation between the timing of an event and the magnitude of the mistakes arising from too-optimistic or too-pessimistic predictions of growth. In this example, future growth is $g(t) = \frac{.02}{1+\gamma t}$, $\gamma \geq 0$. The parameter γ determines growth's speed of decrease. For $\gamma = 0$, growth is constant at 2% per year; as $\gamma \to \infty$, growth falls almost immediately from 2% to 0. We also use the intermediate value $\gamma = 0.0133$, for which annual growth falls to 1% after 75 years, and then gradually falls to 0. This example is broadly consistent with some complex policy-driven models, for which the current growth rate is 1.5–2% and is expected to decline over time. Our example assumes that the true value is $\gamma = 0.0133$; $\gamma = 0$ implies false optimism, and $\gamma = \infty$ implies false pessimism about growth.

If the consumption discount rate (CDR) is constant, at r, then the consumption discount factor is e^{-rt}. If, instead, the CDR is a function of time, $r(t)$, then the consumption discount factor for a future time, t, is $e^{-X(t)t}$, with $X(t)$ equal to the average discount rate from today (time 0) and time t:

$$X(t) = \frac{\int_0^t r(\tau)\,d\tau}{t}.$$

The consumption discount factor, used to evaluate an exchange between the present and t periods in the future, depends on the CDRs at all intervening periods. Using $\rho = 0.01$, $\eta = 2$, and $g(t) = \frac{.02}{1+\gamma t}$ with $\gamma = 0.0133$, the Ramsey formula implies $r(t) = 0.01 + 2 \times \frac{.02}{1+0.0133t}$; it falls over time from 5% to 1%, reaching the intermediate 3% level after 75 years. Under growth optimism ($\gamma = 0$), $r(t) = 0.05$ and under growth pessimism ($\gamma = \infty$), $r(t) = 0.01$. The short-run growth predictions are similar under $\gamma = 0$ and $\gamma = .0133$ and are very different for $\gamma = \infty$. In contrast, the long-run growth predictions are similar under $\gamma = 0.0133$ and $\gamma = \infty$ and are very different under $\gamma = 0$.

The three scenarios with $\gamma = 0$ (growth is constant at 2%), $\gamma = 0.0133$ (described above), and $\gamma = \infty$ (future growth is 0) illustrate the policy importance of assumptions about growth over long stretches of the future. For each of these scenarios, we ask: "What is society's maximum willingness to pay (measured in dollars), in perpetuity, to avoid a $100

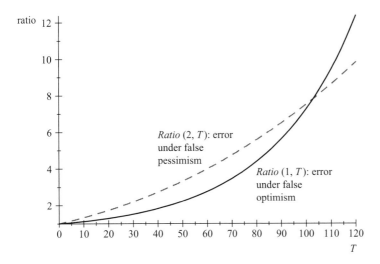

Figure J.1
Ratios of WTP, defined in equation J.1.

perpetual loss in consumption beginning T years in the future?"[1] Denote this willingness to pay (WTP) as $WTP(\gamma, T)$, a function of T and γ.

To show the policy relevance of assumptions about future growth, we consider the ratios of $WTP(\gamma, T)$ for different values of γ and T:

$$Ratio(1, T) = \frac{WTP(\gamma = 0.0133, T)}{WTP(\gamma = 0, T)}; \quad Ratio(2, T) = \frac{WTP(\gamma = \infty, T)}{WTP(\gamma = 0.0133, T)} \tag{J.1}$$

For example, if $Ratio(1, T) = 10$, then the planner is willing to spend 10 times the amount to avoid the event when growth falls ($\gamma = 0.0133$) compared to when growth is constant at 2% ($\gamma = 0$). Because we assume that $\gamma = 0.0133$ describes actual growth, $Ratio(1, T)$ equals the magnitude of the error if we are too optimistic about growth, and $Ratio(2, T)$ equals the error if we are too pessimistic. The "error" is the understatement or overstatement of WTP, relative to the correct WTP when we know $\gamma = 0.0133$.

Figures J.1 and J.2 show graphs of these two ratios as functions of the event time, T. The first figure graphs these two ratios as T varies from 0 to 120 years, and the second figure shows the ratios as T varies from 120 to 220 years. By using two figures, we can see how the scale of the comparison depends on the event time, T. For example:

---

1 Section 19.2.1 addresses a similar question, but here we measure the trade-off in dollars instead of utility, and we take into account the possibility of growth.

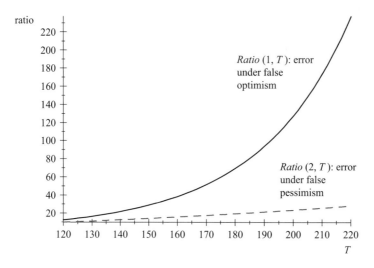

Figure J.2
Ratios of WTP, defined in equation J.1.

- If the event time is $T = 50$, $Ratio(1, 50) = 2.2$, and $Ratio(2, 50) = 3.3$. In this case, the error (in calculating the correct WTP) arising from to being too pessimistic is $\frac{3.3}{2.2} 100\% = 150\%$ of the error arising from being too optimistic.
- If the event time is $T = 200$, $Ratio(1, 200) = 127.5$ and $Ratio(2, 200) = 23.4$. In this case, the error (in calculating the true WTP) arising from being too optimistic is $\frac{127.5}{23.4} 100\% = 544\%$ of the error arising from being too pessimistic.

This example illustrates that the cost-benefit analysis of a public investment with a payoff in the near future (e.g., the next century) is sensitive to near-term growth. In contrast, the cost-benefit analysis of a public investment with a payoff in the distant future is much more sensitive to growth rates over long spans of future time. We probably know much less about growth in the distant compared to the near future. Overestimates of future growth lead to too low an estimate of willingness to pay to avoid future damages. Underestimates of future growth lead to too high an estimate of willingness to pay.

References

Abbott, J., and J. Wilen. 2009. "Regulating of Fisheries Bycatch with Common-Pool Output Quotas." *Journal of Environmental Economics and Management* 57:195–204.

Abbott, J., and J. Wilen. 2011. "Dissecting the Tragedy: A Spatial Model of Behavior in the Commons." *Journal of Environmental Economics and Management* 62:386–401.

Abbott, J., B. Garber-Yonts, and J. Wilen. 2010. "Employment and Remuneration Effects of IFQs in the Bering Seas/Aleutian Islands Crab Fisheries." *Marine Resource Economics* 25:333–354.

Acciavatti, A. 2015. "The Ganges Water Crisis." *New York Times*, June 17.

Aisbett, E., L. Karp, and C. Mcausland. 2010. "Police Powers, Regulatory Takings and the Efficient Compensation of Domestic and Foreign Investors." *Economic Record* 86 (274):367–383.

Aker, J. 2010. "Information from Markets Near and Far: Mobile Phones and Agricultural Markets in Niger." *American Economic Journal: Applied Economics* 2:46–59.

Aldy, J. 2013. "Eliminating Fossil Fuel Subsidies." The Hamilton Project, Brookings, Institution, Washington, DC.

Alix-Garcia, J., A. de Janvry, E. Sadoulet, and J. Torres. 2009. "Payment for Eco-System Services Program." In *Payments for Environmental Services in Agricultural Landscapes*, edited by L. Lipper, T. Sakuyama, R. Stringer, and D. Zilberman, 163–188. New York: Springer-Verlag.

Anderson, J., C. M. Anderson, J. Chu, J. Meredith et al. 2015. "The Fishery Performance Indicators: A Management Tool for Triple Bottom Line Outcomes." *PLoS ONE* 10 (5). http://journals.plos.org/plosone/article?id=10.1371/journal.pone.0122809.

Anderson, S., R. Kellog, and S. Salant. 2016. "Hotelling under Pressure." *Journal of Political Economy* (forthcoming).

Angeletos, G., D. Laibson, A. Repetto, J. Tobacman, and S. Weinberg. 2001. "The Hyperbolic Consumption Model: Calibration, Simulation and Empirical Evaluation." *Journal of Economic Perspectives* 15:47–68.

Anthoff, D., and R. Tol. 2010. "On International Equity Weights and National Decision Making on Climate Change." *Journal of Environmental Economics and Management* 60 (3): 14–20.

Aranson, R. 2012. "Property Rights in Fisheries: How Much Can Individual Transferable Quotas Accomplish?" *Review of Environmental Economics and Policy* 10.1093/reep/res011.

Arnason, R., K. Kelleher, and R. Willmann. 2009. *The Sunken Billions: The Economic Justification for Fisheries Reform*. Washington, DC: World Bank, Agriculture and Rural Development.

Arrow, K., M. Cropper, C. Gollier, B. Groom et al. 2012. "How Should Benefits and Costs Be Discounted in an Intergenerational Context?" Resources for the Future Discussion Paper 12–53.

Asheim, G., W. Buchholz, and C. Withagen. 2003. "The Hartwick Rule: Myths and Facts." *Environmental and Resource Economics* 25:29–150.

Auerbach, A., and J. Hines. 2002. "Taxation and Economic Efficiency, vol. 1." In *Handbook of Public Economics*, edited by A. Auerbach and M. Feldstein, 1347–1421. Amsterdam: North Holland.

Baerenklau, K., K. Schwabe, and A. Dinar. 2015. "The Residential Water Demand Effect of Increasing Block Rate Water Budgets." *Land Economics* 90:683–699.

Barbier, E. 2011. *Capitalizing on Nature: Ecosystems as Natural Assets*. Cambridge: Cambridge University Press.

Barrett, S. 2003. *Environment and Statecraft*. Oxford: Oxford University Press.

Barro, R. 2006. "Rare Disasters and Asset Markets in the Twentieth Century." *Quarterly Journal of Economics* 121:823–866.

Berbel, J., C. Gutierrez-Martin, J. Rodriguez-Diaz, E. Camacho, and P. Montesinos. 2015. "Literature Review on Rebound Effect of Water Saving Measures and Analysis of a Spanish Case Study." *Water Resource Management* 29:663–678.

Berck, P., and G. Helfand. 2010. *The Economics of the Environment*. Boston: Pearson.

Berck, P., and J. Perloff. 1984. "An Open Access Fishery with Rational Expectations." *Econometrica* 52:489–506.

Berck, P., and M. Roberts. 1996. "Natural-Resource Prices: Will They Ever Turn Up?" *Journal of Environmental Economics and Management* 31:65–78.

Boadway, R., and M. Keen. 2010. "Theoretical Perspectives on Resource Tax Design." In *The Taxation of Petrolem: Principles, Problems, and Practice*, edited by P. Daniel, M. Keen, and C. McPherson, 163–188. Oxon, UK: Routledge.

Bohn, H., and R. Deacon. 2000. "Ownership Risk, Investment, and the Use of Natural Resources." *American Economic Review* 90:526–549.

Bolster, J. 2015. "Where Have All the Cod Gone?" Op ed, *New York Times*, January 2.

Bovenberg, A. 1999. "Green Tax Reforms and the Double Dividend: An Updated Reader's Guide." *International Tax and Public Finance* 6:421–443.

Bovenberg, A., and F. van der Ploeg. 1994. "Environmental Policy, Public Finance, and the Labour Market in a Second-Best World." *Journal of Public Economics* 55:349–390.

Boyce, J. 2013. "Externality Regulation in Oil and Gas." In *Encyclopedia of Energy, Natural Resources, and Environmental Economics*, edited by J. Shogren, 154–168. Amsterdam: Elsevier.

Braxton, J. 2009. "The Ogallala Aquifer: Saving a Vital U.S. Water Source." *Scientific American*, March. https://www.scienti.camerican.com/article/the-ogallala-aquifer/.

Bromley, D. 2015. "Correcting the Whimsies of U.S. Fisheries Policies." *Choices* 30:1–7.

Bryce, R. 2015. "The Hidden Corn Ethanol Tax—How Much Does the Renewable Fuel Standard Cost Motorists?" Issues Brief 32, Manhattan Institute, New York.

Bulte, E., and E. Barbier. 2005. "Trade and Renewable Resources in a Second Best World: An Overview." *Environmental and Resource Economics* 30:423–463.

Cerda, R. 2007. "Market Power and Primary Commodity Prices: The Case of Copper." *Applied Economics Letters* 14:775–778.

Chermak, J. M., and R. Patrick. 1995. "A Well-Based Cost Function and the Economics of Exhaustible Resources: The Case of Natural Gas." *Journal of Environmental Economics and Management* 28:174–189.

Chermak, J. M., and R. Patrick. 2001. "A Microeconometric Test of the Theory of Exhaustible Resources." *Journal of Environmental Economics and Management* 42:82–103.

Chermak, J. M., and R. Patrick. 2002. "Comparing Tests of the Theory of Exhaustible Resources." *Resource and Energy Economics* 24:301–325.

Chetty, R., A. Looney, and K. Kraft. 2009. "Salience and Taxation: Theory and Evidence." *American Economic Review* 99:1145–1177.

Chichilnisky, G. 1994. "North-South Trade and the Global Environment." *American Economic Review* 84:851–874.

Chong, H., and D. Sunding. 2006. "Water Markets and Trading." *Annual Review of Environment and Resources* 31:239–264.

Chu, C. 2009. "Thirty Years Later: The Global Growth of ITQs and Their Influences on Stock Status in Marine Fisheries." *Fish and Fisheries* 10:217–230.

Clark, C. 1996. *Mathematical Bioeconomics*. New York: Wiley Interscience.

Clark, G. 2008. *A Farewell to Alms: A Brief Economic History of the World*. Princeton, NJ: Princeton University Press.

Coady, D., I. Parry, L. Sears, and B. Shang. 2015. "How Large Are Global Energy Subsidies?" Working Paper WP/15/105, International Monetary Fund, Washington, DC.

Conover, C. 2010. "Congress Should Account for the Excess Burden of Taxation." Policy Analysis, October 13, Cato Institute, Washington, DC.

Conrad, J. 2010. *Resource Economics*, Second ed. Cambridge: Cambridge University Press.

Copeland, B. R., and M. S. Taylor. 2009. "Trade, Tragedy, and the Commons." *American Economic Review* 99:725–749.

Costello, C. 2012. "Introduction to the Symposium on Rights-Based Fisheries Management." *Review of Environmental Economics and Policy* 10.1093/reep/res011.

Costello, C., S. Gaines, and J. Lynham. 2008. "Can Catch Shares Prevent Fisheries Collapse?" *Science* 321: 1678–1681.

Costello, C., J. Lynham, S. Lester, and S. Gaines. 2010. "Economic Incentives and Global Fisheries Incentives." *Annual Review of Resource Economics* 2:299–318.

Dasgupta, P. 2001. *Human Well-Being and the Natural Environment*. Oxford: Oxford University Press.

Dasgupta, P., and G. Heal. 1974. "The Optimal Depletion of Exhaustible Resources." *Review of Economic Studies* 41:3–28.

Dasgupta, P., and G. Heal. 1979. *Economic Thoery and Exhaustible Resources*. Cambridge: Cambridge University Press.

Daubanes, J., and S. Andrade de Sa. 2014. "Taxing the Rent of Non-renewable Resource Sectors: A Theoretical Note." Working Paper 1149, Economics Department, Organisation for Econamic Co-operation and Development, Paris.

Deacon, R. 2012. "Fishery Management by Harvester Co-ops." *Review of Environmental Economics and Policy* 10.1093/reep/res011.

Deacon, R., D. Parker, and C. Costello. 2013. "Reforming Fisheries: Lessons from a Self-Selected Cooperative." *Journal of Law and Economics* 56:83–125.

de Janvry, A., K. Emerick, M. Gonzalez-Navarro, and E. Sadoulet. 2015. "Delinking Land Rights from Land Use: Certification and Migration in Mexico." *American Economic Review* 105:3125–3149.

Dietz, T., E. Ostrom, and P. C. Stern. 2003. "The Struggle to Govern the Commons." *Science* 302:1907–1912.

Diewert, W. E., D. A. Lawrence, and F. Thompson. 1998. "The Marginal Cost of Taxation and Regulation." In *Handbook of Public Finance*, edited by F. Thomson and M. T. Green, 135–172. New York: Marcel Decker.

Dillon, K. 2014. "Ogallala Water Continues to Pour Onto Farm Fields Despite Decades of Dire Forecasts." LJWorld.com, September 27. http://www2.ljworld.com/news/2014/sep/27/ogallala-water-continues-pore-farm -fields-despite-/.

Di Maria, C., I. Lange, and E. van der Werf. 2013. "Should we be worried about the Green Paradox? Announcement Effects of the Acid Rain Program." *European Economic Review* 69:143–162.

Dinar, A., and D. Zilberman. 1991. "The Economics of Resource Conservation, Pollution-Reduction Technology Selection: The Case of Irrigation Water." *Resource Energy* 13:323–348.

Dyck, A., and U. R. Sumaila. 2010. "Economic Impact of Ocean Fish Populations in the Global Fishery." *Journal of Bioeconomics* 12:227–243.

Ekeland, I., and A. Lazrak. 2010. "The Golden Rule When Preferences Are Time Inconsistent." *Mathematical and Financial Economics* 4 (1):29–55.

Ellerman, A., and J. Montero. 1998. "The Declining Trend in Sulfur Dioxide Emissions: Implications for Allowance Prices." *Journal of Environmental Economics and Policy* 36:26–45.

Ellis, G., and R. Halvorsen. 2002. "Estimation of Market Power in a Nonrenewable Resource Industry." *Journal of Political Economy* 110:883–899.

Epstein, L., and S. Zinn. 1991. "Substitutition, Risk Aversion, and the Temporal Behavior of Consumption and Asset Returns." *Journal of Political Economy* 99:263–286.

Fama, E., and K. French. 2004. "The Capital Asset Pricing Model: Theory and Evidence." *Journal of Economic Perspectives* 18:25–46.

Farzin, Y. 1984. "The Effect of the Discount Rate on Depeletion of Exhaustible Resources." *Journal of Political Economy* 92:841–851.

Farzin, Y. 1995. "Technological Change and the Dynamics of Resource Scarcity Measures." *Journal of Environmental Economics and Management* 29:105–120.

Feldstein, M. 1977. "The Surprising Incidence of a Tax on Pure Rent: A New Answer to an Old Question." *Journal of Political Economy* 85:349–360.

Fenichel, E. P., and J. K. Abbott. 2014. "Natural Capital: From Metaphor to Measurement." *Journal of the Association of Environmental and Resource Economics* 1:1–27.

Fenske, J. 2012. "Imachi Nkwu: Trade and the Commons." CSAE Working Paper WPS/2012-19, Department of Economics, University of Oxford, England.

Fisher, A. 1981. *Resource and Environmental Economics*. Cambridge: Cambridge University Press.

Fowlie, M. 2009. "Incomplete Environmental Regulation, Imperfect Competition, and Emissions Leakage." *American Economic Journal: Economic Policy* 1:72–112.

Fowlie, M., and J. Perloff. 2013. "Distributing Pollution Rights in Cap-and-Trade Programs: Are Outcomes Independent of Allocation?" *Review of Economics and Statistics* 95:1640–1652.

Fowlie, M., S. Holland, and E. Mansur. 2012. "What Do Emissions Markets Deliver and to Whom? Evidence from Southern California's NO_x Trading Program." *American Economic Review* 102:965–993.

Funk, M. 2014. *The Wreck of the Kulluk*. Deca. https://www.decastories.com/kulluk/.

Galbraith, K. 2012. "Texas Supreme Court Rules in Favor of Landowers' Water Rights." *Texas Tribune*, February 24.

Gaudet, G. 2007. "Natural Resource Economics under the Rule of Hotelling." *Canadian Journal of Economics* 40:1003–1059.

Gentry, W. 2007. "A Review of the Evidence of the Incidence of the Corporate Income Tax." OTA Paper 101, U.S. Department of Treasury, Washington, DC.

Gerlagh, R. 2011. "Too Much Oil." *CESifo Economic Studies* 57:79–102.

Gerlagh, R., and M. Liski. 2012. "Carbon Prices for the Next Thousand Years." CESIFO Working Paper 3855.

Gillingham, K., W. Nordhaus, D. Anthoff, G. Blanford et al. 2015. "Modeling Uncertainty in Climate Change: A Multi-Model Comparison." Cowles Foundation Discussion Paper No. 2022.

Glaeser, E., and J. Kohlhase. 2004. "Cities, Regions, and the Decline of Transport Costs." *Papers in Regional Science* 83:197–228, DOI: 10.1007/s10110-003-0183-x.

Gollier, C. 2014. "Evaluation of Long-Dated Investments Under Uncertain Growth Trend, Volatility, and Catastrophes." Working paper, Toulouse School of Economics, Tovlouse.

Golosov, M., J. Hassler, P. Krusell, A. Tsyvinski. 2014. "Optimal Taxs on Fossil Fules in General Equilibrium." *Econometrica* 82:41–88.

Goolsbee, A. 1998. "Taxes, Organizational Forms and the Deadweight Loss of Corporate Income Tax." *Journal of Public Economics* 69:143–152.

Goolsbee, A. 2006. "The Value of Broadband and the Deadweight Loss of Taxing New Technology." *B.E. Journal of Economic Analysis and Policy* 5. https://doi.org/10.1515/1538-0645.1505.

Gordon, H. S. 1954. "The Economic Theory of a Common-Property Resource: The Fishery." *Journal of Political Economy* 62:124–142.

Gordon, R. 2015. *The Rise and Fall of American Growth*. Princeton, NJ: Princeton University Press.

Goulder, L. 1995. "Environmental Taxation and the Double Dividend." *International Tax and Public Finance* 2:157–183.

Grafton, R. Q., T. Kompas, and R. Hilborn. 2007. "Economics of Overexploitation Revisited." *Science* 318: 1601–1604.

Griffin, R. 2012. "The Origins and Ideals of Water Resource Economics in the United States." *Annual Review of Resource Economics* 4:353–377.

Griffin, R. 2016. *Water Resource Economics: The Analysis of Scarcity, Policies, and Projects*, second ed. Cambridge, MA: MIT Press.

Griffin, R., and S. Hsu. 1993. "The Potential for Water Market Efficiency When Instream Flows Have Value." *American Journal of Agricultural Economics* 75:292–303.

Halvorsen, R., and T. Smith. 1991. "A Test of the Theory of Exhaustible Resources." *Quarterly Journal of Economics* 106:123–140.

Hamilton, J. 2011. "Nonlinearities and the Macroeconomic Effects of Oil Prices." *Macroeconomic Dynamics* 15:364–378.

Hamilton, K. 2003. "Sustaining Economic Welfare: Estimating Changes in Total and Per Capita Wealth." *Environment, Development, and Sustainability* 5:3419–3436.

Hardin, G. 1968. "The Tragedy of the Commons." *Science* 162:1243–1248.

Hartwick, J. 1977. "Intergenerational Equity and the Investing of Rents from Exhaustible Resources." *American Economic Review* 67:972–974.

Hartwick, J. 2011. "Green National Income and Green National Product." *Annual Review of Resource Economics* 3:21–35.

Hartwick, J., and N. Olewiler. 1986. *The Economics of Natural Resource Use*. New York: Harper and Row.

Heal, G. 1976. "The Relationship between Price and Extraction Cost for a Resource with a Backstop Technology." *Bell Journal of Economics* 7:371–378.

Heal, G., and M. Barrow. 1980. "The Relationship between Interest Rates and Metal-Price Movements." *Review of Economic Studies* 47:161–182.

Hines, J. 2008. "Excess Burden of Taxation." In *The New Palgrave Dictionary of Economics*, second ed. edited by L. Blume and S. Durlauf. Basingstoke, UK: Palgrave Macmillan.

Hintermann, B. 2015. "Market Power in Emission Permit Markets: Theory and Evidence from the EU ETS." *Environmental and Resource Economics*. DOI: 10.1007/s10640-015-9939-4.

Hnyilicza, E., and R. Pindyck. 1976. "Pricing Policies for a Two-Part Exhaustible Resource Cartel: The Case of OPEC." *European Economic Review* 8:139–154.

Hoel, M. 2008. "Bush Meets Hotelling: The Effects of Improved Renewable Energy Technology on Greenhouse Gas Emissions." Working paper, University of Oslo, Oslo.

Hoel, M. 2012. "The Supply Side of CO_2 with Country Heterogeneity." *Scandanavian Journal of Economics* 113:846–865.

Holland, S. 2012. "Emissions Taxes Versus Intensity Standards: Second-Best Environmental Policies with Incomplete Regulation." *Journal of Environmetnal Economics and Management* 63:375–387.

Holland, S., J. Hughes, C. Knittel, and N. Parker. 2015. "Some Inconvenient Truths about Climate Change Policy: The Distributional Impacts of Tranportation Policies." *Review of Economics and Statistics* 97:1052–1079.

Homans, F. R., and J. Wilen. 1997. "A Model of Regulated Open Access Resource Use." *Journal of Environmental Economics and Management* 32:1–21.

Homans, F. R., and J. Wilen. 2005. "Markets and Rent Dissipation in Regulated Open Access Fisheries." *Journal of Environmental Economics and Management* 49:381–404.

Hotelling, H. 1931. "The Economics of Exhaustible Resources." *Journal of Political Economy* 39:137–175.

Howitt, R. 1994. "Empirical Analysis of Water Market Institutions." *Resource and Energy Economics* 16: 357–371.

Huang, L., and M. Smith. 2014. "The Dynamic Efficiency Costs of Common-Pool Resource Exploitation." *American Economic Review* 104:4071–4103.

Intelligence Community Assessment. 2012. *Global Water Security*. ICA 2012-08, February 2. https://fas.org/irp/nic/water.pdf.

International Energy Agency. 2011. "Joint Report by IEA, OPEC, OECD, and World Bank of Fossil-Fuel and Other Subsidies." https://www.oecd.org/g20/topics/energy-environment-green-growth/49090716.pdf.

Interagency Working Group. 2013. "Technical Update of the Social Cost of Carbon." Washington, DC: U.S. Environmental Protection Agency.

International Scientific Committee for Tuna. 2011. "Report of the Albacore Working Group Stock Assessment Workshop." http://www.pcouncil.org/wp-content/uploads/E1b_ATT1_AWG_STKASSMT_SEPT 2011BB.pdf.

Iverson, T. 2015. "Optimal Carbon Taxes with Non-constant Time Preference." http://mpra.ub.uni-muenchen.de/43264/.

Jensen, S., and C. Traeger. 2014. "Optimal Climate Change Mitigation under Long-Term Growth Uncertainty: Stochastic Integrated Assessment and Analytic Findings." *European Economic Review* 69:104–125.

Johnson, R., and G. Libecap. 1982. "Contracting Problems and Regulation: The Case of the Fishery." *American Economic Review* 72:1005–1022.

Judd, K. 1985. "Redistributive Taxation in a Simple Perfect Foresight Model." *Journal of Public Economics* 28:59–83.

Kaffine, D. 2009. "Quality and the Commons: The Surf Gangs of California." *Journal of Law and Economics* 52:727–743.

Kamien, M., and N. Schwartz. 1991. *Dynamic Optimization*, second ed. Amsterdam: North Holland.

Karp, L. 2005. "Global Warming and Hyperbolic Discounting." *Journal of Public Economocs* 89:261–282.

Karp, L. 2016. "Discounting Utility and the Evaluation of Climate Policy." In *The Economics of the Global Environment—Catastrophic Risks in Theory and Practice*, edited by G. Chichilnisky and A. Rezai. New York: Springer.

Karp, L. and I. H. Lee. 2003. "Time Consistent Policies." *Journal of Economic Theory* 112:353–364.

Karp, L., and A. Rezai. 2015. "Trade and Resource Sustainability with Asset Markets." Working paper. Department of Agriculture and Resource Economics, University of California, Berkeley.

Karp, L., and M. Stevenson. 2012. "Green Industrial Policy: Trade and Theory." Working Paper, World Bank, Washington, DC., https://openknowledge.worldbank.org/handle/10986/12081.

Kassler, D. 2015. "California Supreme Court Won't Budge on Water Rates." *Sacramento Bee*, July 23.

Kilian, L. 2009. "Not All Oil Price Shocks Are Alike: Disentangling Demand and Supply Shocks in the Crude Oil Market." *American Economic Review* 99:1053–1069.

Kolbert, E. 2014. *The Sixth Extinction: An Unnatural History*. New York: Henry Holt and Co.

Krause, S., F. Boano, M. Cuthbert, J. Fleckenstein, and J. Lewandowski. 2014. "Understanding Process Dynamics at Aquifer-Surface Water Interfaces: An Introduction to the Special Section on New Modeling Approaches and Novel Experimental Technologies." *Water Resources Research* 50:1847–1855.

Krautkraemer, J. 1998. "Nonrenewable Resource Scarcity." *Journal of Economic Literature* 36:2065–2107.

Kronenberg, T. 2008. "Should We Worry about Failure of the Hotelling Rule?" *Journal of Economic Surveys* 22:774–793.

Kubiszewski, I., R. Costanza, C. Franco, P. Lawn et al. 2013. "Beyond GDP: Measuring and Achieving Global Genuine Progress." *Ecological Economics* 93:57–68.

Kurlansky, M. 1998. *Cod: A Biography of the Fish that Changed the World*. London: Penguin Books.

Laibson, D. 1997. "Golden Eggs and Hyperbolic Discounting." *Quarterly Journal of Economics* 62:443–478.

Lee, J., J. A. List, and M. Strazicich. 2006. "Nonrenewable Resource Prices: Deterministic or Stochastic Trends?" *Journal of Environmental Economics and Management* 51:354–370.

Lemoine, D. 2015. "The Climate Risk Premium." Working paper, University of Arizona, Tucson.

Lemoine, D. 2016. "Green Expectations: Current Effects of Anticipated Carbon Pricing." forthcoming, *Review of Economics and Statistics*.

Lemoine, D., and I. Rudik. 2015. "Steering the Climate System: Using Inertia to Lower the Cost of Policy." Working paper 14-03, University of Arizona, Tucson.

Lemoine, D., and C. Traeger. 2014. "Watch Your Step: Optimal Policy in a Tipping Climate." *American Economic Journal: Economic Policy* 6:1–31.

Leonhardt, D. 2012. "A Climate Proposal Beyond Cap and Trade." *New York Times*, October 12.

Lin, C., and G. Wagner. 2007. "Steady State Growth in a Hotelling Model of Resource Extraction." *Journal of Environmental Economics and Management* 54:68–83.

Lipsey, R., and K. Lancaster. 1956. "The General Theory of Second Best." *Review of Economic Studies* 24:11–32.

Livernois, J. 1987. "Empirical Evidence on the Characteristics of Extractive Technologies: The Case of Oil." *Journal of Environmental Economics and Management* 14:72–86.

Livernois, J. 2009. "On the Emprical Significance of the Hotelling Rule." *Review of Environmental Economics and Policy* 3:21–41.

Livernois, J., and R. Uhler. 1987. "Extraction Costs and the Economics of Nonrenewable Resources." *Journal of Political Economy* 95:1195–1203.

Livernois, J., H. Thille, and X. Zhang. 2006. "A Test of the Hotelling Rule Using Old-Growth Timber." *Canadian Journal of Economics* 39:163–186.

Llavador, H., J. Roemer, and J. Silvestre. 2016. *Sustainability for a Warming Planet*. Cambridge, MA: Harvard University Press.

Lontzek, T., Y. Cai, K. Judd, and T. Lenton. 2015. "Stochastic Integrated Assessment of Climate Tipping Points Indicates the Need for Strict Climate Policy." *Nature Climate Change* 5:441–444.

Lovett, I. 2016. "California Surfers Look to Courts for Relief against the 'Bay Boys.' " *New York Times*, April 14.

Lund, D. 2009. "Rent Taxation for Nonrenewable Resources." *Annual Review of Resource Economics* 1, 10.1146/annurev.resource.050708.144216.

Malischek, R., and C. Tode. 2015. "A Test of the Theory of Nonrenewable Resouces—Controlling for Exploration and Market Power." Institute of Energy Economics, University of Cologne, Cologne, Germany.

Mangel, M. 1985. *Decision and Control in Uncertain Resource Systems*. Cambridge, MA: Academic Press.

McAusland, C. 2003. "Voting for Pollution Policy: The Importance of Income Inequality and Openness to Trade." *Journal of International Economics* 61(2):425–451.

McAusland, C. 2008. "Trade, Politics and the Environment: Tailpipe vs. Smokestack." *Journal of Environmental Economics and Management* 55:52–71.

Mcguire, V. 2007. "Changes in Water Level and Storage in the High Plains Aquifer, Predevelopment to 2005." U.S. Geological Survey Fact Sheet 2007-3029. Washington, DC. https://pubs.usgs.gov/fs/2007/3029/pdf/FS2007 3029.pdf.

Mehra, R. 2006. "The Equity Premium Puzzle: A Review." *Foundations and Trends in Finance* 2:1–81.

Miller, M., and C. Upton. 1985. "A Test of the Hotelling Valuation Principle." *Journal of Political Economy* 93:1–25.

Mitra, T., G. Asheim, W. Buchholz, and C. Withagen. 2013. "Characterizing the Sustainability Problem in an Exhaustible Resource Model." *Journal of Economic Theory* 148:2164–2182.

Nair, C. 2014. "Tackling a Drought in Iran." *New York Times*, November 4.

National Research Council. 2011. *Renewable Fuel Standard: Potential Economic and Environmental Effects of U.S. Biofuel Policy*. Washington, DC: National Academies Press.

Newell, R., J. Sanchirico, and S. Kerr. 2005. "Fishing Quota Markets." *Journal of Environmental Economics and Management* 49:437–462.

NOOA Fisheries. 2016. "Status of U.S. Fisheries." http://www.nmfs.noaa.gov/sfa/fisheries_eco/status_of _fisheries/.

Nordhaus, W. 1982. "How Fast Should We Graze the Global Commons?" *American Economic Review* 72: 242–246.

Nordhaus, W. 2008. *A Question of Balance*. New Haven, CT: Yale University Press.

OECD. 2012. *OCED Factbook 2011-2012: Economic, Environmental, and Social Statistics*. http://www.oecd -ilibrary.org/economics/oecd-factbook-2011-2012_factbook-2011-en.

Okum, A. 1975. *Equality and Efficiency: The Big Tradeoff*. Washington, DC: Brookings Institution.

Ostrom, E. 1990. *Governing the Commons: The Evolution of Institutions for Collective Action*. Cambridge: Cambridge University Press.

Ostrom, E. 2007. "A Diagnostic Approach for Going beyond Panaceas." *Proceedings of the National Academy of Sciences, USA* 104 (39):15181–15187.

Parry, I., D. Heine, E. Lis, And S. Li. 2014. *Getting Energy Prices Right: From Principle to Practice*. Washington, DC: International Monetary Fund.

Pfeiffer, L., and C. Lin. 2014. "Does Efficient Irrigation Technology Lead to Reduced Groundwater Extraction? Empirical Evidence." *Journal of Environmental and Economic Management* 67:189–208.

Pindyck, R. 1978. "The Optimal Exploration and Production of Nonrenewable Resources." *Journal of Political Economy* 86:841–861.

Pindyck, R. 1980. "Uncertainty and Exhaustible Resource Markets." *Journal of Political Economy* 88:1203–1225.

Pindyck, R. 1987. "On Monopoly Power in Extractive Resource Markets." *Journal of Environmental Economics and Management* 14:128–142.

Pindyck, R. 1999. "The Long-Run Evolution of Energy Prices." *Energy Journal* 20:1–27.

Pittel, K., R. van der Ploeg, and C. Withagen. 2014. *Climate Policy and Nonrenewable Resources: the Green Paradox and Beyond*. Cambridge, MA: MIT Press.

Porcher, S. 2014. "Efficiency and Equity in Two-Part Tariffs: The Case of Residential Water Rates." *Applied Economics* 46:539–555.

Pottinger, L. 2009. "Why Africa Should Shun Hydroelectric Megaprojectes." *World Rivers Review* 24:6–7.

Prakash, A., and M. Potoski. 2007. "Collective Action through Voluntary Environmental Programs: A Club Theory Perspective." *Policy Studies Journal* 35:773–792.

Ramsey, F. 1928. "A Mathematical Theory of Savings." *Economic Journal* 38:543–559.

Reisner, M. 1987. *Cadillac Dessert: The American West and Its Disappearing Water*. New York: Viking.

Reuters. 2014. "Shell Says Fossil Fuel Reserves Won't Be 'Stranded' by Climate Regualtion." May 19. http://www.reuters.com/article/shell-climatechange-idUSL6N0O54CB20140519.

Ricke, K. L., and K. Caldeira. 2014. "Maximum Warming Occurs about One Decade After a Carbon Dioxide Emission." *Environmental Research Letters* 9, http://dx.doi.org/10.1088/1748-9326/9/12/124002.

Roemer, J. 2009. "Equality: Its Justification, Nature, and Domain." In *The Oxford Handbook of Economic Inequality*, edited by W. Salverda, B. Noland, and T. Smeeding, 139-187. Oxford: Oxford University Press.

Sabin, P. 2013. *The Bet: Paul Ehrlich, Julian Simon, and Our Gamble over Earth's Future*. New Haven, CT: Yale University Press.

Schaefer, M. 1954. "Some Aspects of the Dynamics of Population Important to the Management of Commercial Marine Fisheries." *Bulletin of the Inter-American Tropical Tuna Commission* 1:26–56.

Schoengold, K., and D. Zilberman. 2007. "The Economics of Water, Irrigation, and Development." In *Handbook of Agricultural Economics*, edited by R. Evenson and P. Pingali, 2933–2977. Amsterdam: Elsevier.

Schwartz, J. 2015. "Norway Will Divest from Coal in Push Against Climate Change." *New York Times*, June 5.

Schwartzmay, N. 2015. "Water Pricing in Two Thirsty Cities: In One, Guzzlers Pay More and Use Less." *New York Times*, May 6.

Sen, A. 1987. *On Ethics and Economics*. London: Blackwell.

Sharp, R., and U. Sumaila. 2009. "Quantification of U.S. Marine Subsidies." *North American Journal of Fisheries Management* 29:18–32.

Sijm, J., K. Neuhoff, and Y. Chen. 2006. "CO_2 Cost Pass Through and Windfall Profits in the Power Sector." *Climate Policy* 6:49–72.

Sinclair, P. 1992. "High Does Nothing and Rising Is Worse: Carbon Taxes Should Keep Declining to Cut Harmful Emissions." *Manchester School* 60 (1):41–52.

Sinn, H. 2008. "Public Policies against Global Warming: A Supply Side Approach." *International Tax and Public Finance* 15:360–394.

Slade, M. 1984. "Tax Policy and the Supply of Exhaustible Resources." *Land Economics* 60:133–147.

Slade, M., and H. Thille. 1997. "Hotelling Confronts CAPM: A Test of the Theory of Exhaustible Resources." *Canadian Journal of Economics* 30:685–708.

Slade, M., and H. Thille. 2009. "Whither Hotelling: Tests of the Theory of Exhaustible Resources." *Annual Review of Resource Economics* 1:239–259.

Smith, M. 2012. "The New Fisheries Economies: Incentives Across Many Margins." *Annual Review of Resource Economics* 4:379–402.

Smith, V. 1977. "Water Deeds: A Proposed Solution to the Water Valuation Problem." *Arizona Review* 26:7–10.

Solow, R. 1974a. "The Economics of Resources or the Resources of Economics." *Review of Economic Studies* 41:29–46.

Solow, R. 1974b. "Intergenerational Equity and Exhaustible Resources." *American Economic Review* 64:1–14.

Squires, D., and N. Vestergaard. 2013. "Technical Change and the Commons." *Review of Economics and Statistics* 95:1769–1787.

Steward, D., P. Bruss, X. Yang, S. Staggenborg, S. Welch, and M. Apley. 2013. "Tapping Unsustainable Groundwater Stores for Agricultural Production in the High Plains Aquifer of Kansas, Projections to 2110." *Proceedings of the National Academy of Sciences, USA* 110, www.pnas.org/cgi/doi/10.1073/pnas.1220351110.

Stiglitz, J., A. Sen, AND J. P. Fitoussi. 2009. "Report by the Commission on the Measurement of Economic Performance and Social Progress." CMEPSP. http://www.cfr.org/world/report-commission-measurement-economic-performance-social-progress/p22847.

Stollery, K. R. 2008. "Mineral Depletion with Cost as the Extraction Limit." *Journal of Environmental Economics and Management* 10:151–165.

Strambro, E., J. Downen, M. Hogue, L. Pace, P. Jakus, and T. Grijalva. 2014. "An Analysis of a Transfer of Federal Lands to the State of Utah." Public Lands Coordination Office, Office of the Governor, Salt Lake City, Utah.

Straub, L., and I. Werning. 2015. "Positive Long Run Capital Taxation: Chamley-Judd Revisited." Working paper, Massachusetts Institute of Technology, Cambridge.

Sumaila, U., W. Cheung, V. Lam, D. Pauly, and S. Herrick. 2011. "Climate Change Impacts on the Biophysics and Economics of World Fisheries." *Nature Climate Change*. DOI: 10.1038/nclimate1301.

Sumaila, U., V. Lam, F. Le Manach, W. Wartz, and D. Pauly. 2013. "Global Fisheries Subsidies." Report to the European Parliament. http://www.europarl.europa.eu/RegData/etudes/note/join/2013/513978/IPOL-PECH_NT(2013)513978_EN.pdf.

Tietenberg, T. 2006. *Environmental and Natural Resource Economics*, seventh ed. Boston: Pearson.

Timilsinia, G., L. Kurdgelashvili, and P. Narbel. 2011. "A Review of Solar Energy." Policy Research Working paper 5845, Wold Bank, Washington, DC.

Traeger, C. 2014. "Why Uncertainty Matters—Discounting under Intertemporal Risk Aversion and Ambiguity." *Economic Theory* 56:627–664.

Tritch, R. 2015. "President Obama Could Unmask Big Political Donors." *New York Times*, March 24.

Tsur, Y., and A. Zemel. 2003. "Optimal Transition to Backstop Substitutes for Nonrenewable Resources." *Journal of Economic Dynamics and Control* 27:551–572.

United Nations. 2005. *Millennium Ecosystem Assessment*. http://www.maweb.org/en/index.aspx.

USDA. 2016. "Sugar & Sweeteners." http://www.ers.usda.gov/topics/crops/sugar-sweeteners.

U.S. Energy Information Administration. 2014. *Annual Energy Outlook 2014*. Washington, DC. DOE/IEA-0383(2014).

van der Ploeg, R., and C. Withagen. 2012. "Is There Really a Green Paradox?" *Journal of Environmental Economics and Management* 64:342–363.

van der Werf, E., and C. Di Maria. 2012. "Imperfect Environmental Policy and Polluting Emissions: The Green Paradox and Beyond." *International Review of Environmental Resource Economicst* 6:153–194.

Weitzman, M. 1976a. "On the Welfare Significance of National Product in a Dynamic Economy." *Quarterly Journal of Economics* 90:156–162.

Weitzman, M. 1976b. "The Optimal Development of Resource Pools." *Journal of Economic Theory* 12:351–364.

Weitzman, M. 1999. "Pricing the Limits to Growth From Mineral Depletion." *Quarterly Journal of Economics* 114:691–706.

Weitzman, M. 2009. "On Modeling and Interpreting the Economics of Catastrophic Climate Change." *Review of Economics and Statistics* 91:1–19.

Weninger, Q. 1999. "Assessing Efficiency Gains from Individual Transferable Quota: An Application to the Mid-Atlantic Surf Clam and Ocean Quahog Fishery." *American Journal of Agricultural Economics* 80:750–764.

Weninger, Q., and J. R. Waters. 2003. "Economic Benefits of Management Reform in the Northern Gulf of Mexico Reef Fish Fishery." *Journal of Environmental Economcis and Managment* 46:207–230.

Whittington, D., J. Boland, and V. Foster. 2002. *Water Tariffs and Subsidies in South Asia.* Washington, DC: World Bank.

Wilen, J., J. Cancino, and H. Uchida. 2012. "The Economics of Territorial Use Rights Fisheries." *Review of Environmental Economics and Policy*, 10.1093/reep/res011.

Wilson, E. 2016. *Half-Earth: Our Planet's Fight for Life.* Cambridge, MA: Harvard University Press.

Winter, R. 2014. "Innovation and the Dynamic of Global Warming." *Journal of Environmental Economic and Management* 68:124–140.

Wittenberg, A. 2014. "Data-Driven Regulation A Big Hit with U.S. Scallop Industry." Greenwire, December 17. http://www.eenews.net/greenwire/2014/12/17/stories/1060010703.

World Bank. 2014a. *Fish to 2030: Prospects for Fisheries and Aquaculture.* Washington, DC.

World Bank. 2014b. *The Little Green Data Book 2014.* Washington, DC.

World Bank. 2014c. *State and Trends of Carbon Pricing 2014.* Washington, DC: World Bank Group Climate Change.

World Commission on Environment and Development. 1987. *Our Common Future [The Bruntland Report].* Oxford: Oxford University Press.

Zhang, J., and M. D. Smith. 2011. "Estmation of a Generalized Fishery Model." *Review of Economics and Statistics* 93:690–699.

Index

Page numbers in italics indicate tables, figures, and textboxes.